ROCK FILE 4 is a must for every aware Rock listener. It contains a deeply researched article on the influential, behind-the-scene A & R men and a fascinating study of American radio. But above all there are the charts, a unique record of accurate information covering twenty years of hits from both sides of the Atlantic and incorporating some of the material originally published in ROCK FILE 1, now a long out-of-print collector's item. The ROCK FILE series provides a superb reference work for everybody who has ever questioned the who, when, or why of Rock music.

Also available in Panther Books

ROCK FILE 2 – (ed.) Gillett
ROCK FILE 3 – (eds.) Gillett & Frith
ENCYCLOPEDIA OF ROCK (in 3 vols.) (eds.) Hardy & Laing
MAKING TRACKS – Charlie Gillett
WRITINGS AND DRAWINGS OF BOB DYLAN
JOURNEY THROUGH AMERICA WITH THE ROLLING STONES – R. Greenfield
DIARY OF A ROCK 'N' ROLL STAR – Ian Hunter Patterson
ERIC CLAPTON – John Pidgeon
FLAME – John Pidgeon

Rock File 4

Edited by Charlie Gillett and Simon Frith

Panther

Granada Publishing Limited
First published in 1976 by Panther Books Ltd
Frogmore, St Albans, Herts AL2 2NF

A Panther Original

Made and printed in Great Britain by
Cox & Wyman Ltd, London, Reading and Fakenham
Set in Monotype Times

CONTENTS

INTRODUCTION 7

THE A & R MEN 25
Simon Frith

AMERICAN RADIO TODAY 47
Paul Gambaccini

PREFACE TO THE LOG OF HITS 57

THE LOG OF AMERICAN / BRITISH TOP 20 HITS, 1955–74 67
Stephen Nugent, with Pete and Annie Fowler

AMERICAN CHART-TOPPERS, 1955–74 371

BRITISH CHART-TOPPERS, 1955–74 386

ROLL CALL OF HIT MAKERS 398

ACKNOWLEDGMENTS

Grateful thanks to the editors and publishers of the publications which allowed us to use their research facilities in compiling the chart logs, namely *Billboard*, *Music Week*, *Record Mirror* and the *New Musical Express*.

For permission to reprint reviews, thanks to the editors of the *New Musical Express* (for Charles Shaar Murray's review of 10cc's *Original Soundtrack* and for Mick Farren's review of the Bay City Rollers' *Once Upon A Star*), Detroit *Creem* (for Lester Bangs' review of Barry White's *Just Another Way to Say I Love You*), *Phonograph Record Magazine*, Hollywood (for Greg Shaw's review of Elton John's *Captain Fantastic and the Brown Dirt Cowboy*), and *Street Life* (for Simon Frith's review of the Eagles *Greatest Hits*).

CONTRIBUTORS

Charlie Gillett is co-producer for Oval Records, the author of *The Sound of the City* and *Making Tracks*, and hosts 'Honky Tonk' and 'Single File' on BBC Radio London.

Simon Frith teaches Sociology at the University of Warwick, writes for *Street Life* and *Creem*, and contributed a chapter to *The Soul Book*.

Stephen Nugent is an American anthropologist currently living in Brazil.

Paul Gambaccini is *Rolling Stone*'s man in London, where he presents Radio One's weekly American survey on Saturdays.

Pete and Annie Fowler live in Macclesfield, where Pete teaches and records for Oval.

INTRODUCTION

Back again, bigger and better, here's *Rock File Four*. As usual, the bulk of the book is taken up by the log of chart hits, which Stephen Nugent has extended to include every entry to *Billboard's* American top twenty from 1955 to 1974. The Fowler's log of British hits, begun in *Rock File One*, has been updated to the end of 1974.

Continuing his survey of the British music business, Simon Frith investigates the men who plan and produce the year's releases, and files his report (not many hits, for all those releases) in 'The A & R Men'. From a different standpoint, Paul Gambaccini reports on his experiences as programme director on a radio station in Boston, Mass., in 'American Radio Today'.

Developing the idea of 'Five Performers of the Year', the editors have identified the five performers who made the most impact, artistically and/or commercially, in the past year: Elton John, the Bay City Rollers, the Eagles, Barry White and 10cc. Rather than amplify our reasons for choosing them, we have reproduced five album reviews which simultaneously illustrate typical contemporary critical approaches in the music press.

Elton John
Captain Fantastic and the Brown Dirt Cowboy (MCA)

by Greg Shaw*

The time has come to acknowledge just how big Elton John has become. His pre-eminence has come to pass so gradually that the present magnitude of his importance has yet to fully sink in. Indeed, an observer from outside the world of pop might well conclude that such artists as Olivia Newton-John, David Essex, Alice Cooper, or Tony Orlando and Dawn were at the top of the heap, judging from mass-media coverage. On this year's nationally televised American Music Awards, Olivia walked away with an armload of statuettes, and even Roy Clark won three or four. Elton John, though nominated in several categories, finished empty-handed. And it was the same at the Grammys.

But despite all indications to the contrary, Reg Dwight is the biggest phenomenon in modern-day rock. His songs are on every radio station, every hour of every day; the old ones as well as the new. If the singles charts were based solely on airplay, the Beatles' long-standing record of eight songs in the Hot 100 during one week would be quickly forgotten; it's been over a year since Elton had less than that many on the air. I've been spinning my dial for the last six hours, and there hasn't been two minutes when EJ wasn't on some station, with everything from 'Your Song' and 'Daniel' to 'Saturday Night' and his three current hits, 'Philadelphia Freedom', 'Pinball Wizard' and 'Someone Saved My Life Tonight'. These, plus three or four others, seem to be on constant rotation. A leading LA Top 40 now calls itself 'Your Number One Elton John Station', while another 'Plays More Elton John Than Anybody', and in New York a major station claims to be 'Your Official Elton John Spot On the Dial'. Not since Murray the K was the Fifth Beatle has there been anything like it.

It's no wonder a lot of people were caught off-guard. While everyone was out looking for the Next Big Thing, Elton quietly strolled in and took the throne. It was so unexpected; both Elvis and the Beatles had appeared as overnight sensations, out of darkest left field. Elton, growing in full public view, proved the old axiom that the obvious often masks the greatest surprises.

The easiest explanation is simply that the time is right; ten years since anything stupendous has occurred, three years of pop revival leading up to the need for some catalyst to emerge, and a new generation ready to crown its own superstars. And in the absence of anything new and overwhelming they could rally round (Bowie was just a little too far out, and no one else, from Lou Reed to the New York Dolls to the Raspberries to any of the other Great White Hopes, came close to correctly gauging what the masses were looking for in a Seventies Sensation), everyone seemed to latch on to Elton as the best thing around that wasn't left over from the Sixties. Given that, and the additional support of the older generations, Elton John's audience has become, over the last twelve months, demographically enormous. Everybody likes Elton.

His break with tradition extends into every facet of Elton's career. His music exists, if not in a vacuum, in a place of its own; it has set no stylistic trends, spawned no imitators, and not even one novelty record (Elvis had some fifty of these odd tributes; the Beatles over 200). His appeal to fans is not primarily as a sex symbol. He has inspired no new hair styles, no generation gap, no riots. Last tour, lines began forming at the box office three days before it opened. On his next, there'll be no trouble selling out Shea Stadium, or the Astrodome if he so chooses. He has nine platinum albums; this one had sold a million before it was even released. And all without fuss, without controversy.

Elton John is anything but controversial. His funny glasses and flamboyant costumes are his only concession to gimmickry, and neither his activities nor his music appear to be revolutionary in any sense. He's simply ubiquitous; a new single every few weeks, a new album every few months, constant appearances in movies, tennis matches, soccer games, everywhere you look except television, which is sure to follow. And, in everything he does, an unfaltering sense of image (loving his role and playing it to the hilt), a bit of humour, and a consistent, undeniable excellence.

If the need for re-evaluation has just caught up with us, it seems to be on Elton's mind too. His latest album is a conscious look at his past, and a surprisingly bitter reflection on the years of struggle, as if indignation were only now sinking in, along with awareness of his true worth. Of course it's hard to say how much Taupin's lyrics reflect Elton's feelings (in fact, much of the sourness seems to be Bernie's), although they must be pretty close in their thinking. With the songs on this album, and the lavish array of scrapbooks packaged with it (particularly the comic strip that caricatures many of those most influential in their career), Elton and Bernie seem to be standing at a new plateau, secure enough in their success to attempt expunging certain memories and settling a few old scores. Not that it's all rancour, but after two albums of material with plenty of pop charisma but little personal commentary, it's quite a change of pace.

The title song opens things up, setting the tone for most of what follows, stating a theme as it were:

'The Captain and the Kid
Stepping in the ring,
From here on sonny
It's a long and lonely climb . . .'†

These are the most literal of the song's lyrics; the rest of this six-minute autobiography is told in Taupin's typically oblique style ('Fantastic the feedback/The honey the hive could be holding/For there's weak winged young sparrows/That starve in the winter'†). Somehow the point is put across without the need of a linear story line, thanks to Elton's ability to transmit the most abstract impressions in the phrasings of his voice, the turn of a melody, or the slightest touch of a keyboard.

No poetry disguises the intent of 'Bitter Fingers', a vicious indictment of England's notorious Denmark Street music publishers (the same power-mad money mongers who have borne the brunt of more than one Ray Davies diatribe). There was a time when Elton and Bernie, as staff writers with the huge Dick James organization, were required to churn out pretty tunes on demand, which Taupin in particular seems to have found unconscionably degrading (although it could be argued that such discipline has played an important role in the formative years of many great songwriters, perhaps even Taupin and John). This seems to be something they needed to get out of their systems.

Although 'Philadelphia Freedom' is not to be found here, another track from the same session, with a lovely Gene

Page orchestral arrangement, provides some of the album's finest music. 'Tell Me When the Whistle Blows', which Taupin wrote in memory of his younger days on the road, inspired one of Elton's more charming melodies, and marks a pleasant interlude before the weighty statement that closes out the side.

In an album that is, if anything, over-serious, 'Someone Saved My Life Tonight' stands out as a slice of genuine profundity, revealing a side of Elton previously unseen, a depth of feeling barely touched in his more typical cavortings. This is Elton's song all the way, poking open an old wound dating from what must be the major turning point in his life, when only the last-minute intervention of a friend (the redoubtable John Baldry, whose picture accompanies the printed lyrics without explanation) rescued him from a hasty marriage he never really wanted, turning him instead to his music. Singing about himself, Elton has never been so moving; when he screams 'Damn it! Listen to me good . . .' it's as real as he's ever gotten.

The only thing that approaches its intensity is 'We All Fall in Love Sometimes', their most effective love ballad since 'Your Song', to which it seems somehow obscurely dedicated. A delicate, touching, tune that builds to a pitched climax, it blends smoothly into 'Curtains', whose cryptic, opaque lyrics offer no indication of what a powerful piece of music this song becomes, as it extends the mood of the previous song to one long, eloquent consummation. It reminds me in a way of the best parts of *Abbey Road*; a more fully realized concept of what the Beatles were reaching for there.

If this album is meant as a testimonial to the partnership of Elton John and Bernie Taupin, there can be no better example of how far their teamwork has evolved than the music contained here. Though it by no means eclipses their earlier work, somehow the underlying unity which emerges, the lyric book which makes Taupin's contribution more easily distinguishable (and understandable), and the album's unremitting emotional tone, all cast new light on the remarkable process by which Elton John transforms mere lyrics (however sophisticated) and mere musicians (however brilliant they may be – and certainly are) into a gestalt that defies analysis.

His best songs don't merely set words to music, they use both lyrics and basic melody as a starting point from which elaborately constructed moods are explored, often culminating in tonal crescendos that completely overshadow the songs' origins. Elton John's music has become refined now to the point where almost every song he does achieves that kind of impact, helped along by producer Gus Dudgeon and the rest of the team that, with *Captain Fantastic and the Brown Dirt Cowboy*, should finally receive proper recognition for their part in creating (we may as well face it) the only true pop Phenomenon of our times. This is the Year of Elton John, and this is the album that, in retrospect, may prove to be the focal point of his career.

* From *Phonograph Record* magazine, used by permission.
† c 1975 Big Pig Music.

Barry White
Just Another Way To Say I Love You (20th Century)

by Lester Bangs*

Right. This molasses-voiced monument to unashamed bulbosity and the death of Isaac Hayes knows so goddam many ways to say those three little words that you don't even think he's beating them to death unless you're rational. I seriously doubt if most of the people reading this like Barry White; most of his audience is either black (and I'm not talking about *Young Americans*) or incredibly straight and middle-class.

But listen. I was converted. I went down to see him at Olympia Stadium right here in my Motor City, plunged myself into the middle of an audience that looked like Africa in a sportin' hat with a sprinkle seasoning of gays and white folk who were just plain *weird* – old moms and dads, nut and bolt joiners off the factory line, lonely pubescent girls . . .

The only reason I went, of course, was that the tickets were free, and I wanted to take out this girl who was real big on Mr B. She turned out to be a dud (refused to kiss me at midnight on New Year's Eve, said something about 'you've got bad breath' – I'd like to see Barry write a song about *that*), but somehow in the process of trying to feel her leg and getting weird looks back while almost being put to sleep by the Ohio Players and then staring in a minor league, scaled down version of something approximating awe (don't wanna get carried away with the superlatives here, that's how us critics lose our credibility) at The Barry White Show in all its opulent glory . . . somehow, some way, somewhere just this side of the rainbow there's a place for us, all of us, and Barry White is mapping out this so to speak virgin turf.

See, first of all this massive orchestra comes out, all dressed in tuxedos and black ties (even the women), and starts sawing away (even the harpist was sawing) at 'Love's Theme', which the first five thousand times I heard it on the radio I did find truly pleasant. They ocean on like this for a bit, then Barry makes his first *Grand Appearance*, and damn my fillings if he ain't a stunner, nineteen hundred pounds of pure lumbering animal, makes Leslie West look like Steve Tyler, wrapped in a coal-red cape fit to put your eyes out. But this is only a preliminary sort of preview: what he's doing is leading out the Love Unlimited Singers. By hand. What a gentleman, transcends the debonair he do, really lives up to his image maybe better'n Lou Reed even, he's yanking the pore li'l things out under his humongous red wing just to see to it that their sweetkooze don't get hassled by any rampaging perverts who might be lurking in an audience of otherwise stolid, simple, upstanding, *loving* Barry White fans. Then the LU Singers do a straight Supremes imitation lounge act that's quite boring actually, and after 20 or 30 minutes of that The Man returns, Himself, In The Flesh, magisterially resplendent as he takes the stage, the orchestra lurching into one after another of his hits while he does (*all* he does) is walk around the stage (which is in the centre of the arena) in a circle, moaning the word '*love*' over and over in a stupefyingly insinuative basso, while he bestows his big loving eyes on various sweetbuns in the audience, and every once in awhile he'll reach out to take a rose from or merely squeeze the hands of these panting lovelies for one tremulous second which they'll carry with them, unlike certain communicable diseases, for the rest of their lives.

The old boob does this for a half hour or so, then wanders off to his dressing room. '*Looove . . . looove . . . looove . . .*' *And that's it! What an easy gig!* I have never been so jealous since I missed the chance to produce *Four Way Street*. The crowd, of course, eats it up.

I never saw anything quite so immaculately vacant, and after an experience like that (the best part was seeing a guy get murdered a few feet from our car while waiting to get out of the post-concert traffic jam) my whole attitude towards the Big B underwent a radical change. I actually left his songs on when they came on the radio. I was diggin' where the cat was comin' from and where he was goin', as a matter of fact the sooner he gets there the better, but in the meantime I'm gonna wallow in each new B.W. single like a vat of cocoa butter even if I still can't tell 'em apart. As an even more special bonus, I've got a whole new *album* of Barry White masterpieces, and you can bet I play it all the time. You gotta do something when you get tired of the Dictators 'cause you've played 'em thirteen times in a row.

I don't have to tell you what kind of a treat you're in for if you fork over your hard earned for *Just Another Way To Say I Love You* – Barry White is one artiste you can *trust*. But there is a special surprise herein for his fans and those of us, that special élite cadre who have come to consider him not just another globulous crossover act but something more akin to a *god*; Barry has mouthed '*looove*' so many different ways you'd think the man would be hard pressed by now to come up with a new one, but he's succeeded. His technique: slide ever-so-gently, like a palm going down a shoulder to a tit in a movie house, from simple declarations of undying devotion into the realm of prurient interest and ultimately to outright HOT DRIPPING KOOZODELIC BUTTERED

SOUL, er . . . anyway, *It* happens on 'Love Serenade (Part I)': starting out as a typically tropical B.W. instrumental deck, the big fella trots out his tonsils and slides them up some truly titillational stuff: 'Take it off . . . Baby, take it *all* off . . . I want you the way you came into the world . . . I don' wanna feel no clothes . . . I don' wanna see no panties . . . Take off that bra*ssièrre*, my dear . . . Everybody's gone . . . We're gonna take the receiver off the phone . . . Because baby, you and me, *heh* . . . *This night*, we're gonna get it on . . .'

Jesus, is this ever volatile stuff! If you look at it one way, just reading those words cold, it could be interpreted as a rape scene. Or even listening to Barry's unctuous, pooze-ooze voice. It is conceivable that this man is dangerous; at any rate, there is absolutely no question that he's gonna get what he's after.

* From *Creem* magazine, used by permission.

10cc

The Original Soundtrack (Mercury)

by Charles Shaar Murray*

Ain't no getting round it: 10cc make brilliant records.

Unfortunately, they suffer from the crippling delusion that cutesy lighting and pain-threshold volume constitute an acceptable substitute for stage presence, but once they scuttle into Strawberry Studios and get stuck into their composing, arranging, producing, engineering, overdubbing, compressing, mixing and so on and so forth, they mess your mind around a treat.

Like its predeccessors *10cc* and *Sheet Music*, *The Original Soundtrack* is a triumph for technique, not simply *playing* technique (which is what is usually referred to when slinging the term around), but applied technique exemplified in every single aspect of the record. The playing *is* superb throughout, but the production and engineering are exemplary (except that 'The Second Sitting Of The Last Supper', which is 'eavy, has to be played extremely loud before it begins to sound as dynamic as it should. Jimmy Page's production secrets are *still* secret), the melodies are exquisite, the lyrics are absolutely the sharpest, wittiest and most adroitly constructed that I've heard since . . . since 10cc's last album.

In addition, unlike most other bands blessed with a superabundance of technique, 10cc demonstrate an unparalleled ability to *utilize* said technique instead of simply falling in love with their own abilities and remaining content to demonstrate them until the proverbial cows come home to roost or do whatever cows do after work.

This being said, allow me to lay on you a theoretical proposition closely followed by a value judgment, on condition that I wander through the album immediately afterwards and justify both proposition and judgment on route.

Proposition: 10cc are *not*, as has been claimed, the new Beatles. (Anybody who demonstrates an ability to write songs gets saddled with that particular tag, which is by now hopelessly devalued, especially since Pilot are obviously the new Badfinger.)

What they *really* are is the new Mothers of Invention.

Value judgment: I hate this record, a hatred which escalates in direct proportion to my admiration for it, which in turn escalates every time I hear it.

If we start on the outside edge of the first side and set off in the general direction of the label, the first thing we encounter is 8 minutes and 39 seconds of something entitled 'Une Nuit In Paris'.

It's a very Mothers-ish piece set in some hell which a mischievous set designer has disguised as a caricature of music hall Paris complete with people dropping glasses and muttering 'Sacré bleu!', whores, bent coppers, street hustlers, con men, comic landladies and a demoniacally insistent refrain which sneers, 'One night in Paris is like a year in any other place/One night in Paris will wipe the smile off your pretty face/One girl in Paris is like loving every woman/One night in Paris may be your last!'

Sung with almost comic viciousness, the mock-French accent and the heavy on-the-loud pedal rumba beat gives it a teeth-on-edge air of menace which leaves the listener thoroughly shook up and totally unprepared for 10cc's next little assault on his sense of calm and spiritual well-being.

'I'm Not in Love' is superficially sweet and innocent, something like a Philly studio band performing a Lennon song with a McCartney vocal.

The trouble with 10cc is that their sweet songs are all booby-trapped. You pick up what looks like a new-born kitten and find that it's a transistorized sabre toothed tiger with vampiric tendencies.

The protagonist of this one insists that he's not in love despite overwhelming evidence to the contrary and that he only keeps his lady's pic on the wall because 'it hides a nasty stain that's lying there'. Half-way through, it's split by a horrific dream sequence in which a girl's voice repeats mechanically 'Be quiet – big boys don't cry.'

Well, there's two ways you can take that. Either the singer is really in love and doesn't have the courage to admit it – which is incredibly sad when you think about it – or else he really is faking it, which is even sadder.

Either way, it shows a considerable lack of faith in humanity.

The next song, by comparison, is pure comic relief, being about a black-mailing *papparozzo* who shoots doity pictures of a lady only to have her husband order a dozen prints, send them to *Playboy* and boost her into a movie star.

Over on the second side we find the band slipping effortlessly into another musical style – Intelligent Heavy Metal – for the heaviest song on the album, 'The Second Sitting For The Last Supper', which is a cry of rage and pain against the way we've all been betrayed by Christianity.

Lyrics please, maestro:

> '*Another nigger on the woodpile, another honky on the dole/another trip from the 15th floor, the greatest story ever told was wrong, so wrong . . . another Guru in the money, another mantra in the mail/An easy way from rags to riches, God's little acre up for sale.*'

Got it? One more time, please.

'The second coming of the Holy Ghost, we need a pocketful of miracles/ two thousand years and he ain't come yet, we kept his seat warm and the table set/the second sitting for the last supper.'

Okay, George Harrison – back on your head.

(Parenthetical note for technique freaks: 10cc's principal lyrical and musical technique is the juxtaposition of incongruous clichés to provide a whole that is infinitely greater than the sum of the parts – which is basically Uncle Frank's turf. But just as Zappa is probably the outstanding example in rock of the old riff about the cynic simply being a frustrated romantic, 10cc come on like kamikaze kids dedicated to trashing for trashing's sake – rock and roll nihilism run intellectual riot, working on the basic governing principle that one devastating lyric is worth half an hour of power chords and blood-enriched peanut butter any day of the goddam week.)

The angelic voice of Kevin Godley is next unleashed upon a defenceless little song entitled 'Brand New Day', which is so crushingly banal that if it was anybody but 10cc you'd write it off as being simply dumb.

As it is 10cc you haveta check out the lyrics and do a double-take when you finally suss what Godley's actually singing, which is: '*You work all day, you sweat and strain/It's getting late, them pearly gates might close before you reach them/Here boy, there boy, the devil got you running everywhere boy/ I smell cooking and it might be you . . .*'

I'm not sure I like this. I mean, there are negative world views and negative world views but this she is bloody ridiculous.

Onwards.

Next up is the best song about a dealer since Mayfield's 'Superfly' song-cycle.

Again, a quick flashenheimer of the lyrics: '*He's never got the stuff if you come to him without money/ he hasn't got the time for the people who are down on their knees/but if the price is right you won't be asking him where it came from,*' which is really telling it the way it unfortunately is.

Again that's pure comic relief compared to the next one, unbelievably entitled 'Life Is A Minestrone'. The corollary, you'll be glad to know, is that 'death is a cold lasagne'.

This one moves like a 'Lady Madonna' dancing on a red-hot floor and contains more gorgeous lyrical flashes, one of which does in M. Ferrari by observing 'love is the fire of flaming brandy upon a crêpe suzette'. The others I'll leave you to dig out for yourselves.

Finally, 'The Film Of My Love' utilizes every single verbal and musical cliché about movies.

Voici: '*A clapper board kiss, there's an Oscar in this, a hit or a miss, whatever/a box office wedding, a première for two, we'll be on location forever.*' It's so close to the real thing that it's damn near as intolerable as the songs in Marx Brothers movies (apart from Groucho's, that is).

Okay, that's the album. As you may have gathered I find *The Original Soundtrack* an awesome achievement on all levels, but its unrelenting hatred for anything outside of Strawberry Studios is ultimately as loathsome as the mindless complacency that it so brilliantly seeks to subvert.

I mean, what kinda childhoods did these guys have?

In the final analysis, Uncle Frank has the most apposite line, which goeth like this: '*Your whole attitude stinks, I say, and the life you lead is completely empty.*' Zappa always made it clear, at least by inference, where he stood socially and politically.

All 10cc show us is where they *don't* stand, and by doing so, they've painted themselves into a social, if not artistic, corner.

The Original Soundtrack is brilliant. And I hate it.

* From *New Musical Express*, used by permission.

Bay City Rollers
Once Upon A Star Bell

by Mick Farren*

If we forget for the moment that the Bay City Rollers are the biggest thing in the under-sixteen market since crunchy peanut butter, ignore that they've developed a style of dress that represents a sanitized version of Manchester United's notorious North End, and if we even overlook that the B.C.R.s are all pretty enough to cause instant reaction in teeny flesh, it gives us a unique chance to examine the music behind the pop phenomenon.

What we seem to be confronted with is a rather low energy surf music revival band. This in itself would be a fine and glorious thing if it wasn't that all the cuts on this album have a slight but noticeable air of lethargy about them. The combination of this, plus an extraordinary set of influences, makes the whole deal a little disturbing.

'Bye Bye Baby' has the sound of something Brian Wilson might have knocked out on an off day. 'The Disco Kid' has a certain similarity to the Lovin' Spoonful's 'Summer in the City', except it's been put through a wringer until all Sebastian's sweaty dynamism has been squeezed out, leaving the B.C.R.'s tune with the consistency of a dish rag that's seen better days.

'La Belle Jeanne' is an infinitely forgettable ballad with the kind of stupid pseudo-frog romanticism that McCartney wallowed in on 'Michelle'.

'When Will You Be Mine?' is possibly the most confusing cut on the whole record. It's pretty much a straight lift from the Everly Brothers' 'When Will I Be Loved?', except the guitar, vocals and entire structure have all been put through the de-energizing process to the point it sounds like Don and Phil stumbling round in a slow tranquillizer daze.

'Angel Baby' is a doo-wop ballad that could be a Rubettes' tune. It comes complete with spoken middle and suffers from the same slowed down effect.

The standard 'Keep On Dancing' is attacked in a more

sprightly manner. At least it doesn't drag, but it could be a filler track on an album by any middle-grade harmony orientated band.

On to side two and we have 'Once Upon A Star'. This is the B.C.R.'s homage to the Beatles. And down to vocal sound, guitar, everything in fact, it amounts to a careful reconstruction of the *Rubber Soul* period.

There's no actual homage to the Stones, although an Uncle Keith guitar riff figures prominently on 'Let's Go', which is the closest the band gets to high energy. 'Oh Marlina' quickly wipes out the mood with another travelogue romance chant. 'My Teenage Heart' could have easily been a hit for Bobby Vee in 1961; 'Rock and Roll Honeymoon' attempts to get down with glitter band pulse drumming, greaser echo and a lot of shouting, but it fails to really get anywhere. The final cut, 'Beautiful Dreamer', is the kind of dirge that cocker spaniels would excel at if dogs could sing. There's some third-rate Harrison 'While My Guitar Gently Weeps' style picking thrown in for good measure.

Now don't get me wrong. This album isn't all bad. Admittedly I'd never ever play it from choice, but it is tidily played and neatly produced. It's nothing if not competent. What appalls me is that the B.C.R.s, who seem to be the apple of the adolescent's eye, should come out with such a massive display of negative energy.

Maybe it's because they're just too pretty, they feel they don't have to try all that hard. The little girls will love them whatever they do. Perhaps they should remember that it's this kind of under-achievement that caused the decline and fall of one Elvis Presley.

Another alternative is that they're too isolated. In the '64–'67 vintage period of British singles the competition was conscious and intense. Pirate radio gave us such a massive coverage of new releases that in terms of hit 45s, everyone's arse was up for grabs. Townshend, Marriot, Jagger/Richard and Lennon/McCartney, no matter how big they were, constantly worked on outdoing each other with conscious creative writing, production techniques and little sound goodies that would grab both punters' imaginations and their quids.

Today's emergent stars seem to be cocooned in a closed world where, as long as their management can wheel and deal them into the 'Top of the Pops' slots and they brush their teeth regularly and smile nice, their records will always sell.

As long as B.C.R.s continue to work in this kind of over-comfortable environment, their music will never rise above the pedestrian.

* From *New Musical Express*, used by permission.

Eagles
Their Greatest Hits 1971–1975 (Asylum)

by Simon Frith*

Well the cover gets nought. It's got tricksy writing like in a *Beano* quiz, so that you have to hold it up to the light and squint horizontally to read it. And no information: no group names, no recording dates, no guide to the albums from which these tracks came. Shoddy for a greatest hits package 'cause this record isn't for Eagles cognoscenti – they'll have all these songs already. This one's for people like me, who aren't sure and the cover isn't convincing.

But I'll give the music five: the best American pop album since 'The Best of Bread'. It was the great 'Lyin' Eyes' which made me realize: the Eagles are not a country rock group, they're progressive middle-of-the-road. The right words are: professional, versatile, calculated, crafty, brilliant. Anne Nightingale likes them and Noel Edmonds, and they haunt the dreams of every Radio One producer. In fact I can't think why I ever thought they were country rock – their dominant sound is not the steel guitar, the fiddle, nasal voices; it's the floating production of clean harmonies and acoustic rhythms and restrained strings and the occasional carefully wild guitar solo. The sounds of classy pop, LA not Nashville, Lobo's the person they remind me of.

There's a dearth of good pop at present; the Eagles are the best, and their greatest hits are wonderful and much more satisfying than their pretentious 'real' albums. What we have here is AM sensibility at its most precise – maudlin and droopy and romantic. Searching for love but frightened with it or, in their words, 'lookin' for a lover who won't blow my cover'. Deep male fears of women as hard, treacherous, exploiters, milking men of the best of their love, taking them to the limit and leaving. No wonder the Eagles were drawn to the myth of the 'Desperado', the lonely noble cowboy, doing without everyone because people (and especially female people) kill.

It's unsexy music, narcissistic. 'I want to sleep with you,' they sing in 'Peaceful Easy Feeling', 'in the desert tonight.' And I believe them, sleep is safest. Songs of impotence and I love them and play them over and over.

* From *Street Life*, used by permission.

THE A & R MEN
by Simon Frith

Introduction

I've been surveying the year of singles again (see the accompanying League Table) and come to the conclusion that 1974–5 was a dull year up in the charts. There was no dominant group or style but a series of over-worked formulae – white (Glitter Band, Mud, Kenny) and black (Barry White, Stylistics, George McCrae). The year's best singles were the successful *outsiders*; they refreshed simply by having charm (Billy Swan's 'I Can Help', Pete Wingfield's '18 With A Bullet', Ace's 'How Long') and vitality (Rupie Edward's 'Ire Feeling', Jim Gilstrap's 'Swing Your Daddy', Labelle's 'Lady Marmalade'). The year's only 'new' fad were the Bay City Rollers – and their success meant more to tartan patch makers than to the music biz; the year's biggest surprise hits, Tammy Wynette's 'Stand By Your Man' and 'D-I-V-O-R-C-E', were cut seven years ago; the only chart regulars to enhance (rather than exploit) their reputation were 10cc with 'I'm Not In Love'. For the rest, it was all grist to the nostalgia mill, and I can't hear 1974–5 as being very *significant*.

Part of the reason for this was that nothing much was happening to the *taste* for pop; audiences seemed happy enough in their various grooves and, with the exception of the hard-faced Roller girls, there was no musical fanaticism about, no uniforms that needed badges. By 1974 record companies had come to terms with the new selling media – commercial radio and discos. Commercial radio turned out to need little attention. It's clear what sound the major stations are trying for – progressive MOR, the easy-listening records from American FM – but, as yet, they seem to have little effect on singles sales.

Everyone, on the other hand, is now convinced of the selling power of discos. In 1974–5 there were more hits from more releases on more labels than ever before (so much for the economic crisis); it was a good year for American, and particularly black American, records; pop reggae made a chart reappearance – all this can be attributed to the energy with which the disco audience was pursued. Disco djs were swamped with singles and big English companies scurried madly through the catalogues of obscure American ones to find potential dancing hits. The results were various: Island, for instance, completely failed to find success with their USA Series, while Pye's Disco Demand Series managed to get the most mindless (and white) aspects of Northern Soul into the national charts; Jonathan King's UK label, a pioneer of the use of discos, didn't have a single hit and was joined in lack of success by Atlantic, Stax, and even Tamla and Philadelphia, the soul labels that were the first to get regular white sales; their places were taken by new names – Jay Boy, All Platinum – and the sharpest operator of all turned out to be Wes Farrell, veteran of family audience marketing (the Partridge Family), now making music for the New York disco crowds. Disco Tex, on Farrell's Chelsea label, was the cynical success of the year.

Disco Tex was a symptom: 1974–5 was a very *pop* year, very commercial. The music wasn't very interesting, nor was its audience; what was fascinating was the state of the record *industry*. No company had any particular advantage – no Beatles (Apple, for the first time, fell from the top of the League), no secret mailing list; competition was real. And so the event of the year was the bankruptcy of the B & C; Trojan empire. Maybe *Rock File*'s League Tables do reveal something – we recorded Trojan's lack of success last year, and Decca, bottom of 1973–4's Losers' Division with 1 hit from 110 releases, cut their output down to 45 (they still only managed two hits though – the anglicized version of Gilbert Becaud's 'Little Love And Understanding', and 'Hold On To Love', from Peter Skellern, who shortly thereafter signed with Island). Certainly the questions raised by the year's singles statistics are about the business: why did Phonogram have so much more success with its US labels (Avco, Mercury, All Platinum) than Decca with its releases on London? Why did Rak continue to thrive while UK faded? How did Magnet, a label established solely on the success of Alvin Stardust, manage to take off as an important all-round independent?

Rock critics are always looking in vain for *musical* trends, but the only continuing trend in Britain in the 1970s has been a business one, the diversification of the industry. Until (and during) the British Pop Explosion of the mid-sixties the music business was dominated by four companies (EMI, Decca, Pye, Philips); since then their influence has slowly been weakened. This process has had two sources: independent producers and independent labels.

Independent producers function, in creative terms, as mini record companies: the producer finds and contracts his own acts, records them at his own expense and brings the finished tape to a record company; the company presses and releases it on one of its own labels and pays a royalty on every copy sold to the producer. If the record flops then it's a cheap deal for a record company which has been spared the production costs; if the record's a success, the company has to pay out a higher royalty on every copy sold than if it had put the record together itself. Independent production was pioneered by the successful writer/producer/A & R men of the late sixties – Roger Cook and Roger Greenaway, Tony Macaulay, Tony Hatch; there are now few successful pop operators who *don't* work as independents. The implications of this for the pop business are obvious: even if the producers' records finally *emerge* on the major labels, the origins of pop singles are now much more diverse.

Independent labels began differently, as a response to the *rock* market. By the late sixties Britain's major companies were aware of their ineptness with the new, album-oriented, audience and began to set up their own progressive labels – Harvest (EMI), Vertigo (Phonogram), Dawn (Pye), Deram and Nova (Decca) – to compete with the new rock independents – Island, Immediate Chrysalis. The independents have had the better of this competition, but, on the other hand, the situation soon stabilized. The only new progressive label in the last couple of years has been Virgin and the most significant competition for rock acts these days is with American labels – RCA, for example, got Bowie, A & M Rick Wakeman, Warners Rod Stewart.

A second source of independence has been the musicians themselves. Inspired by business acumen (they'd give themselves a better economic deal) and claiming idealism (they'd offer fellow artists a better economic *and* creative deal) a number of labels have followed the Beatles' Apple – the Moody Blues' Threshold, ELP's Manticore, Deep Purple's Purple and Oyster, Rolling Stones, Elton John's Rocket, and, most recently, Led Zeppelin's Swansong, the Kinks' Konk, George Harrison's Dark Horse. Only Rocket and Swansong could claim to have had much success with their signings (Kiki Dee and Bad Company, respectively) and the major companies have preserved close enough ties with all these labels to continue to draw a share of the superstars' earnings.

But there is a third and more threatening source of new company – independent producers going the whole hog. Larry Page's Penny Farthing label, one of the earliest of these, had a bad year in 1974–5, but Micky Most's Rak maintained its astonishing record and was joined in success by a sudden din of new labels – Peter Shelley's Magnet; Gull, set up by MCA's A & R men when MCA decided to stop signing British acts; GTO, the label of Dick Leahy, Bell's ex-manager; Don Arden's Jet; State, run by ex-Polydor men John Fruin and Wayne Bickerton.

Apart from the progressive Gull, these labels are unashamedly pop oriented and their bosses have mostly worked in A & R – they know how the big companies operate. They also know that in an unashamedly pop year, with nothing much of musical interest going on, there is an even bigger onus than usual on A & R departments to come up with successful 'product' . . .

A & R Men

A & R stands for Artists and Repertoire: an A & R man is responsible for what music goes out on a company's label –

for getting artists signed to the label, for keeping them there (or dismissing them) and for the records that are issued in their names. Though in the short term a record company's success may reflect the effectiveness of its *salesmen* – pluggers, press office, distributors, sales reps – in the long run success depends on A & R judgments – who to sign, how to record and present them to the public. In 1971 EMI could still claim that:

> Using hundreds of promotion men and over a thousand salesmen EMI has the power to stimulate demand both in quantity and quality . . .*

But in reply to the question 'What percentage of winners is a company like EMI looking for?' their Managing Director said 'If you got twenty per cent winners, real winners, of course you would be doing very well.' and *Rock File*'s League Tables show that EMI achieve nothing like that ratio, despite their army of salesmen. When it comes to the crunch it is the A & R men who, like football managers, have to carry the can for failure and their job (again like football management) requires diverse skills:

(a) *Talent spotting*

The terrible Warning that hangs over every A & R man's bed concerns the Beatles: Would *You* Have Turned Them Down? And certainly a large part of an A & R man's time is taken up with watching and listening to unknown acts, assessing their potential. But this is only one form of talent spotting. Another is poaching, picking up an act when its contract with a rival company runs out. There are various reasons for doing this; sometimes the hope is to revitalize a fading career; sometimes the move involves a complete change of musical direction; sometimes the new company simply offers an act a greater freedom to carry on doing what it's doing, in the belief that it has yet to reach its maximum

* This is quoted in Michael Wale's *Vox Pop*, from which I have also taken the comment on success rate.

market. In these deals an A & R department is offering 'sympathy' as well as money and this was obviously a key element in, for example, Island's 1974–5 signings of Kevin Ayers, John Cale, and Peter Skellern. At a more cynical level a company might simply outbid its rivals for a known successful act; the decision is based on a straight calculation – what is the act's earning power? What can we afford to offer? A big label can always outbid a small label (and so Mercury got 10cc from UK) but can't always avoid *over* bidding (as I'd bet RCA did for the Kinks). These signings are the equivalent of transfer deals in soccer – even with the most established stars judgments still have to be made about future playing potential.

A & R men don't just judge acts, they've also got to be able to spot *records*, and this, again, in various contexts. First, there are all the tape deals being offered – are they worth it? Jonathan King's skill, for example, has always been with sounds rather than acts – who else would have heard the possibilities of 'Wave Your Knickers In The Air'? Then, there are the US catalogues to go through. The master here is Nigel Grainge at Phonogram, who's interested not just in what might hit but also in what *won't*; he doesn't like releasing records needlessly and so, for instance, did not bother to release All Platinum's American follow up to Shirley's 'Shame, Shame, Shame'. Thirdly, record companies are now aware of the profits to be made from an astute re-release. It was nifty work on Anchor's part to issue Brian Hyland's 'Sealed With A Kiss' just in time for the summer of '75, and Decca's good judgment got the Chi-Lites' 'Have You Seen Her?' into the top three twice in four years, but the re-release of the year was 'Stand By Your Man', as CBS found an unexpected source of wealth in their back catalogue. There's less money lost if an oldie flops and the profits of a successful re-release are consequently greater – going through back numbers is now part of the A & R routine.

(b) *Accounting*

All A & R decisions are basically financial (that's what they mean by 'potential') and the calculations have to be precisely made. Companies don't just sign a group and leave them to get on with it, they have to weigh the necessary investment against the possible returns. There are obvious questions to be asked: how ready is the act to record? How much rehearsing time does it need? What advance should it get for equipment? What recording costs are necessary? How much help should the company give with organizing gigs and tours and publicity?

The answers are not absolute but depend on one simple consideration – how much is the act going to earn? And this is where the problems start: not only may companies calculate this all wrong, but they can't avoid (though they rarely admit this) splitting their acts into potential divisions, and a future Division One act is going to get more investment than a possible Division Three-er. The latter musicians inevitably feel neglected and this becomes one of the major causes of transfer deals – a Third Division act with one company hopes to be treated as First Division with another (perhaps the clearest example of such neglect, and the misjudgment that it involved, was Apple's treatment of James Taylor). Meanwhile, a potential First Division act which fails involves a company in such heavy losses that it is often loath to admit it and merely redoubles its efforts (and expenditure). It's not unknown for an A & R man to become so obsessed with an act which he and no one else believes in that he not only neglects his other signings but even gives up the search for anyone new. Even if such an act does eventually sell records, its success may not be profitable – too much money has been spent in getting it there. This year, for example, A & M got a hit with Supertramp, and Vertigo scored with Alex Harvey, but their future sales are going to have to be long lasting to make up for their past records of failure.

It is in this context that competition between record companies is unequal – some have much more capital to risk than others. John Peel was an excellent talent spotter for his Dandelion label but never had the necessary money to bankroll his protégés. Clifford T Ward, Kevin Coyne, Medicine Head have all had greater success with their subsequent, wealthier labels, and Peel couldn't even afford to *sign* Roxy Music and T. Rex – he knew they were Division One acts but couldn't provide the production and promotion costs they'd need to prove it.

Another calculation A & R departments have to make in signing an act concerns the *balance* of their label. There are two strategies. Some companies like to dangle a finger in every pie – if teenybop idols are selling they'll sign a teenybop idol; if it's drug-crazed hippies then they'll have one of them; if discos are a market then they'll make disco music. The problem with this is that a label's identity may become so diffuse that it can attract neither musicians nor audiences from the special scenes it's trying to cover; and so companies have created their own special labels (Harvest, etc.), while others have tried to change identity with huge, well-publicized, signings (CBS with rock acts in the sixties; a number of pop labels with black acts in the seventies).

The alternative is to *begin* by developing a specific identity and only sign acts that match it. The independent rock companies are an example, Island and Charisma; their hope was to build up an audience that trusted the label and would listen sympathetically to any act on it. But Tamla Motown has been the most successful 'identity label'; Tamla music became identified as a specific genre. Trouble arises when tastes change – specialist labels have nothing to fall back on. Some are content to remain specialist, catering for their small but sure soul or folk or jazz minority; but any company which has had a taste of mass success is under-pressure to diversify. In America Motown developed its own progressive (Rare Earth) and pop (Mowest) labels, to add white and non-soul acts to its lists; Island have deliberately built up an A & R team with diverse tastes, in order to widen their spread of music.

All these calculations rest on assessment of the market, on an understanding of how records get *sold*. A & R men have to know about Radio 1 and *Top Of The Pops*, about discos and the college circuit. A record is rarely made without reference to who it's being made *for*; A & R men are inevitably involved in the problems of publicity and promotion.

No wonder that their recording contracts go into such detail: 'The Company shall have the right to choose which tracks shall be issued as singles, which on albums, and which not at all; the Company shall have the right to decide when recorded material shall be released; the Company shall have the right to decide how an album shall be presented – the order of the tracks, the design of the sleeve; the Company shall have the right to decide the title of an album and of all the tracks thereon; the Company reserve the right to re-arrange, remix, re-record the Company's product . . .'

The fact is that A & R men are operators, dealers. Talent spotting is the easy part; then come the years of handling the acts (and their managers), of coming to terms with independent producers (and their tapes); of negotiating the rights to American tracks. It all needs careful thought, careful calculation, careful *accounting* (and over their desks hang the balance sheets).

(c) *Producing*

The A & R man is responsible for transforming the potential of the talent he's signed into a saleable product and traditionally his most important role was as record producer. At EMI, for example, Cliff Richard was the responsibility of Norrie Paramour, the Beatles of George Martin; both men were part of the A & R team, both were expected to supervise recordings, to arrange and engineer and realize their acts' music. These days an A & R department's production role need not be so direct; the job is still to get the right sound but this means, more and more, getting the right *outside* producer and studio and engineer. Derek Green of A & M explained the eighteen-month gap between signing Andy Fairweather-Low and recording him, this way:

The reason the first album took so long was because we

> were searching around for the right producer. We approached all the big names, but none of them could hear the potential in the music. They all said no. Then we finally got through to Elliot Mazer, Neil Young's producer. Although he liked some of the stuff, he wasn't too sure about it at first. We eventually persuaded him . . .*

(This is also a good example of a company's desperate faith in an act for which they've just paid a lot of money. If I'd been told by 'all the big names' that they couldn't hear 'the potential in the music' I think I'd've given up.)

(d) *Management*

An artist is bound to a record company by a contract which demands so much 'product' per year; the A & R department have to ensure that the terms of the contract are met. But, in the end, there's no way to *force* a musician to make music, and certainly no way to force an act to make *good* (or commercial) music. Enforcing a contract means keeping everyone happy; preventing freak-outs and piss-abouts, papering over group cracks, having the lads (or lasses) on the road when they should be on the road, in the studio when they should be in the studio; keeping the costs down, the spirits up. Man management (with the help and hindrance of the acts' own managers) – it's like football again and just as important a part of the job. I'm convinced that Island's success, for example, has rested on its patient coping with the occasional waywardness of its acts.

Talent spotters, accountants, producers, managers, and all the time with one eye on the market and one on head office; it's not surprising that A & R men pop up from a variety of backgrounds: *writers* (Richard Williams went from *Melody Maker* to Island, Pete Frame from *Zig Zag* to Charisma, Andrew Bailey from *Rolling Stone* and *The Evening Standard* to Bell): *musicians* (Dave Dee is with Atlantic, Muff Winwood, ex-Spencer Davis Group, with Island); *disc jockeys*

* In an interview with Rob Partridge in *Melody Maker*.

(ex-BBC man Alan Black is with Polydor; Nigel Grainge of Phonogram and Pete Waterman of Magnet both ran discos); *promotion men* and *salesmen* (the internal route, followed by Ian Ralfini and Martin Wyatt of Anchor, by Peter Summerfield of Pye, Robin Blanchflower of CBS).

The variety of people in A & R makes for a variety of company styles. I have been describing A & R in general terms, the outline of the job. But, as the League Tables show, the job gets done differently, well and badly, with different emphases. Different companies experience different pressures.

Pye

Pye is best described as a middle-of-the-road company; a long-established British pop label, it had its share of success in the sixties (the Kinks, Petula Clark, the Searchers) but never picked up a superstar and has been singularly unenterprising in its rock signings – the only big success on Dawn was Mungo Jerry, signed through a tie-up with Red Bus Productions. The A & R director is Peter Prince, the A & R manager Peter Summerfield; the way they work provides a clear picture of the state of mainstream British pop, 1974–5.

They still get the tapes trickling in ('99 per cent rubbish'), they still travel the country viewing acts, following up tips, but the basic signing the A & R men do these days ('a couple a week') is on a package deal with an independent producer/writer/artist team. Pye claim a special advantage in these deals – many of the most successful independent producers (Tony Hatch, John Schroeder, Tony Macaulay) are ex-Pye men. So Pye got the Hatch/Des Parton/Sweet Sensation singles, and so they landed the world's biggest selling single of 1974, Biddu's production of Carl Douglas's 'Kung Fu Fighting' (on the other hand, they didn't get the Biddu Orchestra album – he did that deal with Epic).

The second A & R task is sorting through American material. Pye have the rights to a number of American labels and a variety of ways of dealing with them. Some tracks simply appear on the Pye International label, one-off arrangements; some US labels – Buddah, Kama Sutra, Stax – retain their identity. With Buddah the English A & R men decide on what and what not to release – Gladys Knight's hit 'Try To Remember'/'The Way We Were', for example, was not an American 45 until Pye had it in the British charts ten; with 20th Century, by contrast, Pye had to follow the Americans' release policy and 20th Century now has its own English office.

Pye have also had a long-time (and rather surprising) access to obscure soul singles, through the passion of John Abbey and his Contempo label. The company were comparatively slow to appreciate the full potential of the disco market, but when they did, they had the contacts, the understanding, the material, to do it full justice; Pye's Disco Demand Series run by Dave MacAleer, succeeded with its odd combination of straight soul, doctored backing tracks ('Footsee'), and English made-for-disco products like Wayne Gibson's 'Under My Thumb'. The label's mixture of cynicism and purism seems a basic part of Pye's attitude to soul; their latest venture is the Right On label, whose releases will be decided by Dave Godin, an obsessional soul collector/writer.

Pye has had reasonable success with its tape deals and American labels but the hard point remains that the label has few successful acts of its own and has a very poor hit-to-release ratio (both Pye and Pye International are low in our Losers' Division). The A & R department claim that this reflects the essential MOR character of their music, that some of their singles function simply to get a bit of Radio 2 play, to keep an artist in the public ear so that they'll buy his albums; but the majority sink without trace. They also dismiss the British market as being of diminishing importance in world sales (Des O'Connor, I was surprised to learn, is 'big in Japan'). Maybe so, but it sounds as though Pye is becoming a minor, specialist, MOR label, its pop success confined to the tape deals negotiated with shrewder operators than its own A & R department.

CBS

CBS is a telling contrast to Pye, a major American label which not only smoothly added rock to its distinguished classical and pop catalogues but in doing so became, with Dylan and Sly and Paul Simon and Janis Joplin, a *leading* rock label. In England the A & R director, Dan Loggins, is an American, and his team have divided responsibilities: Robin Blanchflower, A & R manager, is the traditional English show-biz figure; Alan Bown works as talent scout and artist liaison; Nicky Graham, Paul Phillips, and Michael Gane are staff producers. The English A & R men make none of the decisions about the company's American material, have no interest in one-off or short-term contracts, and are wary of tape deals with independent producers (though two of their biggest sellers, David Essex and the Wombles, reached them this way).

Their basic brief is to sign acts which are going to last, and what they have to remember is that CBS has got an amazing line-up already – there's no point in signing anyone who's not different or better than the company's existing talent. The tapes come in, as everywhere else, but for CBS these are a minor measure of potential. How does the act perform live? How does it *look*? Has it got the material/appeal/originality/guts on which to base a *career*?

Behind these questions lies an attitude that clearly comes from American CBS: the relationship between a record company and *all* its artists should be very close; a record company has responsibilities beyond the formal terms of a contract – to be involved with promotion and publicity and management, to *look after* its musicians. And so CBS has one of the few British A & R departments in which *everyone* can (and does) still produce; it has one of the few to appreciate the importance of local radio as a source of tour promotion (making special interview and jingle tapes, tying single releases into this strategy).

But CBS remains a schizophrenic company: it is essentially American (two-thirds of its releases) and has American, album-oriented, attitudes – careful and tactical talent spotting, supportive production and management, well organized tours, and so on; singles are thought of as album fodder. But at the same time CBS is an old-fashioned English pop label, with the Wombles and Tammy Jones and a manipulative appreciation of the importance of *Top Of The Pops* and the centre-spread in the *Sunday Mirror*. The consequence of this is not that CBS does particularly badly, but that it should do better! The company has signed a number of *rock* acts (Kokomo, Starry Eyed and Laughing, A Band Called O) which have the right style for *pop* (Top Twenty) success – the question is whether they will get it with CBS. So far they've fallen through the hole in the middle of the company: the pop A & R men aren't comfortable with rock, the rock A & R men aren't comfortable with singles. And so the most successful CBS pop act is the Wombles.

EMI

EMI is big like the BBC, and still recovering from the Beatles. Big means complex: Harvest and Capitol have their own staff, some American labels have their own logos, other American material is issued on EMI International, the EMI label is left with 'everything from Queen to Cilla Black'. The Beatles were such a huge success that the company only realized later that they'd been carried through the sixties despite an archaic organization. The EMI label has started again from scratch, shedding the over-large team of staff producers and talent scouts and faded stars, trying to change the image from grand old man of British pop, to a new and *thrusting* young label.

EMI's A & R team (Nick Mobbs, Martin Clark, Ian McLintock) is genuinely obsessed with talent spotting. They don't believe that anything much is going to come in and so they go out – on the road, round the clubs, glued to *New Faces* and the *Melody Maker*'s folk/rock contests. Cockney Rebel were watched in clubs; Be Bop De Luxe (who ended up on Harvest) created a local (Yorkshire) buzz which reached EMI via a record shop's enthusiasm to a company salesman. The importance of these signings (and Pilot and

Queen) wasn't just for themselves but also to encourage others. EMI would now like a couple of *really* heavy acts (and privately the A & R men believe that Harvest has lost its way – neither commercially successful, nor convincingly progressive; they'd like EMI to move into its territory).

The label is happy to sign tape deals, take one-off records, but they're more interested in the long term and here their talent-spotting instincts pull two ways – on the one hand it's safer to deal with established acts ('if they've been together for a long time they must have *something*') who've got live experience, their own management, a 'professional' outlook, but on the other hand it's more *exciting* to develop a talent from nowhere, and the department has its own eight-track studio and the dream of finding something on the rough tape that *will* turn out to be magic when the right knobs are pulled.

For acts that are signed, EMI's A & R department plays the same supervisory role as in any other company – getting the right producer, thrashing out release policy – but they are much more *cost* conscious than anyone else I spoke to, everything has to be *accounted* for. Not because EMI is hard up (no signs of a recession there) but because it is so rich – it is so *easy* for a group to lose a thousand quid on a silly single that the A & R department have a special duty to make sure that they don't. The weekly A & R conference is joined by marketing men – the A & R department has to justify what it's been doing.

Maybe in consequence EMI are open in admitting that far too many of their singles flop and that *Rock File*'s League Tables are an accurate guide to a company's success. They try *never* to release a single that they don't believe will be a chart hit and the only exceptions are for occasional 'political' reasons (which I take to mean that if one of their major artists sends in an appalling track as his next single they have to take it) and the few 'catalogue sellers' – records which make a five-figure sale but over a long period to a steady market – Cliff fans, Northern soul regulars.

Singles success is not, of course, the *major* concern of a record company – there's far more money in albums; but the overall aim is to have successful *acts*, who will sell records of all sorts. This includes singles and EMI well know that the top twenty is still by far the best break for an act. Their failure with singles *is* a failure of A & R judgment and they'll only make one additional comment: for them, Radio 1 remains the essential medium for singles sales ('we are their slaves'); they experience the 'sub-cultural pressure' to pre-guess the BBC's taste, and they believe that the station is slowly drifting towards an MOR sound – just when they're trying to shift the EMI label the other way.

Magnet

Magnet was started when writer/producer Peter Shelley played his tape of 'Alvin Stardust' singing 'My Coo Coo Ca Choo' to accountant Michael Levy and persuaded him that it was a chart cert and the good basis for a new record company. Within two years Magnet has become one of Britain's most successful independent labels, ambitious enough to handle more than just its own productions. The company's day-to-day A & R man is Pete Waterman, an influential Midlands dj who came to Shelley's attention when he helped break Alvin Stardust. His original job was to find soul and reggae singles for possible Magnet release, but now it's he who goes through *all* the tapes, goes out spotting (he found Adrian Baker). He takes anything interesting to Shelley and they take their joint thoughts to Levy's weekly decision-making conference.

Magnet follows the A & R strategy developed by Dick Leahy at Bell in the early seventies: Limited Output, Intense Promotion. They are looking for *hit singles*, reject all offers of heavy bands, don't even pretend to be able to handle someone like 10cc. They want a *record*; they don't care who the performer is, how they look, if they perform live (Magnet knew nothing about Susan Cadogan, for example, when they bought 'Hurts So Good' from Dip); they're not even interested in potential – they want the hit *now*. Their only questions are: is it good material? does it come across? does it *sound* right?

Pete Waterman is one of the few A & R men who has direct contact with the kids who buy his company's records – he plays to them in his disco, sells to them in his soul shop. His kids buy records, not acts, and Magnet's 'servicing' role is performed accordingly: so, 'Hurt So Good' was remixed to bring the voice forward, ethnic reggae was turned into disco-pop by astute knob-fiddling; now Waterman produces Susan Cadogan himself – the result is no longer reggae, but given what happens to other women in reggae (nothing) I doubt if Susan minds.

As a small company Magnet can't *afford* many failures, they haven't got enough of a cross-subsidy effect from established artists' steady sales – hence the intense promotion. They *don't* believe that Radio 1 is everything (though they're good at Radio 1 games: Adrian Baker made special jingles for Tony Blackburn and Noel Edmonds to support 'Sherry'; having played the jingle the djs followed through with the record, an effective ploy with a distinctive sound. Pete Wingfield used the same tactic with '18 With A Bullet'); they have an extensive disco mailing list (probably the most effective there is, except for Nigel Grainge's at Phonogram) and claim to get about 400 very valuable reaction letters on everything they release. Four of their 1974–5 hits were 'cross-overs' – got radio play as a result of their disco popularity.

Success brings its own pressures. Peter Shelley, with his own musical ambitions, no longer has time to look after Alvin Stardust so Magnet went outside, to Roger Greenaway. The result, 'Sweet Cheating Rita', was Stardust's first flop. Independent producers also come in with unsolicited tapes which clutter Pete Waterman's office, some of them good (Guys and Dolls), some of them unusable.

There are foreign affairs: Epic handle Magnet material in the States, Germany is the company's best market. Already new calculations are being made: does it sound right for *Europe*? As the output increases will promotion become less intense? Can Magnet continue along their single-minded way?

Last Words

There are getting on for 150 A & R departments in the British record industry; four is a tiny sample, unrepresentative, etc. But I wasn't looking for laws or patterns; I was simply trying to find out what A & R men did, which was the best image – evil genius? show-biz hack? musicians' friend? office stooge? All of these, I suppose, and I am tempted to generalize.

One of the few laws of pop sociology says that the quality of the music is in direct proportion to the number of record companies producing it. The argument is most clearly developed in Charlie Gillett's *Sound of the City*: he shows that rock 'n' roll emerged from the studios of competitive independent labels and was emasculated as these labels were absorbed into the majors. But the emergence of the new pop labels in Britain over the last few years has *not* improved anything. I admire Rak and the early UK, Bell and Magnet, for their success, but in musical terms their output is rubbish, lowest common denominator pop, they've hardly issued a single between them that I've kept. The same goes for all those independent producers: these days people go out on their own not because they can't make it with the majors, but because they can make it only too well – what's at issue isn't taste but profit. And so my new law goes: the bigger the company, the more likely it is to sign someone original, issue something interesting.

The essence of A & R is risk-taking; nothing is certain except, maybe, that if the Beatles got back together again, their first album would go straight to No. 1 (but would their first single?). A lot of an A & R man's time is taken up with weighing odds; like any race-goer he's got to judge conditions and form. The A & R man is constrained by the condition of his company, of his market, of his selling media, and his form book has a list of every hit, everything that's *already* worked. There are very few *real* gamblers in British pop, the music only develops when a loony comes along and rewrites the form book. Virgin are the only company gambling a bit madly at the moment, experimenting in the singles market, with little success so far – if they ever win big, other A & R men, their risks reduced, will suddenly turn out to share Virgin tastes.

The gambling metaphor rests on the peculiar relationship between music and money that is the heart of the record industry. Hang around company men, get involved in company concerns and you start talking (as I have in this piece) in company terms: music = product, audience = market, success = sales. What music actually is – notes and words, passion and energy – gets lost in the analysis of company policy, market breakdown, media exploitation. And yet . . . Hang out some more and you find that it's the rare A & R man who isn't *really* into music as music – it's how he got into the job in the first place. And what's weird is that the music he's *into* is not usually the music he's putting out. I can forgive the enthusiasm for trash hits (spoiled by success), and I can understand *not* signing acts (too risky), but I *can't* understand the extraordinary amount of trash *flops* that come pouring out of every label on singles and albums. The only possible explanatory concept is 'professionalism'. There's a great mystique in the business about the professional approach (getting it *together*) – to performing, managing, writing, recording. And, as in football, the 'great professional' is usually the great bore.

In *Rock File 1* I wrote a piece on Holyground, a studio in Yorkshire that was trying to work as a collective record company. One of Holyground's aims was to break up the usual division of rock labour, to give musicians greater control, to avoid making music product. The studio's best musician was Bill Nelson; he now leads Be Bop De Luxe, signed to Harvest, just beginning to dent the American glitter market. There's less idealism about these days. Odd eccentric labels do still appear (Oval, Rubber, Rampant) but I don't know what happened to Holyground and I now see the future somewhere else: the essence of a healthy rock scene is what's happening live. I've concluded that most records (and all discos) are bad for music. A good example: the pub rock story, when it comes to be written, is going to be most instructive and I'll bet on this conclusion in advance: *every* pub group gave more pleasure live than *any* of them has or ever will on record.

I dunno where that leaves A & R men.

THE ROCK FILE LEAGUE TABLE OF RECORD LABELS, 1974–75[1]

(Qualification for inclusion: at least 1 hit and 5 releases[2])

Position (This year)	(Last year)	*Label*	*No. of hits*	*No. of releases*	*% of hits*
Division 1 (Labels with at least 1 hit per 5 releases)					
1	6	Avco	5	7	71·4
2	12 =	Jay Boy	7	13	53·8
3	—	All Platinum	3	7	42·9
4 =	2	Rak	12	34	35·3
4 =	7	MGM	6	17	35·3
6	10	Magnet	8	24	33·3
7	19	Brunswick	4	13	30·8
8	4	Bell	14	46	30·4
9	—	State	3	11	27·3
10	16	Vertigo	4	15	26·7
11 =	—	Chelsea	4	16	25
11 =	—	Jet	2	8	25
13	33	Mercury	4	18	22·2
14 =	12 =	Chrysalis	2	10	20
14 =	22 =	Rocket	1	5	20
Division 2 (Labels with at least 1 hit per 10 releases)					
16 =	11	Island	6	33	18·2
16 =	8	Mam	2	11	18·2
18 =	—	GTO	4	24	16·7
18 =	—	Spector	1	6	16·7
20	—	20th Century	4	25	16
21 =	17 =	RSO	2	16	12·4
21 =	—	Arista	2	16	12·4
23 =	29 =	Chess/Janus	1	9	11·1
23 =	21	Bradleys	4	36	11·1
25	—	Pye Disco Demand	2	19	10·5
26 =	1	Apple	1	10	10
26 =	9	Bus Stop	1	10	10
Division 3 (Labels with at least 1 hit per 20 releases)					
28	—	Cactus	3	31	9·7
29	5	Monument	1	11	9·1
30	—	Gull	1	12	8·3
31	—	Spark	2	25	8
32	28	CBS/Epic	17	214	7·9
33	26	A & M	4	55	7·3
34	43 =	EMI	10	145	6·9

35	20	Tamla Motown	4	62	6·5
36	27	RCA	9	141	6·4
37	32	DJM	5	83	6
38	—	Buddah/Kama Sutra	2	35	5·7
39	38	Mooncrest	1	18	5·6
40	15	Philadelphia	1	20	5

Losers Division [3]
(Labels with less than 1 hit per 20 releases)

41	24	Polydor	6	121	4·96
42	34	Warner/Reprise	4	84	4·8
43 =	—	ABC	2	43	4·7
43 =	—	Capitol	2	43	4·7
45	47	Decca	2	45	4·4
46 =	41	U.A.	4	92	4·3
46 =	35 =	Charisma	1	23	4·3
48	29 =	Pye International	1	24	4·2
49	—	Private Stock	1	25	4
50	—	Anchor	1	28	3·6
51	43 =	Pye	4	118	3·4
52	—	Elektra/Asylum	1	30	3·3
53	43 =	London	1	39	2·6
54	46	Atlantic	2	80	2·5
55	—	Trojan etc.	3	123	2·4
56	37	MCA	1	54	1·9
57	39	Philips	1	66	1·5

Notes
1. This table was compiled with the aid of *The New Singles* (for releases) and the charts provided for the BBC by BMRB – a record is a hit if it gets into the BMRB top twenty. The period covered is September 1, 1974 to August 31, 1975 and the table includes all the releases and hits of this period; it includes, therefore, some hits that were released before September and some releases that became hits after August. This is not strictly fair to individual record companies but any other method is impractical and the table does balance out from year to year. For previous years see *Rock File 2* and *3*. In 1974–5 (last year's figures in brackets) there were 208 hits (181) from 3032 releases (2707), a success rate of 6·9% (6·7). 125 of the hits were British (120), 5 European (7), 6 Jamaican (0) and 72 from the USA (54) – of which 10 (10) were re-released oldies.

2. The following labels had hits from less than five releases: T. Rex (1 from 2); Dark Horse (1 from 3).

3. Note that the following labels had no hits at all, despite releasing 20 singles or more: Torpedo (20); Stax (20); Penny Farthing (33); UK (38); Dawn (37); Contempo (50).

AMERICAN RADIO TODAY
by Paul Gambaccini

'Nobody in town believes it!' stormed an infuriated Ken Shelton, Music Director of WBZ-FM in Boston. 'The fix *has* to be in somewhere. No one is getting requests for it, and we're not getting sales reports from the stores. Besides, *no* record jumps like that.'

The leap from 23 to 5 on the *Billboard* singles chart achieved by Tony Orlando and Dawn's 'He Don't Love You (Like I Love You)' in the third week of April, 1975, did indeed look suspicious, for no record had taken that big a jump since Wings' 'Live And Let Die' shot from 21 to 3 in the summer of 1973. But whereas 'Live And Let Die' peaked at number 2, as did 'The Horse' by Cliff Nobles and Co., which took the extraordinary rise from 21 to 2 in 1968, 'He Don't Love You (Like I Love You)' followed through to the No. 1 position on May 3, 1975.

'It *was* a big jump,' an Elektra official conceded the week of Dawn's unusual leap. 'But it was selling nationwide, and it was getting airplay. After the big deal we did to get Tony Orlando it was decided that if any single was going to be a hit this month, it would be his. The national promotion director made sure of that: he pushed that one personally.'

The three weeks in the life of 'He Don't Love You' had illustrated several aspects of how records are broken in the United States. Local radio stations rely largely on local sales and requests to determine their charts, while the trade magazines are heavily influenced by the local lists in compiling their surveys. Promotion is thus heavily focussed on the local station and music directors like Ken Shelton, who in the course of one week may receive a phone call from Al Martino, a Wombles sweatshirt, and an invitation to a Foghat pie-throwing party at a local roller derby. When the national charts feature records not selling in several major markets, radio station personnel get suspicious, for good reasons or not. They tend to add a record doing very well on the national chart, and if it fails locally they feel burned.

Because the number of stations playing pop music is

literally in the thousands, there are many ways by which a song may be broken. Unlike British promotion men, who spend half their lives pacing the halls of Broadcasting House hoping against hope to get their records programmed on the BBC and at least another one-quarter trying to get their soul titles played in discos, American promo men have any number of opportunities at hand to break a title. Local radio-syndicated programmes, local television, and national late-night television concerts offer more outlets for rock than Britons have ever seen.

Sometimes a hit is broken without record company initiative altogether. Rosalie Trombley, the programming genius of CKLW, serving Detroit from Windsor, Ontario, played 'Bennie and the Jets' as an album cut from *Goodbye Yellow Brick Road*. She received great listener response, but so did a local soul station. The result was that MCA released 'Bennie And The Jets' as an A-side single in America and promoted it in the soul market as well as in Elton John's traditional pop audience. The record went gold, entered the top twenty of the national soul charts, and proved to be the second biggest record of John's American career.

Trombley has broken so many off-the-wall No. 1 hits, including Harry Mancini's 'Love Theme From *Romeo And Juliet*', Bobby Goldsboro's 'Honey', and Terry Jacks' 'Seasons In The Sun', that CKLW has acquired a reputation as a 'barometer' station. If a pop record breaks in the heavily black Detroit market, it is considered a certain national smash by radio programmers, and many doubting stations add the record. When Roger Whittaker's 'The Last Farewell' zoomed from 22 to 4 on CKLW, many music directors threw in the towel and added the unlikely hit to their rotation schedule. If a soul record reaches the top three of the CKLW chart, it has historically been a good bet that it will break nationally within three months.

Detroit is not the only barometer market in the United States. Boston, considered the most British city in America, appropriately breaks British singles, most recently Queen's 'Killer Queen', Leo Sayer's 'Long Tall Glasses', Ace's 'How Long', and Pilot's 'Magic'. New York, for years notorious as the last market to go on a hit, has become the focal point of the Stateside disco craze, the result being that WABC, once the despair of America's promo men for its minuscule playlist, is now the first major station on disco cross-overs.

'I'm in the radio business, not the record business,' WABC Programme Director Rick Sklar has stated. He is interested not so much in breaking records as in maintaining the highest ratings possible. 'We play middle-of-the-road music,' he told a radio programming conference in 1974. 'Middle-of-the-road is what people in our demographic range want to hear at the moment. There is no MOR sound, but there are MOR records.'

Sklar thus added the Hues Corporation's 'Rock The Boat' in the summer of 1974 after the record achieved fifteen thousand sales in New York City off discotheque play. Programming the single increased sales enough to put the record in the *Billboard* chart, and once there the record was home. The exact same sequence has been followed in the cases of several records since, including George McCrae's 'Rock Your Baby', Shirley & Co's 'Shame Shame Shame', Eddie Harris' 'Hijack', and Consumer Rapport's 'Ease On Down The Road'.

The last record had another factor in its favour. It was the catchiest tune from the all-black Broadway version of *The Wizard of Oz*, *The Wiz*. When the play won the hearts of New Yorkers, eventually winning the Antoinette Perry Award for the Best Musical of the year, the single version of the song started to sell and pick up disco play. Songs from entertainment productions traditionally do better in America than Britain. If an entertainment reaches the level of mass market acceptance, the popularity of the theme tune is assured, unless the song is absolutely diabolical. Barbra Streisand's 'The Way We Were' and Marvin Hamlisch's 'The Entertainer' both went to number one, and even Mike Oldfield's 'Tubular Bells' became a gold single in an edit he didn't authorize when billed as 'Theme From *The Exorcist*'.

Stations across the country are anxious to find out what the barometer stations are breaking and what their fellow stations are playing, and a small industry has blossomed to fill that need. Each trade magazine carries a playlist column while several prominent tipsheets inform broadcasters what records are getting key plays.

The trade magazine playlist pioneer was Kal Rudman, who wrote an R & B column in *Music Business* in the mid-sixties. After *Music Business* died with the top forty British invasion, Rudman resurfaced writing pop and R & B columns for *Record World*. These weekly pieces became industry legends, asserting in strong language that certain unlikely records were going to become hits. They almost always became so, rendering the suggestion that Rudman was receiving gifts from record companies almost redundant. Although it is true that he championed many unusual Columbia releases, such as Clint Holmes' 'Playground In My Mind', Dr. Hook's 'Cover Of *Rolling Stone*', and Loudon Wainwright's 'Dead Skunk', it is also true that these records became major American hits. 'I only write about a record I believe in,' Rudman asserted when asked if his consultancy fees hurt his judgment. In 1974 he discontinued the *Record World* column, saying 'I was only competing with myself, wasn't I?' and concentrating his full efforts on his tipsheet and radio programming conference.

The winner and still champion of the tipsheet sweepstakes is the long-lived Bill Gavin Report. The veteran California broadcaster/publisher is read coast-to-coast for his airplay reports, weighted airplay charts, and personal opinions. He is one of the few tipsters whose *personal* opinion is given much value, and it was his praise of Paul Anka's '(You're) Having My Baby' as tasteful as well as commercial that helped get the record away.

When Rudman left *Record World* the magazine recognized it had lost one of its most popular features. The editors launched a section called AM Airplay Report which quickly paled into insignificance compared to other innovative trade services. The Radio Active chart in *Cashbox* lists singles in rank order of percentage of stations adding them during the week, and thus a quick reference is available for programmers making local playlist additions. *Billboard*'s Singles Report has turned out to be the most informative of the lot. The editors divide the country into regions, pick key stations in each to supply weekly playlist additions and chart jumpers, and print these with a summary on what records are moving in each region.

These trade magazine features allow programmers to see what they should be adding far less expensively than if they subscribed to the tipsheets. The high cost of the sheets is a direct result of their low, specialized circulation.

A perfect example of what one can discover from the trade playlist features is that 'Shaving Cream' could go from the twenties to number one in medium-sized metropolitan areas. This novelty disc, recorded by Benny Bell with vocalist Paul Wynn in 1946, was ignored when originally released, presumably because its repetitious play on the unspoken word 'shit' is rather risqué and because it has no melodic virtues. The record broke in 1975 in a most unusual fashion. Dr. Demento, the Los Angeles-based disc jockey whose weekly programme of bizarre pop singles is syndicated across America, featured 'Shaving Cream' on his chart of strange listener favourites. WNBC in New York, which runs Dr. Demento, promoted him by featuring 'Shaving Cream' in a trailer that ran during the Bruce Morrow show. Morrow, long New York's most popular evening disc jockey, received numerous requests to play the novelty in its entirety. He did, and the song debuted at number 24 on the WNBC chart. Vanguard Records dug out the master, re-released the number as a single, and saw it go into the national Hot 100 off New York sales. Several stations went on to the record on that basis, and two reported to the *Billboard* Singles Report that the record had leaped from the twenties to number one in their town. This kind of report helps spread a record on to stations whose programmers follow the trades.

Record companies themselves try to clue radio stations in on their prime pushes by circulating weekly news-sheets. The main goal here, other than to get records on to playlists, is to mask the hype with enough humour or information to get programmers interested in reading the bleeding things. Warner Brothers' *Circular* seems to win this competition hands down, featuring both instructive articles and witty contests. Atlantic's mailout is generally a catalogue of chart positions, tour dates and release schedules. Buddah and Elektra have mailouts to their promotion men and women which deserve mention, Buddah's for its unmasked desperation and Elektra/Asylum's for the prose.

Sometimes a record breaks without radio entirely. Television proved it had surprising power in breaking singles when two dirges featured as theme tunes of teleplays about dying women went to No. 1 in 1973. John Denver's 'Sunshine On My Shoulder' and Jim Croce's 'Time In A Bottle' went to No. 1 after being the signature song of *Sunshine* and *She Lives*, respectively.

It had long been known that a series could sell records, from Ricky Nelson to the Monkees and the Archies. Lately the merchandizing emphasis has been placed on the hosts of variety series, such as Tony Orlando, Mac Davis and Cher. Mac Davis sang his then-current American hit 'Rock And Roll (I Gave You The Best Years Of My Life)' three times on his short-lived programme.

TV appearances coupled with concentrated promotion can increase sales significantly. When Chicago had an hour-long special of their own in 1974, all of their LPs reappeared on the *Billboard* chart. Half the battle of selling a record is getting it into the shops, and with an investment of in-store promotional aids tying Chicago's back-catalogue to their TV special, Columbia was able to restock the stores with all of the group's albums.

But it is always difficult to tell whether the albums listed as making gains in the bottom section of the industry album charts are actually selling, since these numbers are awarded in fickle fashion. The personal preferences of the chart compilers, opinions as to what dealers should stock as catalogue material, and judgments as to which albums are likely to move in the weeks ahead have as much effect on the listings as actual sales. Industry insiders are always trying to figure out which of the three major trade charts is most accurate at any given time.

The subjectiveness of the charts occasionally reflects itself in spectacularly disparate listings. Uriah Heep's *Sweet Freedom* was number ten on the *Cashbox* album chart when it wasn't even in *Billboard*'s top thirty. David Essex's 'Rock On' was number one in *Cashbox* during a week when it wasn't in the *Billboard* top ten.

Billboard itself had some astonishing chart trends from mid-1974 to mid-1975. During one six-week stretch every number one single became number twelve the next week, a statistical improbability. During the first four months of 1975 only two records in the number one position retained that slot the next week, both Elton John singles; the number two singles otherwise automatically ascended to number one.

The chart listings are vitally important to most AM programmers, but there still remain a few FM stations which dare to programme without the express guidance of *Billboard* and its ilk. WBCN-FM in Boston, for example, maintains a library of literally thousands of albums and singles in the studio itself, enabling the disc jockey to exercise one of the widest selections in commercial radio. It is true that some singles and albums are set aside into recommended categories, but the dj can still decide when these records are to be featured.

In contrast are the tight structures of WBZ and WRKD, the two AM giants in Boston. (Although WHDH is mostly music and occasionally number one in the city, it plays fewer current discs.) At WBZ, where this writer worked for several months as Executive Producer and sat in on weekly music meetings, a majority vote of a 'music meeting' panel is required to approve the addition of a record to the playlist, which is not set at a specific number but tends to be on the shy side of thirty. The General Manager, Programme Director, Music Director, Executive Producer, and a disc jockey usually sit in. Since at least two of these figures do not come from distinctly musical backgrounds, a record is judged on its sound as much as on any artistic merit.

In the weeks this writer voted, many hits were rejected for airplay on the basis that they were not suitable for 25–49 year old housewives, considered the bulk of the daytime audience.

Elton John's 'The Bitch Is Back' was banned by the Westinghouse network for the use of the word 'bitch', but it wouldn't have been played anyway because of its freneticism. 'Fire' by the Ohio Players, an American number one, was dismissed out of hand as being 'too raucous', which the Music Director, a black, often sadly equated with 'too black'. William DeVaughn's 'Be Thankful For What You Got' was considered too soul-oriented, while Paul McCartney's 'Junior's Farm' was flipped in favour of 'Sally G', the easier side.

On the other hand, many easy-listening records that were not actual big sellers were passed, including several Charlie Rich singles and everything released by Helen Reddy. WBZ's programming decisions are typical of American stations which see themselves as being contemporary middle-of-the-road, and it is for these stations that *Billboard* publishes its Easy Listening Chart, based primarily on airplay. This approach is in conflict with Rick Sklar's philosophy 'There is no MOR sound, but there are MOR records.'

WRKO tends to dance to the tune piped by RKO headquarters in California. The local Music Director, a young woman, can make some decisions and recommendations on the local level, particularly in light of sales returns, but final decisions often come from chain headquarters in California. She was mortified when she had to go on Telly Savalas' 'If', a colossal stiff in America which failed to make the top 100, and was the object of gleeful jibes from other Boston programmers for weeks.

WRKO has another unusual feature in that its records are all played at the wrong speed. 'I play them all between 45 1/2 and 47 1/2 (r.p.m.),' WRKO programming consultant Paul Drew revealed in November, 1974. 'Sometimes I have to adjust. For example, I have to call KHJ (Los Angeles HQ) tomorrow and tell them to slow down "Please Mr. Postman", it sounds too fast now. I once had "Bridge Over Troubled Water" on too fast, and it sounded like Mickey Mouse.' One WRKO employee revealed that when a commercial for the Jackson Five's *Dancing Machine* was played, several people ran into the studio, fearing the cartridge was defective. It was actually being played at its correct speed, but they had heard the single played at the wrong speed for so long they mistook WRKO-real for real-real.

Drew and other major AM programmers tend to discriminate against length in general. American radio philosophy is that if a record lasts only three minutes instead of three-fifteen, there is far less chance of the listener tuning out, and for the sake of ratings tune-out must be avoided at all costs. The general manager of CKLW recently announced that singles over 3:30 had virtually no chance on his station, unless they were by Elton John or were 'Hey Jude'. The increased speed, shortened length, and restricted playlist all help give AM radio an essentially manic flavour that keeps listeners tuned through the commercials.

An occasional record by a local hero can help. Aerosmith's 'Dream On' was Boston's number one hit of 1973, although it never entered the *Billboard* top thirty.* 'La Grange' by Z.Z. Top spent nearly half a year on *Billboard*'s Hot 100, mainly on sales from the Southwest. Sometimes a local hit breaks nationally, to thrill the rock historian. 'In The Year 2525' went to number one in Nebraska before reaching the national charts in 1969. 'The Mouse' by local television star Soupy Sales hit number three on New York's WMCA in 1965, placing the record on the national chart, where it eventually peaked in the fifties.

But most records follow the tried-but-true road of Broadway plays. They are tried out in middle markets, and if successful there are added on the major stations. It sounds boring, but with thousands of stations the variations are nearly infinite. Besides, there is always the incentive of recognition, that goes to a programming pioneer. 'Last year we got gold records for breaking "Hooked On A Feeling" and "Just You And Me",' Ken Shelton enthused. 'I'm hoping "Magic" and "Killer Queen" go gold, because if they do, we get gold records, for breaking them.'

* 'Dream On' was reissued in 1975, when it did belatedly climb into *Billboard* top ten.

PREFACE TO THE LOG OF AMERICAN AND BRITISH TOP 20 HITS

The American material was compiled by Stephen Nugent from *Billboard*, January 1955 through December 1974. Below, *Billboard*'s managing editor Eliot Tiegel explains the process of computing each week's top 100 records, from which our top twenty is drawn.

The British material, which is printed in italics, was compiled by Pete and Annie Fowler from the *New Musical Express* (January 1955 through December 1958), *Record Mirror* (January 1959 through December 1968), and *Music Week* (formerly called *Record Retailer*, January 1969 through December 1974).* The *Music Week* chart is compiled by the British Market Research Bureau in association with the BBC and the British record industry. Here, Alisa Walker of BMRB explains the procedure.

How The Charts Are Compiled

Part 1: Britain

by Alisa Walker (*British Market Research Bureau*).

What causes the most anger, anguish and controversy within the record industry of any country? The answer is simple – The Charts, that weekly sampling of sales which purports to be a guide to the best-selling singles and albums. They are everybody's favourite Aunt Sally, criticized for being inaccurate, accused of being rigged, a cause for joy and celebration when a company's records are doing well, a source of irritation and frustration when they aren't. In fact, charts

* A print strike prevented *Record Mirror* from going to press from July 4 to August 9, 1959, when the *New Musical Express* chart was used. Because no chart is compiled in Britain during Christmas week, every record which was in the previous week's chart has been credited with an extra week as the same position.

are largely misunderstood, with an industry which lives by them often unaware of the systems by which they are devised. In the UK, for instance, only firm sales across the counter are considered, in America the amount of airplay is an important factor, in France the chart is based on an independent sampling of the record-buying public.

In this series, *Music Week* examines methods of chart-compilation in five different countries.

The charts used by *Music Week* and the BBC are compiled by the British Market Research Bureau, which is a long-established company engaged in a wide range of other market research activities. BMRB has been compiling the charts since the beginning of 1969 and the financial backing for the charts comes from *Music Week* and the BBC, of course, but also substantially from the record companies through their organization, the British Phonographic Industry. Currently the annual cost of producing the charts is in excess of £56,000. All aspects of the charts are discussed on a regular basis with these organizations.

The aim of the charts is to provide the best possible estimate, within the finance available, of the relative popularity of records and the measure of popularity which is used in sales to individual consumers. As will be seen elsewhere in this survey of record charts, sales to individuals are not the only thing which might be used to measure popularity, and this aspect will be discussed later.

The sales figures which are used to compile the charts are obtained from a panel of dealers, who write down in a special booklet the serial numbers of records as they sell them across the counter. The panel used by BMRB numbers 300 out of the 4,000 or so dealers in this country which stock a full range of records. The panel is designed to represent all the different types of shops selling records, in the correct proportions. Lists of dealers are provided by the major record companies and these lists are used to establish the profile of record shops in this country and the sample is then selected to represent this universe.

Obviously, it is very easy to select a list of record shops

that is fully representative of the business in Great Britain, by size of shop, area, type of shop and so on: it is quite another matter to persuade all those shops to provide detailed information to BMRB about their sales each week. Fortunately, there are dealers who are willing to carry out this quite onerous task and a little bit of persuasion sometimes brings in a few of the dealers who are not so enthusiastic initially. However, there are still problems which arise with the sample of shops, so that it is never a perfect representation of the universe. One of these problems is the unwillingness of two important multiples, Boots and Smiths, to provide comprehensive sales information from a sample of their shops. However, the third of the large multiples, Woolworths, has been providing sales information from a sample of its stores and these have been included in the chart compilations since the beginning of this year. BMRB continually makes efforts to improve the representativeness of the panel of shops and obviously there is a certain amount of turnover among the panel which is part of this process.

Each week, BMRB sends a new 'diary' to the members of the panel to arrive by Friday, and the dealer starts using the diary on Monday morning, noting down the serial numbers of each record as he sells it. The dealer continues with this process throughout the week and he then posts the diary in the envelope provided by BMRB, after he closes the shop on Saturday night. The diaries are then delivered to BMRB first thing on Monday morning: if they do not arrive in the first post they are too late to be used, given the tight time schedule involved in processing the charts.

When the diaries arrive at BMRB, Wyn Barton and her team check each diary individually, crossing through all the blank spaces so that nothing can be added to the information and looking for patterns of sales which might appear suspicious or unusual.

The diaries are then counted to establish exactly which ones have arrived on time (these days it is in excess of 75 per cent most weeks), so that if any area (or any shop size) is under-represented because of postal problems, the diaries which have arrived from that area can be given an additional weighting to redress the balance. This process continues all through Monday morning, with about five people working on it, and the information is then transferred on to punched cards ready for feeding into the computer. Each serial number is individually tapped out by a punch card operator and this process takes about 60 girl-hours every week. Sometime during the course of Monday night the punch cards are taken to the computer, and the sales information is processed to produce a chart ready for use on Tuesday morning.

The chart produced by the computer is just a list of serial numbers which must be translated into titles and artists, but even when this has been done, the process is far from complete. Wyn Barton starts work before seven o'clock each Tuesday morning and scrutinizes the chart which the computer has provided. Sometimes there are serial numbers to be added together (for example, if a particular record is available on an import number as well as the British number), or incorrectly written serial numbers to be totalled (which often happens when a company introduces a new prefix, until the dealers and their assistants get used to it). Eventually, a Top 50 Singles chart is compiled and the breakers are selected and then the charts are telephoned through to *Music Week* and the BBC.

At this stage the chart is still provisional, for there are further security checks which must be carried out before the chart may be published and broadcast. One of these checks is a series of telephone calls to 50 record dealers who are *not* part of the panel to check whether the patterns of sales revealed in the chart compiled from the panel of shops is reflected amongst record shops which do not compile chart returns. Each new entry, fast-riser and breaker has to pass a statistical test at this telephone check and if there are insufficient correct answers for a record it must be taken out of the charts. Only when all the records have satisfactorily passed the telephone check can the chart be confirmed to *Music Week* and the BBC.

In addition to the charts themselves, the data is used to compile record company share statistics: these are provided to the BPI member-companies who subscribe to the charts and they are also used to compile the Market Survey which *Music Week* publishes every quarter. These company and label shares take into account *all* sales, not just sales of items which appear in the charts: There are a few questions which crop up again and again in connection with the charts and some of these will be outlined below and answers given.

How accurate are the charts?

As far as reflecting the overall sales pattern in Britain is concerned, there are two important factors which must be right: the sample of shops must be as close to representing reality as possible, and the shops which complete returns must do the job well. If both these things work perfectly the charts will give a very accurate picture of the relative sales levels of different records, although, since the chart is based on a sample of shops and not on all shops, there will still be some inaccuracies. However, we know that it is the case that neither the sample of shops nor the task that they carry out is perfect: we have noted some of the drawbacks of the sample of shops above, and it is obvious that dealers will sometimes forget to write down a serial number, or make a mistake once in a while. However, we believe that imperfections of this nature are not systematic and do not affect particular records or companies more than others.

A further problem is that the number one sells very much more than the number two in the average week, and the number two much more than the number three and so on. This is true until the position 30 is reached, and after this the records are all selling at very much the same level. This means that the charts are attempting to measure differences which are in fact very small, and it means that inaccuracies will occur at the lower end of the chart.

How well are the charts coping with these problems, then? Last year, BMRB carried out a validation exercise covering 100 singles and 100 albums: the record companies were asked to provide ex-factory sales information for the records selected and to give these sales for the whole 'life' of the record in the case of singles and for six months in the case of albums. Generally speaking there was a very close relationship between these figures and those provided by BMRB's panel of shops, although there are a few which do not quite fit the pattern as well as the others.

Another illustration of the reliability of the chart information lies in the Forecasts which are denoted in the *Music Week* chart by an arrow. These forecasts are calculated by BMRB on the basis of the sales information from the panel of shops, and in four cases out of five the forecast is proved correct on the following week.

Why do the dealers have to write down all record sales when so few records ever reach the charts?

If only a selection of records were covered for compiling the charts, it would never be quite certain that something had not been excluded from the list to be covered which should have been included. With the system employed, every record gets an equal chance of being recorded in the diaries and this must be a fairer system. Additionally, the company share information has to take into account the sales of records that are not in the charts, as well as the top sellers.

Why can't an easier system be devised that would make the dealers' job easier?

The only system we can think of which would be scrupulously fair and which would also cut down the work the dealer has to do would be one using serial number tags on records. The dealer would merely have to remove a tear-off or sticky tag from each record and return these to BMRB: this would obviously be an easier and more foolproof system than the one used at present, but the costs of converting all the necessary machinery to tag records in this way has proved an obstacle to this development.

Why use dealers' sales at all – why not manufacturers' sales?

The charts are produced every week and they must reflect sales on a weekly basis therefore. If manufacturers' sales were used, there would be all sorts of unusual patterns occurring, particularly at the beginning of a record's life, when more records may be sent out to shops in the first week than in any other week of the record's life. By counting sales over the counter, these bulk sales patterns do not occur.

Why are shops included in the BMRB panel which do not necessarily stock the vast majority of releases? Why not use just those shops which have the widest range of records in stock?

The charts as compiled by BMRB are designed to measure the relative popularity of records, as measured by sales. A sale is a sale wherever it takes place, and if it takes place in a shop which only stocks the Top 30 singles, it is a sale worth counting as much as the one which takes place in a singles specialist outlet. The main thing to ensure is that the smaller range shop is not over-represented in the panel: at the same time, the picture would be quite wrong if the chart were compiled from shops which stock a very wide range of singles to the exclusion of the non-specialist.

Part 2: America

Eliot Tiegel (*Billboard*)

Billboard Magazine's charts – the national surveys of pop, country, classical, easy listening, jazz and soul music, are a powerful tool used by all facets of the music, recording, broadcasting, and talent buying-selling segments of the entertainment industry.

To many people the methodology of preparing these national surveys is one major mystery, as well it should be, since this is a herculean task which amazes many people week after week.

Yet there is an organized, sound basis for preparing the statistics, based on field research which involves an alert, aggressive and musically oriented staff of young, hip researchers working out of the magazine's Los Angeles headquarters.

Bill Wardlow, the director of chart operations, is the

contact man for representatives of all the record labels who come up to the magazine's offices early in the week to bring up new product and provide information on airplay action and sales movement of product already released which the company wants *Billboard* to be alert to.

Billboard never relies on what a record manufacturer tells the research staff in terms of what that information will do for a chart position. Instead, the information is used as guideline, often alerting the research staff to be on the watch for a product which is being released or is being promoted in a major way and sometimes this can mean exposure in the marketplace.

As for the methodology for the Hot 100: This chart is compiled from a panel of dealers and one-stops representing thousands of dealers. 'We also eyeball rackjobber chart listings by such major firms as Heilicher, ABC Record & Tape Sales and Musical Isle in compiling the Hot 100,' Wardlow says.

'The dealers and one-stops utilized in our panel which we telephone weekly on Friday and Monday, are dealers recommended to us by all record labels.' They are identified to the research staff by the use of a form which breaks down their musical speciality, if any, such as classical, country, pop, plus the percentage of their business which might be software as opposed to hardware (equipment), to make certain they are key music dealers in their market.

'We need to know the key dealer in each market,' Wardlow says. Calls are made by the chart department people using a checksheet which has been prepared and mailed to the sources earlier. 'The checklist includes all those products on the current chart plus additional important products we are checking.'

Wardlow says as many as 185 titles will be checked for the Hot 100 whereas the published chart only lists 100 titles plus ten bubbling-under titles.

'The dealer-one-stops are asked to rate the products as far as movement as very good, good or fair. For very good, we assign 20 points; for good 10 points and for fair five points. We also ask them for their top 15 products and assign 15 points to their first choice working down to one point for number 15. We also use radio from the bottom of the chart to the top. In other words, products can come on to the chart by radio airplay itself or by heavy disco play or by a combination of radio, disco play and sales.

'We canvass over 124 radio stations and these are stations that have been recommended to us by the top record promotion men of all labels.

'We do an overplay of these stations and qualify them as to their importance in moving product saleswise.' Ratings, Wardlow points out, do not always mean a station has the power to affect sales. All of the stations used in the survey also appear in the other radio feature called Singles Radio Action. The stations used for the Hot 100 are rated one, two, four and six depending on their strength in their marketplace. The weight of a single based on its cumulative radio play is totalled and included in the sum total which now includes dealer and one-stops and is printed on a computer sheet for Wardlow's review.

The final chart is made from this Hot 100 computer printout. The printout has the week's sales of each product, the week's top 15 sales points, the total radio points for the week and a comparison of the previous week's points. 'I do not position the chart exactly on the computer printout,' Wardlow says, 'because there are many other factors involved such as whether the artist is on tour, where there are TV spots currently being played on the artist's product, whether there are radio spots on the product and whether the single is tied into an LP or whether the LP is tied into a single because both products would then help each other on their respective charts.

'The computer does not place product on the Hot 100.' All positioning is done by Wardlow on the basis of information at hand.

On calls to radio stations, the researcher gets information on playlists, which songs they are rotating, what new music they are playing, and what extra songs they are using. 'If the product is printed on the station's playlist that week, it is considered for radio points. Our radio input information is cut off as of Tuesday evening. Our last information to come in is from the important RKO General chain.'

Sometimes a single is dropped off the chart after four downward weeks. This was done in the past, Wardlow says, after an item had dropped below 40 and if it had a downward trend after three weeks. But that is not always the case. 'In the case of hot artists they could stay on the chart for many weeks. There is no set figure for how many weeks a single can stay Number One.'

Wardlow emphasizes that by doubling the number of radio stations contacted, the survey now reflects secondary markets as well as major ones. Product is now more current when it makes the chart and the information is being received faster than in the past because all the data is collected by telephone – which speeds up the process by two weeks easily.

Incidentally *Billboard* has been running charts since 1937 – the first music publication to publish national best-selling listings.

Over 1,000 products are checked weekly for the surveys. Once a week after the charts have been put together, Wardlow dictates a justification report explaining the placement of each and every product on all the surveys. It is a record of just what happened and why.

Reprinted with permission by *Billboard* publications

THE LOG OF AMERICAN/BRITISH TOP TWENTY HITS, 1955–74

by

Stephen Nugent, with Pete and Annie Fowler

	Date of chart entry	*Highest position reached*	*Number of weeks in charts*
ABBA			
Waterloo			
(UK) Epic	*20–4–74*	*1*	7
(US) Atlantic	13–7–74	6	7
ACE			
How Long			
(UK) Anchor	*7–12–74*	*20*	*1*
ACE, JOHNNY			
Pledging My Love			
(US) Duke	12–3–55	17	3
ACKLIN, BARBARA			
Love Makes a Woman			
(US) Brunswick	24–8–68	15	3
AD LIBS			
The Boy from New York City			
(US) Blue Cat	13–2–65	8	5
ADDERLY, JULIAN 'CANNONBALL'			
Mercy Mercy Mercy			
(US) Capitol	18–2–67	11	4
AKENS, JEWEL			
The Birds and the Bees			
(US) Era	27–2–65	3	8
ALFIE AND HARRY			
The Trouble with Harry			
(UK) London	*23–3–56*	*15*	*3*
ALICE COOPER			
School's Out			
(US) Warner Brothers	8–7–72	7	7
(UK) Warner Brothers	*22–7–72*	*1*	*9*

	Date of chart entry	*Highest position reached*	*Number of weeks in charts*
ALICE COOPER (cont.)			
Elected			
(UK) Warner Brothers	*14–10–72*	*4*	*7*
Hello Hurray			
(UK) Warner Brothers	*17–2–73*	*6*	*8*
No More, Mr Nice Guy			
(UK) Warner Brothers	*5–5–73*	*10*	*4*
Teenage Lament			
(UK) Warner Brothers	*2–2–74*	*12*	*3*
ALIVE AND KICKING			
Tighter Tighter			
(US) Roulette	4–7–70	7	4
ALLEN, REX			
Don't Go Near the Indians			
(US) Mercury	20–10–62	17	1
ALLISONS			
Are You Sure?			
(UK) Fontana	*12–2–61*	*1*	*12*
ALLMAN BROTHERS BAND			
Ramblin' Man			
(US) Capricorn	22–9–73	2	9
ALLMAN, GREG			
Midnight Rider			
(US) Capricorn	16–2–74	19	2
ALL STAR HIT PARADE (EPs) (Various Artists)			
All Star Hit Parade (Vol. 1)			
(UK) Decca EP	*29–6–56*	*2*	*8*
All Star Hit Parade (Vol. 2)			
(UK) Decca EP	*9–8–57*	*15*	*2*
ALPERT, HERB (AND THE TIJUANA BRASS*)			
Lonely Bull*			
(US) A & M	17–11–62	6	9
Taste of Honey*			
(US) A & M	30–10–65	7	8
Spanish Flea			
(UK) Pye International	*15–1–66*	*3*	*12*
Zorba The Greek*			
(US) A & M	5–2–66	11	4
Work Song*			
(US) A & M	23–7–66	18	3
Mame*			
(US) A & M	17–12–66	19	2

	Date of chart entry	Highest position reached	Number of weeks in charts
ALPERT, HERB (AND THE TIJUANA BRASS (cont.)			
This Guy's In Love With You			
(US) A & M	1–6–68	1	11
(UK) A & M	*20–7–68*	*2*	*11*
AMBOY DUKES			
Journey to the Center of the Earth			
(US) Mainstream	3–8–68	16	6
AMEN CORNER			
Gin House			
(UK) Deram	*2–9–67*	*12*	*5*
Bend Me, Shape Me			
(UK) Deram	*27–1–68*	*3*	*9*
High in the Sky			
(UK) Deram	*17–8–68*	*6*	*9*
Half as Nice			
(UK) Immediate	*8–2–69*	*1*	*7*
Hello Susie			
(UK) Immediate	*5–7–69*	*4*	*6*
AMERICA			
Horse With No Name			
(UK) Warner Brothers	*15–1–72*	*3*	*7*
(US) Warner Brothers	4–3–72	1	12
I Need You			
(US) Warner Brothers	17–6–72	9	5
Ventura Highway			
(US) Warner Brothers	18–11–72	8	6
Tin Man			
(US) Warner Brothers	12–10–74	4	7
AMERICAN BREED			
Bend Me, Shape Me			
(US) Acta	23–12–67	5	8
AMES, ED			
My Cup Runneth Over			
(US) RCA	25–2–67	8	6
Who Will Answer			
(US) RCA	13–1–68	19	2
AMES BROTHERS			
Naughty Lady of Shady Lane			
(US) Victor	1–1–55	3	9
(UK) HMV	*4–2–55*	*6*	*6*
My Bonnie Lassie			
(US) Coral	15–10–55	11	7
It Only Hurts a Little While			
(US) Victor	9–6–56	15	13
Melodie d'Amour			
(US) Victor	28–10–57	12	10

	Date of chart entry	*Highest position reached*	*Number of weeks in charts*
AMES BROTHERS (cont.)			
Pussy Cat			
(US) RCA	27–10–58	17	3
ANDERSON, BILL			
Still			
(US) Decca	25–5–63	8	7
ANDERSON, LYNN			
Rose Garden			
(US) Columbia	2–1–71	3	10
(UK) CBS	*6–3–71*	*3*	*10*
ANDREWS, CHRIS			
Yesterday Man			
(UK) Decca	*21–10–65*	*3*	*11*
To Whom It May Concern			
(UK) Decca	*18–12–65*	*13*	*5*
ANDREWS, EAMONN			
Shifting, Whispering Sands			
(UK) Parlophone	*20–1–56*	*18*	*3*
ANDREWS, LEE, AND THE HEARTS			
Teardrops			
(US) Chess	30–12–57	20	1
ANDY, BOB, AND GRIFFITHS, MARCIA			
Young, Gifted and Black			
(UK) Harry	*21–3–70*	*5*	*8*
Pied Piper			
(UK) Trojan	*3–7–71*	*11*	*5*
ANGELS			
'Til			
(US) Caprice	25–12–61	14	2
My Boyfriend's Back			
(US) Smash	17–8–63	1	10
ANIMALS			
The House of the Rising Sun			
(UK) Columbia	*4–7–64*	*1*	*7*
(US) MGM	15–8–64	1	9
I'm Crying			
(UK) Columbia	*29–9–64*	*8*	*6*
(US) MGM	7–11–64	19	1
Don't Let Me Be Misunderstood			
(UK) Columbia	*13–2–65*	*3*	*7*
(US) MGM	27–3–65	15	2
Bring It On Home To Me			
(UK) Columbia	*17–4–65*	*7*	*8*

	Date of chart entry	Highest position reached	Number of weeks in charts
ANIMALS (cont.)			
We've Gotta Get Out of this Place			
(UK) Columbia	*24–7–65*	*3*	*8*
(US) MGM	18–9–65	13	4
It's My Life			
(UK) Columbia	*6–11–65*	*7*	*6*
Inside Looking Out			
(UK) Decca	*26–2–66*	*12*	*4*
Don't Bring Me Down			
(UK) Decca	*4–6–66*	*6*	*6*
(US) MGM	18–6–66	12	5
(See also ERIC BURDON AND THE ANIMALS; ERIC BURDON AND WAR)			
ANKA, PAUL			
Diana			
(US) ABC–Paramount	12–8–57	2	16
(UK) Columbia	*16–8–57*	*1*	*23*
I Love You Baby			
(UK) Columbia	*8–11–57*	*3*	*13*
You Are My Destiny			
(UK) Columbia	*31–1–58*	*6*	*10*
(US) ABC–Paramount	10–2–58	7	5
Crazy Love			
(US) ABC–Paramount	5–5–58	19	1
All of a Sudden My Heart Sings			
(US) ABC–Paramount	26–1–59	15	5
(UK) Columbia	*31–1–59*	*10*	*9*
Lonely Boy			
(US) ABC–Paramount	8–6–59	1	12
(UK) Columbia	*9–8–59*	*3*	*12*
Put Your Head On My Shoulder			
(US) ABC–Paramount	21–9–59	2	12
(UK) Columbia	*31–10–59*	*7*	*8*
It's Time to Cry			
(US) ABC–Paramount	7–12–59	4	9
Puppy Love			
(US) ABC–Paramount	7–3–60	2	9
My Home Town			
(US) ABC–Paramount	13–6–60	8	7
Summer's Gone			
(US) ABC–Paramount	24–10–60	11	3
Story of My Love			
(US) ABC–Paramount	13–2–61	16	2
Tonight My Love, Tonight			
(US) ABC–Paramount	17–4–61	13	4
Dance On Little Girl			
(US) ABC–Paramount	19–6–61	10	5
Love Me Warm and Tender			
(US) RCA	31–3–62	12	5
(UK) RCA	*7 4–62*	*19*	*2*

	Date of chart entry	*Highest position reached*	*Number of weeks in charts*
ANKA, PAUL (cont.)			
Steel Guitar, Glass of Wine and You			
(US) RCA	16–6–62	13	4
Eso Beso			
(US) RCA	8–12–62	19	1
(You're) Having My Baby			
(US) United Artists	10–8–74	1	8
(UK) United Artists	*12–10–74*	*6*	*6*
One Man Woman, One Woman Man (with ODIA COATES)			
(US) United Artists	21–12–74	7	7
ANNETTE			
Tall Paul			
(US) Disneyland	2–2–59	7	8
First Name Initial			
(US) Vista	11–1–60	20	1
O, Dio Mio			
(US) Vista	14–3–60	10	5
Pineapple Princess			
(US) Vista	19–9–60	11	5
ANN-MARGARET			
I Just Don't Understand			
(US) RCA	4–9–61	17	2
ANTHONY, BILLY			
This Ole House			
(UK) Columbia	*7–1–55*	*12*	*4*
ANTHONY, RAY			
Peter Gunn Theme			
(US) Capitol	2–2–59	8	9
ANTHONY, RICHARD			
If I Loved You			
(UK) Columbia	*9–5–64*	*18*	*3*
APOLLO 100			
Joy			
(US) Mega	29–1–72	6	8
APPLEJACKS			
Mexican Hat Rack			
(US) Cameo	20–10–58	16	5
Tell Me When			
(UK) Decca	*21–3–64*	*7*	*8*
Like Dreamers Do			
(UK) Decca	*4–7–64*	*20*	*1*
APPLEWHITE, CHARLIE			
Blue Star			
(UK) Brunswick	*23–9–55*	*20*	*1*

	Date of chart entry	Highest position reached	Number of weeks in charts
ARBORS			
The Letter			
(US) Date	5–4–69	20	2
ARCHIES			
Sugar Sugar			
(US) Calendar	23–8–69	1	15
(UK) RCA	*18–10–69*	*1*	*17*
Jingle Jangle			
(US) Kirshner	3–1–70	10	7
ARDEN, TONI			
Padre			
(US) Decca	30–6–58	18	2
ARGENT			
Hold Your Head Up			
(UK) Epic	*1–4–72*	*5*	*6*
(US) Epic	5–8–72	5	6
God Gave Rock and Roll to You			
(UK) Epic	*21–4–73*	*18*	*1*
ARMSTRONG, LOUIS			
Theme from Threepenny Opera			
(US) Columbia	17–3–56	20	1
(UK) Philips	*20–4–56*	*8*	*7*
Hello Dolly			
(US) Kapp	14–3–64	1	16
(UK) London	*13–6–64*	*4*	*8*
Wonderful World			
(UK) Stateside	*16–3–68*	*1*	*16*
ARMY GAME (Cast from the TV Show)			
The Army Game			
(UK) HMV	*6–6–58*	*5*	*6*
ARNOLD, EDDY			
Make the World Go Away			
(US) RCA	27–11–65	6	7
(UK) RCA	*5–3–66*	*8*	*10*
ARRIVAL			
Friends			
(UK) Decca	*17–1–70*	*8*	*5*
I Will Survive			
(UK) Decca	*20–6–70*	*16*	*4*
ARROWS			
A Touch Too Much			
(UK) RAK	*8–6–74*	*8*	*5*

	Date of chart entry	*Highest position reached*	*Number of weeks in charts*
ARSENAL FC			
Good Old Arsenal			
(UK) Pye	*22–5–71*	*16*	*1*
ASHTON, GARDNER AND DYKE			
Resurrection Shuffle			
(UK) Capitol	*30–1–71*	*3*	*8*
ASSEMBLED MULTITUDE			
Overture from Tommy			
(US) Atlantic	15–8–70	16	4
ASSOCIATION			
Along Comes Mary			
(US) Valiant	2–7–66	7	4
Cherish			
(US) Valiant	10–9–66	1	8
Windy			
(US) Warner Brothers	10–6–67	1	11
Never My Love			
(US) Warner Brothers	16–9–67	2	10
Everything That Touches You			
(US) Warner Brothers	24–2–68	10	5
ATOMIC ROOSTER			
Tomorrow Night			
(UK) B & C	*6–3–71*	*11*	*5*
Devils Answer			
(UK) B & C	*24–7–71*	*4*	*6*
ARNOLD, P. P.			
First Cut is the Deepest			
(UK) Immediate	*10–6–67*	*18*	*3*
ATTWELL, WINIFRED			
Let's Have Another Party (Medley)			
(UK) Philips	*7–1–55*	*2*	*2*
Let's Have Another Ding Dong (Medley)			
(UK) Decca	*4–11–55*	*3*	*10*
Poor People of Paris			
(UK) Decca	*16–3–56*	*1*	*15*
Port Au Prince			
(UK) Decca	*18 5–56*	*18*	*6*
Left Bank			
(UK) Decca	*20–7–56*	*14*	*4*
Make It a Party (Medley)			
(UK) Decca	*2–11–56*	*7*	*10*
Let's Have a Ball (Medley)			
(UK) Decca	*6–12–57*	*8*	*5*
Piano Party (Medley)			
(UK) Decca	*5–12–59*	*15*	*4*

	Date of chart entry	*Highest position reached*	*Number of weeks in charts*
AUSTIN, SIL			
Slow Walk			
(US) Mercury	8–12–56	19	1
AVALON, FRANKIE			
Dede Dinah			
(US) Chancellor	10–2–58	7	5
Ginger Bread			
(US) Chancellor	28–7–58	9	8
I'll Wait for You			
(US) Chancellor	17–11–58	15	2
Venus			
(US) Chancellor	2–3–59	1	11
Bobby Sox to Stockings			
(US) Chancellor	15–6–59	8	7
Boy Without a Girl			
(US) Chancellor	29–6–59	10	5
Just Ask Your Heart			
(US) Chancellor	21–9–59	7	8
Why			
(US) Chancellor	14–12–59	1	10
(UK) HMV	*16–1–60*	*15*	*3*
AVONS			
Seven Little Girls			
(UK) Columbia	*21–11–59*	*4*	*9*
AZNAVOUR, CHARLES			
She			
(UK) Barclay	*22–6–74*	*1*	*8*
BACHARACH, BURT			
Trains and Boats and Planes			
(UK) London	*29–5–65*	*4*	*7*
BACHELORS			
Charmaine			
(UK) Decca	*2–3–63*	*6*	*9*
Whispering			
(UK) Decca	*21–9–63*	*18*	*1*
Diane			
(UK) Decca	*8–2–64*	*1*	*11*
(US) London	30–5–64	10	5
I Believe			
(UK) Decca	*28–3–64*	*2*	*11*
Ramona			
(UK) Decca	*13–6–64*	*4*	*8*
I Wouldn't Trade You for the World			
(UK) Decca	*29–8–64*	*5*	*11*
No Arms Could Ever Hold You			
(UK) Decca	*12–12–64*	*7*	*7*

	Date of chart entry	*Highest position reached*	*Number of weeks in charts*
BACHELORS (cont.)			
Marie			
(UK) Decca	*29–5–65*	*9*	*6*
(US) London	24–7–65	15	2
Sound of Silence			
(UK) Decca	*26–3–66*	*3*	*8*
Marta			
(UK) Decca	*22–7–67*	*20*	*1*
BACHMAN TURNER OVERDRIVE			
Taking Care of Business			
(US) Mercury	20–7–74	12	5
You Ain't Seen Nothing Yet			
(US) Mercury	19–10–74	1	8
(UK) Mercury	*23–11–74*	*2*	*8*
BAD COMPANY			
Can't Get Enough			
(UK) Island	*29–6–74*	*15*	*1*
(US) Swansong	21–9–74	6	8
BADFINGER			
Come and Get It			
(UK) Apple	*17–1–70*	*4*	*7*
(US) Apple	28–3–70	7	7
No Matter What			
(US) Apple	5–12–70	8	5
(UK) Apple	*23–1–71*	*5*	*8*
Day After Day			
(US) Apple	1–1–72	4	9
(UK) Apple	*12–2–72*	*10*	*5*
Baby Blue			
(US) Apple	15–4–72	14	4
BAEZ, JOAN			
There But For Fortune			
(UK) Fontana	*17–7–65*	*8*	*7*
The Night They Drove Old Dixie Down			
(US) Vanguard	4–9–71	3	11
(UK) Vanguard	*23–10–71*	*6*	*7*
BAKER, LAVERN			
I Cried a Tear			
(US) Atlantic	2–2–59	6	9
BALDRY, LONG JOHN			
Let the Heartaches Begin			
(UK) Pye	*18–11–67*	*1*	*9*
Mexico			
(UK) Pye	*9–11–68*	*15*	*4*

	Date of chart entry	Highest position reached	Number of weeks in charts
BALL, KENNY			
Samantha			
(UK) Pye	*19–2–61*	*7*	*8*
I Still Love You All			
(UK) Pye	*21–5–61*	*18*	*2*
Midnight in Moscow			
(UK) Pye	*11–11–61*	*4*	*14*
(US) Kapp	24–2–62	2	9
March of the Siamese Children			
(UK) Pye	*24–2–62*	*3*	*8*
Green Leaves of Summer			
(UK) Pye	*2–6–62*	*7*	*8*
So Do I			
(UK) Pye	*1–9–62*	*14*	*4*
Suki Yaki			
(UK) Pye	*3–2–63*	*10*	*7*
BALLARD, HANK, AND THE MIDNIGHTERS			
Finger Poppin' Time			
(US) King	25–7–60	7	10
Let's Go Let's Go Let's Go			
(US) King	31–10–60	6	7
BAND			
Rag Mama Rag			
(UK) Capitol	*25–4–70*	*16*	*4*
BANDWAGON			
Breaking Down the Walls of Heartache			
(UK) Direction	*2–11–68*	*4*	*11*
[see also: JOHNSON, JOHNNY AND THE BANDWAGON]			
BARBER, CHRIS			
Petite Fleur			
(UK) Nixa Pye–Nixa	*14–2–59*	*4*	*18*
(US) Laurie	16–2–59	5	6
BARE, BOBBY			
Detroit City			
(US) RCA	27–7–63	16	3
500 Miles From Home			
(US) RCA	9–11–63	10	4
BAR-KAYS			
Soul Finger			
(US) Volt	22–7–67	17	4

	Date of chart entry	*Highest position reached*	*Number of weeks in charts*
BARRETTO, RAY			
El Watusi			
(US) Tico	1–6–63	17	2
BARRON KNIGHTS			
Call Up the Groups			
(UK) Columbia	*18–7–64*	*3*	*9*
Pop! Go the Workers			
(UK) Columbia	*10–4–65*	*5*	*8*
Merrie Gentle Pops			
(UK) Columbia	*25–12–65*	*9*	*5*
Under New Management			
(UK) Columbia	*24–12–66*	*15*	*4*
BARRY, JOHN, ORCHESTRA			
Hit and Miss			
(UK) Parlophone	*27–2–60*	*12*	*8*
Walk Don't Run			
(UK) Parlophone	*18–9–60*	*7*	*9*
Black Stockings			
(UK) Parlophone	*1–1–61*	*13*	*2*
James Bond Theme			
(UK) Columbia	*24–11–62*	*13*	*4*
Theme from 'The Persuaders'			
(UK) CBS	*15–1–72*	*13*	*4*
BARRY, LEN			
1–2–3			
(US) Decca	23–10–65	2	9
(UK) Brunswick	*13–11–65*	*3*	*11*
Like a Baby			
(UK) Brunswick	*5–2–66*	*10*	*4*
BASS, FONTELLA			
Rescue Me			
(US) Checker	30–10–65	4	8
(UK) Chess	*11–12–65*	*11*	*7*
BASSEY, SHIRLEY			
Banana Boat Song			
(UK) Philips	*8–3–57*	*8*	*6*
Kiss Me Honey Honey Kiss Me			
(UK) Philips	*3–1–59*	*4*	*13*
As I Love You			
(UK) Philips	*17–1–59*	*2*	*15*
As Long As He Needs Me			
(UK) Columbia	*31–7–60*	*2*	*17*
You'll Never Know			
(UK) Columbia	*7–5–61*	*3*	*8*
Reach for the Stars			
(UK) Columbia	*29–7–61*	*3*	*10*

	Date of chart entry	*Highest position reached*	*Number of weeks in charts*
BASSEY, SHIRLEY (cont.)			
I'll Get By			
(UK) Columbia	*18–11–61*	*9*	*5*
What Now My Love?			
(UK) Columbia	*22–9–62*	*5*	*10*
I (Who Have Nothing)			
(UK) Columbia	*12–10–63*	*6*	*10*
Goldfinger			
(US) United Artists	6–3–65	8	6
Something			
(UK) United Artists	*4–7–70*	*4*	*12*
For All We Know			
(UK) United Artists	*18–9–71*	*6*	*11*
Never Never Never			
(UK) United Artists	*17–3–73*	*8*	*8*
BAXTER, LES			
Unchained Melody			
(US) Capitol	9–4–55	2	20
(UK) Capitol	*13–5–55*	*10*	*9*
Wake the Town and Tell the People			
(US) Capitol	20–8–55	10	11
Poor People of Paris			
(US) Capitol	25–2–56	1	17
BAY CITY ROLLERS			
Keep On Dancing			
(UK) Bell	*16–10–71*	*9*	*5*
Remember (Sha La La)			
(UK)Bell	*23–2–74*	*6*	*6*
Shang A Lang			
(UK) Bell	*4–5–74*	*2*	*6*
Summerlove Sensation			
(UK) Bell	*3–8–74*	*3*	*7*
All of Me Loves All of You			
(UK) Bell	*19–10–74*	*4*	*6*
B. BUMBLE AND THE STINGERS			
Nut Rocker			
(UK) Top Rank	*28–4–62*	*1*	*11*
(UK) Stateside (re-issue)	*7–7–72*	*19*	*2*
BEACH BOYS			
Surfin' Safari			
(US) Capitol	6–10–62	14	3
Surfin' USA			
(US) Capitol	27–4–63	3	10
Surfer Girl			
(US) Capitol b/w*	24–8–63	7	9
Little Deuce Coupe*			
(US) Capitol	28–9–63	15	2

	Date of chart entry	*Highest position reached*	*Number of weeks in charts*
BEACH BOYS (cont.)			
Be True to Your School			
(US) Capitol	23–11–63	6	7
Fun Fun Fun			
(US) Capitol	29–2–64	5	7
I Get Around			
(US) Capitol	6–6–64	1	12
(UK) Capitol	*25–7–64*	*7*	*8*
When I Grow Up to Be a Man			
(US) Capitol	3–10–64	9	5
Dance Dance Dance			
(US) Capitol	28–11–64	8	5
Do You Wanna Dance?			
(US) Capitol	20–3–65	12	4
Help Me Rhonda			
(US) Capitol	15–5–65	1	8
California Girls			
(US) Capitol	14–8–65	3	7
Little Girl I Once Knew			
(US) Capitol	1–1–66	20	1
Barbara Ann			
(US) Capitol	21–1–66	2	6
(UK) Capitol	*26–2–66*	*3*	*8*
Sloop John B			
(US) Capitol	16–4–66	3	7
(UK) Capitol	*30–4–66*	*2*	*11*
God Only Knows			
*(UK) Capitol b/w***	*6–8–66*	*2*	*9*
Wouldn't It Be Nice**			
(US) Capitol	27–8–66	8	5
Good Vibrations			
(US) Capitol	5–11–66	1	11
(UK) Capitol	*5–11–66*	*1*	*11*
Then I Kissed Her			
(UK) Capitol	*13–5–67*	*4*	*8*
Heroes and Villains			
(US) Capitol	19–8–67	12	3
(UK) Capitol	*2–9–67*	*8*	*5*
Darlin'			
(US) Capitol	3–2–68	19	2
(UK) Capitol	*3–2–68*	*11*	*9*
Do It Again			
(UK) Capitol	*10–8–68*	*1*	*10*
(US) Capitol	14–9–68	20	2
I Can Hear Music			
(UK) Capitol	*22–3–69*	*11*	*7*
Break Away			
(UK) Capitol	*28–6–69*	*6*	*6*
Cottonfields			
(UK) Capitol	*30–5–70*	*5*	*12*

	Date of chart entry	Highest position reached	Number of weeks in charts
BEATLES			
Love Me Do			
(UK) Parlophone	*15–12–62*	*17*	*2*
(US) Tollie (re-issue) b/w*	9–5–64	1	9
Please Please Me			
(UK) Parlophone	*3–2–63*	*2*	*11*
(US) Vee Jay (re-issue)	29–2–64	3	8
From Me to You			
(UK) Parlophone	*27–4–63*	*1*	*16*
She Loves You			
(UK) Parlophone	*31–8–63*	*1*	*24*
(US) Swan (re-issue)	8–2–64	1	12
I Want to Hold Your Hand			
(UK) Parlophone	*7–12–63*	*1*	*13*
(US) Capitol b/w**	25–1–64	1	13
I Saw Her Standing There			
(US) Capitol	7–3–64	14	3
Twist and Shout			
(US) Tollie (re-issue)	21–3–64	2	9
Can't Buy Me Love			
(UK) Parlophone	*28–3–64*	*1*	*9*
(US) Capitol	4–4–64	1	7
Do You Want to Know a Secret			
(US) Vee-Jay (re-issue)	11–4–64	2	8
P.S. I Love You			
(US) Tollie (re-issue)*	23–5–64	10	4
Hard Day's Night			
(UK) Parlophone	*18–7–64*	*1*	*11*
(US) Capitol	25–7–64	1	10
And I Love Her			
(US) Capitol	22–8–64	12	4
Ain't She Sweet			
(US) Atco (re-issue)	22–8–64	19	1
Matchbox			
(US) Capitol	3–10–64	17	3
I Feel Fine			
(UK) Parlophone	*5–12–64*	*1*	*10*
(US) Capitol b/w***	12–12–64	1	8
She's a Woman***			
(US) Capitol	19–12–64	4	6
Eight Days a Week			
(US) Capitol	27–2–65	1	8
Ticket to Ride			
(UK) Parlophone	*17–4–65*	*1*	*9*
(US) Capitol	1–5–65	1	9
Help			
(UK) Parlophone	*31–7–65*	*1*	*10*
(US) Capitol	14–8–65	1	9
Yesterday			
(US) Capitol	2–10–65	1	8

	Date of chart entry	Highest position reached	Number of weeks in charts
BEATLES (cont.)			
Day Tripper			
(UK) Parlophone } *b/w†*	*11–12–65*	*1*	*10*
(US) Capitol }	1–1–66	5	5
We Can Work It Out†			
(US) Capitol	25–12–65	1	9
Nowhere Man			
(US) Capitol	12–3–66	3	7
Paperback Writer			
(UK) Parlophone	*18–6–66*	*1*	*7*
(US) Capitol	18–6–66	1	8
Eleanor Rigby			
(UK) Parlophone } *b/w††*	*13–8–66*	*1*	*9*
(US) Capitol }	17–9–66	11	3
Yellow Submarine††			
(US) Capitol	27–8–66	2	7
Penny Lane			
(UK) Parlophone } *b/w†††*	*25–2–67*	*2*	*8*
(US) Capitol }	11–3–67	1	6
Strawberry Fields†††			
(US) Capitol	11–3–67	8	5
All You Need Is Love			
(UK) Parlophone	*15–7–67*	*1*	*10*
(US) Capitol	5–8–67	1	7
Hello Goodbye			
(UK) Parlophone	*2–12–67*	*1*	*10*
(US) Capitol	9–12–67	1	9
Magical Mystery Tour			
(UK) Parlophone EP	*16–12–67*	*2*	*9*
Lady Madonna			
(UK) Parlophone	*23–3–68*	*1*	*6*
(US) Capitol	30–3–68	4	8
Hey Jude			
(UK) Apple	*14–9–68*	*1*	*10*
(US) Apple	14–9–68	1	16
Revolution			
(US) Apple	21–9–68	12	9
Get Back			
(UK) Apple	*26–4–69*	*1*	*10*
(US) Apple	10–5–69	1	11
Ballad of John and Yoko			
(UK) Apple	*7–6–69*	*1*	*8*
(US) Apple	28–6–69	8	6
Something/Come Together			
(US) Apple	18–10–69	1	14
(UK) Apple	*5–11–69*	*4*	*17*
Let It Be			
(UK) Apple	*14–3–70*	*2*	*6*
(US) Apple	21–3–70	1	11

	Date of chart entry	*Highest position reached*	*Number of weeks in charts*
BEATLES (cont.)			
Long and Winding Road/ For You Blue			
(US) Apple	30–5–70	1	8
BEAU BRUMMELS			
Laugh Laugh			
(US) Autumn	13–2–65	15	4
Just a Little			
(US) Autumn	22–5–65	8	6
BECK, JEFF			
Hi Ho Silver Lining			
(UK) Columbia	*6–5–67*	*14*	*5*
(UK) RAK (re-issue)	*18–11–72*	*17*	*4*
BEDROCKS			
Ob-La-Di-Ob-La-Da			
(UK) Columbia	*4–1–69*	*20*	*1*
BEE GEES			
New York Mining Disaster 1941			
(UK) Polydor	*13–5–67*	*12*	*5*
(US) Atco	17–6–67	14	3
To Love Somebody			
(US) Atco	19–8–67	17	2
Massachusetts			
(UK) Polydor	*30–9–67*	*1*	*10*
(US) Atco	2–12–67	11	4
Holiday			
(US) Atco	11–11–67	16	2
Words			
(UK) Polydor	*2–12–67*	*8*	*7*
(US) Atco	24–2–68	15	4
World			
(UK) Polydor	*10–2–68*	*9*	*10*
I've Gotta Get a Message to You			
(UK) Polydor	*17–8–68*	*1*	*11*
(US) Atco	21–9–68	8	7
I Started a Joke			
(US) Atco	11–1–69	6	7
First of May			
(UK) Polydor	*8–3–69*	*6*	*6*
Don't Forget to Remember			
(UK) Polydor	*23–8–69*	*3*	*11*
Lonely Days			
(US) Atco	9–1–71	3	7
How Can You Mend a Broken Heart			
(US) Atco	10–7–71	1	12

	Date of chart entry	*Highest position reached*	*Number of weeks in charts*
BEE GEES (cont.)			
My World			
(UK) Polydor	*2–12–72*	*16*	*5*
(US) Atco	26–2–72	16	2
Run to Me			
(UK) Polydor	*12–8–72*	*11*	*5*
(US) Atco	9–9–72	16	4
BEGINNING OF THE END			
Funky Nassau			
(US) Alston	26–6–71	15	4
BELAFONTE, HARRY			
Mary's Boy Child			
(US) Victor	5–1–57	15	1
(UK) RCA	*15–11–57*	*1*	*9*
Jamaica Farewell			
(US) Victor	12–1–57	17	5
Banana Boat Song			
(US) Victor	19–1–57	5	13
(UK) HMV	*1–3–57*	*2*	*14*
Mama Look-A-Boobo			
(US) Victor	13–4–57	13	6
Island in the Sun			
(UK) RCA	*21–6–57*	*3*	*22*
Scarlet Ribbons			
(UK) HMV	*20–9–57*	*18*	*2*
Little Bernadette			
(UK) RCA	*22–8–58*	*16*	*4*
Mary's Boy Child			
(UK) RCA (re-entry)	*5–12–58*	*10*	*5*
The Son of Mary			
(UK) RCA	*19–12–58*	*18*	*2*
BELL, ARCHIE, AND THE DRELLS			
Tighten Up			
(US) Atlantic	27–4–68	1	9
I Can't Stop Dancing			
(US) Atlantic	17–8–68	9	5
Here I Go Again			
(UK) Atlantic	*11–11–72*	*11*	*3*
BELL, FREDDIE, AND THE BELL BOYS			
Giddy Up A Ding Dong			
(UK) Mercury	*28–9–56*	*4*	*8*
BELL, WILLIAM. See CLAY, JUDY			
BELL NOTES			
I've Had It			
(US) Time	23–2–59	6	8

	Date of chart entry	*Highest position reached*	*Number of weeks in charts*
BELLS			
Stay Awhile			
(US) Polydor	24–4–71	7	6
BELMONTS			
Tell Me Why			
(US) Sabrina	26–6–61	18	4
(see also: DION)			
BENNETT, BOYD			
Seventeen			
(US) King	23–7–55	5	13
(UK) Parlophone	*23–12–55*	*16*	*1*
BENNETT, CLIFF, AND THE REBEL ROUSERS			
One Way Love			
(UK) Parlophone	*24–10–64*	*9*	*4*
Got to Get You Into My Life			
(UK) Parlophone	*10–9–66*	*6*	*4*
BENNETT, JOE, AND THE SPARKLETONES			
Black Slacks			
(US) ABC–Paramount	9–10–57	18	2
BENNETT, TONY			
Stranger in Paradise			
(UK) Philips	*15–4–55*	*1*	*16*
Close Your Eyes			
(UK) Philips	*16–9–55*	*18*	*1*
Can You Find It in Your Heart			
(US) Columbia	2–6–56	19	1
In the Middle of an Island			
(US) Columbia	9–9–57	9	8
Firefly			
(US) Columbia	13–10–58	20	1
I Left My Heart in San Francisco			
(US) Columbia	20–10–62	19	1
I Wanna Be Around			
(US) Columbia	23–3–63	14	3
Good Life			
(US) Columbia	15–6–63	18	2
BENTON, BROOK			
It's Just a Matter of Time			
(US) Mercury	2–3–59	3	9
Endlessly			
(US) Mercury	18–5–59	12	5
Thank You Pretty Baby			
(US) Mercury	17–8–59	16	5

	Date of chart entry	*Highest position reached*	*Number of weeks in charts*
BENTON, BROOK (cont.)			
So Many Ways			
(US) Mercury	2–11–59	6	9
Baby (with DINAH WASHINGTON)			
(US) Mercury	15–2–60	5	10
Rockin' Good Way (with DINAH WASHINGTON)			
(US) Mercury	13–6–60	7	7
Kiddio			
(US) Mercury b/w*	5–9–60	7	8
Same One			
(US) Mercury*	12–9–60	16	5
Think Twice			
(US) Mercury	13–3–61	11	5
Boll Weevil Song			
(US) Mercury	12–6–61	2	10
Frankie and Johnny			
(US) Mercury	11–9–61	20	2
Revenge			
(US) Mercury	6–1–62	15	2
Shadrack			
(US) Mercury	17–2–62	19	1
Lie to Me			
(US) Mercury	29–9–62	13	3
Hotel Happiness			
(US) Mercury	15–12–62	3	7
Rainy Night in Georgia			
(US) Cotillion	14–2–70	4	9
BERNARD, ROD			
This Should Go On Forever			
(US) Argo	13–4–59	20	1
BERNSTEIN, ELMER			
The Johnny Staccato Theme			
(UK) Capitol	*19–12–59*	*5*	*8*
BERRY, CHUCK			
Maybellene			
(US) Chess	20–8–55	5	10
School Days			
(US) Chess	29–4–57	5	10
Rock and Roll Music			
(US) Chess	25–11–57	8	9
Sweet Little Sixteen			
(US) Chess	24–2–58	2	9
(UK) London	*9–5–58*	*16*	*3*
Johnny B. Goode			
(US) Chess	5–5–58	8	9
Carol			
(US) Chess	29–9–58	18	2

	Date of chart entry	*Highest position reached*	*Number of weeks in charts*
BERRY, CHUCK (cont.)			
Let It Rock/Memphis, Tennessee			
(UK) Pye (re-issue)	*26–10–63*	*6*	*7*
No Particular Place To Go			
(UK) Pye	*23–5–64*	*3*	*7*
(US) Chess	27–6–64	10	4
You Never Can Tell			
(US) Chess	29–8–64	14	3
My Ding-a-Ling (live recording)			
(US) Chess	23–9–72	1	9
(UK) Chess	*11–11–72*	*1*	*10*
Reelin' and Rockin' (live recording)			
(UK) Chess	*24–2–73*	*18*	*2*
BERRY, DAVE, AND THE CRUISERS			
Memphis, Tennessee			
(UK) Decca	*9–11–63*	*19*	*1*
The Crying Game			
(UK) Decca	*22–8–64*	*5*	*7*
Little Things			
(UK) Decca	*10–4–65*	*6*	*6*
Mama			
(UK) Decca	*23–7–66*	*5*	*10*
BERRY, MIKE			
Tribute to Buddy Holly			
(UK) HMV	*28–10–61*	*18*	*1*
Don't You Think It's Time			
(UK) HMV	*20–1–63*	*6*	*7*
BEVERLY SISTERS			
Little Drummer Boy			
(UK) Decca	*14–2–59*	*9*	*11*
Little Donkey			
(UK) Decca	*28–11–59*	*16*	*2*
BIG BEN BANJO BAND			
Let's Get Together Again			
(UK) Columbia	*9–12–55*	*15*	*4*
BIG BOPPER			
Chantilly Lace			
(US) Mercury	29–9–58	6	11
(UK) Mercury	*17–1–59*	*14*	*6*
BIG BROTHER AND THE HOLDING COMPANY			
Piece of My Heart			
(US) Columbia	12–10–68	12	5

	Date of chart entry	*Highest position reached*	*Number of weeks in charts*
BILK, ACKER			
Summer Set			
(UK) Columbia	*16–1–60*	*10*	*11*
Buona Sera			
(UK) Columbia	*25–12–60*	*9*	*8*
That's My Home			
(UK) Columbia	*22–7–61*	*11*	*8*
Creole Jazz			
(UK) Columbia	*4–11–61*	*17*	*1*
Stranger on the Shore			
(UK) Columbia	*25–11–61*	*1*	*39*
(US) Atco	14–4–62	1	13
Frankie and Johnny			
(UK) Columbia	*10–3–62*	*19*	*2*
Lonely			
(UK) Columbia	*13–10–62*	*14*	*4*
A Taste of Honey			
(UK) Columbia	*10–2–63*	*16*	*3*
BILLIE AND LILLIE			
La Dee Dah			
(US) Swan	20–1–58	9	7
Lucky Ladybug			
(US) Swan	26–1–59	14	1
BILLY JOE AND THE CHECKMATES			
Percolator (Twist)			
(US) Dore	24–2–62	10	5
BIRKIN, JANE, AND GAINSBOURG, SERGE			
Je T'Aime Moi Non Plus			
(UK) Fontana	*23–8–69*	*2*	*7*
(UK) Major Minor (re-licence)	*4–10–69*	*1*	*7*
BILL BLACK'S COMBO			
Smokie Pt. II			
(US) Hi	4–1–60	17	3
White Silver Sands			
(US) Hi	28–3–60	9	9
Josephine			
(US) Hi	18–7–60	18	2
Don't Be Cruel			
(US) Hi	10–10–60	11	7
Blue Tango			
(US) Hi	19–12–60	16	1
Hearts of Stone			
(US) Hi	20–3–61	20	1

	Date of chart entry	Highest position reached	Number of weeks in charts
BLACK, CILLA			
Anyone Who Had a Heart			
(UK) Parlophone	*15–2–64*	*1*	*11*
You're My World			
(UK) Parlophone	*16–5–64*	*1*	*10*
It's For You			
(UK) Parlophone	*15–8–64*	*7*	*6*
You've Lost That Lovin' Feeling			
(UK) Parlophone	*23–1–65*	*2*	*5*
I've Been Wrong Before			
(UK) Parlophone	*15–5–65*	*17*	*2*
Love's Just a Broken Heart			
(UK) Parlophone	*29–1–66*	*5*	*6*
Alfie			
(UK) Parlophone	*9–4–66*	*9*	*7*
Don't Answer Me			
(UK) Parlophone	*18–6–66*	*6*	*6*
A Fool Am I			
(UK) Parlophone	*5–11–66*	*13*	*4*
Step Inside Love			
(UK) Parlophone	*30–3–68*	*8*	*5*
Surround Yourself With Sorrow			
(UK) Parlophone	*22–2–69*	*3*	*9*
Conversations			
(UK) Parlophone	*26–7–69*	*7*	*6*
If I Thought You'd Ever Change Your Mind			
(UK) Parlophone	*10–1–70*	*20*	*1*
Something Tells Me (Something's Gonna Happen Tonight)			
(UK) Parlophone	*4–12–71*	*6*	*8*
BLACK, JEANNE			
He'll Have To Stay			
(US) Capitol	16–5–60	4	7
BLACKFOOT SUE			
Standing In The Road			
(UK) DJM	*26–8–72*	*4*	*6*
BLACK SABBATH			
Paranoid			
(UK) Vertigo	*26–9–70*	*4*	*8*
BLAND BILLY			
Let The Little Girl Dance			
(US) Old Town	18–4–60	7	8
(UK) London	*8–5–60*	*18*	*2*
BLAND, BOBBY			
Ain't Nothing You Can Do			
(US) Duke	11–4–64	20	2

	Date of chart entry	*Highest position reached*	*Number of weeks in charts*
BLANE, MARCIE			
Bobby's Girl			
(US) Seville	10–11–62	3	11
BLOODSTONE			
Natural High			
(US) London	23–6–73	10	6
BLOOD, SWEAT AND TEARS			
You've Made Me So Very Happy			
(US) Columbia	29–3–69	2	8
Spinning Wheel			
(US) Columbia	14–6–69	2	10
And When I Die			
(US) Columbia	1–11–69	2	10
Hi-De-Ho			
(US) Columbia	29–8–70	14	3
BLOOM, BOBBY			
Montego Bay			
(UK) Polydor	*12–9–70*	*3*	*8*
(US) MGM	7–11–70	8	6
BLUE, BARRY			
Dancing On A Saturday Night			
(UK) Bell	*11–8–73*	*2*	*9*
Do You Wanna Dance?			
(UK) Bell	*10–11–73*	*7*	*6*
School Love			
(UK) Bell	*16–3–74*	*11*	*5*
BLUE BELLES			
I Sold My Heart To The Junkman			
(US) Newtown	26–5–62	15	3
BLUE CHEER			
Summertime Blues			
(US) Philips	13–4–68	14	6
BLUE MAGIC			
Sideshow			
(US) Atco	29–6–74	8	10
BLUE MINK			
Melting Pot			
(UK) Philips	*29–11–69*	*3*	*10*
Good Morning Freedom			
(UK) Philips	*18–4–70*	*10*	*4*
Our World			
(UK) Philips	*10–10–70*	*17*	*2*

	Date of chart entry	*Highest position reached*	*Number of weeks in charts*
BLUE MINK (cont.)			
Banner Man			
(UK) Regal Zonophone	*5–6–71*	*3*	*9*
Stay With Me			
(UK) Regal Zonophone	*2–12–72*	*11*	*4*
Randy			
(UK) EMI	*14–7–73*	*9*	*5*
BLUE RIDGE RANGERS			
Jambalaya			
(US) Fantasy	17–2–73	16	4
BLUE SWEDE			
Hooked On A Feeling			
(US) EMI	16–3–74	1	9
Never My Love			
(US) EMI	28–9–74	7	4
BLUES IMAGE			
Ride Captain Ride			
(US) Atco	6–6–70	4	9
BLUES MAGOOS			
(We Ain't Got) Nothin' Yet			
(US) Mercury	21–1–67	5	7
BLUE STARS			
Lullaby of Birdland			
(US) Mercury	25–2–56	20	1
BLUNSTONE, COLIN			
Say You Don't Mind			
(UK) Epic	*4–3–72*	*15*	*3*
BOB AND EARL			
Harlem Shuffle			
(UK) Island (re-issue)	*19–4–69*	*7*	*6*
BOB B. SOXX AND THE BLUE JEANS			
Zip-A-Dee-Doo-Dah			
(US) Philles	22–12–62	8	6
BOBETTES			
Mr. Lee			
(US) Atlantic	2–9–75	6	11
BO DIDDLEY			
Say Man			
(US) Checker	26–10–59	20	1
BOLAN, MARC			
Teenage Dream			
(UK) EMI	*9–2–74*	*13*	*3*
[see also: T. REX]			

	Date of chart entry	*Highest position reached*	*Number of weeks in charts*
BONDS, GARY 'U.S.'			
New Orleans			
(US) LeGrand	7–11–60	6	8
(UK) Top Rank	*12–2–61*	*20*	*1*
Quarter To Three			
(US) LeGrand	12–6–61	1	10
(UK) Top Rank	*22–7–61*	*11*	*8*
School Is Out			
(US) LeGrand	7–8–61	5	6
Dear Lady Twist			
(US) LeGrand	27–1–62	9	8
Twist, Twist Señora			
(US) LeGrand	14–4–62	9	6
BONNEY, GRAHAM			
Supergirl			
(UK) Columbia	*30–4–66*	*19*	*1*
BONZO DOG DOO DAH BAND			
I'm The Urban Spaceman			
(UK) Liberty	*30–11–68*	*5*	*10*
BOOKER T AND THE MGs			
Green Onions			
(US) Stax	15–9–62	3	8
Soul Limbo			
(US) Stax	17–8–68	17	4
Hang 'Em High			
(US) Stax	25–1–69	9	6
Time Is Tight			
(US) Stax	26–4–69	6	6
(UK) Stax	*31–5–69*	*4*	*10*
BOONE, DANIEL			
Daddy Don't You Walk So Fast			
(UK) Penny Farthing	*25–9–71*	*17*	*4*
Beautiful Sunday			
(US) Mercury	2–9–72	15	5
BOONE, PAT			
Two Hearts			
(US) Dot	16–4–55	16	6
Ain't It A Shame			
(US) Dot	9–7–55	2	18
(UK) London	*18–11–55*	*7*	*9*
At My Front Door/No Arms Can Ever Hold You			
(US) Dot	29–10–55	7	9
I'll Be Home			
(US) Dot b/w*	18–2–56	5	17
(UK) London	*27–4–56*	*1*	*23*

	Date of chart entry	Highest position reached	Number of weeks in charts
BOONE, PAT (cont.)			
Tutti Frutti			
(US) Dot*	18–2–56	12	5
Long Tall Sally			
(US) Dot	12–5–56	18	2
(UK) London	*24–8–56*	*18*	*2*
I Almost Lost My Mind			
(US) Dot	16–6–56	1	17
(UK) London	*17–8–56*	*14*	*6*
Friendly Persuasion			
(US) Dot b/w**	6–10–56	1	12
(UK) London	*21–12–56*	*3*	*17*
Chains of Love			
(US) Dot**	6–10–56	20	1
Don't Forbid Me			
(US) Dot	5–1–57	1	15
(UK) London	*8–2–57*	*2*	*14*
Why Baby Why			
(US) Dot	30–3–57	6	10
(UK) London	*10–5–57*	*17*	*1*
Love Letters In The Sand			
(US) Dot	20–5–57	1	19
(UK) London	*5–7–57*	*2*	*21*
Remember You're Mine			
(UK) London	*4–10–57*	*5*	*13*
(US) Dot	21–10–57	20	1
April Love			
(US) Dot	11–11–57	1	16
(UK) London	*20–12–57*	*7*	*18*
It's Too Soon To Know			
(US) Dot }	24–2–58	13	5
(UK) London } *b/w****	*11–4–58*	*7*	*8*
A Wonderful Time Up There***			
(US) Dot	10–3–58	10	9
(UK) London	*4–4–58*	*2*	*14*
Sugar Moon			
(US) Dot	19–5–58	11	8
(UK) London	*27–6–58*	*6*	*10*
If Dreams Came True			
(US) Dot	28–7–58	12	5
(UK) London	*19–9–58*	*16*	*5*
I'll Remember Tonight			
(UK) London	*31–1–59*	*17*	*3*
'Twixt Twelve And Twenty			
(US) Dot	13–7–59	17	3
(UK) London	*9–8–59*	*16*	*3*
For A Penny			
(UK) London	*18–7–59*	*19*	*1*
(Welcome) New Lovers			
(US) Dot	21–3–60	18	2

	Date of chart entry	*Highest position reached*	*Number of weeks in charts*
BOONE, PAT (cont.)			
Moody River			
(US) Dot	29–5–61	1	9
(UK) London	*2–7–61*	*16*	*3*
Big Cold Wind			
(US) Dot	18–9–61	19	2
Johnny Will			
(UK) London	*2–12–61*	*3*	*8*
I'll See You In My Dreams			
(UK) London	*10–3–62*	*19*	*2*
Speedy Gonzales			
(US) Dot	14–7–62	6	8
(UK) London	*21–7–62*	*2*	*13*
The Main Attraction			
(UK) London	*1–12–62*	*12*	*7*
BOOTHE, KEN			
Everything I Own			
(UK) Trojan	*5–10–74*	*1*	*9*
BOSWELL, EVE			
Pickin' A Chicken			
(UK) Parlophone	*6–1–56*	*9*	*10*
BOWEN, JIMMY			
I'm Sticking With You			
(US) Roulette	22–4–57	14	3
BOWIE, DAVID			
Space Oddity			
(UK) Philips	*4–10–69*	*5*	*8*
(US) RCA (re-issue)	24–3–73	15	4
Starman			
(UK) RCA	*15–7–72*	*10*	*6*
John I'm Only Dancing			
(UK) RCA	*7–10–72*	*12*	*5*
The Jean Genie			
(UK) RCA	*23–12–72*	*2*	*8*
Drive-In Saturday			
(UK) RCA	*14–4–73*	*3*	*7*
Life On Mars			
(UK) RCA	*7–7–73*	*3*	*8*
Laughing Gnome			
(UK) Deram (re-issue)	*29–9–73*	*6*	*6*
Sorrow			
(UK) RCA	*20–10–73*	*3*	*8*
Rebel Rebel			
(UK) RCA	*23–2–74*	*5*	*5*
Knock On Wood			
(UK) RCA	*28–9–74*	*10*	*4*

	Date of chart entry	*Highest position reached*	*Number of weeks in charts*
BOX TOPS			
The Letter			
(US) Mala	2–9–67	1	10
(UK) Stateside	*30–9–67*	*5*	*8*
Cry Like A Baby			
(US) Mala	23–3–68	2	10
(UK) Bell	*20–4–68*	*15*	*5*
Soul Deep			
(US) Mala	30–8–69	8	2
BOYCE, TOMMY, AND HART BOBBY			
I Wonder What She's Doing Tonight			
(US) A & M	3–2–68	8	7
BRADLEY, JAN			
Mama Didn't Lie			
(US) Chess	16–2–63	14	6
BREAD			
Make It With You			
(US) Elektra	11–7–70	1	12
(UK) Elektra	*29–8–70*	*5*	*7*
It Don't Matter To Me			
(US) Elektra	31–10–70	10	5
If			
(US) Elektra	17–4–71	4	8
Baby I'm-a Want You			
(US) Elektra	13–11–71	3	7
(UK) Elektra	*29–1–72*	*14*	*4*
Everything I Own			
(US) Elektra	19–2–72	5	8
Diary			
(US) Elektra	27–5–72	15	5
Guitar Man			
(US) Elektra	19–8–72	11	5
(UK) Elektra	*28–10–72*	*16*	*2*
Sweet Surrender			
(US) Elektra	2–12–72	15	6
Aubrey			
(US) Elektra	17–3–73	15	3
BREMERS, BEVERLY			
Don't Say You Don't Remember			
(US) Scepter	19–2–72	15	5
BRENDA AND THE TABULATIONS			
Dry Your Eyes			
(US) Dionn	15–4–67	20	2

	Date of chart entry	*Highest position reached*	*Number of weeks in charts*
BRENNAN, WALTER			
Old Rivers			
(US) Liberty	5–5–62	5	6
BRENT, TONY			
Cindy Oh Cindy			
(UK) Columbia	*14–12–56*	*16*	*3*
Dark Moon			
(UK) Columbia	*19–7–57*	*17*	*5*
The Clouds Will Soon Roll By			
(UK) Columbia	*5–9–58*	*16*	*5*
BRESSLAW, BERNARD			
Mad Passionate Love			
(UK) HMV	*12–9–58*	*6*	*9*
BREWER, TERESA			
Let Me Go Lover			
(US) Coral	1–1–55	8	7
(UK) Vogue-Coral	*4–2–55*	*9*	*3*
A Tear Fell			
(US) Coral b/w*	10–3–56	7	14
(UK) Vogue-Coral	*13–4–56*	*2*	*15*
Bo Weevil			
(US) Coral*	7–4–56	17	3
Sweet Old Fashioned Girl			
(US) Coral	7–7–56	9	11
(UK) Vogue-Coral	*13–7–56*	*3*	*13*
Empty Arms			
(US) Coral	6–5–57	18	4
BREWER AND SHIPLEY			
One Toke Over The Line			
(US) Buddah	3–4–71	10	6
BRIGHTER SIDE OF DARKNESS			
Love Jones			
(US) 20th Century	20–1–73	16	5
BRISTOL, JOHNNY			
Hang On In There Baby			
(US) MGM	31–8–74	8	6
(UK) MGM	*7–9–74*	*3*	*7*
BROOK BROTHERS			
Please Help Me, I'm Falling			
(UK) Pye	*14–8–60*	*16*	*1*
Warpaint			
(UK) Pye	*5–3–61*	*6*	*10*
Ain't Gonna Wash For A Week			
(UK) Pye	*19–8–61*	*8*	*6*
Married			
(UK) Pye	*11–11–61*	*17*	*3*

	Date of chart entry	Highest position reached	Number of weeks in charts
BROOKLYN BRIDGE			
Worst That Could Happen			
(US) Buddah	18–1–69	3	7
BROOKS, DONNIE			
Mission Bell			
(US) Era	25–7–60	7	9
BROTHERHOOD OF MAN			
United We Stand			
(UK) Deram	*21–2–70*	*10*	*6*
(US) Deram	20–6–70	13	4
BROTHERS FOUR			
Greenfields			
(US) Columbia	4–4–60	2	11
(UK) Philips	*1–5–60*	*19*	*1*
BROWN, ARTHUR, CRAZY WORLD OF			
Fire			
(UK) Track	*13–7–68*	*1*	*10*
(US) Atlantic	21–9–68	2	10
BROWN, JAMES (*AND THE FAMOUS FLAMES)			
Prisoner Of Love			
(US) King	15–6–63	18	2
Papa's Got A Brand New Bag*			
(US) King	14–8–65	8	6
I Got You (I Feel Good)*			
(US) King	20–11–65	3	9
It's A Man's Man's Man's World*			
(US) King	21–5–66	8	5
(UK) Pye International	*9–7–66*	*13*	*2*
Cold Sweat*			
(US) King	12–8–67	7	6
I Got The Feelin'*			
(US) King	30–3–68	6	9
Licking Stick*			
(US) King	15–6–68	14	4
Say It Loud (I'm Black And I'm Proud)			
(US) King	5–10–68	10	6
Give It Up Or Turn It Loose			
(US) King	15–2–69	15	5
I Don't Want Nobody To Give Me Nothing			
(US) King	10–5–69	20	1
Mother Popcorn Pt. 1			
(US) King	28–6–69	11	8

	Date of chart entry	Highest position reached	Number of weeks in charts
BROWN, JAMES (cont.)			
Get Up I Feel Like Being A Sex Machine (Pt 1 and Pt 2)			
(US) King	8–8–70	15	2
Super Bad (Pt 1 and Pt 2)			
(US) King	31–10–70	13	5
Hot Pants (Pt 1)			
(US) People	24–7–71	15	5
Good Foot (Pt 1)			
(US) Polydor	7–10–72	18	3
BROWN, JOE			
Picture Of You			
(UK) Piccadilly	*2–6–62*	*2*	*14*
It Only Took A Minute			
(UK) Piccadilly	*1–12–62*	*6*	*8*
That's What Love Will Do			
(UK) Piccadilly	*24–2–63*	*3*	*8*
BROWN, MAXINE			
All In My Mind			
(US) Nomar	13–2–61	19	3
BROWNE, JACKSON			
Doctor My Eyes			
(US) Asylum	15–4–72	8	6
BROWNS			
Three Bells			
(US) RCA	10–8–59	1	12
(UK) RCA	*12–9–59*	*5*	*12*
Scarlet Ribbons			
(US) RCA	9–12–59	13	5
Old Lamplighter			
(US) RCA	11–4–60	5	8
BROWNSVILLE STATION			
Smokin' In The Boys' Room			
(US) Big Tree	22–12–73	3	8
BRUBECK, DAVE			
Take Five			
(UK) Fontana	*21–10–61*	*6*	*12*
Unsquare Dance			
(UK) CBS	*9–6–62*	*14*	*4*
BRUCE, TOMMY			
Ain't Misbehavin'			
(UK) Columbia	*5–6–60*	*4*	*10*

	Date of chart entry	*Highest position reached*	*Number of weeks in charts*
BRYANT, ANITA			
Paper Roses			
(US) Carlton	16–5–60	5	9
In My Little Corner Of The World			
(US) Carlton	15–8–60	10	6
Wonderland By Night			
(US) Carlton	31–12–60	18	3
B. T. EXPRESS			
Do It ('Til You're Satisfied)			
(US) Scepter	26–10–74	2	9
BUBBLE PUPPY			
Hot Smoke and Sassafrass			
(US) International Artists	29–3–69	14	3
BUCHANAN AND GOODMAN			
Flying Saucers			
(US) Luniverse	18–8–56	7	10
Flying Saucer The Second			
(US) Luniverse	12–8–57	19	2
BUCKINGHAMS			
King Of A Drag			
(US) U.S.A.	21–1–67	1	9
Don't You Care			
(US) Columbia	22–4–67	6	6
Mercy Mercy Mercy			
(US) Columbia	15–7–67	5	6
Hey Baby (They're Playing Our Song)			
(US) Columbia	7–10–67	12	5
Susan			
(US) Columbia	13–1–68	11	6
BUFFALO SPRINGFIELD			
For What It's Worth			
(US) Atco	4–3–67	7	8
BUOYS			
Timothy			
(US) Scepter	1–5–71	17	4
BURDON, ERIC, AND THE ANIMALS			
See See Rider			
(US) MGM	8–10–66	10	5
Help Me Girl			
(UK) Decca	*12–11–66*	*14*	*4*
When I Was Young			
(US) MGM	6–5–67	15	3

	Date of chart entry	*Highest position reached*	*Number of weeks in charts*
BURDON, ERIC (cont.)			
San Franciscan Nights			
(US) MGM	9–9–67	9	3
(UK) MGM	*4–11–67*	*7*	*5*
Good Times			
(UK) MGM	*7–10–67*	*20*	*1*
Monterey			
(US) MGM	13–1–68	15	2
Sky Pilot			
(US) MGM	20–7–68	14	3
[see also: ANIMALS; ERIC BURDON AND WAR]			
BURDON, ERIC, AND WAR			
Spill The Wine			
(US) MGM	25–7–70	3	9
[see also: WAR]			
BURNETTE, JOHNNY			
Dreamin'			
(US) Liberty	22–8–60	11	7
(UK) London	*7–10–60*	*6*	*10*
You're Sixteen			
(US) Liberty	5–12–60	8	5
(UK) London	*8–1–61*	*5*	*7*
Little Boy Sad			
(US) Liberty	13–3–61	17	3
(UK) London	*9–4–61*	*13*	*6*
God, Country And My Baby			
(US) Liberty	20–11–61	18	1
BURNS, RAY			
Mobile			
(UK) Columbia	*11–12–55*	*4*	*13*
That's How A Love Song Was Born			
(UK) Columbia	*28–8–55*	*14*	*6*
BUSCH, LOU			
Zambesi			
(UK) Capitol	*27–1–56*	*2*	*15*
BUTLER, JERRY			
For Your Precious Love (and the IMPRESSIONS)			
(US) Abner	7–7–58	11	5
He Will Break Your Heart			
(US) Vee Jay	21–11–60	7	9
Moon River			
(US) Vee Jay	27–11–61	11	5
Make It Easy On Yourself			
(US) Vee Jay	1–9–62	20	1

	Date of chart entry	*Highest position reached*	*Number of weeks in charts*
BUTLER, JERRY (cont.)			
Let It Be Me (with BETTY EVERETT)			
(US) Vee Jay	10–10–64	5	7
Never Give You Up			
(US) Mercury	20–7–68	20	1
Hey, Western Union Man			
(US) Mercury	19–10–68	16	5
Only The Strong Survive			
(US) Mercury	29–3–69	4	8
What's The Use Of Breaking Up			
(US) Mercury	11–10–69	20	1
BUTTERSCOTCH			
Don't You Know			
(UK) RCA	*30–5–70*	*17*	*4*
BYGRAVES, MAX			
Mr. Sandman			
(UK) HMV	*21–1–55*	*16*	*1*
Meet Me On The Corner			
(UK) HMV	*18–11–55*	*2*	*11*
Davy Crockett			
(UK) HMV	*17–2–56*	*20*	*1*
Out Of Town			
(UK) HMV	*15–6–56*	*18*	*2*
Heart			
(UK) Decca	*5–4–57*	*14*	*7*
You Need Hands/Tulips From Amsterdam			
(UK) Decca	*16–5–58*	*3*	*21*
My Ukelele			
(UK) Decca	*10–1–59*	*16*	*2*
Jingle Bell Rock			
(UK) Decca	*26–12–59*	*11*	*1*
Fings Ain't What They Used To Be			
(UK) Decca	*13–3–60*	*6*	*8*
Deck Of Cards			
(UK) Pye	*27–10–73*	*13*	*5*
BYRD, CHARLIE. See GETZ, STAN			
BYRDS			
Mr. Tambourine Man			
(US) Columbia	5–6–65	1	9
(UK) CBS	*3–7–65*	*1*	*9*
All I Really Want To Do			
(UK) CBS	*21–8–65*	*9*	*1*
Turn Turn Turn			
(US) Columbia	13–11–65	1	10

	Date of chart entry	Highest position reached	Number of weeks in charts
BYRDS (cont.)			
Eight Miles High			
(US) Columbia	7–5–66	14	3
Chestnut Mare			
(UK) CBS	*27–2–71*	*19*	*1*
BYRNES, ED, AND STEVENS, CONNIE			
Kookie, Kookie (Lend Me Your Comb)			
(US) Warner Brothers	4–5–59	4	8
(UK) Warner Brothers	*1–5–60*	*20*	*1*
C, ROY			
Shotgun Wedding			
(UK) Island	*7–5–66*	*6*	*6*
(UK) UK (re-issue)	*9–12–72*	*8*	*7*
CADETS			
Stranded In The Jungle			
(US) Modern	28–7–55	18	2
CAIOLA, AL			
Bonanza			
(US) United Artists	15–5–61	19	2
CALVERT, EDDIE			
Cherry Pink			
(UK) Columbia	*8–4–55*	*1*	*21*
Stranger In Paradise			
(UK) Columbia	*13–3–55*	*14*	*4*
John and Julie			
(UK) Columbia	*29–7–55*	*6*	*11*
Zambesi			
(UK) Columbia	*9–3–56*	*13*	*5*
Mandy			
(UK) Columbia	*21 2–58*	*9*	*11*
CAMPBELL, GLEN			
Wichita Lineman			
(US) Capitol	23–11–68	3	11
(UK) Ember	*22–2–69*	*7*	*8*
Galveston			
(US) Capitol	15–3–69	4	9
(UK) Ember	*24–5–69*	*14*	*5*
All I Have To Do Is Dream (with BOBBIE GENTRY)			
(UK) Capitol	*13–12–69*	*3*	*10*
Honey Come Back			
(US) Capitol	21–2–70	19	2
(UK) Capitol	*23–5–70*	*4*	*10*

	Date of chart entry	*Highest position reached*	*Number of weeks in charts*
CAMPBELL, GLEN (cont.)			
It's Only Make Believe			
(US) Capitol	17–10–70	10	4
(UK) Capitol	*28–11–70*	*4*	*11*
CAMPBELL, JUNIOR			
Hallelujah Freedom			
(UK) Deram	*28–10–72*	*10*	*5*
Sweet Illusion			
(UK) Deram	*16–6–73*	*15*	*4*
CANNED HEAT			
On The Road Again			
(UK) Liberty	*24–8–68*	*8*	*7*
(US) Liberty	21–9–68	16	2
Going Up The Country			
(US) Liberty	28–12–68	11	7
(UK) Liberty	*15–2–69*	*19*	*1*
Let's Work Together			
(UK) Liberty	*7–2–70*	*2*	*9*
CANNON, ACE			
Tuff			
(US) Hi	24–2–62	17	4
CANNON, FREDDIE			
Tallahassie Lassie			
(US) Swan	1–6–59	6	8
(UK) Top Rank	*22–8–59*	*15*	*2*
Way Down Yonder In New Orleans			
(US) Swan	14–12–59	3	9
(UK) Top Rank	*3–1–60*	*4*	*10*
California Here I Come			
(UK) Top Rank	*27–2–60*	*19*	*2*
The Urge			
(UK) Top Rank	*22–5–60*	*18*	*2*
Palisades Park			
(US) Swan	2–6–62	3	9
(UK) Stateside	*14–7–62*	*20*	*1*
Abigail Beecher			
(US) Warner Brothers	29–2–64	16	2
Action			
(US) Warner Brothers	11–9–65	13	3
CAPITOLS			
Cool Jerk			
(US) Karen	28–5–66	7	8
CAPRIS			
There's A Moon Out Tonight			
(US) Old Town	6–2–61	3	7

	Date of chart entry	*Highest position reached*	*Number of weeks in charts*
CARAVELLES			
You Don't Have To Be A Baby To Cry			
(UK) Decca	*17–8–63*	*6*	*8*
(US) Smash	30–11–63	3	7
CARLTON, CARL			
Everlasting Love			
(US) Back Beat	2–11–74	6	6
CAROSONE, RENATE			
Torero			
(US) Capitol	9–6–58	19	2
CARPENTERS			
Close To You			
(US) A & M	4–7–70	1	13
(UK) A & M	*26–9–70*	*6*	*8*
We've Only Just Begun			
(US) A & M	3–10–70	2	13
For All We Know			
(US) A & M	27–2–71	3	9
Rainy Days and Mondays			
(US) A & M	22–5–71	2	10
Superstar			
(US) A & M (b/w Bless the Beasts and Children)	11–9–71	2	11
(UK) A & M (b/w For All We Know)	*6–11–71*	*18*	*3*
Hurting Each Other			
(US) A & M	29–1–72	2	8
It's Going To Take Some Time			
(US) A & M	27–5–72	12	4
Goodbye To Love			
(US) A & M	12–8–72	7	5
(UK) A & M	*21–10–72*	*9*	*6*
Sing			
(US) A & M	17–3–73	3	9
Yesterday Once More			
(US) A & M	23–6–73	2	9
(UK) A & M	*28–7–73*	*2*	*8*
Top Of The World			
(UK) A & M	*27–10–73*	*5*	*8*
(US) A & M	3–11–73	1	11
Jambalaya			
(UK) A & M	*16–3–74*	*12*	*5*
I Won't Last Another Day Without You			
(US) A & M	11–5–74	7	6
Please Mr. Postman			
(US) A & M	21–12–74	1	8

	Date of chart entry	*Highest position reached*	*Number of weeks in charts*
CARR, CATHY			
Ivory Tower			
(US) Fraternity	28–4–56	6	13
CARR, JOE 'FINGERS'			
Portuguese Washer Women			
(UK) Capitol	*6–7–56*	*20*	*1*
CARR, PEARL, AND JOHNSON, TEDDY			
Sing Little Birdy			
(UK) Columbia	*21–3–59*	*12*	*5*
CARR, VIKKI			
It Must Be Him			
(UK) Liberty	*1–7–67*	*2*	*10*
(US) Liberty	21–10–67	3	6
CARROLL, DON			
Melody Of Love			
(US) Mercury	29–1–55	9	11
CARROLL, RONNIE			
Walk Hand in Hand			
(UK) Philips	*25–7–56*	*13*	*6*
Wisdom Of A Fool			
(UK) Philips	*29–3–57*	*20*	*1*
Roses Are Red			
(UK) Philips	*18–8–62*	*3*	*11*
Say Wonderful Things			
(UK) Philips	*23–3–63*	*6*	*8*
CARSON, JOHNNY			
You Talk Too Much			
(UK) Fontana	*11–12–60*	*18*	*1*
CARSON, KIT			
Band Of Gold			
(US) Capitol	18–2–56	17	1
CARSON, MINDY			
Wake The Town And Tell The People			
(US) Columbia	3–9–55	20	2
CARTER, CLARENCE			
Slip Away			
(US) Atlantic	7–9–68	6	7
Too Weak To Fight			
(US) Atlantic	4–1–69	13	1
Patches			
(US) Atlantic	15–8–70	4	9
(UK) Atlantic	*17–10–70*	*2*	*8*

	Date of chart entry	Highest position reached	Number of weeks in charts
CARTER, MEL			
Hold Me, Thrill Me, Kiss Me			
(US) Imperial	7–8–65	8	7
CASCADES			
Rhythm Of The Rain			
(US) Valiant	2–2–63	3	11
(UK) Warner Brothers	*16–3–63*	*5*	*11*
CASH, ALVIN, AND THE CRAWLERS			
Twine Time			
(US) Mar-V-Lus	6–2–65	14	5
CASH, JOHNNY			
I Walk The Line			
(US) Sun	10–11–56	19	3
Ballad Of A Teenage Queen			
(US) Sun	3–3–58	16	4
Guess Things Happen That Way			
(US) Sun	14–7–58	11	3
Ring of Fire			
(US) Columbia	20–7–63	17	3
A Boy Named Sue			
(US) Columbia	2–8–69	2	10
(UK) CBS	*20–9–69*	*4*	*9*
What Is Truth			
(US) Columbia	9–5–70	19	3
A Thing Called Love			
(UK) CBS	*29–4–72*	*4*	*7*
CASINOS			
Then You Can Tell Me Goodbye			
(US) Fraternity	11–2–67	6	7
CASS, MAMA			
Dream A Little Dream Of Me			
(US) Dunhill	3–8–68	12	4
(UK) RCA	*31–8–68*	*11*	*7*
It's Getting Better			
(UK) Stateside	*20–9–69*	*8*	*7*
[see also: MAMAS AND PAPAS]			
CASSIDY, DAVID			
Cherish			
(US) Bell	27–11–71	9	8
Could It Be Forever?			
(UK) Bell	*22–4–72*	*2*	*9*
How Can I Be Sure?			
(UK) Bell	*16–9–72*	*1*	*8*
Rock Me Baby			
(UK) Bell	*2–12–72*	*11*	*4*

	Date of chart entry	*Highest position reached*	*Number of weeks in charts*
CASSIDY, DAVID (cont.)			
I'm A Clown/Some Kind Of A Summer			
(UK) Bell	*31–3–73*	*3*	*8*
Daydreamer/Puppy Song			
(UK) Bell	*13–10–73*	*1*	*8*
If I Didn't Care			
(UK) Bell	*25–5–74*	*9*	*4*
Please Please Me			
(UK) Bell	*10–8–74*	*16*	*2*
[see also: PARTRIDGE FAMILY]			
CASTAWAYS			
Liar, Liar			
(US) Soma	2–10–65	12	6
CASTELLS			
Sacred			
(US) Era	24–7–61	20	2
CASTOR, JIMMY, BUNCH			
Troglodyte (Cave Man)			
(US) RCA	3–6–72	6	7
CASUALS			
Jesamine			
(UK) Decca	*14–9–68*	*2*	*11*
CATES, GEORGE			
Theme From Picnic/Moonglow			
(US) Coral	5–5–56	4	15
CATHY JEAN AND THE ROOMMATES			
Please Love Me Forever			
(US) Valmor	3–4–61	12	5
CCS			
Whole Lotta Love			
(UK) RAK	*14–11–70*	*13*	*5*
Walking			
(UK) RAK	*27–3–71*	*7*	*7*
Tap Turns On The Water			
(UK) RAK	*18–9–71*	*5*	*7*
CHACKSFIELD, FRANK			
In Old Lisbon			
(UK) Decca	*24–2–56*	*15*	*4*
CHAD AND JEREMY			
Summer Song			
(US) World Artists	26–9–64	7	6

	Date of chart entry	Highest position reached	Number of weeks in charts
CHAD AND JEREMY (cont.)			
Willow Weep For Me			
(US) World Artists	2–1–65	15	4
Before And After			
(US) Columbia	19–6–65	17	3
CHAIRMEN OF THE BOARD			
Give Me Just A Little More Time			
(US) Invictus	21–2–70	3	9
(UK) Invictus	*29–8–70*	*3*	*8*
You've Got Me Dangling On A String			
(UK) Invictus	*21–11–70*	*5*	*10*
Pay To The Piper			
(US) Invictus	2–1–71	13	3
Everything's Tuesday			
(UK) Invictus	*27–2–71*	*12*	*5*
Working On The Building Of Love			
(UK) Invictus	*19–8–72*	*20*	*1*
CHAKACHAS			
Jungle Fever			
(US) Polydor	4–3–72	8	7
CHAMBERLAIN, RICHARD			
Theme From 'Dr. Kildare'			
(UK) MGM	*23–6–62*	*12*	*3*
(US) MGM	30–6–62	10	7
Love Me Tender			
(UK) MGM	*24–11–62*	*15*	*5*
Hi-Lili-Hi-Lo			
(UK) MGM	*9–3–63*	*20*	*1*
All I Have To Do Is Dream			
(US) MGM	23–3–63	14	4
CHAMBERS BROTHERS			
Time Has Come Today			
(US) Columbia	21–9–68	11	5
CHAMPS			
Tequila			
(US) Challenge	10–3–58	1	20
(UK) London	*4–4–58*	*5*	*7*
CHANDLER, GENE			
Duke Of Earl			
(US) Vee Jay	27–1–62	1	11
Just Be True			
(US) Constellation	15–8–64	19	3

	Date of chart entry	Highest position reached	Number of weeks in charts
CHANDLER, GENE (cont.)			
Nothing Can Stop Me			
(US) Constellation	19–6–65	18	1
Groovy Situation			
(US) Mercury	12–9–70	12	4
CHANNEL, BRUCE			
Hey! Baby			
(US) Smash	17–2–62	1	10
(UK) Mercury	*31–3–62*	*2*	*9*
Keep On			
(UK) Bell	*3–8–68*	*11*	*6*
CHANTAYS			
Pipeline			
(US) Dot	13–4–63	4	8
(UK) London	*25–5–63*	*16*	*4*
CHANTELS			
Maybe			
(US) End	10–2–58	15	4
Look In My Eyes			
(US) Carlton	9–10–61	14	4
CHAPIN, HARRY			
Cat's In The Cradle			
(US) Elektra	23–11–74	1	7
CHARLES, JIMMY			
A Million To One			
(US) Promo	5–9–60	5	9
CHARLES, RAY			
What'd I Say			
(US) Atlantic	3–8–59	6	7
Georgia On My Mind			
(US) ABC–Paramount	17–10–60	1	8
One Mint Julep			
(US) Impulse	10–4–61	8	6
Hit The Road Jack			
(US) ABC–Paramount	25–9–61	1	9
(UK) HMV	*21–10–61*	*5*	*7*
Unchain My Heart			
(US) ABC–Paramount	18–12–61	9	6
Hide Nor Hair			
(US) ABC–Paramount	5–5–62	20	1
I Can't Stop Loving You			
(US) ABC–Paramount	26–5–62	1	12
(UK) HMV	*23–6–62*	*1*	*13*
You Don't Know Me			
(US) ABC–Paramount	11–8–62	2	6
(UK) HMV	*29–9–62*	*9*	*8*

	Date of chart entry	*Highest position reached*	*Number of weeks in charts*
CHARLES, RAY (cont.)			
You Are My Sunshine			
(US) ABC–Paramount	15–12–62	7	5
Your Cheating Heart			
(UK) HMV	*29–12–62*	*13*	*4*
Don't Set Me Free			
(US) ABC–Paramount	30–3–63	20	1
Take These Chains From My Heart			
(US) ABC–Paramount	4–5–63	8	6
(UK) HMV	*1–6–63*	*5*	*13*
Busted			
(US) ABC–Paramount	28–9–63	4	8
That Lucky Old Sun			
(US) ABC–Paramount	18–1–64	20	2
Crying Time			
(US) ABC–Paramount	29–1–66	6	6
Together Again			
(US) ABC–Paramount	30–4–66	19	1
Here We Go Again			
(US) ABC	8–7–67	15	4
CHARLES, RAY, SINGERS			
Love Me With All Your Heart			
(US) Command	16–5–64	3	8
CHARLES, SONNY, AND THE CHECKMATES			
Black Pearl			
(US) A & M	14–6–69	13	7
CHARMS			
Hearts Of Stone			
(US) Deluxe	1–1–55	15	4
CHECKER, CHUBBY			
Twist			
(US) Parkway	8–8–60	1	13
Hucklebuck			
(US) Parkway	14–11–60	14	4
Pony Time			
(US) Parkway	6–2–61	1	11
(UK) Columbia	*26–3–61*	*19*	*1*
Let's Twist Again			
(US) Parkway	17–7–61	8	7
(UK) Columbia	*20–1–62*	*2*	*16*
Fly			
(US) Parkway	16–10–61	7	8
Twist (re-issue)			
(US) Parkway	27–11–61	1	15
(UK) Columbia	*13–1–62*	*12*	*5*

	Date of chart entry	Highest position reached	Number of weeks in charts
CHECKER, CHUBBY (cont.)			
Slow Twistin'			
(US) Parkway	17–3–62	3	10
Dancing Party			
(US) Parkway	14–7–62	12	4
(UK) Columbia	*25–8–62*	*19*	*2*
Popeye (Hitchhiker)			
(US) Parkway	20–10–62	10	5
Limbo Rock			
(US) Parkway	27–10–62	2	14
Let's Limbo Some More			
(US) Parkway	16–3–63	20	1
20 Miles			
(US) Parkway	13–4–63	15	2
Birdland			
(US) Parkway	15–6–63	12	3
Loddy Lo			
(US) Parkway	7–12–63	12	4
Hooka Tooka			
(US) Parkway	1–2–64	17	4
CHEECH AND CHONG			
Basketball Jones featuring Tyrone Shoelaces			
(US) Ode	6–10–73	15	4
Earache My Eye featuring Alice Bowie			
(US) Ode	21–9–74	9	4
CHEERS			
Black Denim Trousers (and Motorcycle Boots)			
(US) Capitol	1–10–55	6	9
CHELSEA FC			
Blue Is The Color			
(UK) Penny Farthing	*26–2–72*	*5*	*7*
CHER			
All I Really Want To Do			
(US) Imperial	14–8–65	15	4
(UK) Liberty	*4–9–65*	*9*	*5*
Bang Bang			
(US) Imperial	26–3–66	2	8
(UK) Liberty	*9–4–66*	*3*	*8*
You Better Sit Down Kids			
(US) Imperial	25–11–67	9	7
Gypsies Tramps and Thieves			
(US) Kapp	16–10–71	1	11
(UK) MCA	*13–11–71*	*4*	*9*

	Date of chart entry	*Highest position reached*	*Number of weeks in charts*
CHER (cont.)			
Way Of Love			
(US) Kapp	26–2–72	7	7
Half-Breed			
(US) MCA	15–9–73	1	11
Dark Lady			
(US) MCA	23–2–74	1	8
[see also: SONNY AND CHER]			
CHERRY, DON			
Band Of Gold			
(US) Columbia	24–12–55	5	16
(UK) Philips	*10–2–56*	*6*	*11*
CHESTER, PETE, AND THE CHESTERNUTS			
Ten Swinging Bottles			
(UK) Pye International	*18–12–60*	*14*	*2*
CHICAGO			
I'm A Man			
(UK) Columbia	*24–1–70*	*8*	*5*
Make Me Smile			
(US) Columbia	16–5–70	9	7
25 Or 6 To 4			
(US) Columbia	15–8–70	4	8
(UK) Columbia	*15–8–70*	*7*	*7*
Does Anybody Really Know What Time It Is?			
(US) Columbia	28–11–70	7	9
Free			
(US) Columbia	3–4–71	20	1
Beginnings/Color My World			
(US) Columbia	24–7–71	7	8
Saturday In The Park			
(US) Columbia	26–8–72	3	7
Feelin' Stronger Everyday			
(US) Columbia	21–7–73	10	9
Just You 'n' Me			
(US) Columbia	3–11–73	4	9
(I've Been) Searchin' So Long			
(US) Columbia	20–4–74	9	7
Call On Me			
(US) Columbia	27–7–74	6	5
Wishing You Were Here			
(US) Columbia	16–11–74	11	5
CHICKEN SHACK			
I'd Rather Go Blind			
(UK) Blue Horizon	*7–6–69*	*14*	*5*

	Date of chart entry	Highest position reached	Number of weeks in charts
CHICORY TIP			
Son Of My Father			
(UK) CBS	*5–2–72*	*1*	*10*
What's Your Name?			
(UK) CBS	*17–6–72*	*13*	*1*
Good Grief Christina			
(UK) CBS	*5–5–73*	*17*	*2*
CHIFFONS			
He's So Fine			
(US) Laurie	9–3–63	1	11
(UK) Stateside	*4–5–63*	*16*	*6*
One Fine Day			
(US) Laurie	15–6–63	5	6
Sweet Talkin' Guy			
(US) Laurie	28–5–66	10	6
(UK) London (re-issue)	*1–4–72*	*4*	*7*
CHI-LITES			
Have You Seen Her?			
(US) Brunswick	6–11–71	3	10
(UK) MCA	*29–1–72*	*2*	*7*
Oh Girl			
(US) Brunswick	22–4–72	1	11
(UK) MCA	*24–6–72*	*14*	*3*
Homely Girl			
(UK) Brunswick	*20–4–74*	*5*	*6*
Too Good To Be Forgotten			
(UK) Brunswick	*23–11–74*	*10*	*4*
CHIMES			
Once In A While			
(US) Tag	23–1–61	11	4
CHIPMUNKS. See Seville, David			
CHORDETTES			
Mr. Sandman			
(US) Cadence	1–1–55	1	11
(UK) Columbia	*7–1–55*	*11*	*5*
Eddie My Love			
(US) Cadence	31–3–56	18	3
Born To Be With You			
(US) Cadence	16–6–56	5	13
(UK) London	*31–8–56*	*8*	*8*
Lay Down Your Arms			
(US) Cadence	17–11–56	16	2
Just Between You And Me			
(US) Cadence	21–10–57	19	1

	Date of chart entry	Highest position reached	Number of weeks in charts
CHORDETTES (cont.)			
Lollipop			
(US) Cadence	17–3–58	2	10
(UK) London	*25–4–58*	*6*	*5*
Zorro			
(US) Cadence	16–6–58	17	2
Never On Sunday			
(US) Cadence	17–7–61	13	6
CHRISTIE			
Yellow River			
(UK) CBS	*16–5–70*	*1*	*11*
San Bernardino			
(UK) CBS	*7–11–70*	*7*	*6*
CHRISTIE, LOU			
Two Faces Have I			
(US) Roulette	11–5–63	6	7
Lightnin' Strikes			
(US) MGM	29–1–66	1	8
(UK) MGM	*5–3–66*	*11*	*5*
Rhapsody In The Rain			
(US) MGM	30–4–66	16	1
I'm Gonna Make You Mine			
(US) Buddah	4–10–69	10	5
(UK) Buddah	*4–10–69*	*2*	*8*
CHRISTIE, TONY			
I Did What I Did For Maria			
(UK) MCA	*29–5–71*	*2*	*9*
Is This The Way To Amarillo?			
(UK) MCA	*18–12–71*	*18*	*4*
CINQUETTI, GIGLIOLA			
Non Ho L'Eta			
(UK) Decca	*30–5–64*	*17*	*4*
Go			
(UK) CBS	*25–5–74*	*8*	*4*
CLANTON, JIMMY			
Just A Dream			
(US) Ace	4–8–58	4	12
Go Jimmy Go			
(US) Ace	28–12–59	5	8
Venus In Blue Jeans			
(US) Ace	15–9–62	7	7
CLAPTON, ERIC			
After Midnight			
(US) Atco	12–12–70	18	2

	Date of chart entry	*Highest position reached*	*Number of weeks in charts*
CLAPTON, ERIC (cont.)			
I Shot The Sheriff			
(UK) RSO	*10–8–74*	*9*	*4*
(US) RSO	17–8–74	1	7
[see also: CREAM; DELANEY AND BONNIE; DEREK AND THE DOMINOS]			
CLARK, CLAUDINE			
Party Lights			
(US) Chancellor	11–8–62	5	6
CLARK, DAVE, FIVE			
Glad All Over			
(UK) Columbia	*30–11–63*	*1*	*14*
(US) Epic	14–3–64	6	9
Bits And Pieces			
(US) Epic	18–4–64	4	7
(UK) Columbia	*22–4–64*	*2*	*9*
Do You Love Me			
(US) Epic	23–5–64	11	4
Can't You See That She's Mine			
(UK) Columbia	*13–6–64*	*10*	*6*
(US) Epic	27–6–64	4	7
Because			
(US) Epic	15–8–64	3	7
Everybody Knows			
(US) Epic	31–10–64	15	2
(UK) Columbia (re-issue)	*18–11–67*	*2*	*8*
Anyway You Want It			
(US) Epic	19–12–64	14	6
Come Home			
(US) Epic	13–3–65	14	3
(UK) Columbia	*19–6–65*	*16*	*3*
I Like It Like That			
(US) Epic	24–7–65	7	4
Catch Us If You Can			
(UK) Columbia	*31–7–65*	*5*	*6*
(US) Epic	11–9–65	4	7
Over and Over			
(US) Epic	27–11–65	1	8
At The Scene			
(US) Epic	5–3–66	18	2
Try Too Hard			
(US) Epic	30–4–66	12	2
You Got What It Takes			
(US) Epic	22–4–67	7	6
Red Balloon			
(UK) Columbia	*28–9–68*	*7*	*6*
Good Old Rock And Roll			
(UK) Columbia	*20–12–69*	*7*	*8*

	Date of chart entry	Highest position reached	Number of weeks in charts
CLARK, DAVE, FIVE (cont.)			
Everybody Get Together			
(UK) Columbia	*14–3–70*	*8*	*5*
CLARK, DEE			
Just Keep It Up			
(US) Abner	8–6–59	18	2
(UK) London	*12–9–59*	*19*	*1*
Hey Little Girl			
(US) Abner	21–9–59	20	1
Raindrops			
(US) Vee Jay	29–5–61	2	10
CLARK, PETULA			
Majorca			
(UK) Polygon	*18–2–55*	*13*	*5*
Suddenly There's A Valley			
(UK) Nixa	*25–11–55*	*8*	*10*
With All My Heart			
(UK) Nixa	*2–8–57*	*4*	*16*
Alone			
(UK) Pye Nixa	*22–11–57*	*8*	*9*
Baby Lover			
(UK) Pye Nixa	*14–3–58*	*12*	*4*
Sailor			
(UK) Pye	*15–1–61*	*2*	*10*
Romeo			
(UK) Pye	*2–7–61*	*4*	*11*
My Friend The Sea			
(UK) Pye	*18–11–61*	*10*	*6*
Ya Ya Twist			
(UK) Pye	*21–7–62*	*14*	*4*
Downtown			
(UK) Pye	*21–11–64*	*2*	*12*
(US) Warner Brothers	2–1–65	1	11
I Know A Place			
(UK) Pye	*27–3–65*	*17*	*2*
(US) Warner Brothers	10–4–65	3	7
My Love			
(US) Warner Brothers	22–1–65	1	8
(UK) Pye	*19–2–66*	*4*	*6*
Sign Of The Times			
(US) Warner Brothers	16–4–66	11	3
I Couldn't Live Without Your Love			
(UK) Pye	*16–7–66*	*6*	*7*
(US) Warner Brothers	6–8–66	9	5
Color My World			
(US) Warner Brothers	21–1–67	16	3
This Is My Song			
(UK) Pye	*11–2–67*	*1*	*10*
(US) Warner Brothers	25–3–67	3	7

	Date of chart entry	Highest position reached	Number of weeks in charts
CLARK, PETULA (cont.)			
Don't Sleep In The Subway			
(UK) Pye	*24-6-67*	*12*	*4*
(US) Warner Brothers	24-6-67	5	5
The Other Man's Grass			
(UK) Pye	*13-1-68*	*20*	*1*
Kiss Me Goodbye			
(US) Warner Brothers	23-3-68	15	4
CLARK, ROY			
Yesterday, When I Was Young			
(US) Dot	2-8-69	19	1
CLARK, SANFORD			
Fool			
(US) Dot	25-8-56	9	10
CLASSICS IV			
Spooky			
(US) Imperial	20-1-68	3	9
Stormy			
(US) Imperial	23-11-68	5	9
Traces			
(US) Imperial	1-3-69	2	9
Everyday With You Girl			
(US) Imperial	14-6-69	19	2
CLAY, JUDY AND BELL, WILLIAM			
Private Number			
(UK) Stax	*21-12-68*	*8*	*9*
CLAY, TOM			
What The World Needs Now Is Love/Abraham, Martin and John			
(US) Mowest	31-7-71	8	5
CLEFTONES			
Heart And Soul			
(US) Gee	19-6-61	18	1
CLIFF, JIMMY			
Wonderful World, Beautiful People			
(UK) Trojan	*1-11-69*	*6*	*8*
Wild World			
(UK) Island	*5-9-70*	*8*	*5*
CLIFFORD, BUZZ			
Baby Sittin' Boogie			
(US) Columbia	13-2-61	6	7
(UK) Philips	*19-2-61*	*16*	*10*

	Date of chart entry	Highest position reached	Number of weeks in charts
CLIFFORD, MIKE			
Close To Cathy			
(US) United Artists	27–10–62	12	5
CLIMAX			
Precious Few			
(US) Rocky Road	29–1–72	3	10
CLINE, PATSY			
Walking After Midnight			
(US) Decca	23–3–57	17	3
I Fall To Pieces			
(US) Decca	21–8–61	12	3
Crazy			
(US) Decca	13–11–61	9	5
She's Got You			
(US) Decca	10–3–62	14	5
CLOONEY, ROSEMARY			
This Old House			
(US) Columbia	1–1–55	4	5
(UK) Philips	*7–1–55*	*10*	*5*
Mambo Italiano			
(US) Columbia	1–1–55	17	1
(UK) Philips	*7–1–55*	*3*	*13*
Where Will The Dimple Be?			
(UK) Philips	*20–5–55*	*6*	*13*
Hey There			
(UK) Philips	*30–9–55*	*4*	*11*
Mangos			
(UK) Philips	*24–5–57*	*17*	*1*
COASTERS			
Young Blood			
(US) Atco	27–5–57	18	4
Searchin'			
(US) Atco	27–5–57	5	14
Yakety Yak			
(US) Atco	16–6–58	1	10
(UK) London	*15–8–58*	*12*	*7*
Charlie Brown			
(US) Atco	16–2–59	2	10
(UK) London	*28–3–59*	*5*	*10*
Along Came Jones			
(US) Atco	8–6–59	9	6
Poison Ivy			
(US) Atlantic	14–9–59	7	9
(UK) London	*21–11–59*	*15*	*2*

COATES, ODIA. See ANKA, PAUL

	Date of chart entry	*Highest position reached*	*Number of weeks in charts*
COCHRAN, EDDIE			
Sittin' In The Balcony			
(US) Liberty	20–4–57	18	2
Summertime Blues			
(US) Liberty	1–9–58	8	7
(UK) London	*28–11–58*	*18*	*2*
C'Mon Everybody			
(UK) London	*21–3–59*	*8*	*10*
Three Steps To Heaven			
(UK) London	*8–5–60*	*3*	*12*
Lonely/Sweetie Pie			
(UK) London	*30–9–60*	*19*	*1*
Weekend			
(UK) London	*11–6–61*	*15*	*8*
COCKER, JOE			
With A Little Help From My Friends			
(UK) Regal Zonophone	*19–10–68*	*1*	*8*
Delta Lady			
(UK) Regal Zonophone	*25–10–69*	*10*	*5*
The Letter			
(US) A & M	23–5–70	7	6
Cry Me A River			
(US) A & M	31–10–70	11	5
COCKEREL CHORUS			
Nice One Cyril			
(UK) Young Blood	*10–3–73*	*14*	*5*
COCKNEY REBEL			
Judy Teen			
(UK) EMI	*1–6–74*	*5*	*6*
Mr. Soft			
(UK) EMI	*24–8–74*	*8*	*5*
COFFEY, DENNIS, AND THE DETROIT GUITAR BAND			
Scorpio			
(US) Sussex	4–12–71	6	11
Taurus			
(US) Sussex	8–4–72	18	3
COGAN, ALMA			
Can't Tell A Waltz From A Tango			
(UK) HMV	*7–1–55*	*6*	*6*
Dreamboat			
(UK) HMV	*26–5–55*	*1*	*16*
Banjo's Back In Town			
(UK) HMV	*23–9–55*	*17*	*1*
Go On By			
(UK) HMV	*14–10–55*	*16*	*4*

	Date of chart entry	*Highest position reached*	*Number of weeks in charts*
COGAN, ALMA (cont.)			
Never Do A Tango With An Eskimo			
(UK) HMV	*23–12–55*	*6*	*5*
Twenty Tiny Fingers			
(UK) HMV	*16–12–55*	*17*	*1*
Willie Can			
(UK) HMV	*30–3–56*	*13*	*7*
Middle Of The House			
(UK) HMV	*23–11–56*	*20*	*2*
You Me and Us			
(UK) HMV	*18–1–57*	*18*	*3*
Sugartime			
(UK) HMV	*28–2–58*	*16*	*3*
COLE, COZY			
Topsy II			
(US) Love	13–10–58	3	11
COLE, NAT 'KING'			
A Blossom Fell			
(UK) Capitol	*25–2–55*	*3*	*10*
(US) Capitol	14–5–55	2	18
Darling (Je Vous Aime Beaucoup)			
(US) Capitol	5–3–55	10	13
My One Sin			
(UK) Capitol	*26–8–55*	*17*	*2*
Someone You Love/Forgive My Heart			
(US) Capitol	22–10–55	16	3
Dreams Can Tell A Lie			
(UK) Capitol	*27–1–56*	*10*	*9*
Too Young To Go Steady			
(UK) Capitol	*18–5–56*	*11*	*10*
That's All There Is To That			
(US) Capitol	28–7–56	18	4
Love Me As Though There Were No Tomorrow			
(UK) Capitol	*26–10–56*	*11*	*7*
Night Light			
(US) Capitol	1–12–56	16	4
When I Fall In Love			
(UK) Capitol	*19–4–57*	*2*	*19*
Send For Me			
(US) Capitol	15–7–57	7	12
Looking Back			
(US) Capitol	5–5–58	5	11
That's You			
(UK) Capitol	*22–5–60*	*17*	*5*
Let Your True Love Begin			
(UK) Capitol	*2–12–61*	*19*	*1*

	Date of chart entry	Highest position reached	Number of weeks in charts
COLE, NAT (cont.)			
Let There Be Love (with GEORGE SHEARING)			
(UK) Capitol	*4–8–62*	*11*	*7*
Ramblin' Rose			
(US) Capitol	1–9–62	2	10
(UK) Capitol	*6–10–62*	*5*	*9*
Dear Lonely Hearts			
(US) Capitol	15–12–62	13	4
Those Lazy-Hazy-Crazy Days of Summer			
(US) Capitol	1–6–63	6	7
That Sunday, That Summer			
(US) Capitol	12–10–63	12	5
COLLINS, DAVE AND ANSELL			
Double Barrel			
(UK) Technique	*10–4–71*	*1*	*8*
Monkey Spanner			
(UK) Technique	*3–7–71*	*7*	*8*
COLLINS, JUDY			
Both Sides Now			
(US) Elektra	23–11–68	8	6
(UK) Elektra	*21–2–70*	*14*	*3*
Amazing Grace			
(UK) Elektra	*16–1–71*	*5*	*13*
(US) Elektra	6–2–71	15	5
(UK) Elektra (re-entry)	*20–5–71*	*20*	*1*
COLTRANE, CHI			
Thunder And Lightning			
(US) Columbia	4–11–72	17	3
COMMANDER CODY AND HIS LOST PLANET AIRMEN			
Hot Rod Lincoln			
(US) Paramount	29–4–72	9	7
COMMODORES			
Machine Gun			
(UK) Tamla-Motown	*5–10–74*	*20*	*3*
COMO, PERRY			
Papa Loves Mambo			
(US) Victor	1–1–55	9	4
Home For The Holidays			
(US) Victor	1–1–55	18	2
Koko Mo			
(US) Victor	5–2–55	4	12
Tina Marie			
(US) Victor	27–8–55	6	14

	Date of chart entry	Highest position reached	Number of weeks in charts
COMO, PERRY (cont.)			
Juke Box Baby			
(US) Victor	17–3–56	10	7
Hot Diggity			
(US) Victor	24–3–56	2	14
(UK) HMV	*25–5–56*	*4*	*12*
More			
(US) Victor	30–6–56	9	11
(UK) HMV	*5–10–56*	*10*	*8*
Glendora			
(US) Victor	30–6–56	14	7
(UK) HMV	*19–10–56*	*18*	*2*
Round And Round			
(US) Victor	9–3–57	2	16
Girl With The Golden Braids			
(US) Victor	24–6–57	15	1
Just Born			
(US) Victor	18–11–57	19	2
Magic Moments			
(UK) RCA (b/w)*	*7–2–58*	*1*	*15*
Catch A Falling Star			
(US) Victor	10–2–58	9	12
*(UK) RCA**	*14–3–48*	*9*	*7*
Kewpie Doll			
(US) Victor	28–4–58	12	7
(UK) RCA	*16–5–58*	*9*	*5*
I May Never Pass This Way Again			
(UK) RCA	*6–6–58*	*15*	*4*
Moontalk			
(UK) RCA	*3–10–58*	*17*	*4*
Love Makes The World Go Round			
(UK) RCA	*7–11–58*	*7*	*8*
Mandolins In The Moonlight			
(UK) RCA	*28–11–58*	*15*	*5*
Tomboy			
(UK) RCA	*28–2–59*	*12*	*10*
I Know			
(UK) RCA	*18–7–59*	*11*	*7*
Delaware			
(UK) RCA	*20–2–60*	*3*	*8*
It's Impossible			
(US) RCA	5–12–70	10	10
(UK) RCA	*13–2–71*	*4*	*11*
I Think Of You			
(UK) RCA	*29–5–71*	*14*	*5*
And I Love Her So			
(UK) RCA	*5–5–73*	*3*	*12*
For The Good Times			
(UK) RCA	*22–9–73*	*7*	*10*

	Date of chart entry	*Highest position reached*	*Number of weeks in charts*
CONGREGATION			
Softly Whispering I Love You			
(UK) Columbia	*11–12–71*	*4*	*8*
CONLEY, ARTHUR			
Sweet Soul Music			
(US) Atco	8–4–67	2	9
(UK) Stax	*20–5–67*	*7*	*9*
Funky Street			
(US) Atco	11–5–68	14	3
CONNIFF, RAY, SINGERS			
Somewhere My Love			
(US) Columbia	23–7–66	9	5
CONTOURS			
Do You Love Me?			
(US) Gordy	29–9–62	3	8
CONWAY, RUSS			
More Party Pops (Medley)			
(UK) Columbia	*19–12–58*	*10*	*4*
Side Saddle			
(UK) Columbia	*28–2–59*	*1*	*23*
Roulette			
(UK) Columbia	*23–5–59*	*1*	*16*
China Tea			
(UK) Columbia	*22–8–59*	*4*	*10*
Snow Coach			
(UK) Columbia	*14–11–59*	*6*	*8*
More and More Party Pops (Medley)			
(UK) Columbia	*28–11–59*	*9*	*6*
Royal Event			
(UK) Columbia	*20–2–60*	*14*	*4*
Lucky Five			
(UK) Columbia	*22–5–60*	*9*	*7*
Even More Party Pops (Medley)			
(UK) Columbia	*18–12–60*	*15*	*1*
Pepe			
(UK) Columbia	*8–1–61*	*14*	*3*
Toy Balloons			
(UK) Columbia	*2–12–61*	*7*	*8*
Lesson No. 1			
(UK) Columbia	*24–2–62*	*12*	*4*
COOK, PETER, AND MOORE, DUDLEY			
Goodbye			
(UK) Decca	*17–7–65*	*18*	*3*

	Date of chart entry	*Highest position reached*	*Number of weeks in charts*
COOKE, SAM			
You Send Me Summertime			
(US) Keen	28–10–57	1	15
Only Sixteen			
(UK) HMV	*15–8–59*	*13*	*3*
Wonderful World			
(US) Keen	6–6–60	12	7
Chain Gang			
(US) RCA	12–9–60	2	10
(UK) RCA	*23–9–60*	*9*	*7*
Cupid			
(US) RCA	24–7–61	17	3
(UK) RCA	*5–8–61*	*9*	*8*
Twisting The Night Away			
(US) RCA	17–3–62	9	7
(UK) RCA	*17–3–62*	*6*	*10*
Having A Party			
(US) RCA	14–7–62	17	2
Bring It On Home To Me			
(US) RCA	25–8–62	13	1
Nothing Can Change This Love			
(US) RCA	10–11–62	12	3
Send Me Some Lovin'			
(US) RCA	16–2–63	13	5
Another Saturday Night			
(US) RCA	18–5–63	10	5
Frankie and Johnny			
(US) RCA	31–8–63	14	4
Little Red Rooster			
(US) RCA	23–11–63	11	5
Good News			
(US) RCA	29–2–64	11	4
Good Times			
(US) RCA	4–7–64	11	5
Shake			
(US) RCA	30–1–65	7	5
COOKIES			
Chains			
(US) Dimension	22–12–62	17	3
Don't Say Nothing Bad About My Baby			
(US) Dimension	13–4–63	7	5
COPELAND, KEN			
Pledge of Love			
(US) Imperial	20–5–57	17	1
CORDET, LOUISE			
I'm Just A Baby			
(UK) Decca	*11–8–62*	*13*	*5*

	Date of chart entry	*Highest position reached*	*Number of weeks in charts*
CORNEY, JILL			
Love Me To Pieces			
(US) Columbia	19–8–57	18	4
CORNELIUS BROTHERS AND SISTER ROSE			
Treat Her Like A Lady			
(US) United Artists	29–5–71	3	10
Too Late To Turn Back Now			
(US) United Artists	24–6–72	2	9
CORNELL, DON			
Hold My Hand			
(UK) Vogue-Coral	*7–1–55*	*7*	*3*
Stranger in Paradise			
(UK) Vogue-Coral	*22–4–55*	*19*	*2*
Most Of All			
(US) Coral	28–5–55	20	1
Bible Tells Me So			
(US) Coral	10–9–55	7	9
CORNELL, LYN			
Never On Sunday			
(UK) Decca	*14–10–60*	*18*	*2*
CORONETS			
Twenty Tiny Fingers			
(UK) Columbia	*25–11–55*	*20*	*1*
CORSAIRS			
Smoky Places			
(US) Tuff	10–3–62	12	3
CORTEZ, DAVE 'BABY'			
Happy Organ			
(US) Clock	13–4–59	1	10
Rinky Dink			
(US) Chess	1–9–62	10	4
COSBY, BILL			
Little Ole Man (Uptight-Everythin's Alright)			
(US) Warner Brothers	23–9–67	4	6
COSTA, DON			
Never On Sunday			
(US) United Artists	24–10–60	19	1
COUNT FIVE			
Psychotic Reaction			
(US) Double Shot	1–10–66	5	5

	Date of chart entry	*Highest position reached*	*Number of weeks in charts*
COWBOY CHURCH SUNDAY SCHOOL			
Open Up Your Heart			
(US) Decca	8–1–55	8	16
COWSILLS			
The Rain, The Park And Other Things			
(US) MGM	28–10–67	2	11
Indian Lake			
(US) MGM	29–6–68	10	5
Hair			
(US) MGM	5–4–69	2	10
COX, MICHAEL			
Angela Jones			
(UK) Triumph	*12–6–60*	*8*	*7*
Along Came Caroline			
(UK) HMV	*30–9–60*	*20*	*2*
CRADDOCK, BILLY 'CRASH'			
Rub It In			
(US) ABC	17–8–74	16	4
CRAMER, FLOYD			
Last Date			
(US) RCA	7–11–60	2	13
On The Rebound			
(US) RCA	20–3–61	4	9
(UK) RCA	*16–4–61*	*5*	*8*
San Antonio Rose			
(US) RCA	26–6–61	8	7
CRANE, LES			
Desiderata			
(US) Warner Brothers	13–11–71	8	5
(UK) Warner Brothers	*18–3–72*	*7*	*7*
CRAWFORD, JIMMY			
I Love How You Love Me			
(UK) Columbia	*16–12–61*	*17*	*1*
CRAWFORD, JOHNNY			
Cindy's Birthday			
(US) Del Fi	16–6–62	8	4
Your Nose Is Gonna Grow			
(US) Del Fi	1–9–62	14	2
Rumors			
(US) Del Fi	1–12–62	12	4

	Date of chart entry	*Highest position reached*	*Number of weeks in charts*
CRAZY ELEPHANT			
Gimme Gimme Good Lovin'			
(US) Bell	19–4–69	12	5
(UK) Major Minor	*28–6–69*	*12*	*5*
CRAZY OTTO			
Glad Rag Doll			
(US) Decca	5–3–55	19	2
CREAM			
I Feel Free			
(UK) Reaction	*21–1–67*	*11*	*4*
Strange Brew			
(UK) Reaction	*1–7–67*	*17*	*4*
Sunshine Of Your Love			
(US) Atco	27–7–68	5	8
White Room			
(US) Atco	26–10–68	6	7
Badge			
(UK) Polydor	*26–4–69*	*18*	*3*
CREEDENCE CLEARWATER REVIVAL			
Suzie Q			
(US) Fantasy	12–10–68	11	6
Proud Mary			
(US) Fantasy	22–2–69	2	9
(UK) Liberty	*21–6–69*	*8*	*6*
Bad Moon Rising			
(US) Fantasy	24–5–69	2	10
(UK) Liberty	*23–8–69*	*1*	*11*
Green River			
(US) Fantasy	16–8–69	2	10
(UK) Liberty	*27–12–69*	*19*	*2*
Fortunate Son/Down on the Corner			
(US) Fantasy	15–11–69	3	10
Travellin' Band			
(US) Fantasy (b/w Who'll Stop the Rain?	7–2–70	2	8
(UK) Liberty	*18–4–70*	*8*	*7*
Up Around The Bend			
(US) Fantasy (b/w Run Through The Jungle	9–5–70	4	8
(UK) Liberty	*27–6–70*	*3*	*7*
Long As I Can See The Light			
(US) Fantasy (b/w Looking Out My Back Door)	22–8–70	2	10
(UK) Liberty	*26–9–70*	*20*	*1*

	Date of chart entry	Highest position reached	Number of weeks in charts
CREEDENCE CLEARWATER REVIVAL (cont.)			
Have You Ever Seen The Rain/Hey Tonight			
(US) Fantasy	20–2–71	8	6
Sweet Hitch-Hiker			
(US) Fantasy	7–8–71	6	5
CRESCENDOS			
Oh, Julie			
(US) Nasco	17–2–58	5	8
CRESTS			
16 Candles			
(US) Coed	5–1–59	2	11
Step By Step			
(US) Coed	11–4–60	14	6
Trouble In Paradise			
(US) Coed	1–8–60	20	2
CREW CUTS			
Earth Angel			
(US) Mercury	5–2–55	8	11
(UK) Mercury	*15–4–55*	*4*	*20*
Koko Mo			
(US) Mercury	12–2–55	8	8
Don't Be Angry			
(US) Mercury	7–5–55	14	7
Story Untold			
(US) Mercury	9–7–55	16	4
Gum Drop			
(US) Mercury	27–8–55	10	7
Angels In The Sky			
(US) Mercury	14–1–56	13	9
Seven Days			
(US) Mercury	3–3–56	20	1
CREWE, BOB, GENERATION			
Music To Watch Girls By			
(US) DynoVoice	4–2–67	15	3
CRIBBINS, BERNARD			
Hole In The Ground			
(UK) Parlophone	*24–2–62*	*9*	*10*
Right Said Fred			
(UK) Parlophone	*21–7–62*	*10*	*4*
CRICKETS			
That'll Be The Day			
(US) Brunswick	26–8–57	3	11
(UK) Vogue-Coral	*27–9–57*	*1*	*12*

	Date of chart entry	Highest position reached	Number of weeks in charts
CRICKETS (cont.)			
Oh Boy!			
(US) Brunswick	30–12–57	10	6
(UK) Coral	*10–1–58*	*3*	*12*
Maybe Baby			
(UK) Coral	*21–3–58*	*4*	*8*
(US) Brunswick	31–3–58	18	2
Think It Over			
(UK) Coral	*1–8–58*	*11*	*5*
Don't Ever Change			
(UK) Liberty	*7–7–62*	*5*	*9*
My Little Girl			
(UK) Liberty	*10–2–63*	*17*	*3*
CRITTERS			
Mr. Dieingly Sad			
(US) Kapp	24–9–66	17	4
CROCE, JIM			
You Don't Mess Around With Jim			
(US) ABC	12–8–72	8	5
Operator (That's Not The Way It Feels)			
(US) ABC	25–11–72	17	3
Bad, Bad Leroy Brown			
(US) ABC	9–6–73	1	12
I Got A Name			
(US) ABC	27–10–73	10	6
Time In A Bottle			
(US) ABC	1–12–73	1	11
I'll Have To Say I Love You In A Song			
(US) ABC	6–4–74	9	5
CROSBY, BING			
Count Your Blessings			
(UK) Brunswick	*7–1–55*	*11*	*3*
Stranger In Paradise			
(UK) Brunswick	*29–4–55*	*17*	*2*
White Christmas			
(US) Decca (re-entry)	7–1–56	18	1
(US) Decca (re-entry)	25–12–61	12	2
True Love (with GRACE KELLY)			
(US) Capitol	20–10–56	4	18
(UK) Capitol	*23–11–56*	*4*	*23*
Around The World			
(UK) Brunswick	*24–5–57*	*5*	*14*
CROSBY, STILLS AND NASH			
Marrakesh Express			
(UK) Atlantic	*13–9–69*	*17*	*2*

	Date of chart entry	*Highest position reached*	*Number of weeks in charts*
CROSBY, STILLS, NASH AND YOUNG			
Woodstock			
(US) Atlantic	18–4–70	11	7
Teach Your Children			
(US) Atlantic	25–7–70	16	2
Ohio			
(US) Atlantic	25–7–70	14	3
[see also: YOUNG, NEIL]			
CROW			
Evil Woman Don't Play Your Games With Me			
(US) Ameret	10–1–70	19	2
CRYSTALS			
There's No Other (Like My Baby)			
(US) Philles	6–1–62	20	1
Uptown			
(US) Philles	12–5–62	13	5
He's A Rebel			
(US) Philles	13–10–62	1	10
(UK) London	*13–1–63*	*19*	*1*
He's Sure The Boy I Love			
(US) Philles	9–2–63	11	4
Da Doo Ron Ron			
(US) Philles	18–5–63	3	8
(UK) London	*29–6–63*	*5*	*12*
(UK) Warner Spector (re-issue)	*9–11–74*	*15*	*4*
Then He Kissed Me			
(US) Philles	31–8–63	6	8
(UK) London	*28–9–63*	*2*	*10*
CUFF LINKS			
Tracy			
(US) Decca	11–10–69	9	6
(UK) MCA	*13–12–69*	*4*	*9*
When Julie Comes Around			
(UK) MCA	*11–4–70*	*10*	*6*
CURVED AIR			
Back Street Luv			
(UK) Warner Brothers	*4–9–71*	*4*	*6*
CYMARRON			
Rings			
(US) Entrance	7–8–71	17	2
CYMBAL, JOHNNY			
Mr. Bass Man			
(US) Kapp	6–4–63	16	3
[see also: DEREK]			

	Date of chart entry	*Highest position reached*	*Number of weeks in charts*
CYRKLE			
Red Rubber Ball			
(US) Columbia	11–6–66	2	8
Turn Down Day			
(US) Columbia	10–9–66	16	2
DADDY DEWDROP			
Chick-A-Boom			
(US) Sunflower	24–4–71	9	8
DAKOTAS			
Cruel Sea			
(UK) Parlophone	*10–8–63*	*18*	*4*
[See also: KRAMER, BILLY J.]			
DALE, ALAN			
Sweet and Gentle			
(US) Coral	2–7–55	12	7
DALE, JIM			
Be My Girl			
(UK) Parlophone	*25–10–57*	*2*	*12*
DALE AND GRACE			
I'm Leaving It Up To You			
(US) Montel–Michele	26–10–63	1	10
Stop And Think It Over			
(US) Montel–Michele	15–2–64	8	5
DALTREY, ROGER			
Giving It All Away			
(UK) Track	*28–4–73*	*5*	*6*
I'm Free (with THE LONDON SYMPHONY ORCHESTRA)			
(UK) Ode	*25–8–73*	*13*	*4*
[see also: WHO]			
DAMITA JO			
I'll Be There			
(US) Mercury	31–2–61	12	4
DAMONE, VIC			
On The Street Where You Live			
(US) Columbia	16–6–56	8	12
(UK) Philips	*16–5–58*	*1*	*15*
DANA			
All Kinds of Everything			
(UK) Rex	*4–4–70*	*1*	*8*
Who Put The Lights Out?			
(UK) Rex	*13–3–71*	*14*	*3*

	Date of chart entry	*Highest position reached*	*Number of weeks in charts*
DANA, VIC			
Red Roses for a Blue Lady			
(US) Dolton	20–3–65	10	5
DANIELS, CHARLIE			
Uneasy Rider			
(US) Kama Sutra	4–8–73	9	5
DANKWORTH, JOHNNY			
Experiments With Mice			
(UK) Parlophone	*29–4–56*	*7*	*8*
African Waltz			
(UK) Parlophone	*19–3–61*	*11*	*9*
DANLEERS			
One Summer Night			
(US) Mercury	28–7–58	16	3
DANNY AND THE JUNIORS			
At The Hop			
(US) ABC–Paramount	16–12–57	1	14
(UK) HMV	*17–1–58*	*3*	*13*
Rock And Roll Is Here To Stay			
(US) ABC–Paramount	17–3–58	19	2
DANTE AND THE EVERGREENS			
Alley-Oop			
(US) Madison	20–6–60	15	5
DARIN, BOBBY			
Splish Splash			
(US) Atco	30–6–58	3	10
(UK) London	*29–8–58*	*20*	*1*
Queen Of The Hop			
(US) Atco	11–3–58	9	10
Dream Lover			
(US) Atco	11–5–59	2	11
(UK) London	*6–6–59*	*1*	*15*
Mack The Knife			
(US) Atco	14–9–59	1	19
(UK) London	*3–10–49*	*2*	*12*
Beyond The Sea			
(UK) London	*30–1–60*	*8*	*6*
(US) Atco	8–2–60	6	8
Clementine			
(UK) London	*27–3–60*	*13*	*5*
(Won't You Come Home) Bill Bailey			
(US) Atco	4–7–60	19	1
Artificial Flowers			
(US) Atco	31–10–60	20	1

	Date of chart entry	Highest position reached	Number of weeks in charts
DARIN, BOBBY (cont.)			
Lazy River			
(UK) London	*5–3–61*	*4*	*10*
(US) Atco	20–3–61	14	2
You Must Have Been A Beautiful Baby			
(US) Atco	25–9–61	5	6
(UK) London	*14–10–61*	*18*	*2*
Multiplication			
(UK) London (b/w)*	*6–1–62*	*3*	*8*
Irresistible You*			
(US) Atco	3–2–62	15	3
Things			
(US) Atco	4–8–62	3	6
(UK) London	*4–8–62*	*2*	*12*
You're The Reason I'm Leaving			
(US) Capitol	9–2–63	3	10
18 Yellow Roses			
(US) Capitol	8–6–63	10	4
If I Were A Carpenter			
(US) Atlantic	15–10–66	8	7
(UK) Atlantic	*29–10–66*	*9*	*7*
DARRELL, GUY			
I've Been Hurt			
(UK) Santa Ponsa (re-issue)	*15–9–73*	*12*	*5*
DARREN, JAMES			
Goodbye Cruel World			
(US) Colpix	13–11–61	3	10
(UK) Pye	*6–1–62*	*15*	*3*
Her Royal Majesty			
(US) Colpix	3–3–62	6	5
Conscience			
(US) Colpix	12–5–62	11	5
DARTELLS			
Hot Pastrami			
(US) Dot	11 5 63	11	6
DAVID, ANN MARIE			
Wonderful Dream			
(UK) Epic	*12–5–73*	*13*	*4*
DAVID AND JONATHAN			
Michelle			
(UK) Columbia	*29–1–66*	*11*	*4*
(US) Capitol	12–2–66	18	2
Lovers Of The World Unite			
(UK) Columbia	*20–8–66*	*7*	*7*

	Date of chart entry	Highest position reached	Number of weeks in charts
DAVIES, DAVE			
Death Of A Clown			
(UK) Pye	*29–7–67*	*3*	*7*
DA VINCI, PAUL			
Your Baby Ain't Your Baby Anymore			
(UK) Penny Farthing	*17–8–74*	*20*	*1*
DAVIS, BILLIE			
Tell Him			
(UK) Decca	*9–3–63*	*10*	*5*
DAVIS, MAC			
Baby Don't Get Hooked On Me			
(US) Columbia	19–8–72	1	10
One Hell Of A Woman			
(US) Columbia	22–6–74	11	6
Stop and Smell The Roses			
(US) Columbia	28–9–74	9	6
DAVIS JR., SAMMY			
Something's Gotta Give			
(US) Decca } (b/w*)	4–6–55	9	11
(UK) Brunswick } (b/w*)	*29–7–55*	*11*	*7*
Love Me Or Leave Me*			
(US) Decca	4–6–55	9	11
(UK) Brunswick	*9–9–55*	*8*	*8*
That Ol' Black Magic			
(US) Decca	9–7–55	16	2
(UK) Brunswick	*30–9–55*	*16*	*1*
Hey There			
(UK) Brunswick	*7–10–55*	*19*	*1*
What Kind Of Fool Am I			
(US) Reprise	20–10–62	17	3
The Shelter Of Your Arms			
(US) Reprise	7–3–64	17	2
I've Gotta Be Me			
(US) Reprise	8–2–69	11	7
Candy Man			
(US) MGM	20–5–72	1	9
DAVIS, SKEETER			
End Of The World			
(US) RCA	2–3–63	2	9
(UK) RCA	*13–4–63*	*18*	*4*
I Can't Stay Mad At You			
(US) RCA	12–10–63	7	6

	Date of chart entry	Highest position reached	Number of weeks in charts
SPENCER DAVIS GROUP			
Keep On Running			
(UK) Fontana	*25–12–65*	*1*	*10*
Somebody Help Me			
(UK) Fontana	*2–4–66*	*1*	*7*
When I Come Home			
(UK) Fontana	*17–9–66*	*12*	*4*
Gimme Some Lovin'			
(UK) Fontana	*12–11–66*	*2*	*7*
(US) United Artists	11–2–67	7	6
I'm A Man			
(UK) Fontana	*4–2–67*	*9*	*3*
(US) United Artists	22–4–67	10	4
DAVIS, TYRONE			
Can I Change My Mind			
(US) Dakar	25–1–69	5	7
Turn Back The Hands Of Time			
(US) Dakar	18–4–70	3	8
DAWN (featuring TONY ORLANDO)			
Candida			
(US) Bell	5–9–70	3	11
(UK) Bell	*30–1–71*	*9*	*6*
Knock Three Times			
(US) Bell	12–12–70	1	13
(UK) Bell	*17–4–71*	*1*	*13*
What Are You Doing Sunday?			
(UK) Bell	*14–8–71*	*3*	*7*
Tie A Yellow Ribbon Round The Old Oak Tree			
(US) Bell	24–3–73	1	14
(UK) Bell	*24–3–73*	*1*	*17*
Say, Has Anybody Seen My Sweet Gypsy Rose?			
(US) Bell	11–8–73	3	9
(UK) Bell	*1–9–73*	*12*	*5*
[see also: ORLANDO, TONY]			
DAY, BOBBY			
Rockin' Robin/Over and Over			
(US) Class	1–9–58	2	13
DAY, DORIS			
Ready Willing and Able			
(UK) Philips	*8–4–55*	*7*	*9*
I'll Never Stop Loving You			
(US) Capitol	30–7–55	15	4
(UK) Philips	*21–10–55*	*17*	*3*

	Date of chart entry	*Highest position reached*	*Number of weeks in charts*
DAY, DORIS (cont.)			
Love Me Or Leave Me			
(UK) Philips	*9–9–55*	*20*	*1*
Whatever Will Be Will Be (Que Sera Sera)			
(UK) Philips	*29–6–56*	*1*	*19*
(US) Columbia	14–7–56	2	19
A Very Precious Love			
(UK) Philips	*4–7–58*	*16*	*5*
Everybody Loves A Lover			
(US) Columbia	4–8–58	14	8
Move Over Darling			
(UK) CBS	*11–4–64*	*8*	*8*
DEAN, JIMMY			
Big Bad John			
(US) Columbia	9–10–61	1	12
(UK) Philips	*21–10–61*	*2*	*9*
PT 109			
(US) Columbia	28–4–62	8	6
DE CASTRO SISTERS			
Teach Me Tonight			
(US) Abbott	1–1–55	5	6
(UK) London	*11–2–55*	*20*	*1*
DEE, DAVE, DOZY, BEAKY, MICK AND TITCH			
Hold Tight			
(UK) Fontana	*26–3–66*	*4*	*10*
Hideaway			
(UK) Fontana	*25–6–66*	*10*	*6*
Bend It			
(UK) Fontana	*24–9–66*	*2*	*9*
Save Me			
(UK) Fontana	*17–12–66*	*3*	*7*
Touch Me Touch Me			
(UK) Fontana	*15–4–67*	*8*	*5*
Okay			
(UK) Fontana	*10–6–67*	*4*	*6*
Zabadak			
(UK) Fontana	*21–10–67*	*3*	*8*
Legend of Xanadu			
(UK) Fontana	*24–2–68*	*1*	*8*
Last Night In Soho			
(UK) Fontana	*27–7–68*	*8*	*6*
Wreck Of The Antoinette			
(UK) Fontana	*12–10–68*	*14*	*5*

	Date of chart entry	Highest position reached	Number of weeks in charts
DEE, JOEY, AND THE STARLITERS			
Peppermint Twist			
(US) Roulette	11–12–61	1	13
(UK) Columbia	*13–1–62*	*13*	*6*
Hey Let's Twist			
(US) Roulette	17–3–62	20	1
Shout			
(US) Roulette	14–4–62	6	7
What Kind Of Love Is This			
(US) Roulette	6–10–62	18	2
DEE, KIKI			
Amoureuse			
(UK) Rocket	*8–12–73*	*13*	*5*
I Got The Music In Me			
(UK) Rocket	*12–10–74*	*19*	*1*
(US) Rocket	9–11–74	12	5
DEE, TOMMY			
Three Stars			
(US) Crest	20–4–59	11	4
DEEP PURPLE			
Hush			
(US) Tetragrammaton	31–8–68	4	7
Black Night			
(UK) Harvest	*19–9–70*	*2*	*10*
Strange Kind Of Woman			
(UK) Harvest	*20–3–71*	*8*	*6*
Fireball			
(UK) Harvest	*11–12–71*	*15*	*6*
Smoke On The Water			
(US) Warner Brothers	23–6–73	4	9
DE FRANCO FAMILY			
Heartbeat It's A Lovebeat			
(US) 20th Century	13–10–73	3	9
Save The Last Dance For Me (featuring TONY DE FRANCO)			
(US) 20th Century	22–6–74	18	1
DE JOHN SISTERS			
No More			
(US) Epic	1–1–55	8	9
DEKKER, DESMOND, AND THE ACES			
007			
(UK) Pyramid	*29–7–67*	*14*	*4*

	Date of chart entry	*Highest position reached*	*Number of weeks in charts*
DEKKER, DESMOND (cont.)			
The Israelites			
(UK) Pyramid	*5–4–69*	*1*	*8*
(US) Uni	7–6–69	12	6
It Mek			
(UK) Pyramid	*12–7–69*	*7*	*5*
You Can Get It If You Really Want It			
(UK) Trojan	*5–9–70*	*2*	*10*
DELANEY AND BONNIE AND FRIENDS			
Comin' Home (with ERIC CLAPTON)			
(UK) Atlantic	*10–1–70*	*16*	*2*
Never Ending Song Of Love			
(US) Atco	17–7–71	13	6
Only You Know And I Know			
(US) Atco	6–11–71	20	2
DELEGATES			
Convention '72			
(US) Mainstream	11–11–72	8	3
DELFONICS			
La-La Means I Love You			
(US) Philly Groove	2–3–68	4	9
(UK) Bell (re-issue)	*7–8–71*	*19*	*2*
Didn't I (Blow Your Mind This Time)			
(US) Philly Groove	21–2–70	10	6
DELIVERANCE, see WEISSBERG, ERIC			
DELLS			
There Is			
(US) Cadet	17–2–68	20	3
Stay In My Corner			
(US) Cadet	3–8–68	10	7
Always Together			
(US) Cadet	16–11–68	18	2
Love is Blue/I Can Sing A Rainbow			
(UK) Chess	*9–8–69*	*15*	*3*
Oh, What A Night			
(US) Cadet	13–9–69	10	6
DE LOS RIOS, WALDO			
Mozart Symphony No. 40			
(UK) A & M	*17–4–71*	*5*	*10*

	Date of chart entry	Highest position reached	Number of weeks in charts
DEL VIKINGS			
Come Go With Me			
(US) Dot	6-4-57	5	15
Whispering Bells			
(US) Dot	29-7-57	9	9
DEMENSIONS			
Over The Rainbow			
(US) Mohawk	22-8-60	16	4
DENE, TERRY			
White Sports Coat			
(UK) Decca	*21-6-57*	*18*	*2*
Start Movin'			
(UK) Decca	*16-8-57*	*15*	*2*
Stairway Of Love			
(UK) Decca	*23-5-58*	*16*	*2*
DENNIS, JACKIE			
La Dee Dah			
(UK) Decca	*28-3-58*	*4*	*7*
DENNY, MARTIN			
Quiet Village			
(US) Liberty	11-5-59	4	9
DENVER, JOHN			
Take Me Home Country Roads (with FAT CITY)			
(US) RCA	10-7-71	2	11
Rocky Mountain High			
(US) RCA	3-2-73	9	7
Sunshine On My Shoulder			
(US) RCA	2-3-74	1	10
Annie's Song			
(US) RCA	29-6-74	1	8
(UK) RCA	*31-8-74*	*2*	*9*
Back Home Again			
(US) RCA	19-10-74	5	7
DENVER, KARL			
Marcheta			
(UK) Decca	*18-6-61*	*16*	*8*
Mexicali Rose			
(UK) Decca	*14-10-61*	*7*	*7*
Wimoweh			
(UK) Decca	*3-2-62*	*5*	*12*
Never Goodbye			
(UK) Decca	*7-4-62*	*9*	*8*
A Little Love A Little Kiss			
(UK) Decca	*16-6-62*	*19*	*3*
Still			
(UK) Decca	*7-9-63*	*13*	*10*

	Date of chart entry	Highest position reached	Number of weeks in charts
DEODATO			
Also Sprach Zarathustra			
(US) CTI	24–2–73	2	8
(UK) CTI	*12–5–73*	*7*	*5*
DE PAUL, LYNSEY			
Sugar Me			
(UK) MAM	*26–8–72*	*5*	*6*
Getting A Drag			
(UK) MAM	*23–12–72*	*18*	*3*
Won't Somebody Dance With Me			
(UK) MAM	*3–11–73*	*14*	*5*
No Honestly			
(UK) Jet	*16–11–74*	*7*	*4*
DEREK			
Cinnamon			
(US) Bang	14–12–68	11	7
DEREK AND THE DOMINOS			
Layla			
(US) Atco (re-issue)	1–7–72	10	7
(UK) Polydor (re-issue)	*19–8–72*	*7*	*5*
DE SHANNON, JACKIE			
What The World Needs Now Is Love			
(US) Imperial	26–6–65	7	7
Put A Little Love In Your Heart			
(US) Imperial	9–8–69	4	7
DESMOND, JOHNNY			
Play Me Hearts And Flowers			
(US) Coral	2–4–55	16	5
Yellow Rose Of Texas			
(US) Coral	13–8–55	6	15
DE SYKES, STEPHANIE			
Born With A Smile On My Face			
(UK) Bradleys	*20–7–74*	*2*	*6*
DETERGENTS			
Leader Of The Laundromat			
(US) Roulette	9–1–65	19	1
DETROIT EMERALDS			
Feel The Need In Me			
(UK) Janus	*3–3–73*	*4*	*7*
You Want It, I Got It			
(UK) Westbound	*2–6–73*	*12*	*3*

	Date of chart entry	*Highest position reached*	*Number of weeks in charts*
DETROIT SPINNERS. See SPINNERS			
DE VAUGHN, WILLIAM			
Be Thankful For What You Got			
(US) Roxbury	1–6–74	4	7
DE YOUNG, CLIFF			
My Sweet Lady			
(US) MCA	16–3–74	17	2
DIAMOND, NEIL			
Cherry, Cherry			
(US) Bang	24–9–66	6	6
I Got The Feeling (Oh No No)			
(US) Bang	3–12–66	16	4
You Got To Me			
(US) Bang	4–3–67	18	1
Girl, You'll Be A Woman Soon			
(US) Bang	13–5–67	10	4
Thank The Lord For The Night Time			
(US) Bang	12–8–67	13	5
Sweet Caroline			
(US) UNI	26–7–69	4	9
(UK) UNI (re-issue)	*27–2–71*	*8*	*7*
Holly Holy			
(US) UNI	29–11–69	6	9
Cracklin' Rosie			
(US) UNI	19–9–70	1	10
(UK) UNI	*21–11–70*	*3*	*13*
He Ain't Heavy, He's My Brother			
(US) UNI	19–12–70	20	2
I Am . . . I Said			
(US) UNI	10–4–71	4	7
(UK) UNI	*22–5–71*	*4*	*8*
Stones/Crunchy Granola Suite			
(US) UNI	4–12–71	14	3
Song Sung Blue			
(US) UNI	27–5–72	1	9
(UK) UNI	*17–6–72*	*14*	*4*
Play Me			
(US) UNI	16–9–72	11	5
Walk On Water			
(US) UNI	30–12–72	17	2
Longfellow Serenade			
(US) Columbia	9–11–74	5	5
DIAMONDS			
Why Do Fools Fall In Love?			
(US) Mercury	31–3–56	17	3

	Date of chart entry	*Highest position reached*	*Number of weeks in charts*
DIAMONDS (cont.)			
Church Bells May Ring			
(US) Mercury	2–6–56	20	1
Little Darlin'			
(US) Mercury	30–3–57	2	17
(UK) Mercury	*7–6–57*	*3*	*15*
The Stroll			
(US) Mercury	20–1–58	5	9
She Say (Oom Dooby Doom)			
(US) Mercury	9–3–59	18	3
DICK AND DEEDEE			
Mountain's High			
(US) Liberty	11–9–61	2	6
Young And In Love			
(US) Warner Brothers	20–4–63	17	3
Thou Shalt Not Steal			
(US) Warner Brothers	16–1–65	13	3
DICKENS, LITTLE JIMMY			
May The Bird Of Paradise Fly Up Your Nose			
(US) Columbia	20–11–65	15	3
DI MUCCI, DION. See DION			
DINNING, MARK			
Teen Angel			
(US) MGM	11–1–60	1	11
DINO, DESI, AND BILLY			
I'm A Fool			
(US) Reprise	14–8–65	17	2
DION (*and THE BELMONTS) (†DION DI MUCCI)			
Teenager In Love*			
(US) Laurie	4–5–59	5	10
Where Or When*			
(US) Laurie	18–1–60	3	9
Lonely Teenager			
(US) Laurie	12–12–60	12	6
Runaround Sue			
(US) Laurie	9–10–61	1	11
(UK) Top Rank	*4–11–61*	*12*	*4*
Wanderer			
(US) Laurie	13–1–62	2	11
(UK) HMV	*24–2–62*	*10*	*8*
Lovers Who Wander			
(US) Laurie	12–5–62	3	7

DION (cont.)	*Date of chart entry*	*Highest position reached*	*Number of weeks in charts*
Little Diane			
(US) Laurie	4-8-62	8	5
Love Came To Me			
(US) Laurie	8-12-62	10	4
Ruby Baby			
(US) Columbia	2-2-63	2	8
Donna The Prima Donna†			
(US) Columbia	5-10-63	6	7
Drip Drop†			
(US) Columbia	7-12-63	6	6
Abraham, Martin and John			
(US) Laurie	9-11-68	4	10
DISCO TEX AND THE SEX-O-LETTES			
Get Dancin'			
(UK) Chelsea	*7-12-74*	*8*	*7*
DISTEL, SACHA			
Raindrops Keep Falling On My Head			
(UK) Warner Brothers	*28-2-70*	*10*	*5*
DIXIEBELLS			
(Down At) Papa Joe's			
(US) Soundstage	9-11-63	9	5
Southtown USA			
(US) Soundstage	15-2-64	15	2
DIXIE CUPS			
Chapel Of Love			
(US) Red Bird	16-5-64	1	9
People Say			
(US) Red Bird	8-8-64	12	5
Iko Iko			
(US) Red Bird	22-5-65	20	2
DOBKINS, CARL, JR			
My Heart Is An Open Book			
(US) Decca	29-6-59	3	11
DR. HOOK AND THE MEDICINE SHOW			
Sylvia's Mother			
(US) Columbia	13-5-72	5	8
(UK) CBS	*8-7-72*	*2*	*8*
Cover Of Rolling Stone			
(US) Columbia	17-2-73	6	7
DR. JOHN			
Right Place, Wrong Time			
(US) Atco	2-6-73	9	8

	Date of chart entry	*Highest position reached*	*Number of weeks in charts*
DODD, KEN			
Love Is Like A Violin			
(UK) Columbia	*17–7–60*	*12*	*8*
Tears			
(UK) Columbia	*11–9–65*	*1*	*21*
The River			
(UK) Columbia	*27–11–65*	*3*	*11*
Promises			
(UK) Columbia	*21–5–66*	*6*	*8*
More Than Love			
(UK) Columbia	*20–8–66*	*14*	*4*
Let Me Cry On Your Shoulder			
(UK) Columbia	*4–2–67*	*11*	*3*
Brokenhearted			
(UK) Columbia	*19–12–70*	*15*	*6*
When Love Comes Around Again			
(UK) Columbia	*18–9–71*	*19*	*1*
DOGGETT, BILL			
Honky Tonk, Part Two			
(US) King	15–9–56	2	16
DOLAN, JOE			
Make Me An Island			
(UK) Pye	*19–7–69*	*3*	*10*
Teresa			
(UK) Pye	*22–11–69*	*20*	*1*
You're Such A Good-looking Woman			
(UK) Pye	*28–3–70*	*17*	*5*
DOMINO, FATS			
Ain't It A Shame			
(US) Imperial	16–7–55	16	4
I'm In Love Again			
(US) Imperial	18–5–56	5	13
(UK) London	*24–8–56*	*12*	*5*
Blueberry Hill			
(US) Imperial	20–10–56	4	19
(UK) London	*11–1–57*	*6*	*10*
Blue Monday			
(US) Imperial	19–1–57	9	10
I'm Walkin'			
(US) Imperial	23–3–57	5	11
(UK) London	*19–4–57*	*19*	*1*
Valley Of Tears			
(US) Imperial	24–6–57	13	4
The Big Beat			
(UK) London	*11–4–58*	*20*	*1*

	Date of chart entry	Highest position reached	Number of weeks in charts
DOMINO, FATS (cont.)			
Whole Lotta Lovin'			
(US) Imperial	8–12–58	6	9
Margie			
(UK) London	*30–5–59*	*16*	*2*
I'm Ready			
(US) Imperial	1–6–59	16	4
I Want To Walk You Home			
(US) Imperial (b/w*)	24–8–59	8	7
(UK) London	*7–11–59*	*19*	*2*
I'm Gonna Be A Wheel Someday			
(US) Imperial*	7–9–59	17	2
Be My Guest			
(US) Imperial	16–11–59	8	5
(UK) London	*19–12–59*	*12*	*8*
Country Boy			
(UK) London	*3–4–60*	*18*	*1*
Walkin' To New Orleans			
(US) Imperial	18–7–60	6	7
Three Nights A Week			
(US) Imperial	10–10–60	15	3
My Girl Josephine			
(US) Imperial	5–12–60	14	3
Let The Four Winds Blow			
(US) Imperial	14–8–61	15	3
DONALDSON, BO, AND THE HEYWOODS			
Billy Don't Be A Hero			
(US) ABC	25–5–74	1	9
Who Do You Think You Are?			
(US) ABC	14–9–74	15	3
DON AND JUAN			
What's Your Name?			
(US) Big Top	3–3–62	7	7
DONEGAN, LONNIE			
Rock Island Line			
(UK) Decca	*6–1–56*	*8*	*17*
(US) London	14–4–56	10	7
Lost John			
(UK) Nixa	*27–4–56*	*2*	*14*
Skiffle Session			
(UK) Nixa EP	*6–7–56*	*20*	*1*
Bring A Little Water, Sylvie			
(UK) Pye Nixa	*14–9–56*	*7*	*8*
Don't You Rock Me Daddy-O			
(UK) Pye Nixa	*18–1–57*	*4*	*15*
Cumberland Gap			
(UK) Pye Nixa	*5–4–57*	*1*	*11*

	Date of chart entry	*Highest position reached*	*Number of weeks in charts*
DONEGAN, LONNIE (cont.)			
Puttin' On The Style/Gambling Man			
(UK) Pye Nixa	*7–6–57*	*1*	*18*
Dixie Darling			
(UK) Pye Nixa	*11–10–57*	*10*	*8*
Jack O'Diamonds			
(UK) Pye Nixa	*20–12–57*	*14*	*6*
Grand Coulee Dam			
(UK) Pye Nixa	*25–4–58*	*6*	*9*
Sally Don't You Grieve/Betty Betty Betty			
(UK) Pye Nixa	*11–7–58*	*11*	*6*
Tom Dooley			
(UK) Pye Nixa	*21–11–58*	*3*	*12*
Skiffle Party			
(UK) Pye Nixa EP	*3–1–59*	*18*	*1*
Does Your Chewing Gum Lose Its Flavor On The Bedpost Overnight?			
(UK) Pye Nixa	*7–2–59*	*3*	*10*
(US) Dot	28–8–61	5	6
Fort Worth Jail			
(UK) Pye Nixa	*9–5–59*	*12*	*4*
Battle Of New Orleans			
(UK) Pye	*20–6–59*	*2*	*14*
Sal's Got A Sugar Lip			
(UK) Pye	*19–9–59*	*16*	*3*
My Old Man's A Dustman			
(UK) Pye	*20–3–60*	*1*	*9*
I Wanna Go Home			
(UK) Pye	*22–5–60*	*5*	*9*
Lorelei			
(UK) Pye	*21–8–60*	*11*	*3*
Lively			
(UK) Pye	*20–11–60*	*10*	*4*
Have A Drink On Me			
(UK) Pye	*30–4–61*	*7*	*9*
Michael/Lumbered			
(UK) Pye	*2–9–61*	*6*	*7*
The Commancheros			
(UK) Pye	*27–1–62*	*17*	*3*
The Party's Over			
(UK) Pye	*28–4–62*	*9*	*7*
Pick A Bale Of Cotton			
(UK) Pye	*1–9–62*	*11*	*5*
DONNER, RAL			
Girl Of Me Best Friend			
(US) Gone	29–5–61	19	2

DONNER, RAL (cont.)	*Date of chart entry*	*Highest position reached*	*Number of weeks in charts*
You Don't Know What You've Got (Until You Lose It)			
(US) Gone	7–8–61	4	7
(UK) Parlophone	*28–10–61*	*16*	*2*
She's Everything			
(US) Gone	10–2–62	18	2
DONOVAN			
Catch The Wind			
(UK) Pye	*3–4–65*	*4*	*8*
Colours			
(UK) Pye	*19–6–65*	*4*	*6*
Sunshine Superman			
(US) Epic	13–8–66	1	9
(UK) Pye	*17–12–66*	*2*	*7*
Mellow Yellow			
(US) Epic	26–11–66	2	8
(UK) Pye	*18–2–67*	*8*	*5*
Epistle To Dippy			
(US) Epic	11–3–67	19	2
There Is A Mountain			
(US) Epic	9–9–67	11	4
(UK) Pye	*4–11–67*	*8*	*5*
Jennifer Juniper			
(UK) Pye	*2–3–68*	*5*	*6*
Hurdy Gurdy Man			
(UK) Pye	*8–6–68*	*4*	*7*
(US) Epic	13–7–68	5	7
Atlantis			
(US) Epic	3–5–69	7	8
Babarabbajagal (with JEFF BECK)			
(UK) Pye	*26–7–69*	*12*	*4*
DOOBIE BROTHERS			
Listen To The Music			
(US) Warner Brothers	21–10–72	11	5
Long Train Running			
(US) Warner Brothers	9–6–73	8	7
China Grove			
(US) Warner Brothers	29–9–73	15	4
DOONICAN, VAL			
Walk Tall			
(UK) Decca	*28–11–64*	*3*	*10*
The Special Years			
(UK) Decca	*6–2–65*	*7*	*8*
Elusive Butterfly			
(UK) Decca	*26–3–66*	*5*	*7*
What Would I Be?			
(UK) Decca	*19–11–66*	*2*	*11*
Memories Are Made Of This			
(UK) Decca	*18–3–67*	*11*	*5*

	Date of chart entry	*Highest position reached*	*Number of weeks in charts*
DOONICAN, VAL (cont.)			
If The Whole World Stopped Loving			
(UK) Pye	*4–11–67*	*3*	*13*
If I Knew Then What I Know Now			
(UK) Pye	*23–11–68*	*14*	*3*
Morning			
(UK) Philips	*18–12–71*	*12*	*6*
DOORS			
Light My Fire			
(US) Elektra	1–7–67	1	12
People Are Strange			
(US) Elektra	21–10–67	12	4
Hello, I Love You			
(US) Elektra	20–7–68	1	9
(UK) Elektra	*21–9–68*	*15*	*6*
Touch Me			
(US) Elektra	11–1–69	3	10
Love Her Madly			
(US) Elektra	1–5–71	11	6
Riders On The Storm			
(US) Elektra	14–8–71	14	4
DORSEY, JIMMY			
So Rare			
(US) Fraternity	27–4–57	2	22
DORSEY, LEE			
Ya Ya			
(US) Fury	2–10–61	7	7
Working In A Coalmine			
(US) Amy	20–8–66	8	5
(UK) Stateside	*3–9–66*	*8*	*6*
Holy Cow			
(UK) Stateside	*12–11–66*	*6*	*7*
DORSEY, TOMMY, ORCHESTRA			
Tea For Two Cha-Cha			
(US) Decca	29–9–58	7	9
(UK) Brunswick	*7–11–58*	*4*	*13*
DOUGLAS, CARL			
Kung Fu Fighting			
(UK) Pye	*31–8–74*	*1*	*8*
(US) 20th Century	23–11–74	1	9
DOUGLAS, CRAIG			
Teenager In Love			
(UK) Top Rank	*13–6–59*	*14*	*7*
Only Sixteen			
(UK) Top Rank	*15–8–59*	*1*	*13*

	Date of chart entry	*Highest position reached*	*Number of weeks in charts*
DOUGLAS, CRAIG (cont.)			
Pretty Blue Eyes			
(UK) Top Rank	*23–1–60*	*5*	*9*
Heart Of A Teenage Girl			
(UK) Top Rank	*17–4–60*	*10*	*8*
A Hundred Pounds Of Clay			
(UK) Top Rank	*2–4–61*	*8*	*7*
Time			
(UK) Top Rank	*25–6–61*	*9*	*10*
When My Little Girl Is Smiling			
(UK) Top Rank	*7–4–62*	*9*	*7*
Our Favourite Melodies			
(UK) Decca	*14–7–62*	*9*	*5*
Oh Lonesome Me			
(UK) Decca	*10–11–62*	*15*	*4*
DOUGLAS, MIKE			
The Men In My Little Girl's Life			
(US) Epic	15–1–66	6	5
DOVE, RONNIE			
Right Or Wrong			
(US) Diamond	28–11–64	14	3
One Kiss For Old Times' Sake			
(US) Diamond	24–4–65	14	4
Little Bit Of Heaven			
(US) Diamond	3–7–65	16	5
When Liking Turns To Loving			
(US) Diamond	26–2–66	18	3
Let's Start Over Again			
(US) Diamond	21–5–66	20	1
Cry			
(US) Diamond	24–12–66	18	3
DOVELLS			
Bristol Stomp			
(US) Parkway	25–9–61	2	11
You Can't Sit Down			
(US) Parkway	18–5–63	3	9
DOWELL, JOE			
Wooden Heart			
(US) Smash	24–7–61	1	9
DOZIER, LAMONT			
Trying To Hold On To My Woman			
(US) ABC	9–3–74	15	4
DRAKE, CHARLIE			
Splish Splash			
(UK) Parlophone	*15–8–58*	*7*	*9*
Mr. Custer			
(UK) Parlophone	*30–10–60*	*14*	*4*

	Date of chart entry	*Highest position reached*	*Number of weeks in charts*
DRAKE, CHARLIE (cont.)			
My Boomerang Won't Come Back			
(UK) Parlophone	*7–10–61*	*10*	*5*
DRAMATICS			
Whatcha See Is Whatcha Get			
(US) Volt	21–8–71	9	7
In The Rain			
(US) Volt	18–3–72	5	8
DRAPER, RUSTY			
Seventeen			
(US) Mercury	27–8–55	18	1
Shifting Whispering Sands			
(US) Mercury	8–10–55	6	12
Are You Satisfied			
(US) Mercury	14–1–56	12	5
In The Middle Of The House			
(US) Mercury	13–10–56	20	1
Freight Train			
(US) Mercury	3–6–57	11	3
DREAMLOVERS			
When We Get Married			
(US) Heritage	11–9–61	10	3
DREAM WEAVERS			
It's Almost Tomorrow			
(US) Decca	3–12–55	8	16
(UK) Brunswick	*10–2–56*	*1*	*16*
DRIFTERS			
There Goes My Baby			
(US) Atlantic	13–7–59	2	10
Dance With Me			
(US) Atlantic	16–11–59	15	13
(UK) London	*16–1–60*	*18*	*2*
This Magic Moment			
(US) Atlantic	21–3–60	16	2
Save The Last Dance For Me			
(US) Atlantic	19–9–60	1	12
(UK) London	*21–10–60*	*2*	*13*
I Count The Tears			
(US) Atlantic	30–1–61	17	2
Please Stay			
(US) Atlantic	10–7–61	14	4
Sweets For My Sweet			
(US) Atlantic	16–10–61	16	3
Up On The Roof			
(US) Atlantic	12–1–63	5	7

DRIFTERS (cont.)	*Date of chart entry*	*Highest position reached*	*Number of weeks in charts*
On Broadway			
(US) Atlantic	20–4–63	9	4
Under The Boardwalk			
(US) Atlantic	18–7–64	4	9
Saturday Night At The Movies			
(US) Atlantic	12–12–64	18	3
(UK) Atlantic (re-issue, b/w At The Club)	*6–5–72*	*3*	*9*
Come Over To My Place			
(UK) Atlantic (re-issue)	*16–9–72*	*9*	*6*
Like Sister And Brother			
(UK) Bell	*18–8–73*	*7*	*6*
Kissin' In The Back Row			
(UK) Bell	*22–6–74*	*2*	*8*
Down On The Beach Tonight			
(UK) Bell	*26–10–74*	*7*	*5*
DRISCOLL, JULIE with the AUGER, BRIAN TRINITY			
This Wheel's On Fire			
(UK) Marmalade	*25–5–68*	*5*	*8*
D'RONE, FRANK			
Strawberry Blonde			
(UK) Capitol	*18–12–60*	*13*	*2*
DRUPI			
Vado Via			
(UK) A & M	*12–1–74*	*17*	*2*
DUBLINERS			
Seven Drunken Nights			
(UK) Major Minor	*22–4–67*	*7*	*9*
Black Velvet Band			
(UK) Major Minor	*23–9–67*	*18*	*5*
DUKE, PATTY			
Don't Just Stand There			
(US) United Artists	31–7–65	8	5
DUNCAN, JOHNNY, AND HIS BLUEGRASS BOYS			
Last Train To San Fernando			
(UK) Columbia	*26–7–57*	*2*	*16*
DUNN, CLIVE			
Grandad			
(UK) Columbia	*12–12–70*	*1*	*14*
DUPREE, SIMON, AND THE BIG SOUND			
Kites			
(UK) Columbia	*9–12–67*	*9*	*8*

	Date of chart entry	*Highest position reached*	*Number of weeks in charts*
DUPREES			
You Belong To Me			
(US) Coed	1–9–62	7	6
My Own True Love			
(US) Coed	24–11–62	13	3
Have You Heard			
(US) Coed	14–12–63	18	2
DUSTY, SLIM			
A Pub With No Beer			
(UK) Columbia	*14–2–59*	*3*	*11*
DYLAN, BOB			
The Times They Are A-Changin'			
(UK) CBS	*3–4–65*	*7*	*7*
Subterranean Homesick Blues			
(UK) CBS	*8–5–65*	*9*	*6*
Like A Rolling Stone			
(US) Columbia	21–8–65	2	7
(UK) CBS	*28–8–65*	*4*	*8*
Positively 4th Street			
(US) Columbia	16–10–65	7	5
(UK) CBS	*6–11–65*	*8*	*9*
Can You Please Crawl Out Your Window?			
(UK) CBS	*29–1–66*	*17*	*1*
Rainy Day Women No. 12 And No. 35			
(US) Columbia	30–4–66	2	7
(UK) CBS	*21–5–66*	*7*	*5*
I Want You			
(US) Columbia	30–7–66	20	2
(UK) CBS	*6–8–66*	*16*	*4*
Lay Lady Lay			
(US) Columbia	9–8–69	7	8
(UK) CBS	*27–9–69*	*5*	*7*
Knockin' On Heaven's Door			
(US) Columbia	13–10–73	12	6
(UK) CBS	*20–10–73*	*14*	*4*
DYSON, RONNIE			
(If You Let Me Make Love To You Then) Why Can't I Touch You			
(US) Columbia	8–8–70	8	5
EAGLES			
Take It Easy			
(US) Asylum	1–7–72	12	6
Witchy Woman			
(US) Asylum	28–10–72	9	5

	Date of chart entry	*Highest position reached*	*Number of weeks in charts*
EARL, ROBERT			
I May Never Pass This Way Again			
(UK) Philips	*2–5–58*	*14*	*9*
EAST OF EDEN			
Jig-A-Jig			
(UK) Deram	*8–5–71*	*7*	*6*
EASYBEATS			
Friday On My Mind			
(UK) United Artists	*19–11–66*	*6*	*9*
(US) United Artists	6–5–67	16	5
Hello How Are You			
(UK) United Artists	*27–4–68*	*20*	*1*
ECHOES			
Baby Blue			
(US) Segway	3–4–61	14	6
ECKSTINE, BILLY			
No One But You			
(UK) MGM	*7–1–55*	*3*	*9*
Gigi			
(UK) Mercury	*21–2–59*	*11*	*10*
[see also: VAUGHAN, SARAH]			
EDDY, DUANE			
Rebel-Rouser			
(US) Jamie	7–7–58	6	10
(UK) London	*12–9–58*	*19*	*5*
Cannon Ball			
(US) Jamie	24–11–58	15	5
(UK) London	*3–1–59*	*14*	*4*
The Lonely One			
(UK) London	*20–4–59*	*20*	*1*
Peter Gunn/Yep			
(UK) London	*20–6–59*	*6*	*8*
40 Miles Of Bad Road			
(US) Jamie	13–7–59	9	7
(UK) London	*5–9–59*	*6*	*8*
Some Kinda Earthquake			
(UK) London	*12–12–59*	*7*	*6*
Bonnie Came Back			
(UK) London	*13–2–60*	*9*	*4*
Shazam			
(UK) London	*24–4–60*	*3*	*10*
Because They're Young			
(US) Jamie	13–6–60	4	9
(UK) London	*17–7–60*	*2*	*13*

	Date of chart entry	*Highest position reached*	*Number of weeks in charts*
EDDY, DUANE (cont.)			
Kommotion			
(UK) London	*6–11–60*	*10*	*3*
Pepe			
(UK) London	*1–1–61*	*3*	*8*
(US) Jamie	30–1–61	18	2
Theme From Dixie			
(UK) London	*9–4–61*	*6*	*6*
Ring Of Fire			
(UK) London	*11–6–61*	*13*	*5*
Drivin' Home			
(UK) London	*2–9–61*	*18*	*2*
Deep In The Heart Of Texas			
(UK) RCA	*23–6–62*	*19*	*1*
Ballad Of Paladin			
(UK) RCA	*1–9–62*	*10*	*5*
(Dance With The) Guitar Man			
(UK) RCA	*17–11–62*	*4*	*12*
(US) RCA	1–12–62	12	3
EDISON LIGHTHOUSE			
Love Grows (Where My Rosemary Goes)			
(UK) Bell	*24–1–70*	*1*	*10*
(US) Bell	7–3–70	5	9
EDMUNDS, DAVE			
I Hear You Knocking			
(UK) MAM	*21–11–70*	*1*	*12*
(US) MAM	23–1–71	4	7
Baby I Love You			
(UK) Rockfield	*17–2–73*	*8*	*6*
Born To Be With You			
(UK) Rockfield	*23–6–73*	*5*	*7*
EDWARD BEAR			
Last Song			
(US) Capitol	10–2–73	3	9
EDWARDS, BOBBY			
You're The Reason			
(US) Crest	30–10–61	11	5
EDWARDS, JONATHAN			
Sunshine			
(US) Capricorn	18–12–71	4	10
EDWARDS, RUPIE			
Ire Feelings (Skanga)			
(UK) Cactus	*30–11–74*	*9*	*5*

	Date of chart entry	Highest position reached	Number of weeks in charts
EDWARDS, TOMMY			
It's All In The Game			
(US) MGM	8–9–58	1	14
(UK) MGM	*10–10–58*	*1*	*15*
Love Is All We Need			
(US) MGM	1–12–58	15	5
Please Mr. Sun			
(US) MGM	23–3–59	11	3
I Really Don't Want To Know			
(US) MGM	4–7–60	18	1
8th DAY			
She's Not Just Another Woman			
(US) Invictus	19–6–71	11	6
ELBERT, DONNIE			
Where Did Our Love Go?			
(US) All Platinum	11–12–71	15	3
(UK) London	*22–1–72*	*8*	*5*
I Can't Help Myself			
(UK) Avco	*4–3–72*	*11*	*5*
ELECTRIC INDIAN			
Keem-O-Sabe			
(US) United Artists	27–9–69	16	2
ELECTRIC LIGHT ORCHESTRA			
10538 Overture			
(UK) Harvest	*5–8–72*	*9*	*6*
Roll Over Beethoven			
(UK) Harvest	*3–2–73*	*6*	*5*
Showdown			
(UK) Harvest	*20–10–73*	*12*	*5*
ELECTRIC PRUNES			
I Had Too Much To Dream Last Night			
(US) Reprise	28–1–67	11	6
ELEGANTS			
Little Star			
(US) APT	28–7–58	1	14
ELGINS			
Heaven Must Have Sent You			
(UK) Tamla-Motown (re-issue)	*15–5–71*	*3*	*9*
ELIAS AND HIS ZIG ZAG JIVE FLUTES			
Tom Hark			
(UK) Columbia	*2–5–58*	*2*	*12*

	Date of chart entry	*Highest position reached*	*Number of weeks in charts*
ELLIOTT, BERN, AND THE FENMEN			
Money (That's What I Want)			
(UK) Decca	*14–12–63*	*14*	*4*
ELLIS, SHIRLEY			
Nitty Gritty			
(US) Congress	28–12–63	8	5
Name Game			
(US) Congress	16–1–65	3	8
(UK) London	*22–5–65*	*6*	*8*
Clapping Song			
(US) Congress	10–4–65	8	5
ENGLAND WORLD CUP SQUAD			
Back Home			
(UK) Pye	*2–5–70*	*1*	*9*
ENGLISH, SCOTT			
Brandy			
(UK) Horse	*30–10–71*	*12*	*5*
EPPS, PRESTON			
Bongo Rock			
(US) Original	22–6–59	14	4
EQUALS			
Baby Come Back			
(UK) President	*25–6–68*	*1*	*12*
Viva Bobby Joe			
(UK) President	*16–8–69*	*6*	*8*
Blackskin Blue-Eyed Boys			
(UK) President	*9–1–71*	*9*	*6*
ERNIE			
Rubber Duckie			
(US) Columbia	12–9–70	16	3
ESQUIRES			
Get On Up			
(US) Bunky	7–10–67	11	6
ESSEX			
Easier Said Than Done			
(US) Roulette	22–6–63	1	9
Walkin' Miracle			
(US) Roulette	21–9–63	12	3

	Date of chart entry	*Highest position reached*	*Number of weeks in charts*
ESSEX, DAVID			
Rock On			
(UK) CBS	*1–9–73*	*3*	*7*
(US) Columbia	2–2–74	5	10
Lamplight			
(UK) CBS	*24–11–73*	*7*	*11*
Gonna Make You A Star			
(UK) CBS	*19–10–74*	*1*	*10*
EVANS, MAUREEN			
Like I Do			
(UK) Oriole	*22–12–62*	*3*	*12*
EVANS, PAUL, AND THE CURLS			
Seven Little Girls			
(US) Guaranteed	26–10–59	9	7
(UK) London	*28–11–59*	*16*	*3*
Midnight Special			
(US) Guaranteed	22–2–60	16	4
Happy-Go-Lucky			
(US) Guaranteed	6–6–60	10	6
EVERETT, BETTY			
Shoop Shoop Song (It's In His Kiss)			
(US) Vee Jay	28–3–64	6	7
[see also: BUTLER, JERRY]			
EVERLY BROTHERS			
Bye Bye Love			
(US) Cadence	3–6–57	2	20
(UK) London	*12–7–57*	*6*	*13*
Wake Up Little Susie			
(US) Cadence	7–10–57	1	16
(UK) London	*15–11–57*	*2*	*12*
All I Have To Do Is Dream			
(US) Cadence	28–4–58	1	13
(UK) London (b/w Claudette)	*30–5–58*	*1*	*19*
Bird Dog			
(US) Cadence (b/w*)	18–8–58	2	13
(UK) London	*12–9–58*	*2*	*16*
Devoted To You*			
(US) Cadence	25–8–58	10	5
Problems			
(US) Cadence	24–11–58	2	9
(UK) London	*24–1–59*	*5*	*8*
Take A Message To Mary			
(US) Cadence	4–5–59	16	5
(UK) London (b/w Poor Jenny)	*30–5–59*	*11*	*7*
('Til) I Kissed You			
(US) Cadence	31–8–59	4	11
(UK) London	*12–9–59*	*2*	*14*

	Date of chart entry	*Highest position reached*	*Number of weeks in charts*
EVERLY BROTHERS (cont.)			
Let It Be Me			
(US) Cadence	1–2–60	7	8
Cathy's Clown			
(UK) Warner Brothers	*10–4–60*	*1*	*15*
(US) Warner Brothers	2–5–60	1	12
When Will I Be Loved/Be-Bop-A-Lula			
(US) Cadence	4–7–60	8	5
(UK) London	*10–7–60*	*4*	*12*
So Sad			
(US) Warner Brothers	12–9–60	7	8
(UK) Warner Brothers (b/w Lucille)	*18–9–60*	*4*	*8*
Like Strangers			
(UK) Warner Brothers	*25–12–60*	*12*	*3*
Walk Right Back			
(UK) Warner Brothers (b/w**)	*29–1–61*	*1*	*13*
(US) Warner Brothers (b/w**)	6–3–61	7	6
Ebony Eyes**			
(US) Warner Brothers	24–2–61	8	5
Temptation			
(UK) Warner Brothers	*4–6–61*	*1*	*12*
Muskrat			
*(UK) Warner Brothers (b/w***)*	*30–9–61*	*16*	*1*
Don't Blame Me***			
(US) Warner Brothers	16–10–61	20	1
Crying In The Rain			
(US) Warner Brothers	27–1–62	8	10
(UK) Warner Brothers	*3–2–62*	*6*	*8*
How Can I Meet Her?			
(UK) Warner Brothers (b/w †)	*2–6–62*	*12*	*5*
That's Old Fashioned†			
(US) Warner Brothers	16–6–62	9	3
No One Can Make My Sunshine Smile			
(UK) Warner Brothers	*3–11–62*	*11*	*7*
Price Of Love			
(UK) Warner Brothers	*29–5–65*	*2*	*10*
Love Is Strange			
(UK) Warner Brothers	*6–11–65*	*11*	*4*
EVERY MOTHER'S SON			
Come On Down To My Boat			
(US) MGM	10–6–67	6	8
EXCITERS			
Tell Him			
(US) United Artists	29–12–62	4	7

	Date of chart entry	Highest position reached	Number of weeks in charts
FABARES, SHELLEY			
Johnny Angel			
(US) Colpix	24–3–62	1	10
FABIAN			
Turn Me Loose			
(US) Chancellor	13–4–59	9	8
Tiger			
(US) Chancellor	29–6–59	3	8
Hound Dog Man			
(US) Chancellor	14–12–59	9	7
Friendly World			
(US) Chancellor	21–12–59	12	3
FABRIC, BENT			
Alley Cat			
(US) Atco	8–9–62	7	8
FACES			
Stay With Me			
(UK) Warner Brothers	*15–1–72*	*6*	*5*
(US) Warner Brothers	5–2–72	17	4
Cindy Incidentally			
(UK) Warner Brothers	*17–2–73*	*2*	*7*
Poolhall Richard/I Wish It Would Rain			
(UK) Warner Brothers	*22–12–73*	*8*	*7*
You Can Make Me Dance, Sing, Or Anything (with ROD STEWART)			
(UK) Warner Brothers	*21–12–74*	*6*	*3*
FAIRWEATHER			
Natural Sinner			
(UK) RCA	*8–8–70*	*6*	*6*
FAIRWEATHER-LOW, ANDY			
Reggae Tune			
(UK) A & M	*5–10–74*	*10*	*5*
[see also: AMEN CORNER, FAIRWEATHER]			
FAITH, ADAM			
What Do You Want?			
(UK) Parlophone	*21–11–59*	*1*	*13*
Poor Me			
(UK) Parlophone	*30–1–60*	*1*	*10*
Someone Else's Baby			
(UK) Parlophone	*10–4–60*	*2*	*9*

	Date of chart entry	*Highest position reached*	*Number of weeks in charts*
FAITH, ADAM (cont.)			
Made You			
(UK) Parlophone	*19–6–60*	*3*	*8*
How About That			
(UK) Parlophone	*11–9–60*	*2*	*10*
Lonely Pup			
(UK) Parlophone	*4–12–60*	*5*	*5*
Who Am I/This Is It			
(UK) Parlophone	*29–1–61*	*6*	*7*
Easy Going Me			
(UK) Parlophone	*23–4–61*	*9*	*5*
Don't You Know It?			
(UK) Parlophone	*22–7–61*	*10*	*5*
The Time Has Come			
(UK) Parlophone	*21–10–61*	*5*	*9*
Lonesome			
(UK) Parlophone	*3–2–62*	*12*	*3*
As You Like It			
(UK) Parlophone	*19–5–62*	*5*	*9*
Don't That Beat All			
(UK) Parlophone	*8–9–62*	*8*	*8*
The First Time			
(UK) Parlophone	*5–10–63*	*5*	*8*
We Are In Love			
(UK) Parlophone	*4–1–64*	*11*	*6*
Message to Martha			
(UK) Parlophone	*12–12–64*	*12*	*6*
FAITH, HORACE			
Black Pearl			
(UK) Trojan	*3–10–70*	*13*	*4*
FAITH, PERCY			
Theme From A Summer Place			
(US) Columbia	1–2–60	1	15
(UK) Philips	*27–2–60*	*4*	*12*
FAITHFUL, MARIANNE			
As Tears Go By			
(UK) Decca	*22–8–64*	*9*	*10*
Come And Stay With Me			
(UK) Decca	*27–2–65*	*4*	*7*
This Little Bird			
(UK) Decca	*15–5–65*	*6*	*7*
Summer Night			
(UK) Decca	*7–8–65*	*10*	*5*
FALCONS			
You're So Fine			
(US) Unart	6–7–59	17	3

	Date of chart entry	*Highest position reached*	*Number of weeks in charts*
FAME, GEORGIE			
Yeh, Yeh			
(UK) Columbia	*26–12–64*	*1*	*8*
Get Away			
(UK) Columbia	*2–7–66*	*1*	*7*
Sunny			
(UK) Columbia	*8–10–66*	*13*	*4*
Sittin' In The Park			
(UK) Columbia	*31–12–66*	*12*	*7*
Because I Love You			
(UK) CBS	*15–4–67*	*15*	*2*
Ballad Of Bonnie And Clyde			
(UK) CBS	*30–12–67*	*1*	*8*
(US) Epic	16–3–68	7	9
Peaceful			
(UK) CBS	*9–8–69*	*16*	*1*
[see also: FAME AND PRICE]			
FAME AND PRICE			
Rosetta			
(UK) CBS	*24–4–71*	*11*	*5*
FAMILY			
Strange Band			
(UK) Reprise	*19–9–70*	*11*	*5*
In My Own Time			
(UK) Reprise	*7–8–71*	*4*	*8*
Burlesque			
(UK) Reprise	*21–10–72*	*13*	*4*
FAMILY DOGG			
Way Of Life			
(UK) Bell	*21–6–69*	*6*	*8*
FANCY			
Wild Thing			
(US) Big Tree	24–8–74	14	3
Touch Me			
(US) Big Tree	30–11–74	19	2
FANTASTIC JOHNNY C.			
Boogaloo Down Broadway			
(US) Phil-L.A. of Soul	25–11–67	7	9
FANTASTICS			
Something Old, Something New			
(UK) Bell	*24–4–71*	*9*	*3*
FARDON, DON			
Indian Reservation			
(US) GNP Crescendo	5–10–68	20	2
(UK) Young Blood (re-issue)	*31–10–70*	*3*	*11*

	Date of chart entry	*Highest position reached*	*Number of weeks in charts*
FARGO, DONNA			
Happiest Girl In The Whole USA			
(US) Dot	29–7–72	11	5
Funny Face			
(US) Dot	2–12–72	5	9
FARLOWE, CHRIS			
Out Of Time			
(UK) Immediate	*9–7–66*	*1*	*9*
FELICIANO, JOSÉ			
Light My Fire			
(US) RCA	10–8–68	3	9
(UK) RCA	*12–10–68*	*6*	*8*
FELIX, JULIE			
If I Could			
(UK) RAK	*23–5–70*	*19*	*1*
FENDERMEN			
Mule Skinner Blues			
(US) Soma	27–6–60	5	9
FENTON, SHANE AND THE FENTONES			
I'm A Moody Guy			
(UK) HMV	*4–8–62*	*19*	*1*
[see also: STARDUST, ALVIN]			
FERKO STRING BAND			
Alabama Jubilee			
(US) Media	2–7–55	18	2
(UK) London	*12–8–55*	*20*	*1*
FERRANTE AND TEICHER			
Theme from 'The Apartment'			
(US) United Artists	29–8–60	10	11
Exodus			
(US) United Artists	12–12–60	2	14
(UK) United Artists	*26–2–61*	*6*	*10*
Tonight			
(US) United Artists	20–11–61	8	6
Midnight Cowboy			
(US) United Artists	20–12–69	10	7
FERRY, BRYAN			
A Hard Rain's A-Gonna Fall			
(UK) Island	*13–10–73*	*10*	*5*
The In Crowd			
(UK) Island	*1–6–74*	*13*	*4*

	Date of chart entry	*Highest position reached*	*Number of weeks in charts*
FERRY, BRYAN (cont.)			
Smoke Gets In Your Eyes			
(UK) Island	*28–9–74*	*17*	*2*
[see also: ROXY MUSIC]			
FIELDS, ERNIE			
In The Mood			
(US) Rendezvous	26–10–59	4	10
(UK) London	*9–1–60*	*18*	*1*
FIELDS, GRACIE			
Around The World			
(UK) Columbia	*31–5–57*	*8*	*6*
FIESTAS			
So Fine			
(US) Old Town	25–5–59	11	5
FIFTH DIMENSION			
Go Where You Wanna Go			
(US) Soul City	25–2–67	16	2
Up Up And Away			
(US) Soul City	1–7–67	7	6
Stoned Soul Picnic			
(US) Soul City	29–6–68	3	9
Sweet Blindness			
(US) Soul City	9–11–68	13	2
Aquarius/Let The Sun Shine In			
(US) Soul City	22–3–69	1	14
(UK) Liberty	*24–5–69*	*11*	*4*
Workin' On A Groovy Thing			
(US) Soul City	23–8–69	20	2
Wedding Bell Blues			
(US) Soul City	18–10–69	1	10
(UK) Liberty	*14–2–70*	*16*	*1*
One Less Bell To Answer			
(US) Bell	5–12–70	2	12
Love's Lines, Angles and Rhymes			
(US) Bell	17–4–71	19	1
Never My Love			
(US) Bell	23–10–71	12	5
(Last Night) I Didn't Get To Sleep At All			
(US) Bell	20–5–72	8	7
If I Could Reach You			
(US) Bell	28–10–72	10	6
FIFTH ESTATE			
Ding Dong The Witch Is Dead			
(US) Jubilee	17–6–67	11	4

	Date of chart entry	Highest position reached	Number of weeks in charts
FINNEGAN, LARRY			
Dear One			
(US) Old Town	14–4–62	11	4
FIREBALLS			
Quite A Party			
(UK) Pye	*5–8–61*	*20*	*1*
Bottle Of Wine			
(US) Atco	10–2–68	9	6
[see also: GILMER, JIMMY]			
FIRST CHOICE			
Armed and Extremely Dangerous			
(UK) Bell	*9–6–73*	*16*	*3*
Smarty Pants			
(UK) Bell	*18–8–73*	*9*	*5*
FIRST CLASS			
Beach Baby			
(UK) UK	*13–7–74*	*13*	*4*
(US) UK	7–9–74	4	6
FIRST EDITION			
Just Dropped In (To See What Condition My Condition Was In)			
(US) Reprise	2–3–68	5	6
But You Know I Love You			
(US) Reprise	8–3–69	19	1
[see also ROGERS, KENNY AND THE FIRST EDITION]			
FISHER, EDDIE			
I Need You Now			
(US) Victor	1–1–55	4	5
(UK) HMV	*21–1–55*	*1*	*19*
Wedding Bells			
(UK) HMV	*18–3–55*	*5*	*11*
Count Your Blessings			
(US) Victor	1–1–55	5	5
Heart			
(US) Victor	4–6–55	15	7
Song Of The Dreamer			
(US) Victor	3–9–55	16	5
Dungaree Doll			
(US) Victor	31–12–55	7	11
Cindy, Oh Cindy			
(US) Victor	3–11–56	10	12
(UK) HMV	*23–11–56*	*5*	*13*

	Date of chart entry	Highest position reached	Number of weeks in charts
FISHER, TONI			
Big Hurt			
(US) Signet	30–11–59	3	12
FITZGERALD, ELLA			
Swinging Shepherd Blues			
(UK) HMV	*23–5–58*	*15*	*3*
Mack The Knife			
(UK) HMV	*1–5–60*	*20*	*1*
FIVE AMERICANS			
Western Union			
(US) Abnak	1–4–67	5	6
FIVE MAN ELECTRICAL BAND			
Signs			
(US) Lionel	31–7–71	3	8
FIVE STAIRSTEPS			
O-Oh Child			
(US) Buddah	4–7–70	8	8
FLACK, ROBERTA			
First Time Ever I Saw Your Face			
(US) Atlantic	25–3–72	1	14
(UK) Atlantic	*24–6–72*	*14*	*4*
Where Is The Love (with DONNY HATHAWAY)			
(US) Atlantic	8–7–72	5	8
Killing Me Softly With His Song			
(US) Atlantic	10–2–73	1	12
(UK) Atlantic	*3–3–73*	*6*	*8*
Feel Like Makin' Love			
(US) Atlantic	20–7–74	1	8
FLAMINGOS			
I Only Have Eyes For You			
(US) End	22–6–59	11	7
FLEETWOOD MAC			
Albatross			
(UK) Blue Horizon	*14–12–68*	*1*	*13*
Man Of The World			
(UK) Immediate	*19–4–69*	*2*	*9*
Oh Well			
(UK) Reprise	*11–10–69*	*2*	*9*
Green Manalishi			
(UK) Reprise	*30–5–70*	*10*	*9*
Albatross			
(UK) CBS (re-issue)	*2–6–73*	*2*	*8*

	Date of chart entry	*Highest position reached*	*Number of weeks in charts*
FLEETWOODS			
Come Softly To Me			
(US) Dolphin	16–3–59	1	10
(UK) London	*25–4–59*	*6*	*8*
Mr. Blue			
(US) Dolton	21–9–59	1	14
Tragedy			
(US) Dolton	22–5–61	10	4
FLOWERPOT MEN			
Let's Go To San Francisco			
(UK) Deram	*9–9–67*	*4*	*7*
FLOYD, EDDIE			
Knock On Wood			
(UK) Atlantic	*15–4–67*	*19*	*5*
Bring It On Home To Me			
(US) Stax	7–12–68	17	5
FLYING MACHINE			
Smile A Little Smile For Me			
(US) Congress	25–10–69	5	8
FOCUS			
Sylvia			
(UK) Polydor	*10–2–73*	*4*	*6*
Hocus Pocus			
(UK) Polydor	*24–2–73*	*20*	*1*
(US) Sire	12–5–73	9	7
FONTANA, WAYNE (AND THE MINDBENDERS*)			
Um Um Um Um Um Um*			
(UK) Fontana	*31–10–64*	*5*	*7*
Game Of Love*			
(UK) Fontana	*13–2–65*	*2*	*7*
(US) Fontana	3–4–65	1	8
Just A Little Bit Too Late*			
(UK) Fontana	*10–7–65*	*20*	*1*
Come On Home			
(UK) Fontana	*4–6–66*	*16*	*3*
Pamela Pamela			
(UK) Fontana	*7–1–67*	*11*	*6*
FONTANE SISTERS			
Hearts Of Stone			
(US) Dot	1–1–55	1	14
Rock Love			
(US) Dot	12–3–55	19	1
Seventeen			
(US) Dot	27–8–55	6	13

	Date of chart entry	Highest position reached	Number of weeks in charts
FONTANE SISTERS (cont.)			
Daddy-O			
(US) Dot	3–12–55	11	5
Eddie My Love			
(US) Dot	24–3–56	12	7
FORD, CLINTON			
Too Many Beautiful Girls			
(UK) Oriole	*19–8–61*	*20*	*1*
FORD, EMILE, AND THE CHECKMATES			
What Do You Want To Make Those Eyes At Me For?			
(UK) Pye	*31–10–59*	*1*	*17*
Slow Boat To China			
(UK) Pye	*30–1–60*	*4*	*10*
You'll Never Know What You're Missing Till You Try			
(UK) Pye	*5–6–60*	*18*	*2*
Them There Eyes			
(UK) Pye	*24–10–60*	*20*	*1*
Counting Teardrops			
(UK) Pye	*25–12–60*	*6*	*6*
FORD, FRANKIE			
Sea Cruise			
(US) Ace	30–3–59	14	5
FORD, TENNESSEE ERNIE			
Give Me Your Word			
(UK) Capitol	*21–2–55*	*1*	*24*
Ballad Of Davy Crockett			
(US) Capitol	19–3–55	6	15
(UK) Capitol	*13–1–56*	*3*	*7*
Sixteen Tons			
(US) Capitol	19–11–55	1	17
(UK) Capitol	*6–1–56*	*1*	*11*
FORTUNE, LANCE			
Be Mine			
(UK) Pye	*13–2–60*	*5*	*6*
FORTUNES			
You've Got Your Troubles			
(UK) Decca	*17–7–65*	*2*	*9*
(US) Press	18–9–65	7	6
Here It Comes Again			
(UK) Decca	*21–10–65*	*4*	*7*
This Golden Ring			
(UK) Decca	*12–3–66*	*15*	*2*

	Date of chart entry	*Highest position reached*	*Number of weeks in charts*
FORTUNES (cont.)			
Here Comes That Rainy Day Feeling Again			
(US) Capitol	3–7–71	15	5
Freedom Come, Freedom Go			
(UK) Capitol	*2–10–71*	*6*	*7*
Storm In A Teacup			
(UK) Capitol	*12–2–72*	*7*	*6*
FOUNDATIONS			
Baby, Now That I've Found You			
(UK) Pye	*21–10–67*	*1*	*9*
(US) UNI	20–1–68	11	8
Back On My Feet Again			
(UK) Pye	*17–2–68*	*18*	*4*
Build Me Up Buttercup			
(UK) Pye	*7–12–68*	*2*	*9*
(US) UNI	1–2–69	3	10
In The Bad Bad Old Days			
(UK) Pye	*22–3–69*	*8*	*7*
FOUR ACES			
Mr. Sandman			
(US) Decca	1–1–55	10	7
(UK) Brunswick	*7–1–55*	*9*	*5*
Melody Of Love			
(US) Decca	29–1–55	11	13
Stranger In Paradise			
(UK) Brunswick	*20–5–55*	*6*	*6*
Love Is A Many Splendored Thing			
(US) Decca	3–9–55	1	20
(UK) Brunswick	*18–11–55*	*2*	*13*
Woman In Love			
(US) Decca	24–12–55	19	1
(UK) Brunswick	*26–10–56*	*19*	*1*
FOUR JACKS AND A JILL			
Master Jack			
(US) RCA	8–6–68	18	1
FOUR LADS			
Moments to Remember			
(US) Columbia	10–9–55	3	23
No, Not Much			
(US) Columbia	11–2–56	3	15
Standing On The Corner			
(US) Columbia	19–5–56	3	13
Who Needs You			
(US) Columbia	23–2–57	14	7

	Date of chart entry	*Highest position reached*	*Number of weeks in charts*
FOURMOST			
Hello Little Girl			
(UK) Parlophone	*5–10–63*	*9*	*7*
I'm In Love			
(UK) Parlophone	*1–2–64*	*17*	*4*
A Little Lovin'			
(UK) Parlophone	*2–5–64*	*6*	*8*
FOUR PENNIES			
Juliet			
(UK) Philips	*25–4–64*	*1*	*10*
I Found Out The Hard Way			
(UK) Philips	*15–8–64*	*14*	*3*
Black Girl			
(UK) Philips	*28–11–64*	*20*	*2*
Until It's Time For You To Go			
(UK) Philips	*6–11–65*	*19*	*3*
FOUR PREPS			
Twenty-Six Miles			
(US) Capitol	24–2–58	4	9
Big Man			
(US) Capitol	19–5–58	5	9
(UK) Capitol	*20–6–58*	*2*	*12*
Down By The Station			
(US) Capitol	18–1–60	13	8
More Money For You And Me (Medley)			
(US) Capitol	25–9–61	17	1
FOUR SEASONS (featuring FRANKIE VALLI*)			
Sherry			
(US) Vee Jay	8–9–62	1	10
(UK) Stateside	*20–10–62*	*8*	*10*
Big Girls Don't Cry			
(US) Vee Jay	27–10–62	1	13
(UK) Stateside	*27–1–63*	*13*	*5*
Walk Like A Man			
(US) Vee Jay	2–2–63	1	9
(UK) Stateside	*13–4–63*	*12*	*6*
Candy Girl			
(US) Vee Jay	27–7–63	3	8
Dawn (Go Away)			
(US) Philips	15–2–64	3	8
Stay			
(US) Vee Jay	21–3–64	16	4
Ronnie*			
(US) Philips	25–4–64	6	6

	Date of chart entry	*Highest position reached*	*Number of weeks in charts*
FOUR SEASONS (cont.)			
Rag Doll*			
(US) Philips	27–6–64	1	10
(UK) Philips	*4–9–64*	*2*	*9*
Save It For Me*			
(US) Philips	19–9–64	10	4
Big Man In Town*			
(US) Philips	5–12–64	20	2
Bye Bye Baby*			
(US) Philips	6–2–65	12	3
Let's Hang On*			
(US) Philips	30–10–65	3	12
(UK) Philips	*4–12–65*	*4*	*11*
Working My Way Back To You*			
(US) Philips	19–2–66	9	4
Opus 17 (Don't Worry 'Bout Me)*			
(US) Philips	4–6–66	13	5
(UK) Philips	*25–6–66*	*20*	*1*
I've Got You Under My Skin*			
(US) Philips	24–9–66	9	5
(UK) Philips	*15–10–66*	*12*	*5*
Tell It To The Rain*			
(US) Philips	7–1–67	10	4
Beggin'*			
(US) Philips	8–4–67	16	2
C'mon Marianne*			
(US) Philips	1–7–67	9	5
[see also: WONDER WHO]			
FOUR TOPS			
Baby I Need Your Loving			
(US) Motown	19–9–64	11	5
I Can't Help Myself			
(US) Motown	29–5–65	1	11
(UK) Tamla-Motown (re-issue)	*4–4–70*	*10*	*5*
It's The Same Old Song			
(US) Motown	7–8–65	5	7
Something About You			
(US) Motown	27–11–65	19	3
Shake Me, Wake Me (When It's Over)			
(US) Motown	19–3–66	18	2
Reach Out I'll Be There			
(US) Motown	24–9–66	1	9
(UK) Tamla-Motown	*15–10–66*	*1*	*11*
Standing In The Shadows Of Love			
(US) Motown	31–12–66	6	7
(UK) Tamla-Motown	*14–1–67*	*6*	*4*
Bernadette			
(US) Motown	25–3–67	4	6
(UK) Tamla-Motown	*15–4–67*	*8*	*5*

	Date of chart entry	Highest position reached	Number of weeks in charts
FOUR TOPS (cont.)			
Seven Rooms Of Gloom			
(US) Motown	10–6–67	14	4
(UK) Tamla-Motown	*1–7–67*	*12*	*5*
You Keep Running Away			
(US) Motown	14–10–67	19	1
Walk Away Renee			
(UK) Tamla-Motown	*23–12–67*	*3*	*8*
(US) Motown	24–2–68	14	4
If I Were A Carpenter			
(UK) Tamla-Motown	*23–3–68*	*7*	*6*
(US) Motown	8–6–68	20	2
Yesterday's Dream			
(UK) Tamla-Motown	*7–9–68*	*20*	*1*
What Is Man?			
(UK) Tamla-Motown	*28–6–69*	*16*	*2*
Do What You Gotta Do			
(UK) Tamla-Motown	*11–10–69*	*20*	*1*
It's All In The Game			
(UK) Tamla-Motown	*20–6–70*	*5*	*9*
Still Water (Love)			
(US) Motown	3–10–70	11	7
(UK) Tamla-Motown	*17–10–70*	*10*	*6*
Simple Game			
(UK) Tamla-Motown	*9–10–71*	*3*	*8*
Keeper Of The Castle			
(US) Dunhill	16–12–72	10	6
(UK) Probe	*16–12–72*	*18*	*1*
Ain't No Woman (Like The One I've Got)			
(US) Dunhill	10–3–73	4	9
Are You Man Enough			
(US) Dunhill	25–8–73	15	3
[see also: SUPREMES]			
FOXX, INEZ AND CHARLIE			
Mockingbird			
(US) Symbol	17–8–63	7	6
FRANCIS, CONNIE			
Who's Sorry Now?			
(US) MGM	3–3–58	4	11
(UK) MGM	*11–4–58*	*1*	*20*
I'm Sorry I Made You Cry			
(UK) MGM	*4–7–58*	*12*	*8*
Stupid Cupid			
(UK) MGM (b/w Carolina Moon)	*22–8–58*	*1*	*17*
(US) MGM	8–9–58	17	4
I'll Get By			
(UK) MGM	*21–11–58*	*19*	*1*

	Date of chart entry	Highest position reached	Number of weeks in charts
FRANCIS, CONNIE (cont.)			
Fallin'			
(UK) MGM	*28–11–58*	*20*	*1*
You Always Hurt The One You Love			
(UK) MGM	*10–1–59*	*12*	*5*
My Happiness			
(US) MGM	22–12–58	2	11
(UK) MGM	*21–2–59*	*3*	*11*
Lipstick On Your Collar (b/w*)			
(US) MGM	8–6–59	5	10
(UK) MGM	*11–7–59*	*4*	*13*
Frankie*			
(US) MGM	8–6–59	9	7
Plenty Good Lovin'			
(UK) MGM	*5–9–59*	*14*	*3*
Among My Souvenirs			
(UK) MGM	*12–12–59*	*8*	*5*
(US) MGM	21–12–59	7	6
Mama			
(US) MGM (b/w **)	28–3–60	8	5
(UK) MGM (b/w Robot Man)	*15–5–60*	*2*	*13*
Teddy**			
(US) MGM	4–4–60	17	1
Everybody's Somebody's Fool			
(US) MGM (b/w ***)	30–5–60	1	12
(UK) MGM	*14–8–60*	*6*	*10*
Jealous Of You***			
(US) MGM	20–6–60	19	2
My Heart Has A Mind Of Its Own			
(US) MGM	28–9–60	1	12
(UK) MGM	*30–10–60*	*2*	*7*
Many Tears Ago			
(US) MGM	22–11–60	7	9
(UK) MGM	*15–1–61*	*13*	*2*
Where The Boys Are			
(US) MGM	6–2–61	4	9
(UK) MGM	*19–3–61*	*7*	*6*
Breakin' In A Brand New Heart			
(US) MGM	1–5–61	7	6
(UK) MGM	*25–6–61*	*14*	*1*
Together			
(US) MGM	10–7–61	6	8
(UK) MGM	*9–9–61*	*10*	*6*
(He's My) Dreamboat			
(US) MGM	23–10–61	14	3
Baby's First Christmas†			
(UK) MGM	*9–12–61*	*17*	*1*
When The Boy In Your Arms			
(US) MGM (b/w †)	18–12–61	10	6

	Date of chart entry	*Highest position reached*	*Number of weeks in charts*
FRANCIS, CONNIE (cont.)			
Don't Break The Heart That Loves You			
(US) MGM	3–3–62	1	8
Second Hand Love			
(US) MGM	2–6–62	7	5
Vacation			
(US) MGM	18–8–62	9	4
(UK) MGM	*18–8–62*	*10*	*4*
I'm Gonna Be Warm This Winter			
(US) MGM	26–1–63	18	1
Follow The Boys			
(US) MGM	6–4–63	17	3
FRANKLIN, ARETHA			
I Never Loved A Man The Way I Loved You			
(US) Atlantic	25–3–67	9	7
Respect			
(US) Atlantic	13–5–67	1	9
(UK) Atlantic	*8–7–67*	*10*	*5*
Baby I Love You			
(US) Atlantic	12–8–67	4	7
Natural Woman			
(US) Atlantic	14–10–67	8	6
Chain Of Fools			
(US) Atlantic	23–12–67	2	9
(Sweet Sweet Baby) Since You've Been Gone			
(US) Atlantic (b/w *)	9–3–68	5	8
Ain't No Way*			
(US) Atlantic	4–5–68	16	2
Think			
(US) Atlantic	25–5–68	7	8
House That Jack Built			
(US) Atlantic (b/w **)	31–8–68	6	6
I Say A Little Prayer**			
(UK) Atlantic	*24–8–68*	*4*	*8*
(US) Atlantic	14–9–68	10	5
See Saw			
(US) Atlantic	7–12–68	14	5
The Weight			
(US) Atlantic	22–3–69	19	2
Share Your Love With Me			
(US) Atlantic	6–9–69	13	3
Eleanor Rigby			
(US) Atlantic	6–12–69	17	2
Call Me/Son Of A Preacher Man			
(US) Atlantic	21–3–70	13	4

	Date of chart entry	Highest position reached	Number of weeks in charts
FRANKLIN, ARETHA (cont.)			
Don't Play That Song			
(US) Atlantic	5–9–70	11	5
(UK) Atlantic	*12–9–70*	*13*	*5*
You're All I Need			
(US) Atlantic	3–4–71	19	1
Bridge Over Troubled Waters/ Brand New Me			
(US) Atlantic	1–5–71	6	8
Spanish Harlem			
(US) Atlantic	14–8–71	2	9
(UK) Atlantic	*23–10–71*	*14*	*3*
Rock Steady			
(US) Atlantic	20–11–71	9	5
Day Dreaming			
(US) Atlantic	1–4–72	5	9
Angel			
(US) Atlantic	1–9–73	20	1
Until You Come Back (That's What I'm Gonna Do)			
(US) Atlantic	29–12–73	3	12
I'm In Love			
(US) Atlantic	25–5–74	19	3
FRED, JOHN, AND HIS PLAYBOY BAND			
Judy In Disguise (With Glasses)			
(US) Paula	23–12–67	1	11
(UK) Pye	*20–1–68*	*3*	*7*
FREDDIE AND THE DREAMERS			
If You Gotta Make A Fool Of Somebody			
(UK) Columbia	*1–6–63*	*3*	*9*
I'm Telling You Now			
(UK) Columbia	*17–8–63*	*2*	*8*
(US) Tower	27–3–65	1	7
You Were Made For Me			
(UK) Columbia	*23–11–63*	*3*	*10*
Over You			
(UK) Columbia	*29–2–64*	*13*	*6*
I Love You Baby			
(UK) Columbia	*6–6–64*	*16*	*3*
I Understand			
(UK) Columbia	*5–12–64*	*5*	*8*
Do The Freddie			
(US) Mercury	5–6–65	18	1

	Date of chart entry	Highest position reached	Number of weeks in charts
FREE			
All Right Now			
(UK) Island	*20–6–70*	*2*	*11*
(US) A & M	19–9–70	4	10
(UK) Island (re-issue)	*11–8–73*	*15*	*3*
My Brother Jake			
(UK) Island	*15–5–71*	*4*	*7*
Little Bit Of Love			
(UK) Island	*17–6–72*	*13*	*5*
Wishing Well			
(UK) Island	*20–1–73*	*7*	*5*
FREEMAN, BOBBY			
Do You Want To Dance?			
(US) Josie	26–5–58	5	11
C'mon and Swim			
(US) Autumn	8–8–64	5	6
FREEMAN, ERNIE			
Raunchy			
(US) Imperial	25–11–57	12	9
FREE MOVEMENT			
I've Found Someone Of My Own			
(US) Decca	9–10–71	5	7
FRIEND AND LOVER			
Reach Out Of The Darkness			
(US) Verve Forecast	22–6–68	10	6
FRIENDS OF DISTINCTION			
Grazin' In The Grass			
(US) RCA	17–5–69	6	8
Going In Circles			
(US) RCA	1–11–69	15	6
Love Me Or Let Me Be Lonely			
(US) RCA	4–4–70	6	8
FRIJID PINK			
House Of The Rising Sun			
(US) Parrot	14–3–70	7	7
(UK) Deram	*25–4–70*	*4*	*8*
FROMAN, JANE			
I Wonder			
(UK) Capitol	*17–6–55*	*14*	*4*
FULLER, BOBBY, FOUR			
I Fought The Law			
(US) Mustang	26–2–66	9	5

	Date of chart entry	*Highest position reached*	*Number of weeks in charts*
FURY, BILLY			
Maybe Tomorrow *(UK) Decca*	*11–4–59*	*17*	*4*
Colette *(UK) Decca*	*6–3–60*	*18*	*2*
That's Love *(UK) Decca*	*5–6–60*	*20*	*1*
Halfway To Paradise *(UK) Decca*	*21–5–61*	*4*	*18*
Jealousy *(UK) Decca*	*9–9–61*	*4*	*7*
I'd Never Find Another You *(UK) Decca*	*9–12–61*	*4*	*12*
Letter Full Of Tears *(UK) Decca*	*17–3–62*	*20*	*1*
Last Night Was Made For Love *(UK) Decca*	*19–5–62*	*4*	*11*
Once Upon A Dream *(UK) Decca*	*11–8–62*	*7*	*8*
Because Of Love *(UK) Decca*	*10–11–62*	*18*	*1*
Like I've Never Been Gone *(UK) Decca*	*2–3–63*	*3*	*10*
When Will You Say I Love You? *(UK) Decca*	*25–5–63*	*3*	*9*
In Summer *(UK) Decca*	*3–8–63*	*5*	*8*
Somebody Else's Girl *(UK) Decca*	*12–10–63*	*18*	*2*
Do You Really Love Me Too (Fool's Errand) *(UK) Decca*	*11–1–64*	*13*	*5*
I Will *(UK) Decca*	*9–5–64*	*14*	*6*
It's Only Make Believe *(UK) Decca*	*1–8–64*	*10*	*5*
I'm Lost Without You *(UK) Decca*	*6–2–65*	*16*	*3*
In Thoughts Of You *(UK) Decca*	*7–8–65*	*9*	*5*
GALLERY			
Nice To Be With You (US) Sussex	27–5–72	4	7
GARDNER, DON AND FORD, DEE DEE			
I Need Your Loving (US) Fire	28–7–62	20	2

	Date of chart entry	Highest position reached	Number of weeks in charts
GARFUNKEL, ART			
All I Know			
(US) Columbia	13–10–73	9	7
[see also: SIMON AND GARFUNKEL]			
GARLAND, JUDY			
The Man That Got Away			
(UK) Philips	*10–6–55*	*18*	*2*
GARNETT, GALE			
We'll Sing In The Sunshine			
(US) RCA	14–9–64	4	9
GAYE, MARVIN			
Pride And Joy			
(US) Tamla	6–7–63	10	4
You're A Wonderful One			
(US) Tamla	4–4–64	15	5
Once Upon A Time (with MARY WELLS)			
(US) Motown (b/w *)	6–6–64	19	3
What's The Matter With You Baby? (with MARY WELLS)*			
(US) Motown	4–7–64	17	1
Try It Baby			
(US) Tamla	4–7–64	15	5
How Sweet It Is (To Be Loved By You)			
(US) Tamla	2–1–65	6	7
I'll Be Doggone			
(US) Tamla	17–4–65	8	6
Ain't That Peculiar			
(US) Tamla	30–10–65	8	7
It Takes Two (with KIM WESTON)			
(US) Tamla	18–2–67	14	3
(UK) Motown	*18–2–67*	*16*	*5*
Ain't No Mountain High Enough (with TAMMI TERRELL)			
(US) Tamla	15–7–67	19	2
Your Precious Love (with TAMMI TERRELL)			
(US) Tamla	14–10–67	5	7
If I Could Build My Whole World Around You (with TAMMI TERRELL)			
(US) Tamla	30–12–67	10	4
Ain't Nothing Like The Real Thing (with TAMMI TERRELL)			
(US) Tamla	18–5–68	8	5

	Date of chart entry	*Highest position reached*	*Number of weeks in charts*
GAYE, MARVIN (cont.)			
You're All I Need To Get By (with TAMMI TERRELL)			
(US) Tamla	24–8–68	7	5
(UK) Motown	*16–11–68*	*19*	*1*
I Heard It Through The Grapevine			
(US) Tamla	30–11–68	1	13
(UK) Motown	*1–3–69*	*1*	*10*
Too Busy Thinking About My Baby			
(US) Tamla	24–5–69	4	10
(UK) Motown	*16–8–69*	*5*	*8*
That's The Way Love Is			
(US) Tamla	27–9–69	7	6
Onion Song (with TAMMI TERRELL)			
(UK) Motown	*29–11–69*	*9*	*8*
Abraham, Martin and John			
(UK) Tamla-Motown	*30–5–70*	*9*	*7*
What's Going On			
(US) Tamla	13–3–71	2	11
Mercy Mercy (The Ecology)			
(US) Tamla	24–7–71	4	8
Inner City Blues (Make Me Want To Holler)			
(US) Tamla	30–10–71	9	4
Trouble Man			
(US) Tamla	13–1–73	7	6
Let's Get It On			
(US) Tamla	4–8–73	1	15
[see also: ROSS, DIANA]			
GAYNOR, GLORIA			
Never Can Say Goodbye			
(US) MGM	28–12–74	9	7
G-CLEFS			
I Understand (Just How You Feel)			
(US) Terrace	23–10–61	9	7
(UK) London	*16–12–61*	*20*	*1*
GEILS, J., BAND			
Must Of Got Lost			
(US) Atlantic	14–12–74	12	4
GENE AND DEBBE			
Playboy			
(US) TRX	13–4–68	17	3
GENTRY, BOBBIE			
Ode To Billie Joe			
(US) Capitol	19–8–67	1	10
(UK) Capitol	*7–10–67*	*13*	*6*

	Date of chart entry	*Highest position reached*	*Number of weeks in charts*
GENTRY, BOBBIE (cont.)			
I'll Never Fall In Love Again			
(UK) Capitol	*13–9–69*	*1*	*10*
[see also: CAMPBELL, GLEN]			
GENTRYS			
Keep On Dancing			
(US) MGM	2–10–65	4	7
GEORDIE			
All Because Of You			
(UK) EMI	*14–4–73*	*6*	*6*
Can You Do It?			
(UK) EMI	*23–6–73*	*13*	*4*
GEORGE, BARBARA			
I Know			
(US) AFO	6–1–62	3	8
GERRARD, DANYEL			
Butterfly			
(UK) CBS	*2–10–71*	*11*	*5*
GERRY AND THE PACEMAKERS			
How Do You Do It?			
(UK) Columbia	*23–3–63*	*1*	*10*
(US) Laurie (re-issue)	15–8–64	10	5
I Like It			
(UK) Columbia	*8–6–63*	*1*	*12*
(US) Laurie (re-issue)	31–10–64	17	2
You'll Never Walk Alone			
(UK) Columbia	*19–10–63*	*1*	*14*
I'm The One			
(UK) Columbia	*25–1–64*	*2*	*9*
Don't Let The Sun Catch You Crying			
(UK) Columbia	*25–4–64*	*6*	*6*
(US) Laurie	13–6–64	4	7
I'll Be There			
(US) Laurie	19–1–65	14	3
(UK) Columbia	*3–4–65*	*12*	*4*
Ferry Cross The Mersey			
(UK) Columbia	*9–1–65*	*8*	*7*
(US) Laurie	27–2–65	6	7
GETZ, STAN AND BYRD, CHARLIE			
Desafinado			
(US) Verve	10–11–62	15	5
(UK) HMV	*15–12–62*	*13*	*5*
GETZ, STAN AND GILBERTO, ASTRUD			
Girl From Ipanema			
(US) Verve	27–6–64	5	8

	Date of chart entry	*Highest position reached*	*Number of weeks in charts*
GIBB, ROBIN			
Saved By The Bell			
(UK) Polydor	*19–7–69*	*2*	*10*
[see also: BEE GEES]			
GIBBS, GEORGIA			
Tweedle Dee			
(US) Mercury	5–2–55	3	17
(UK) Mercury	*22–4–55*	*20*	*1*
Dance With Me Henry			
(US) Mercury	2–4–55	2	16
GIBSON, DON			
Oh Lonesome Me			
(US) Victor	14–4–58	8	11
Sea Of Heartbreak			
(UK) RCA	*2–9–61*	*14*	*7*
GILKYSON, TERRY, AND THE EASYRIDERS			
Marianne			
(US) Columbia	23–2–57	5	10
GILLIES, STUART			
Amanda			
(UK) Philips	*7–4–73*	*13*	*5*
GILMER, JIMMY, AND THE FIREBALLS			
Sugar Shack			
(US) Dot	28–9–63	1	12
Daisy Petal Pickin'			
(US) Dot	25–1–64	15	4
GLAHE, WILL			
Liechtensteiner Polka			
(US) London	16–12–57	19	2
GLAZER, TOM, AND THE CHILDREN'S CHORUS			
On Top Of Spaghetti			
(US) Kapp	29–6–63	14	3
GLITTER, GARY			
Rock And Roll			
(UK) Bell (Part 2)	*24–6–72*	*2*	*10*
(US) Bell	26–8–72	7	5
I Didn't Know I Loved You Till I Saw You Rock And Roll			
(UK) Bell	*30–9–72*	*4*	*7*

	Date of chart entry	*Highest position reached*	*Number of weeks in charts*
GLITTER, GARY (cont.)			
Do You Wanna Touch Me			
(UK) Bell	*27–1–73*	*2*	*7*
Hello Hello I'm Back Again			
(UK) Bell	*7–4–73*	*2*	*10*
I'm The Leader Of The Gang			
(UK) Bell	*21–7–73*	*1*	*8*
I Love You Love Me Love			
(UK) Bell	*17–11–73*	*1*	*12*
Remember Me This Way			
(UK) Bell	*30–3–74*	*3*	*6*
Always Yours			
(UK) Bell	*15–6–74*	*1*	*6*
Oh Yes, You're Beautiful (with GLITTER BAND)			
(UK) Bell	*23–11–74*	*2*	*6*
GLITTER BAND			
Angel Face			
(UK) Bell	*30–3–74*	*4*	*7*
Just For You			
(UK) Bell	*17–8–74*	*10*	*4*
Let's Get Together			
(UK) Bell	*26–10–74*	*8*	*5*
[see also: GLITTER, GARY]			
GODSPELL			
Day By Day			
(US) Bell	22–7–72	13	4
GOLDEN EARRING			
Radar Love			
(UK) Track	*12–1–74*	*7*	*6*
(US) Track	6–7–74	13	5
GOLDSBORO, BOBBY			
See The Funny Little Clown			
(US) United Artists	22–2–64	9	5
Little Things			
(US) United Artists	13–3–65	13	4
Honey			
(US) United Artists	6–4–68	1	11
(UK) United Artists	*4–5–68*	*2*	*11*
Autumn Of My Life			
(US) United Artists	3–8–68	19	2
Watching Scotty Grow			
(US) United Artists	6–2–71	11	5
Summer (The First Time)			
(UK) United Artists	*18–8–73*	*9*	*5*
Hello Summertime			
(UK) United Artists	*17–8–74*	*14*	*6*

	Date of chart entry	*Highest position reached*	*Number of weeks in charts*
GOODIES			
The Inbetweenies/Father Christmas Do Not Touch Me			
(UK) Bradleys	*21–12–74*	*7*	*5*
GOODWIN, RON			
Blue Star			
(UK) Parlophone	*28–10–55*	*20*	*1*
GOONS			
I'm Walking Backwards For Christmas			
(UK) Decca	*6–7–56*	*4*	*8*
Bloodnock's Rock And Roll/Ying Tong Song			
(UK) Decca	*14–9–56*	*3*	*8*
Ying Tong Song			
(UK) Decca (re-issue)	*4–8–73*	*9*	*4*
GORE, LESLEY			
It's My Party			
(US) Mercury	25–5–63	1	9
(UK) Mercury	*6–7–63*	*9*	*6*
Judy's Turn To Cry			
(US) Mercury	27–7–63	5	7
She's A Fool			
(US) Mercury	26–10–63	5	9
You Don't Own Me			
(US) Mercury	18–1–64	2	8
That's The Way Boys Are			
(US) Mercury	18–4–64	12	4
Maybe I Know			
(US) Mercury	29–8–64	14	3
(UK) Mercury	*24–10–64*	*20*	*1*
Sunshine, Lollipops and Rainbows			
(US) Mercury	24–7–65	13	3
California Nights			
(US) Mercury	18–3–67	16	2
GORME, EYDIE			
Yes My Darling Daughter			
(UK) CBS	*30–6–62*	*10*	*5*
Blame It On The Bossa Nova			
(US) Columbia	16–2–63	7	8
[see also: LAWRENCE, STEVE]			
GOULET, ROBERT			
My Love Forgive Me			
(US) Columbia	2–1–65	16	2

	Date of chart entry	*Highest position reached*	*Number of weeks in charts*
GRACIE, CHARLIE			
Butterfly			
(US) Cameo	2–3–57	7	12
(UK) Parlophone	*17–5–57*	*12*	*3*
Fabulous			
(UK) Parlophone	*21–6–57*	*8*	*13*
Wanderin' Eyes			
(UK) London	*30–8–57*	*6*	*11*
I Love You So Much It Hurts			
(UK) London	*30–8–57*	*14*	*2*
GRAMMER, BILLY			
Gotta Travel On			
(US) Monument	15–12–58	4	12
GRAND FUNK (RAILROAD*)			
We're An American Band*			
(US) Capitol	25–8–73	1	10
Walk Like A Man			
(US) Capitol	19–1–74	19	2
Locomotion			
(US) Capitol	13–4–74	1	10
Shinin' On			
(US) Capitol	10–8–74	11	4
GRANT, EARL			
The End			
(US) Decca	29–9–58	7	11
GRANT, GOGI			
Suddenly There's A Valley			
(US) Era	15–10–55	14	9
Wayward Wind			
(US) Era	19–5–56	1	19
(UK) London	*29–6–56*	*9*	*9*
GRASS ROOTS			
Let's Live For Today			
(US) Dunhill	10–6–67	8	6
Midnight Confession			
(US) Dunhill	28–9–68	5	10
I'd Wait A Million Years			
(US) Dunhill	30–8–69	15	4
Temptation Eyes			
(US) Dunhill	13–3–71	15	5
Sooner Or Later			
(US) Dunhill	10–7–71	9	5
Two Divided By Love			
(US) Dunhill	20–11–71	16	3

	Date of chart entry	*Highest position reached*	*Number of weeks in charts*
GRAY, DOBIE			
The 'In' Crowd			
(US) Charger	6–2–65	13	3
Drift Away			
(US) Decca	21–4–73	5	9
GREAN, CHARLES RANDOLPH SOUNDS			
Quentin's Theme			
(US) Ranwood	19–7–69	13	5
GREAVES, R.B.			
Take A Letter Maria			
(US) Atco	8–11–69	2	10
GREGORY, IAN			
Time Will Tell			
(UK) Pye	*4–12–60*	*17*	*3*
GREEN, AL			
Tired Of Being Alone			
(US) Hi	18–9–71	11	10
(UK) London	*23–10–71*	*4*	*6*
Let's Stay Together			
(US) Hi	25–12–71	1	12
(UK) London	*22–1–72*	*7*	*7*
Look What You Done For Me			
(US) Hi	15–4–72	4	9
I'm Still In Love With You			
(US) Hi	29–7–72	3	8
You Ought To Be With Me			
(US) Hi	18–11–72	3	8
Call Me (Come Back Home)			
(US) Hi	17–3–73	10	6
Here I Am (Come Take Me)			
(US) Hi	4–8–73	10	8
Living For You			
(US) Hi	19–1–74	19	1
Sha La La (Makes Me Happy)			
(US) Hi	23–11–74	7	7
(UK) London	*21–12–74*	*20*	*1*
GREENBAUM, NORMAN			
Spirit In The Sky			
(US) Reprise	21–3–70	3	10
(UK) Reprise	*4–4–70*	*1*	*11*
GREENE, GARLAND			
Jealous Kind Of Fellow			
(US) UNI	1–11–69	20	1

	Date of chart entry	*Highest position reached*	*Number of weeks in charts*
GREENE, LORNE			
Ringo			
(US) RCA	14-11-64	1	9
GREYHOUND			
Black And White			
(UK) Trojan	*3-7-71*	*6*	*8*
Moon River			
(UK) Trojan	*29-1-72*	*12*	*3*
I Am What I Am			
(UK) Trojan	*29-4-72*	*20*	*1*
GUESS WHO			
Those Eyes			
(US) RCA	3-5-69	6	9
Laughing			
(US) RCA	9-8-69	10	5
No Time			
(US) RCA	31-1-70	5	7
American Woman (b/w No Sugar Tonight)			
(US) RCA	4-4-70	1	12
(UK) RCA	*4-7-70*	*19*	*1*
Hand Me Down World			
(US) RCA	29-8-70	17	3
Share The Land			
(US) RCA	21-11-70	10	5
Rain Dance			
(US) RCA	2-10-71	19	2
Clap For The Wolfman			
(US) RCA	31-8-74	6	7
GUITAR, BONNIE			
Dark Moon			
(US) Dot	6-5-57	8	7
GUN			
Race With The Devil			
(UK) CBS	*7-12-68*	*8*	*7*
GUTHRIE, ARLO			
City Of New Orleans			
(US) Reprise	7-10-72	18	4
HALEY, BILL, AND THE COMETS			
Shake, Rattle And Roll			
(US) Decca	1-1-55	12	4
(UK) Brunswick	*7-1-55*	*4*	*11*
Dim Dim The Lights			
(US) Decca	1-1-55	11	7

	Date of chart entry	*Highest position reached*	*Number of weeks in charts*
HALEY, BILL (cont.)			
Rock Around The Clock			
(UK) Brunswick	*7-1-55*	*17*	*2*
(US) Decca	21-5-55	1	22
(UK) Brunswick (re-entry)	*14-10-55*	*1*	*17*
(UK) Brunswick (re-entry)	*21-9-56*	*5*	*11*
(UK) MCA (re-issue)	*6-4-68*	*20*	*1*
(UK) MCA (re-issue)	*6-7-74*	*12*	*5*
Mambo Rock			
(US) Decca	19-3-55	18	1
(UK) Brunswick	*15-4-55*	*14*	*2*
Razzle Dazzle			
(US) Decca	23-7-55	15	2
(UK) Brunswick	*28-9-56*	*13*	*4*
Burn That Candle			
(US) Decca	31-12-55	20	2
Rock-a-Beatin' Boogie			
(UK) Brunswick	*6-1-56*	*4*	*8*
See You Later Alligator			
(US) Decca	28-1-56	6	12
(UK) Brunswick	*9-3-56*	*7*	*11*
(UK) Brunswick (re-entry)	*28-9-56*	*12*	*6*
Saints Rock And Roll			
(UK) Brunswick	*1-6-56*	*5*	*22*
Rockin' Through The Rye			
(UK) Brunswick	*17-8-56*	*3*	*19*
Rip It Up			
(UK) Brunswick	*16-11-56*	*4*	*14*
Don't Knock The Rock			
(UK) Brunswick	*8-3-57*	*7*	*7*
Rock The Joint			
(UK) Brunswick	*1-2-57*	*20*	*1*
HALL, LARRY			
Sandy			
(US) Strand	28-12-59	15	5
HALL, TOM T.			
I Love			
(US) Mercury	2-2-74	12	5
HAMILTON IV, GEORGE			
Rose And A Baby Ruth			
(US) ABC-Paramount	24-11-56	6	11
Why Don't They Understand?			
(US) ABC-Paramount	27-1-58	17	2
Abilene			
(US) RCA	10-8-63	15	2

	Date of chart entry	Highest position reached	Number of weeks in charts
HAMILTON, ROY			
Unchained Melody			
(US) Epic	30–4–55	9	13
Don't Let Go			
(US) Epic	10–2–58	13	4
You Can Have Her			
(US) Epic	6–3–61	12	2
HAMILTON, RUSS			
We Will Make Love			
(UK) Oriole (b/w)*	*7–6–57*	*2*	*16*
Rainbow*			
(US) Kapp	19–8–57	7	11
Wedding Ring			
(UK) Oriole	*18–10–57*	*20*	*1*
HAMILTON, JOE FRANK AND REYNOLDS			
Don't Pull Your Love			
(US) Dunhill	19–6–71	4	8
HAMLICH, MARVIN			
The Entertainer			
(US) MCA	27–4–74	3	9
HAMMOND, ALBERT			
It Never Rains In Southern California			
(US) Mums	25–11–72	5	8
Free Electric Band			
(UK) Mums	*11–8–73*	*19*	*1*
HAPPENINGS			
See You In September			
(US) B. T. Puppy	6–8–66	3	8
Go Away Little Girl			
(US) B. T. Puppy	22–10–66	12	4
I Got Rhythm			
(US) B. T. Puppy	6–5–67	3	7
My Mommy			
(US) B. T. Puppy	5–8–67	13	4
HARDY, FRANÇOISE			
All Over The World			
(UK) Pye	*17–4–65*	*16*	*7*
HARNELL, JOE, AND ORCHESTRA			
Fly Me To The Moon Bossa Nova			
(US) Kapp	9–2–63	14	4

	Date of chart entry	Highest position reached	Number of weeks in charts
HARPER'S BIZARRE			
59th Street Bridge Song			
(US) Warner Brothers	25–3–67	13	4
HARRIS, ANITA			
Just Loving You			
(UK) CBS	*29–7–67*	*6*	*15*
HARRIS, JET			
Theme From 'The Man With The Golden Arm'			
(UK) Decca	*1–9–62*	*12*	*7*
HARRIS, JET AND MEEHAN, TONY			
Diamonds			
(UK) Decca	*20–1–63*	*1*	*10*
Scarlett O'Hara			
(UK) Decca	*4–5–63*	*2*	*10*
Applejack			
(UK) Decca	*14–9–63*	*4*	*7*
HARRIS, MAX			
Gurney Slade			
(UK) Philips	*27–11–60*	*10*	*4*
HARRIS, RICHARD			
MacArthur Park			
(US) Dunhill	1–6–68	2	8
(UK) RCA	*6–7–68*	*4*	*7*
HARRIS, ROLF			
Tie Me Kangaroo Down			
(UK) Columbia	*24–7–60*	*7*	*8*
(US) Epic	29–6–63	3	5
Sun Arise			
(UK) Columbia	*10–11–62*	*3*	*12*
Two Little Boys			
(UK) Columbia	*29–11–69*	*1*	*15*
HARRIS, THURSTON			
Little Bittle Pretty One			
(US) Aladdin	4–11–57	6	8
HARRISON, GEORGE			
My Sweet Lord (b/w Isn't It A Pity?)			
(US) Apple	5–12–70	1	12
(UK) Apple	*23–1–71*	*1*	*12*
What Is Life			
(US) Apple	13–3–71	10	6

	Date of chart entry	*Highest position reached*	*Number of weeks in charts*
HARRISON, GEORGE (cont.)			
Give Me Love			
(US) Apple	2–6–73	1	9
(UK) Apple	*9–6–73*	*8*	*6*
Dark Horse			
(US) Apple	28–12–74	15	3
[see also: BEATLES]			
HARRISON, NOEL			
Windmills Of Your Mind			
(UK) Reprise	*15–3–69*	*8*	*9*
HARRISON, WILBERT			
Kansas City			
(US) Fury	4–5–59	1	10
HARRY J AND THE ALL STARS			
The Liquidator			
(UK) Trojan	*15–11–69*	*9*	*13*
HART, FREDDIE			
Easy Loving			
(US) Capitol	30–10–71	17	5
HATHAWAY, DONNY. See FLACK, ROBERTA			
HAVENS, RICHIE			
Here Comes The Sun			
(US) Stormy Forest	15–5–71	16	4
HAWKINS, EDWIN, SINGERS			
Oh Happy Day			
(US) Pavillion	10–5–69	4	3
(UK) Buddah	*31–5–69*	*2*	*8*
[see also: MELANIE]			
HAWKWIND			
Silver Machine			
(UK) United Artists	*22–7–72*	*3*	*10*
HAYES, BILL			
Ballad Of Davy Crockett			
(US) Cadence	26–2–55	1	20
(UK) London	*6–1–56*	*2*	*9*
HAYES, ISAAC			
Theme From 'Shaft'			
(US) Enterprise/MGM	23–10–71	1	10
(UK) Stax	*4–12–71*	*4*	*8*

	Date of chart entry	*Highest position reached*	*Number of weeks in charts*
HAYMAN, RICHARD AND AUGUST, JAN			
Theme From 'Three Penny Opera'			
(US) Mercury	25–2–56	12	6
HAZLEWOOD, LEE. See SINATRA, NANCY			
HEAD, MURRAY (WITH THE TRINIDAD SINGERS)			
Superstar			
(US) Decca (re-issue)	22–5–71	14	5
HEAD, ROY			
Treat Her Right			
(US) Back Beat	25–9–65	2	7
HEATH, TED			
Faithful Hussar			
(UK) Decca	*3–8–56*	*18*	*3*
Swingin' Shepherd Blues			
(UK) Decca	*28–3–58*	*3*	*10*
HEBB, BOBBY			
Sunny			
(US) Philips	30–7–66	2	8
(UK) Philips	*1–10–66*	*12*	*3*
HEDGEHOPPERS ANONYMOUS			
It's Good News Week			
(UK) Decca	*21–10–65*	*5*	*6*
HEINZ			
Just Like Eddie			
(UK) Decca	*24–8–63*	*5*	*10*
HELLO			
Tell Him			
(UK) Bell	*30–11–74*	*6*	*5*
HELMS, BOBBY			
My Special Angel			
(US) Decca	4–11–57	7	12
Jingle Bell Rock			
(US) Decca	6–1–58	6	3
Jacqueline			
(UK) Brunswick	*8–8–58*	*20*	*1*
HELMS, JIMMY			
Gonna Make You An Offer You Can't Refuse			
(UK) Cube	*3–3–73*	*8*	*5*

	Date of chart entry	Highest position reached	Number of weeks in charts
HENDERSON, JOE 'MR PIANO'			
Sing It With Joe			
(UK) Polygon	*3–6–55*	*14*	*7*
Trudie			
(UK) Pye Nixa	*8–8–58*	*14*	*6*
HENDERSON, JOE			
Snap Your Fingers			
(US) Todd	16–6–62	8	6
HENDRIX, JIMI, EXPERIENCE			
Hey Joe			
(UK) Polydor	*21–1–67*	*6*	*5*
Purple Haze			
(UK) Track	*15–4–67*	*3*	*8*
And The Wind Cries Mary			
(UK) Track	*20–5–67*	*6*	*5*
Burning Of The Midnight Lamp			
(UK) Track	*9–9–67*	*18*	*4*
All Along The Watchtower			
(US) Reprise	19–10–68	20	2
(UK) Track	*2–11–68*	*5*	*6*
Voodoo Chile			
(UK) Track	*7–11–70*	*1*	*10*
HENRY, CLARENCE 'FROGMAN'			
But I Do			
(US) Argo	27–3–61	4	7
(UK) Pye International	*7–5–61*	*5*	*11*
You Always Hurt The One You Love			
(US) Argo	5–6–61	12	5
(UK) Pye International	*15–7–61*	*9*	*8*
HERD			
From The Underworld			
(UK) Fontana	*7–10–67*	*6*	*8*
Paradise Lost			
(UK) Fontana	*20–1–68*	*15*	*3*
I Don't Want Our Loving To Die			
(UK) Fontana	*4–5–68*	*5*	*8*
HERMAN'S HERMITS			
I'm Into Something Good			
(UK) Columbia	*4–9–64*	*1*	*10*
(US) MGM	21–11–64	13	6
Show Me Girl			
(UK) Columbia	*5–12–64*	*19*	*3*
Silhouettes			
(UK) Columbia	*27–2–65*	*3*	*9*
(US) MGM	17–4–65	5	9

	Date of chart entry	Highest position reached	Number of weeks in charts
HERMAN'S HERMITS (cont.)			
Can't You Hear My Heartbeat?			
(US) MGM	6–3–65	2	8
Mrs. Brown You've Got A Lovely Daughter			
(US) MGM	17–4–65	1	10
Wonderful World			
(UK) Columbia	*1–5–65*	*7*	*7*
(US) MGM	12–6–65	4	6
I'm Henry VIII I Am			
(US) MGM	10–7–65	1	8
Just A Little Bit Better			
(UK) Columbia	*18–9–65*	*15*	*5*
(US) MGM	9–10–65	7	4
A Must To Avoid			
(UK) Columbia	*8–1–66*	*6*	*7*
(US) MGM	8–1–66	8	6
Listen People			
(US) MGM	26–2–66	3	6
You Won't Be Leaving			
(UK) Columbia	*16–4–66*	*20*	*2*
Leaning On A Lamp Post			
(US) MGM	23–4–66	9	5
This Door Swings Both Ways			
(UK) Columbia	*9–7–66*	*18*	*2*
(US) MGM	30–7–66	12	4
Dandy			
(US) MGM	15–10–66	5	6
No Milk Today*			
(UK) Columbia	*15–10–66*	*7*	*7*
There's A Kind Of A Hush			
(US) MGM (b/w*)	11–3–67	4	6
(UK) Columbia	*25–2–67*	*7*	*7*
Don't Go Out In The Rain (You're Going To Melt)			
(US) MGM	22–7–67	18	1
I Can Take Or Leave Your Loving			
(UK) Columbia	*27–1–68*	*11*	*6*
Sleepy Joe			
(UK) Columbia	*11–5–68*	*12*	*6*
Sunshine Girl			
(UK) Columbia	*3–8–68*	*8*	*8*
Something's Happening			
(UK) Columbia	*4–1–69*	*6*	*9*
My Sentimental Friend			
(UK) Columbia	*3–5–69*	*2*	*7*
Years May Come, Years May Go			
(UK) Columbia	*21–2–70*	*7*	*7*

[see also: NOONE, PETER]

	Date of chart entry	Highest position reached	Number of weeks in charts
HEYWOOD, EDDIE			
Soft Summer Breeze			
(US) Mercury	4–8–56	12	12
Canadian Sunset (with HUGO WINTERHALTER)			
(US) Victor	11–8–56	2	18
HIBBLER, AL			
Unchained Melody			
(US) Decca	9–4–55	5	18
(UK) Brunswick	*13–5–55*	*2*	*17*
He			
(US) Decca	1–10–55	7	20
After The Lights Go Down Low			
(US) Decca	15–9–56	15	5
HIGHWAYMEN			
Michael			
(US) United Artists	7–8–61	1	10
(UK) HMV	*9–9–61*	*1*	*9*
Cotton Fields			
(US) United Artists	13–1–62	13	7
HILL, BENNY			
Pepys' Diary/Gather in the Mushrooms			
(UK) Pye	*5–2–61*	*13*	*5*
Harvest of Love			
(UK) Pye	*1–6–63*	*20*	*2*
Ernie (The Fastest Milkman In The West)			
(UK) Columbia	*20–11–71*	*1*	*10*
HILL, VINCE			
Take Me To Your Heart Again			
(UK) Columbia	*22–1–66*	*13*	*1*
Edelweiss			
(UK) Columbia	*18–2–67*	*2*	*11*
Roses of Picardy			
(UK) Columbia	*3–6–67*	*13*	*4*
Look Around			
(UK) Columbia	*30–10–71*	*12*	*6*
HILLSIDE SINGERS			
I'd Like To Teach The World To Sing			
(US) Metromedia	1–1–72	13	5
HILLTOPPERS			
Kentuckian Song			
(US) Dot	13–8–55	20	1

	Date of chart entry	*Highest position reached*	*Number of weeks in charts*
HILLTOPPERS (cont.)			
Only You			
(US) Dot	12–11–55	9	12
(UK) London	*27–1–56*	*3*	*21*
Marianne			
(US) Dot	16–2–57	8	11
(UK) London	*5–4–57*	*20*	*1*
HILTON, RONNIE			
I Still Believe			
(UK) HMV	*7–1–55*	*4*	*8*
Veni Vidi Vici			
(UK) HMV	*7–1–55*	*12*	*4*
A Blossom Fell			
(UK) HMV	*11–3–55*	*10*	*7*
Stars Shine In Your Eyes			
(UK) HMV	*26–8–55*	*13*	*7*
Yellow Rose Of Texas			
(UK) HMV	*11–11–55*	*15*	*2*
Young And Foolish			
(UK) HMV	*10–2–56*	*17*	*3*
No Other Love			
(UK) HMV	*20–4–56*	*1*	*13*
Who Are We			
(UK) HMV	*13–7–56*	*6*	*8*
Two Different Worlds			
(UK) HMV	*23–11–56*	*13*	*7*
Around The World			
(UK) HMV	*24–5–57*	*4*	*15*
HINTON, JOE			
Funny			
(US) Back Beat	26–9–64	13	4
HIRT, AL			
Java			
(US) RCA	8–2–64	4	9
Cotton Candy			
(US) RCA	30–5–64	15	2
HOCKRIDGE, EDMUND			
Young And Foolish			
(UK) Nixa	*17–2–56*	*10*	*7*
Fountains Of Rome			
(UK) Pye Nixa	*7–9–56*	*17*	*4*
HODGES, EDDIE			
I'm Gonna Knock On Your Door			
(US) Cadence	21–8–61	12	3
(UK) London	*23–9–61*	*20*	*1*
(Girls Girls Girls) Made To Love			
(US) Cadence	21–7–62	14	5

	Date of chart entry	*Highest position reached*	*Number of weeks in charts*
HOLDEN, ROD			
Love You So			
(US) Donna	16–5–60	7	7
HOLLIDAY, MICHAEL			
Nothin' to Do			
(UK) Columbia	*30–3–56*	*20*	*1*
Gal With The Yaller Shoes			
(UK) Columbia	*15–6–56*	*13*	*3*
Hot Diggity			
(UK) Columbia	*22–6–56*	*14*	*4*
Story Of My Life			
(UK) Columbia	*17–1–58*	*1*	*14*
Stairway Of Love			
(UK) Columbia	*23–5–58*	*3*	*11*
Starry Eyed			
(UK) Columbia	*2–1–60*	*2*	*9*
HOLLIES			
Searchin'			
(UK) Parlophone	*28–9–63*	*12*	*6*
Stay			
(UK) Parlophone	*14–12–63*	*8*	*10*
Just One Look			
(UK) Parlophone	*7–3–64*	*2*	*9*
Here I Go Again			
(UK) Parlophone	*30–5–64*	*4*	*7*
We're Through			
(UK) Parlophone	*3–10–64*	*7*	*7*
Yes I Will			
(UK) Parlophone	*20–2–65*	*9*	*7*
I'm Alive			
(UK) Parlophone	*12–6–65*	*1*	*10*
Look Through Any Window			
(UK) Parlophone	*11–9–65*	*4*	*8*
If I Needed Someone			
(UK) Parlophone	*15–1–66*	*20*	*1*
I Can't Let Go			
(UK) Parlophone	*5–3–66*	*2*	*6*
Bus Stop			
(UK) Parlophone	*25–6–66*	*5*	*7*
(US) Imperial	3–9–66	5	6
Stop Stop Stop			
(UK) Parlophone	*22–10–66*	*2*	*8*
(US) Imperial	19–11–66	7	6
On A Carousel			
(UK) Parlophone	*25–2–67*	*4*	*7*
(US) Imperial	29–4–67	11	7
Carrie Anne			
(UK) Parlophone	*10–6–67*	*3*	*8*
(US) Epic	29–7–67	9	6

	Date of chart entry	Highest position reached	Number of weeks in charts
HOLLIES (cont.)			
King Midas In Reverse			
(UK) Parlophone	*14–10–67*	*18*	*3*
Jennifer Eccles			
(UK) Parlophone	*13–4–68*	*7*	*6*
Listen To Me			
(UK) Parlophone	*19–10–68*	*11*	*6*
Sorry Suzanne			
(UK) Parlophone	*15–3–69*	*3*	*7*
He Ain't Heavy He's My Brother			
(UK) Parlophone	*11–10–69*	*3*	*8*
(US) Epic	28–2–70	7	7
I Can't Tell The Bottom From The Top			
(UK) Parlophone	*2–5–70*	*7*	*5*
Gasoline Alley Bred			
(UK) Parlophone	*17–10–70*	*14*	*4*
Long Cool Woman			
(US) Epic	22–7–72	2	9
Air That I Breathe			
(UK) Polydor	*23–2–74*	*2*	*7*
(US) Epic	29–6–74	6	7
HOLLOWAY, BRENDA			
Every Little Bit Hurts			
(US) Tamla	30–5–64	13	4
HOLLY, BUDDY			
Peggy Sue			
(US) Coral	2–12–57	3	13
(UK) Coral	*3–1–58*	*6*	*12*
Listen To Me			
(UK) Coral	*14–3–58*	*16*	*1*
Rave On			
(UK) Coral	*27–6–58*	*5*	*12*
Early In The Morning			
(UK) Coral	*29–8–58*	*17*	*2*
It Doesn't Matter Anymore			
(UK) Coral	*7–3–59*	*1*	*19*
(US) Coral	16–3–59	13	4
Peggy Sue Got Married			
(UK) Coral	*12–9–59*	*14*	*8*
Baby I Don't Care			
(UK) Coral	*2–7–61*	*13*	*7*
Reminiscing			
(UK) Coral	*6–10–62*	*17*	*2*
Brown Eyed Handsome Man			
(UK) Coral	*16–3–63*	*3*	*10*
Bo Diddley			
(UK) Coral	*15–6–63*	*4*	*8*

	Date of chart entry	Highest position reached	Number of weeks in charts
HOLLY, BUDDY (cont.)			
Wishing			
(UK) Coral	*14–9–63*	*10*	*7*
[see also: CRICKETS]			
HOLLYWOOD ARGYLES			
Alley-Oop			
(US) Lute	13–6–60	1	10
HOLLYWOOD FLAMES			
Buzz Buzz Buzz			
(US) Ebb	20–1–58	11	3
HOLMAN, EDDIE			
Hey There Lonely Girl			
(US) ABC	24–1–70	2	8
(UK) ABC (re-issue)	*26–10–74*	*4*	*7*
HOLMES, CLINT			
Playground In My Mind			
(US) Epic	26–5–73	2	10
HOMBRES			
Let It Out			
(US) Verve Forecast	28–10–67	12	5
HOMER AND JETHRO			
Battle Of Kookamouga			
(US) RCA	21–9–59	14	5
HONDELLS			
Little Honda			
(US) Mercury	17–10–64	9	5
HONEYBUS			
I Can't Let Maggie Go			
(UK) Deram	*14–4–68*	*8*	*6*
HONEYCOMBS			
Have I The Right?			
(UK) Pye	*8–8–64*	*1*	*11*
(US) Interphon	17–10–64	5	7
That's The Way			
(UK) Pye	*4–9–65*	*12*	*7*
HONEY CONE			
Want Ads			
(US) Hot Wax	8–5–71	1	11
Stick Up			
(US) Hot Wax	4–9–71	11	7
One Monkey Don't Stop No Show			
(US) Hot Wax	1–1–72	15	4

	Date of chart entry	*Highest position reached*	*Number of weeks in charts*
HOPKIN, MARY			
Those Were The Days			
(UK) Apple	*14–9–68*	*1*	*14*
(US) Apple	12–10–68	2	11
Goodbye			
(UK) Apple	*19–4–69*	*2*	*8*
(US) Apple	17–5–69	13	4
Temma Harbour			
(UK) Apple	*7–2–70*	*6*	*6*
Knock Knock Who's There?			
(UK) Apple	*28–3–70*	*2*	*7*
Think About Your Children			
(UK) Apple	*14–11–70*	*19*	*2*
HORTON, JOHNNY			
Battle Of New Orleans			
(US) Columbia	18–5–59	1	14
(UK) Philips	*18–7–59*	*16*	*1*
Sink The Bismarck			
(US) Columbia	28–3–60	3	10
North To Alaska			
(US) Columbia	7–11–60	4	14
(UK) Philips	*8–1–61*	*15*	*4*
HOT BUTTER			
Popcorn			
(UK) Pye International	*29–7–72*	*5*	*8*
(US) Musicor	16–9–72	10	6
HOT CHOCOLATE			
Love Is Life			
(UK) RAK	*22–8–70*	*6*	*8*
I Believe In Love			
(UK) RAK	*11–9–71*	*8*	*6*
Brother Louie			
(UK) RAK	*28–4–73*	*7*	*6*
Emma			
(UK) RAK	*23–3–74*	*3*	*7*
HOTLEGS			
Neanderthal Man			
(UK) Fontana	*25–7–70*	*2*	*9*
HOTSHOTS			
Snoopy Versus The Red Baron			
(UK) Mooncrest	*16–6–73*	*4*	*8*
HUDSON, FORD			
Pick Up The Pieces			
(UK) A & M	*1–9–73*	*8*	*4*

	Date of chart entry	Highest position reached	Number of weeks in charts
HUDSON, FORD (cont.)			
Burn Baby Burn			
(UK) A & M	*2–3–74*	*15*	*4*
[see also: STRAWBS]			
HUES CORPORATION			
Rock The Boat			
(US) RCA	22–6–74	1	7
(UK) RCA	*3–8–74*	*6*	*5*
Rockin' Soul			
(US) RCA	16–11–74	18	2
HUGHES, JIMMY			
Steal Away			
(US) Fame	1–8–64	17	3
HUMAN BEINZ			
Nobody But Me			
(US) Capitol	13–1–68	8	8
HUMBLE PIE			
Natural Born Bugie			
(UK) Immediate	*30–8–69*	*4*	*7*
HUMPERDINCK, ENGELBERT			
Release Me			
(UK) Decca	*11–2–67*	*1*	*15*
(US) Parrot	6–5–67	4	8
There Goes My Everything			
(UK) Decca	*3–6–67*	*2*	*13*
(US) Parrot	29–7–67	20	1
The Last Waltz			
(UK) Decca	*26–8–67*	*1*	*21*
Am I That Easy To Forget?			
(UK) Decca	*20–1–68*	*3*	*9*
(US) Parrot	27–1–68	18	3
Man Without Love			
(UK) Decca	*4–5–68*	*2*	*9*
(US) Parrot	22–6–68	19	1
Les Bicyclettes De Belsize			
(UK) Decca	*12–10–68*	*5*	*7*
The Way It Used To Be			
(UK) Decca	*15–2–69*	*3*	*9*
I'm A Better Man			
(UK) Decca	*23–8–69*	*16*	*4*
Winterworld Of Love			
(UK) Decca	*22–11–69*	*7*	*9*
(US) Parrot	24–1–70	16	2
Another Time Another Place			
(UK) Decca	*2–10–71*	*13*	*4*
Too Beautiful To Last			
(UK) Decca	*25–3–72*	*14*	*4*

	Date of chart entry	Highest position reached	Number of weeks in charts
100 PROOF AGED IN SOUL			
Somebody's Been Sleepin'			
(US) Hot Wax	24–10–70	8	6
HUNTER, IVORY JOE			
Since I Met You Baby			
(US) Atlantic	14–12–56	12	9
HUNTER, TAB			
Young Love			
(US) Dot	19–1–57	1	14
(UK) London	*8–2–57*	*1*	*17*
Ninety-Nine Ways			
(UK) London	*12–4–57*	*5*	*10*
(US) Dot	13–4–57	11	5
HUSKY, FERLIN			
Gone			
(US) Capitol	30–3–57	4	13
Wings Of A Dove			
(US) Capitol	9–1–61	12	8
HYLAND, BRIAN			
Itsy Bitsy Teenie Weenie Yellow Polka Dot Bikini			
(UK) London	*10–7–60*	*9*	*8*
(US) Leader	11–7–60	1	10
Let Me Belong To You			
(US) ABC-Paramount	25–9–61	20	1
Ginny Come Lately			
(UK) HMV	*19–5–62*	*5*	*12*
Sealed With A Kiss			
(US) ABC-Paramount	7–7–62	3	8
(UK) HMV	*18–8–62*	*3*	*10*
Joker Went Wild			
(US) Philips	3–9–66	20	1
Gypsy Woman			
(US) UNI	7–11–70	3	9
HYMAN, DICK, TRIO			
Theme From 'Threepenny Opera'			
(US) MGM	11–2–56	9	11
(UK) MGM	*16–3–56*	*9*	*9*
IAN, JANIS			
Society's Child			
(US) Verve	8–7–67	14	3
IDES OF MARCH			
Vehicle			
(US) Warner Brothers	25–4–70	2	7

	Date of chart entry	Highest position reached	Number of weeks in charts
IFIELD, FRANK			
I Remember You			
(UK) Columbia	*14–7–62*	*1*	*21*
(US) Vee Jay	29–9–62	5	5
Lovesick Blues			
(UK) Columbia	*27–10–62*	*1*	*15*
Wayward Wind			
(UK) Columbia	*3–2–63*	*1*	*10*
Nobody's Darling But Mine			
(UK) Columbia	*20–4–63*	*4*	*10*
I'm Confessin'			
(UK) Columbia	*6–7–63*	*1*	*12*
Don't Blame Me			
(UK) Columbia	*18–1–64*	*8*	*7*
IKETTES			
I'm Blue (The Gong-Gong Song)			
(US) Atco	17–2–62	19	3
IMPALAS			
Sorry, I Ran All The Way Home			
(US) Cub	20–4–59	2	10
IMPRESSIONS			
Gypsy Woman			
(US) ABC-Paramount	4–12–61	20	2
It's All Right			
(US) ABC-Paramount	26–10–63	4	8
Talking About My Baby			
(US) ABC-Paramount	1–2–64	12	5
I'm So Proud			
(US) ABC-Paramount	9–5–64	14	4
Keep On Pushing			
(US) ABC-Paramount	11–7–64	10	5
You Must Believe Me			
(US) ABC-Paramount	3–10–64	15	4
Amen			
(US) ABC-Paramount	26–12–64	7	5
People Get Ready			
(US) ABC-Paramount	20–3–65	14	2
We're A Winner			
(US) ABC	17–2–68	14	4
Finally Got Myself Together (I'm A Changed Man)			
(US) Curtom	20–7–74	17	2
[see also: BUTLER, JERRY]			
INGMANN, JORGEN			
Apache			
(US) Atco	27–2–61	2	10

	Date of chart entry	Highest position reached	Number of weeks in charts
INGRAM, LUTHER			
(If Loving You Is Wrong) I Don't Want To Be Right			
(US) Koko	24-6-72	3	11
INK SPOTS			
Melody Of Love			
(UK) Parlophone	*29-4-55*	*14*	*4*
INTRUDERS			
Cowboys To Girls			
(US) Gamble	13-4-68	6	9
She's A Winner			
(UK) Philadelphia International (re-issue)	*20-7-74*	*14*	*5*
IRISH ROVERS			
Unicorn			
(US) Decca	20-4-68	7	7
IRWIN, BIG DEE (with LITTLE EVA			
Swinging On A Star			
(UK) Colpix	*21-12-63*	*7*	*9*
ISLANDERS			
Enchanted Sea			
(US) Mayflower	9-11-59	15	3
ISLEY BROTHERS			
Twist And Shout			
(US) Wand	28-7-62	17	4
This Old Heart Of Mine			
(US) Tamla	2-4-66	12	4
(UK) Tamla-Motown	*2-11-68*	*3*	*9*
I Guess I'll Always Love You			
(UK) Tamla-Motown	*1-2-69*	*11*	*5*
It's Your Thing			
(US) T-Neck	5-4-69	2	10
Behind A Painted Smile			
(UK) Tamla-Motown	*3-5-69*	*5*	*7*
Put Yourself In My Place			
(UK) Tamla-Motown	*27-9-69*	*13*	*2*
Love The One You're With			
(US) T-Neck	7-8-71	18	2
That Lady			
(US) T-Neck	8-9-73	6	10
(UK) Epic	*20-10-73*	*14*	*2*
Summer Breeze			
(UK) Epic	*15-6-74*	*16*	*3*
IVES, BURL			
A Little Bitty Tear			
(US) Decca	13-1-62	9	8
(UK) Brunswick	*10-2-62*	*12*	*7*

	Date of chart entry	*Highest position reached*	*Number of weeks in charts*
IVES, BURL (cont.)			
Funny Way Of Laughin'			
(US) Decca	28–4–62	10	5
Call Me Mr. In-Between			
(US) Decca	25–8–62	19	1
IVY LEAGUE			
Funny How Love Can Be			
(UK) Piccadilly	*13–2–65*	*8*	*6*
Tossing And Turning			
(UK) Piccadilly	*10–7–65*	*3*	*8*
IVY THREE			
Yogi			
(US) Shell	29–8–60	8	6
JACKS, TERRY			
Seasons In The Sun			
(US) Bell	16–2–74	1	10
(UK) Bell	*23–3–74*	*1*	*9*
If You Go Away			
(UK) Bell	*13–7–74*	*8*	*4*
JACKSON, DEON			
Love Makes The World Go Round			
(US) Carala	12–3–66	11	5
JACKSON, JERMAINE			
Daddy's Home			
(US) Motown	10–2–73	9	7
[see also: JACKSON FIVE]			
JACKSON, MICHAEL			
Got To Be There			
(US) Motown	13–11–71	4	11
(UK) Tamla-Motown	*26–2–72*	*5*	*5*
Rockin' Robin			
(US) Motown	25–3–72	2	9
(UK) Tamla-Motown	*10–6–72*	*3*	*7*
I Wanna Be Where You Are			
(US) Motown	8–7–72	16	3
Ain't No Sunshine			
(UK) Tamla-Motown	*2–9–72*	*8*	*6*
Ben			
(US) Motown	16–9–72	1	9
(UK) Tamla-Motown	*2–12–72*	*7*	*8*
[see also: JACKSON FIVE]			
JACKSON, STONEWALL			
Waterloo			
(US) Columbia	22–6–59	4	9

	Date of chart entry	Highest position reached	Number of weeks in charts
JACKSON FIVE			
I Want You Back			
(US) Motown	13–12–69	1	13
(UK) Tamla-Motown	*14–2–70*	*2*	*9*
ABC			
(US) Motown	21–3–70	1	11
(UK) Tamla-Motown	*23–5–70*	*8*	*5*
The Love You Save (b/w I Found That Girl)			
(US) Motown	6–6–70	1	11
(UK) Tamla-Motown	*15–8–70*	*7*	*4*
I'll Be There			
(US) Motown	26–9–70	1	14
(UK) Tamla-Motown	*5–12–70*	*4*	*11*
Mama's Pearl			
(US) Motown	13–2–71	2	7
Never Can Say Goodbye			
(US) Motown	10–4–71	2	10
Maybe Tomorrow			
(US) Motown	21–8–71	20	1
Sugar Daddy			
(US) Motown	8–1–72	10	5
Little Bitty Pretty One			
(US) Motown	13–5–72	13	4
Lookin' Through The Windows			
(US) Motown	19–8–72	16	2
(UK) Tamla-Motown	*25–11–72*	*9*	*3*
Corner Of The Sky			
(US) Motown	9–12–72	18	2
Doctor My Eyes			
(UK) Tamla-Motown	*24–2–73*	*9*	*5*
Hallelujah Day			
(UK) Tamla-Motown	*30–6–73*	*20*	*2*
Dancing Machine			
(US) Motown	13–4–74	2	13
JACKY			
White Horses			
(UK) Philips	*27–4–68*	*10*	*9*
[see also: LEE, JACKIE]			
JACOBS, DICK			
Petticoats Of Portugal			
(US) Coral	8–12–56	20	1
JAGGERZ			
The Rapper			
(US) Kama Sutra	21–2–70	2	9

	Date of chart entry	*Highest position reached*	*Number of weeks in charts*
JAMES, DICK			
Robin Hood			
(UK) Parlophone	*20–1–56*	*14*	*8*
Garden Of Eden			
(UK) Parlophone	*25–1–57*	*18*	*2*
JAMES, JONI			
How Important Can It Be			
(US) MGM	19–2–55	8	13
You Are My Love			
(US) MGM	5–11–55	15	6
There Goes My Heart			
(US) MGM	17–11–58	19	1
JAMES, SONNY			
Young Love			
(US) Capitol	12–1–57	2	14
(UK) Capitol	*8–2–57*	*11*	*7*
JAMES, TOMMY			
Draggin' The Line			
(US) Roulette	10–7–71	4	8
[see also: JAMES, TOMMY, AND THE SHONDELLS]			
JAMES, TOMMY, AND THE SHONDELLS			
Hanky Panky			
(US) Roulette	25–6–66	1	8
I Think We're Alone Now			
(US) Roulette	18–3–67	4	10
Mirage			
(US) Roulette	20–5–67	10	5
Gettin' Together			
(US) Roulette	23–9–67	18	2
Mony Mony			
(US) Roulette	18–5–68	3	9
(UK) Roulette	*6–7–68*	*1*	*11*
Crimson And Clover			
(US) Roulette	4–1–69	1	13
Sweet Cherry Wine			
(US) Roulette	12–4–69	7	6
Crystal Blue Persuasion			
(US) Roulette	28–6–69	2	11
Ball Of Fire			
(US) Roulette	8–11–69	19	2
JAN AND ARNIE			
Jennie Lee			
(US) Arwin	2–6–58	8	7

	Date of chart entry	Highest position reached	Number of weeks in charts
JAN AND DEAN			
Baby Talk			
(US) Dore	24–8–59	10	6
Surf City			
(US) Liberty	22–6–63	1	10
Honolulu Lulu			
(US) Liberty	28–9–63	11	5
Drag City			
(US) Liberty	4–1–64	10	5
Dead Man's Curve			
(US) Liberty	11–4–64	8	7
Little Old Lady From Pasadena			
(US) Liberty	11–7–64	3	7
Ride The Wild Surf			
(US) Liberty	24–10–64	16	2
JANKOWSKI, HORST			
A Walk In The Black Forest			
(US) Mercury	19–6–65	12	5
(UK) Mercury	*7–8–65*	*3*	*12*
JARMELS			
Little Bit Of Soap			
(US) Laurie	11–9–61	12	2
JAY AND THE AMERICANS			
She Cried			
(US) United Artists	21–4–62	5	8
Come A Little Bit Closer			
(US) United Artists	24–10–64	3	7
Let's Lock The Door (And Throw Away The Key)			
(US) United Artists	23–1–65	11	5
Cara Mia			
(US) United Artists	26–6–65	4	8
Some Enchanted Evening			
(US) United Artists	25–9–65	13	5
Sunday And Me			
(US) United Artists	18–12–65	18	2
This Magic Moment			
(US) United Artists	1–2–69	6	8
Walkin' In The Rain			
(US) United Artists	31–1–70	19	2
JAY AND THE TECHNIQUES			
Apples, Peaches, Pumpkin Pie			
(US) Smash	26–8–67	6	9
Keep The Ball Rollin'			
(US) Smash	2–12–67	14	4

	Date of chart entry	Highest position reached	Number of weeks in charts
JAYNETTS			
Sally Go Round The Roses			
(US) Tuff	14–9–63	2	7
JEFFERSON AIRPLANE			
Somebody To Love			
(US) RCA	27–5–67	5	6
White Rabbit			
(US) RCA	15–7–67	8	5
JEFFREY JOE GROUP			
My Pledge Of Love			
(US) Wand	26–7–69	14	4
JELLY BEANS			
I Wanna Love Him So Bad			
(US) Red Bird	25–7–64	9	5
JENSEN, KRIS			
Torture			
(US) Hickory	3–11–62	20	1
JETHRO TULL			
Living In The Past			
(UK) Island	*14–6–69*	*3*	*6*
(US) Chrysalis (re-issue)	16–12–72	11	6
Sweet Dream			
(UK) Chrysalis	*5–11–69*	*7*	*5*
Witches Promise/Teacher			
(UK) Chrysalis	*31–1–70*	*4*	*5*
Life Is A Long Song			
(UK) Chrysalis	*25–9–71*	*11*	*5*
Bungle In The Jungle			
(US) Chrysalis	21–12–74	12	5
JIMENEZ, JOSÉ			
Astronaut			
(US) Kapp	2–10–61	19	1
JIVE FIVE			
My True Story			
(US) Beltone	28–8–61	3	6
JOHN, ELTON			
Your Song			
(US) UNI	9–1–71	8	7
(UK) DJM	*6–2–71*	*7*	*6*
Rocket Man			
(UK) DJM	*6–5–72*	*2*	*8*
(US) UNI	17–6–72	6	8

	Date of chart entry	*Highest position reached*	*Number of weeks in charts*
JOHN, ELTON (cont.)			
Honky Cat			
(US) UNI	9–9–72	8	4
Crocodile Rock			
(UK) DJM	*11–11–72*	*5*	*10*
(US) MCA	30–12–72	1	12
Daniel			
(UK) DJM	*27–1–73*	*4*	*6*
(US) MCA	5–5–73	2	9
Saturday Night's All Right For Fighting			
(UK) DJM	*14–7–73*	*7*	*5*
(US) MCA	25–8–73	12	6
Goodbye Yellow Brick Road			
(UK) DJM	*6–10–73*	*6*	*7*
(US) MCA	17–11–73	2	9
Candle In The Wind			
(UK) DJM (b/w)*	*9–3–74*	*11*	*6*
Bennie And The Jets*			
(US) MCA	16–3–74	1	11
Don't Let The Sun Go Down On Me			
(UK) DJM	*15–6–74*	*16*	*5*
(US) MCA	13–7–74	2	6
The Bitch Is Back			
(UK) DJM	*5–10–74*	*15*	*2*
(US) MCA	5–10–74	4	7
Lucy In The Sky With Diamonds			
(UK) DJM	*30–11–74*	*10*	*7*
(US) MCA	14–12–74	1	8
JOHN, LITTLE WILLIE			
Talk To Me Talk To Me			
(US) King	26–5–58	20	1
Sleep			
(US) King	31–10–60	13	4
JOHN, ROBERT			
The Lion Sleeps Tonight			
(US) Atlantic	5–2–72	3	11
JOHNNIE AND JOE			
Over The Mountain			
(US) Chess	1–7–57	8	7
JOHNNY AND THE HURRICANES			
Red River Rock			
(US) Warwick	24–8–59	5	10
(UK) London	*10–10–59*	*2*	*14*

	Date of chart entry	*Highest position reached*	*Number of weeks in charts*
JOHNNY AND THE HURRICANES (cont.)			
Reveille Rock			
(UK) London	*26–12–59*	*8*	*4*
Beatnik Fly			
(US) Warwick	7–3–60	15	5
(UK) London	*13–3–60*	*9*	*10*
Down Yonder			
(UK) London	*5–6–60*	*9*	*5*
Rocking Goose			
(UK) London	*14–10–60*	*3*	*10*
Ja Da			
(UK) London	*12–2–61*	*14*	*3*
Old Smokey			
(UK) Decca	*2–7–61*	*12*	*3*
JOHNSON, BETTY			
I Dreamed			
(US) Bally	9–2–57	12	5
Little Blue Man			
(US) Atlantic	31–3–58	19	2
JOHNSON, BRYAN			
Looking High High High			
(*UK*) *Decca*	*3–4–60*	*17*	*1*
JOHNSON, JOHNNY, AND THE BANDWAGON			
Sweet Inspiration			
(UK) Bell	*22–8–70*	*10*	*5*
Blame It On The Pony Express			
(UK) Bell	*19–12–70*	*7*	*8*
[see also: BANDWAGON]			
JOHNSON, LAURIE			
Sucu Sucu			
(UK) Pye	*30–9–61*	*5*	*8*
JOHNSON, MARV			
You've Got What It Takes			
(US) United Artists	11–1–60	10	8
(UK) London	*6–2–60*	*4*	*10*
I Love The Way You Love			
(US) United Artists	28–3–60	9	8
Move Two Mountains			
(US) United Artists	17–10–60	20	1
I'll Pick A Rose For My Rose			
(UK) Tamla-Motown	*8–2–69*	*10*	*6*
JOHNSON, TEDDY see CARR, PEARL			

	Date of chart entry	Highest position reached	Number of weeks in charts
JOHNSTON BROTHERS			
Hernando's Hideaway			
(UK) Decca	*7–10–55*	*1*	*13*
JO JO GUNNE			
Run Run Run			
(UK) Asylum	*15–4–72*	*6*	*7*
JON AND ROBIN AND THE IN CROWD			
Do It Again A Little Bit Slower			
(US) Abnak	17–6–67	18	2
JONES, JACK			
Wives And Lovers			
(US) Kapp	21–12–63	14	4
The Race Is On			
(US) Kapp	10–4–65	15	3
JONES, JIMMY			
Handy Man			
(US) Cub	25–1–60	2	12
(UK) MGM	*13–3–60*	*4*	*18*
Good Timin'			
(US) Cub	9–5–60	3	9
(UK) MGM	*12–6–60*	*1*	*10*
JONES, JOE			
You Talk Too Much			
(US) Roulette	24–10–60	3	6
JONES, PAUL			
High Time			
(UK) HMV	*29–10–66*	*4*	*8*
I've Been A Bad Bad Boy			
(UK) HMV	*28–1–67*	*5*	*6*
JONES, TOM			
It's Not Unusual			
(UK) Decca	*20–2–65*	*1*	*9*
(US) Parrot	15–5–65	10	6
What's New Pussycat?			
(US) Parrot	10–7–65	3	8
(UK) Decca	*28–8–65*	*11*	*5*
With These Hands			
(UK) Decca	*31–7–65*	*13*	*4*
Not Responsible			
(UK) Decca	*4–6–66*	*18*	*4*
Green Green Grass Of Home			
(UK) Decca	*19–11–66*	*1*	*15*
(US) Parrot	28–1–67	11	5

	Date of chart entry	*Highest position reached*	*Number of weeks in charts*
JONES, TOM (cont.)			
Detroit City			
(UK) Decca	*4–3–67*	*8*	*6*
Funny Familiar Forgotten Feelings			
(UK) Decca	*29–4–67*	*7*	*7*
I'll Never Fall In Love Again			
(UK) Decca	*5–8–67*	*2*	*10*
(US) Parrot (re-issue)	23–8–69	6	11
I'm Coming Home			
(UK) Decca	*2–12–67*	*2*	*12*
Delilah			
(UK) Decca	*9–3–68*	*2*	*12*
(US) Parrot	8–6–68	15	2
Help Yourself			
(UK) Decca	*27–7–68*	*3*	*10*
A Minute Of Your Time			
(UK) Decca	*14–12–68*	*15*	*7*
Love Me Tonight			
(UK) Decca	*17–5–69*	*9*	*6*
(US) Parrot	21–6–69	13	6
Without Love (There Is Nothing)			
(UK) Decca	*20–12–69*	*10*	*6*
(US) Parrot	10–1–70	5	7
Daughters Of Darkness			
(UK) Decca	*25–4–70*	*5*	*9*
(US) Parrot	23–5–70	13	4
I (Who Have Nothing)			
(US) Parrot	5–9–70	14	5
(UK) Decca	*5–9–70*	*16*	*1*
She's A Lady			
(UK) Decca	*30–1–71*	*13*	*5*
(US) Parrot	27–2–71	2	10
Till			
(UK) Decca	*30–10–71*	*2*	*10*
Young New Mexican Puppeteer			
(UK) Decca	*8–4–72*	*6*	*6*
JOPLIN, JANIS			
Me And Bobby McGee			
(US) Columbia	27–2–71	1	10
[see also: BIG BROTHER AND THE HOLDING COMPANY]			
JUDGE DREAD			
Big Six			
(UK) Big Shot	*23–9–72*	*11*	*8*
Big Seven			
(UK) Big Shot	*23–12–72*	*8*	*7*
Big Eight			
(UK) Big Shot	*28–4–73*	*14*	*5*

	Date of chart entry	*Highest position reached*	*Number of weeks in charts*
JUICY LUCY			
Who Do You Love?			
(UK) Vertigo	*4-4-70*	*14*	*4*
JUNE, ROSEMARY			
I'll Be With You In Appleblossom Time			
(UK) Pye	*7-2-59*	*12*	*4*
JUSTICE, JIMMY			
When My Little Girl Is Smiling			
(UK) Pye	*21-4-62*	*9*	*7*
Ain't That Funny			
(UK) Pye	*23-6-62*	*8*	*7*
Spanish Harlem			
(UK) Pye	*15-9-62*	*20*	*1*
JUSTIS, BILL			
Raunchy			
(US) Philips International	25-11-57	3	11
(UK) London	*14-2-58*	*11*	*4*
KAEMPFERT, BERT			
Wonderland By Night			
(US) Decca	28-11-60	1	13
Red Roses For A Blue Lady			
(US) Decca	27-2-65	11	7
KALIN TWINS			
When			
(US) Decca	7-7-58	5	9
(UK) Brunswick	*25-7-58*	*1*	*16*
Forget Me Not			
(US) Decca	27-10-58	12	6
KALLEN, KITTY			
My Coloring Book			
(US) RCA	2-2-63	18	1
KANE, EDEN			
Well I Ask You			
(UK) Decca	*28-5-61*	*1*	*16*
Get Lost			
(UK) Decca	*16-9-61*	*7*	*5*
Forget Me Not			
(UK) Decca	*27-1-62*	*4*	*10*
I Don't Know Why			
(UK) Decca	*26-5-62*	*7*	*8*
Boys Cry			
(UK) Fontana	*22-2-64*	*8*	*7*

	Date of chart entry	*Highest position reached*	*Number of weeks in charts*
KASENATZ KATZ SINGING ORCHESTRAL CIRCUS			
Quick Joey Small			
(UK) Buddah	*1–2–69*	*19*	*1*
KAYE SISTERS			
Paper Roses			
(UK) Philips	*31–7–60*	*10*	*8*
[see also: THREE KAYES; FRANKIE VAUGHAN]			
K.C. AND THE SUNSHINE BAND			
Queen Of Clubs			
(UK) Jay Boy	*7–9–74*	*7*	*6*
Sound Your Funky Horn			
(UK) Jay Boy	*21–12–74*	*17*	*1*
K-DOE, ERNIE			
Mother-In-Law			
(US) Minit	10–4–61	1	9
KEATING, JOHNNY			
Theme From 'Z Cars'			
(UK) Piccadilly	*10–3–62*	*8*	*10*
KEITH			
98.6			
(US) Mercury	21–1–67	7	6
KELLER, JERRY			
Here Comes Summer			
(US) Kapp	3–8–59	14	3
(UK) London	*29–8–59*	*2*	*12*
KELLY, GRACE. See CROSBY, BING			
KELLY, KEITH			
Ooh! La La			
(UK) Parlophone	*17–4–60*	*13*	*6*
Listen Little Girl/Uh Huh			
(UK) Parlophone	*31–7–60*	*15*	*4*
KENDRICKS, EDDIE			
Keep On Truckin'			
(US) Tamla	22–9–73	1	13
(UK) Tamla-Motown	*15–12–73*	*18*	*1*
Boogie Down			
(US) Tamla	2–2–74	2	10

	Date of chart entry	*Highest position reached*	*Number of weeks in charts*
KENNER, CHRIS			
I Like It Like That			
(US) Instant	10–7–61	2	8
KENNY			
Heart Of Stone			
(UK) RAK	*17–3–73*	*11*	*6*
KIDD, JOHNNY, AND THE PIRATES			
Shakin' All Over			
(UK) HMV	*26–6–60*	*3*	*12*
Restless			
(UK) HMV	*7–10–60*	*18*	*2*
I'll Never Get Over You			
(UK) HMV	*10–8–63*	*4*	*10*
Hungry For Love			
(UK) HMV	*7–12–63*	*20*	*1*
KIM, ANDY			
Baby, I Love You			
(US) Steed	12–7–69	9	8
Be My Baby			
(US) Steed	12–12–70	17	2
Rock Me Gently			
(US) Capitol	10–8–74	1	9
(UK) Capitol	*28–9–74*	*2*	*5*
KING, B.B.			
The Thrill Is Gone			
(US) Blues Way	14–2–70	15	4
KING, BEN E.			
First Taste Of Love*			
(UK) London	*15–1–61*	*16*	*3*
Spanish Harlem			
(US) Atco (b/w*)	27–2–61	10	5
Stand By Me			
(US) Atco	29–5–61	4	7
Amor			
(US) Atco	4–9–61	18	1
Don't Play That Song			
(US) Atco	2–6–62	11	4
[see also: DRIFTERS]			
KING, CAROLE			
It Might As Well Rain Until September			
(UK) London	*6–10–62*	*3*	*9*

	Date of chart entry	Highest position reached	Number of weeks in charts
KING, CAROLE (cont.)			
It's Too Late (b/w I Feel The Earth Move)			
(US) Ode	5–6–71	1	12
(UK) A & M	*28–8–71*	*6*	*6*
So Far Away/Smackwater Jack			
(US) Ode	25–9–71	14	5
Sweet Seasons			
(US) Ode	12–2–72	9	6
Jazzman			
(US) Ode	5–10–74	2	8
KING, CLAUDE			
Wolverton Mountain			
(US) Columbia	23–6–62	6	10
KING, DAVE			
Memories Are Made Of This			
(UK) Decca	*17–2–56*	*5*	*13*
You Can't Be True To Two			
(UK) Decca	*20–4–56*	*11*	*7*
Story Of My Life			
(UK) Decca	*24–1–58*	*20*	*1*
KING, JONATHAN			
Everyone's Gone To The Moon			
(UK) Decca	*7–8–65*	*4*	*7*
(US) Parrot	30–10–65	17	3
[see also: SAKHARIN; WEATHERMEN]			
KING, SOLOMON			
She Wears My Ring			
(UK) Columbia	*20–1–68*	*3*	*11*
KING BROTHERS			
White Sports Coat			
(UK) Parlophone	*7–6–57*	*6*	*11*
In The Middle Of An Island			
(UK) Parlophone	*20–9–57*	*19*	*3*
Standing On The Corner			
(UK) Parlophone	*17–4–60*	*9*	*5*
KING CURTIS			
Soul Twist			
(US) Enjoy	28–4–62	17	2
KING FLOYD			
Groove Me			
(US) Chimneyville	26–12–70	6	10
KING HARVEST			
Dancing In The Moonlight			
(US) Perception	27–1–73	13	7

	Date of chart entry	Highest position reached	Number of weeks in charts
KINGSMEN			
Louie Louie			
(US) Wand	7–12–63	2	10
Money			
(US) Wand	11–4–64	16	4
Jolly Green Giant			
(US) Wand	6–2–65	4	7
KINGSTON TRIO			
Tom Dooley			
(US) Capitol	13–10–58	1	5
(UK) Capitol	*21–11–58*	*4*	*12*
Tijuana Jail			
(US) Capitol	6–4–59	12	5
MTA			
(US) Capitol	6–7–59	15	4
Worried Man			
(US) Capitol	19–10–59	20	1
Reverend Mr. Black			
(US) Capitol	27–4–63	8	6
KINKS			
You Really Got Me			
(UK) Pye	*22–8–64*	*1*	*9*
(US) Reprise	7–11–64	7	8
All Day And All Of The Night			
(UK) Pye	*7–11–64*	*2*	*9*
(US) Reprise	23–1–65	7	6
Tired Of Waiting For You			
(UK) Pye	*30–1–65*	*1*	*7*
(US) Reprise	3–4–65	6	6
Everybody's Gonna Be Happy			
(UK) Pye	*10–4–65*	*11*	*3*
Set Me Free			
(UK) Pye	*12–6–65*	*9*	*6*
See My Friend			
(UK) Pye	*21–8–65*	*10*	*4*
Till The End Of The Day			
(UK) Pye	*25–12–65*	*8*	*8*
Well Respected Man			
(US) Reprise	29–1–66	13	5
Dedicated Follower Of Fashion			
(UK) Pye	*12–3–66*	*4*	*8*
Sunny Afternoon			
(UK) Pye	*18–6–66*	*1*	*9*
(US) Reprise	10–9–66	14	4
Dead End Street			
(UK) Pye	*3–12–66*	*5*	*9*
Waterloo Sunset			
(UK) Pye	*20–5–67*	*2*	*7*

	Date of chart entry	Highest position reached	Number of weeks in charts
KINKS (cont.)			
Autumn Almanac			
(UK) Pye	*28–10–67*	*3*	*7*
Days			
(UK) Pye	*3–8–68*	*12*	*6*
Lola			
(UK) Pye	*11–7–70*	*2*	*10*
(US) Reprise	10–10–70	9	6
Apeman			
(UK) Pye	*2–1–71*	*5*	*9*
Supersonic Rocketship			
(UK) RCA	*17–6–72*	*16*	*3*
KIRBY, KATHY			
Dance On			
(UK) Decca	*31–8–63*	*11*	*5*
Secret Love			
(UK) Decca	*16–11–63*	*4*	*11*
Let Me Go Lover			
(UK) Decca	*7–3–64*	*10*	*6*
You're The One			
(UK) Decca	*30–5–64*	*17*	*2*
KISSON, MAC AND KATIE			
Chirpy Chirpy Cheep Cheep			
(US) ABC	2–10–71	20	2
KITT, EARTHA			
Under The Bridges Of Paris			
(UK) HMV	*4–4–55*	*7*	*9*
KNICKERBOCKERS			
Lies			
(US) Challenge	22–1–66	20	1
KNIGHT, GLADYS, AND THE PIPS			
Letter Full Of Tears			
(US) Fury	10–2–62	19	1
Take Me In Your Arms And Love Me			
(UK) Tamla-Motown	*22–7–67*	*13*	*3*
I Heard It Through The Grapevine			
(US) Soul	25–11–67	2	11
End Of Our Road			
(US) Soul	9–3–68	15	4
Nitty Gritty			
(US) Soul	13–9–69	19	1
Friendship Train			
(US) Soul	13–12–69	17	3
If I Were Your Woman			
(US) Soul	9–1–71	9	7

	Date of chart entry	Highest position reached	Number of weeks in charts
KNIGHT, GLADYS (cont.)			
I Don't Want To Do Wrong			
(US) Soul	3–7–71	17	5
Help Me Make It Through The Night			
(UK) Tamla-Motown	*9–12–72*	*11*	*8*
Neither Of Us (Wants To Say Goodbye)			
(US) Soul	3–3–73	2	9
Daddy Could Swear I Declare			
(US) Soul	7–7–73	19	1
Midnight Train To Georgia			
(US) Buddah	29–9–73	1	12
I've Got To Use My Imagination			
(US) Buddah	22–12–73	4	9
The Best Thing That Ever Happened To Me			
(US) Buddah	23–3–74	3	9
On And On			
(US) Buddah	22–6–74	5	7
[see also: PIPS]			
KNIGHT, JEAN			
Mr. Big Stuff			
(US) Stax	26–6–71	2	11
KNIGHT, ROBERT			
Everlasting Love			
(US) Rising Sons	11–11–67	13	4
(UK) Monument (re-issue)	*30–3–74*	*19*	*2*
Love On A Mountain Top			
(UK) Monument	*15–12–73*	*10*	*9*
KNIGHT, SONNY			
Confidential			
(US) Dot	15–12–56	20	2
KNOX, BUDDY			
Party Doll			
(US) Roulette	9–3–57	2	13
Hula Love			
(US) Roulette	30–9–57	12	8
KOKOMO			
Asia Minor			
(US) Felsted	27–3–61	8	5
KONGOS, JOHN			
He's Gonna Step On You Again			
(UK) Fly	*12–6–71*	*4*	*8*
Tokoloshe Man			
(UK) Fly	*27–11–71*	*4*	*7*

	Date of chart entry	*Highest position reached*	*Number of weeks in charts*
KOOL AND THE GANG			
Jungle Boogie			
(US) De Lite	26–1–74	4	11
Hollywood Swinging			
(US) De Lite	8–6–74	6	7
KRAMER, BILLY J., AND THE DAKOTAS			
Do You Want To Know A Secret?			
(UK) Parlophone	*11–5–63*	*2*	*12*
Bad To Me			
(UK) Parlophone	*10–8–63*	*1*	*9*
(US) Imperial (b/w*)	20–6–64	9	5
I'll Keep You Satisfied			
(UK) Parlophone	*16–11–63*	*4*	*6*
Little Children*			
(UK) Parlophone	*7–3–74*	*1*	*9*
(US) Imperial	16–5–64	7	9
From A Window			
(UK) Parlophone	*8–8–64*	*10*	*4*
Trains Boats And Planes			
(UK) Parlophone	*29–5–65*	*12*	*4*
KRISTOFFERSON, KRIS			
Why Me			
(US) Monument	3–11–73	16	3
KUBAN, BOB, AND THE IN-MEN			
Cheater			
(US) Musicland USA	26–2–66	12	4
KUNZ, CHARLIE			
Piano Medley			
(UK) Decca	*14–1–55*	*16*	*1*
LAINE, CLEO			
You'll Answer To Me			
(UK) Fontana	*16–9–61*	*4*	*9*
LAINE, FRANKIE			
Rain Rain Rain			
(UK) Philips	*7–1–55*	*8*	*9*
In The Beginning			
(UK) Philips	*11–3–55*	*20*	*1*
Cool Water			
(UK) Philips	*24–6–55*	*2*	*22*
Strange Lady In Town			
(UK) Philips	*15–7–55*	*6*	*13*
Humming Bird			
(UK) Philips	*11–11–55*	*16*	*1*

	Date of chart entry	*Highest position reached*	*Number of weeks in charts*
LAINE, FRANKIE (cont.)			
Hawkeye			
(UK) Philips	*25–11–55*	*7*	*8*
Sixteen Tons			
(UK) Philips	*20–1–56*	*10*	*3*
Woman In Love			
(UK) Philips	*14–9–56*	*1*	*19*
Moonlight Gambler			
(UK) Philips	*28–12–56*	*13*	*9*
(US) Columbia	29–12–56	3	13
Love Is A Golden Ring			
(UK) Philips	*10–5–57*	*19*	*2*
Rawhide			
(UK) Philips	*14–11–59*	*11*	*11*
LANE, RONNIE			
How Come			
(UK) GM	*26–1–74*	*11*	*4*
[see also: FACES; SMALL FACES]			
LANG, DON			
Cloudburst			
(UK) HMV	*4–11–55*	*16*	*4*
Witch Doctor			
(UK) HMV	*23–5–58*	*5*	*10*
LANSON, SNOOKY			
It's Almost Tomorrow			
(US) Dot	17–12–55	20	1
LANZA, MARIO			
Drinking Song			
(UK) HMV	*4–2–55*	*13*	*1*
I'll Walk With God			
(UK) HMV	*18–2–55*	*18*	*1*
(UK) HMV (re-entry)	*6–5–55*	*20*	*1*
Serenade			
(UK) HMV	*22–4–55*	*15*	*3*
LARKS			
The Jerk			
(US) Money	19–12–64	7	7
LA ROSA, JULIUS			
Domani			
(US) Cadence	30–7–55	13	4
Torero			
(UK) *RCA*	*1–8–58*	*15*	*3*
LA SALLE, DENISE			
Trapped By A Thing Called Love			
(US) Westbound	9–10–71	13	5

	Date of chart entry	Highest position reached	Number of weeks in charts
LAWRENCE, LEE			
Suddenly There's A Valley			
(UK) Columbia	*2–12–55*	*14*	*3*
LAWRENCE, STEVE			
Party Doll			
(US) Coral	16–3–57	10	11
Pretty Blue Eyes			
(US) ABC-Paramount	14–12–59	9	11
Footsteps			
(US) ABC-Paramount	4–4–60	7	6
(UK) HMV	*10–4–60*	*9*	*9*
Portrait Of My Love			
(US) United Artists	24–4–61	9	6
Go Away Little Girl			
(US) Columbia	8–12–62	1	12
I Want To Stay Here (with EYDIE GORME)			
(UK) CBS	*31–8–63*	*3*	*8*
LAWRENCE, VICKI			
The Night The Lights Went Out In Georgia			
(US) Bell	24–3–73	1	10
LEANDROS, VICKY			
Come What May			
(UK) Philips	*22–4–72*	*2*	*8*
LED ZEPPELIN			
Whole Lotta Love			
(US) Atlantic	20–12–69	4	9
Immigrant Song			
(US) Atlantic	16–1–71	16	3
Black Dog			
(US) Atlantic	12–2–72	15	2
D'Yer Mak'Er			
(US) Atlantic	29–12–73	20	1
LEE, BRENDA			
Sweet Nothin's			
(US) Decca	29–2–60	4	11
(UK) Brunswick	*3–4–60*	*5*	*14*
I'm Sorry			
(US) Decca	20–6–60	1	13
(UK) Brunswick (b/w)*	*3–7–60*	*10*	*10*
That's All You Gotta Do*			
(US) Decca	27–6–60	6	6
I Want To Be Wanted			
(US) Decca	3–10–60	1	9

	Date of chart entry	*Highest position reached*	*Number of weeks in charts*
LEE, BRENDA (cont.)			
Rockin' Around The Christmas Tree			
(US) Decca	26–12–60	14	2
(UK) Brunswick	*8–12–62*	*5*	*5*
Emotions			
(US) Decca	23–1–61	7	6
Let's Jump The Broomstick			
(UK) Brunswick	*12–2–61*	*15*	*3*
You Can Depend On Me			
(US) Decca	10–4–61	6	7
Dum, Dum			
(US) Decca	3–7–61	4	9
Fool No. 1			
(US) Decca	30–10–61	3	8
(UK) Brunswick	*18–11–61*	*18*	*2*
Break It To Me Gently			
(US) Decca	27–1–62	4	9
Speak To Me Pretty			
(UK) Brunswick	*21–4–62*	*3*	*8*
Everybody Loves Me But You			
(US) Decca (b/w**)	5–5–62	6	6
Here Comes That Feeling**			
(UK) Brunswick	*7–7–62*	*5*	*8*
Heart In Hand			
(US) Decca (b/w***)	11–8–62	15	3
It Started All Over Again***			
(UK) Brunswick	*6–10–62*	*15*	*5*
All Alone Am I			
(US) Decca	20–10–62	3	9
(UK) Brunswick	*27–1–63*	*7*	*8*
Losing You			
(UK) Brunswick	*20–4–63*	*10*	*8*
(US) Decca	4–5–63	6	7
I Wonder			
(UK) Brunswick	*27–7–63*	*14*	*5*
Grass Is Greener			
(US) Decca	2–11–63	17	2
As Usual			
(US) Decca	28–12–63	12	6
(UK) Brunswick	*18–1–64*	*5*	*10*
Is It True?			
(UK) Brunswick	*26–9–64*	*17*	*3*
(US) Decca	14–11–64	17	3
Too Many Rivers			
(US) Decca	17–7–65	13	3
Coming On Strong			
(US) Decca	12–11–66	11	5

	Date of chart entry	Highest position reached	Number of weeks in charts
LEE, CURTIS			
Pretty Little Angel Eyes			
(US) Dunes	31–7–61	7	5
LEE, DICKEY			
Patches			
(US) Smash	8–9–62	6	9
I Saw Him Yesterday			
(US) Smash	12–1–63	14	5
Laurie			
(US) TCF-Hall	3–7–65	14	3
LEE, JACKIE			
The Duck			
(US) Mirwood	8–1–66	14	3
LEE, JACKIE			
Rupert			
(UK) Pye	*13–2–71*	*14*	*5*
[see also: JACKY]			
LEE, LEAPY			
Little Arrows			
(UK) MCA	*7–9–68*	*2*	*13*
(US) Decca	30–11–68	16	2
LEE, PEGGY			
Mr. Wonderful			
(UK) Brunswick	*24–5–57*	*5*	*13*
Fever			
(US) Capitol	28–7–58	8	7
(UK) Capitol	*22–8–58*	*5*	*8*
Is That All There Is?			
(US) Capitol	18–10–69	11	5
LEEDS UNITED FC			
Leeds United			
(UK) Chapter One	*13–5–72*	*10*	*5*
LEFT BANKE			
Walk Away Renee			
(US) Smash	8–10–66	5	7
Pretty Ballerina			
(US) Smash	18–2–67	15	3
LEMON PIPERS			
Green Tambourine			
(US) Buddah	6–1–68	1	9
(UK) Pye International	*24–2–68*	*7*	*6*

	Date of chart entry	Highest position reached	Number of weeks in charts
LENNON, JOHN (*and the PLASTIC ONO BAND)			
Give Peace A Chance*			
(UK) Apple	*19–7–69*	*2*	*7*
(US) Apple	16–8–69	14	4
Cold Turkey*			
(UK) Apple	*5–11–69*	*14*	*5*
Instant Karma			
(UK) Apple	*21–2–70*	*5*	*6*
(US) Apple	14–3–70	3	10
Power To The People*			
(UK) Apple	*20–3–71*	*7*	*6*
(US) Apple	24–4–71	11	4
Imagine*			
(US) Apple	30–10–71	3	7
Happy Christmas (War Is Over)* (with the HARLEM COMMUNITY CHOIR)			
(UK) Apple	*16–12–72*	*4*	*5*
Mind Games			
(US) Apple	15–12–73	18	3
Whatever Gets You Through The Night			
(US) Apple	19–10–74	1	6
[see also: BEATLES]			
LENNON SISTERS			
Tonight You Belong To Me			
(US) Coral	20–10–56	15	4
LESTER, KETTY			
Love Letters			
(US) Era	24–3–62	5	7
(UK) London	*5–5–62*	*4*	*7*
LETTERMEN			
The Way You Look Tonight			
(US) Capitol	2–10–61	13	6
When I Fall In Love			
(US) Capitol	18–12–61	7	8
Come Back Silly Girl			
(US) Capitol	31–3–62	17	2
Theme From 'Summer Place'			
(US) Capitol	31–7–65	16	2
Goin' Out Of My Head/Can't Take My Eyes Off You			
(US) Capitol	27–1–68	7	6
Hurt So Bad			
(US) Capitol	30–8–69	12	6

	Date of chart entry	*Highest position reached*	*Number of weeks in charts*
LEWIS, BARBARA			
Hello Stranger			
(US) Atlantic	8–6–63	3	7
Baby I'm Yours			
(US) Atlantic	7–8–65	11	5
Make Me Your Baby			
(US) Atlantic	23–10–65	11	4
LEWIS, BOBBY			
Tossin' And Turnin'			
(US) Beltone	12–6–61	1	15
One Track Mind			
(US) Beltone	18–9–61	9	3
LEWIS, GARY, AND THE PLAYBOYS			
This Diamond Ring			
(US) Liberty	30–1–65	1	9
Count Me In			
(US) Liberty	24–4–65	2	7
Save Your Heart For Me			
(US) Liberty	24–7–65	2	7
Everybody Loves A Clown			
(US) Liberty	16–10–65	4	6
She's Just My Style			
(US) Liberty	1–1–65	3	7
Sure Gonna Miss Her			
(US) Liberty	26–3–66	9	4
Green Grass			
(US) Liberty	28–5–66	8	5
My Heart's A Symphony			
(US) Liberty	13–8–66	13	4
(You Don't Have To) Paint Me A Picture			
(US) Liberty	29–10–66	15	2
Sealed With A Kiss			
(US) Liberty	17–8–68	19	3
LEWIS, JERRY			
Rock-a-Bye Your Baby To A Dixie Melody			
(US) Decca	22–12–56	12	9
(UK) Brunswick	*8–2–57*	*12*	*5*
LEWIS, JERRY LEE			
Whole Lotta Shakin' Goin' On			
(US) Sun	19–8–57	3	13
(UK) London	*4–10–57*	*8*	*7*
Great Balls Of Fire			
(US) Sun	9–12–57	2	11
(UK) London	*20–12–57*	*1*	*11*

	Date of chart entry	*Highest position reached*	*Number of weeks in charts*
LEWIS, JERRY LEE (cont.)			
Breathless			
(US) Sun	17–3–58	7	6
(UK) London	*18–4–58*	*8*	*5*
High School Confidential			
(UK) London	*24–1–59*	*10*	*5*
Lovin' Up A Storm			
(UK) London	*2–5–59*	*20*	*1*
What'd I Say			
(UK) London	*30–4–61*	*8*	*7*
LEWIS, LINDA			
Rock A Doodle			
(UK) Raft	*7–7–73*	*15*	*3*
LEWIS, RAMSEY, TRIO			
'In' Crowd			
(US) Argo	4–9–65	5	8
Hang On Sloopy			
(US) Cadet	11–12–65	11	4
Wade In The Water			
(US) Cadet	10–9–66	19	2
LEYTON, JOHN			
Johnny Remember Me			
(UK) Top Rank	*29–7–61*	*1*	*12*
Wild Wind			
(UK) Top Rank	*30–9–61*	*2*	*7*
Son This Is She			
(UK) HMV	*9–12–61*	*12*	*4*
Lonely City			
(UK) HMV	*26–5–62*	*14*	*5*
LIBERACE			
Unchained Melody			
(UK) Philips	*17–6–55*	*20*	*1*
LIEUTENANT PIGEON			
Mouldy Old Dough			
(UK) Decca	*23–9–72*	*1*	*11*
Desperate Dan			
(UK) Decca	*13–1–73*	*17*	*3*
LIGHTFOOT, GORDON			
If You Could Read My Mind			
(US) Reprise	6–2–71	5	8
Sundown			
(US) Reprise	18–5–74	1	10
Carefree Highway			
(US) Reprise	26–10–74	10	4

	Date of chart entry	*Highest position reached*	*Number of weeks in charts*
LIMMIE AND THE FAMILY COOKING			
You Can Do Magic			
(UK) Avco	*4–8–73*	*3*	*7*
Walking Miracle			
(UK) Avco	*20–4–74*	*6*	*5*
LIND, BOB			
Elusive Butterfly			
(US) World Pacific	19–2–66	5	7
(UK) Fontana	*26–3–66*	*5*	*5*
LINDEN, KATHY			
Billy			
(US) Felsted	21–4–58	12	4
Goodbye Jimmy Goodbye			
(US) Felsted	25–5–59	11	4
LINDISFARNE			
Meet Me On The Corner			
(UK) Charisma	*11–3–72*	*5*	*6*
Lady Eleanor			
(UK) Charisma	*20–5–72*	*3*	*6*
LINDSAY, MARK			
Arizona			
(US) Columbia	24–1–70	10	7
[see also: REVERE, PAUL AND THE RAIDERS]			
LITTLE ANTHONY AND THE IMPERIALS			
Tears On My Pillow			
(US) End	8–9–58	4	10
I'm On The Outside (Looking In)			
(US) DCP	3–10–64	15	2
Goin' Out Of My Head			
(US) DCP	5–12–64	6	9
Hurt So Bad			
(US) DCP	27–2–65	10	5
Take Me Back			
(US) DCP	17–8–65	16	3
LITTLE CAESAR AND THE ROMANS			
Those Oldies But Goodies			
(US) Del Fi	12–6–61	9	6
LITTLE DIPPERS			
Forever			
(US) University	22–2–60	9	6

	Date of chart entry	Highest position reached	Number of weeks in charts
LITTLE EVA			
The Locomotion			
(US) Dimension	28–7–62	1	10
(UK) London	*22–9–62*	*2*	*12*
(UK) London (re-issue)	*19–8–72*	*11*	*5*
Keep Your Hands Off			
(US) Dimension	1–12–62	12	6
Let's Turkey Trot			
(US) Dimension	23–3–63	20	1
(UK) London	*30–3–63*	*13*	*5*
[see also: Irwin, Big Dee]			
LITTLE RICHARD			
Long Tall Sally			
(US) Specialty	21–4–56	13	7
(UK) London	*15–2–57*	*3*	*14*
The Girl Can't Help It			
(UK) London (b/w)*	*15–3–57*	*9*	*10*
She's Got It			
*(UK) London**	*22–3–57*	*15*	*4*
Jenny Jenny			
(US) Specialty	1–7–57	14	8
(UK) London	*13–9–57*	*11*	*5*
Lucille			
(UK) London	*5–7–57*	*10*	*7*
Keep A-Knockin'			
(US) Specialty	14–10–57	8	7
Good Golly Miss Molly			
(UK) London	*7–3–58*	*8*	*7*
(US) Specialty	10–3–58	10	3
Baby Face			
(UK) London	*10–1–59*	*2*	*11*
By The Light Of The Silvery Moon			
(UK) London	*4–4–59*	*15*	*3*
Bamalama Loo			
(UK) London	*27–6–64*	*20*	*1*
LITTLE TONY			
Too Good			
(UK) Decca	*2–1–60*	*13*	*4*
LIVINGSTONE, DANDY			
Suzanne Beware Of The Devil			
(UK) Horse	*23–9–72*	*14*	*5*
LOBO			
Me And You And A Dog Named Boo			
(US) Big Tree	1–5–71	5	8
(UK) Philips	*3–7–71*	*4*	*9*

	Date of chart entry	*Highest position reached*	*Number of weeks in charts*
LOBO (cont.)			
I'd Love You To Want Me			
(US) Big Tree	28–10–72	2	7
(UK) UK (re-issue)	*22–6–74*	*5*	*6*
Don't Expect Me To Be Your Friend			
(US) Big Tree	27–1–73	8	7
LOCKLIN, HANK			
Please Help Me I'm Falling			
(US) RCA	4–7–60	8	10
(UK) RCA	*4–9–60*	*10*	*10*
LOGGINS AND MESSINA			
Your Mama Don't Dance			
(US) Columbia	23–12–72	4	8
Thinking Of You			
(US) Columbia	19–5–73	18	3
My Music			
(US) Columbia	8–12–73	16	3
LOGGINS, DAVE			
Please Come To Boston			
(US) Epic	20–7–74	5	7
LOLITA			
Sailor (Your Home Is In The Sea)			
(US) Kapp	28–11–60	5	10
LONDON, JULIE			
Cry Me A River			
(US) Liberty	10–12–55	13	8
LONDON, LAURIE			
He's Got The Whole World In His Hands			
(UK) Parlophone	*29–11–57*	*12*	*8*
(US) Capitol	31–3–58	2	13
LONG, SHORTY			
Here Comes The Judge			
(US) Soul	15–6–68	8	7
LOOKING GLASS			
Brandy (You're A Fine Girl)			
(US) Epic	8–7–72	1	11
LOPEZ, TRINI			
If I Had A Hammer			
(US) Reprise	17–8–63	3	8
(UK) Reprise	*21–9–63*	*4*	*11*
Lemon Tree			
(US) Reprise	20–2–65	20	2

	Date of chart entry	Highest position reached	Number of weeks in charts
LORDAN, JERRY			
Who Could Be Bluer?			
(UK) Parlophone	*20–2–60*	*14*	*6*
LOREN, SOPHIA. See SELLERS, PETER			
LOS BRAVOS			
Black Is Black			
(UK) Decca	*16–7–66*	*2*	*9*
(US) Press	17–9–66	4	6
I Don't Care			
(UK) Decca	*8–10–66*	*16*	*3*
LOS INDIOS TABAJERAS			
Maria Elena			
(US) RCA	26–10–63	6	6
(UK) RCA	*16–11–63*	*5*	*11*
LOS MACHUCAMBOS			
Pepito			
(UK) Decca	*26–8–61*	*19*	*2*
LOSS, JOE			
Theme From 'Maigret'			
(UK) HMV	*21–4–62*	*20*	*1*
Must Be Madison			
(UK) HMV	*17–11–62*	*20*	*2*
LOUDERMILK, JOHN D.			
The Language Of Love			
(UK) RCA	*20–1–62*	*13*	*3*
LOVE AFFAIR			
Everlasting Love			
(UK) CBS	*13–1–68*	*1*	*10*
Rainbow Valley			
(UK) CBS	*11–5–68*	*5*	*8*
A Day Without Love			
(UK) CBS	*5–10–68*	*6*	*7*
One Road			
(UK) CBS	*15–3–69*	*16*	*3*
Bringing On Back The Good Times			
(UK) CBS	*2–8–69*	*9*	*5*
LOVE SCULPTURE			
Sabre Dance			
(UK) Parlophone	*14–12–68*	*6*	*8*

	Date of chart entry	*Highest position reached*	*Number of weeks in charts*
LOVE UNLIMITED			
Walking In The Rain With The One I Love			
(US) UNI	27–5–72	14	4
(UK) UNI	*8–7–72*	*14*	*4*
LOVE UNLIMITED ORCHESTRA			
Love Theme			
(US) 20th Century	5–1–74	1	11
(UK) Pye International	*9–2–74*	*10*	*6*
LOVIN' SPOONFUL			
Do You Believe In Magic			
(US) Kama Sutra	25–9–65	9	5
You Didn't Have To Be So Nice			
(US) Kama Sutra	8–1–66	10	4
Daydream			
(US) Kama Sutra	19–3–66	2	8
(UK) Pye	*23–4–66*	*2*	*8*
Did You Ever Have To Make Up Your Mind?			
(US) Kama Sutra	21–5–66	2	7
Summer In The City			
(US) Kama Sutra	30–7–66	1	8
(UK) Kama Sutra	*30–7–66*	*8*	*7*
Rain On The Roof			
(US) Kama Sutra	5–11–66	10	5
Nashville Cats			
(US) Kama Sutra	14–1–67	8	4
Darlin' Be Home Soon			
(US) Kama Sutra	11–3–67	15	2
Six O'Clock			
(US) Kama Sutra	3–6–67	18	2
LOWE, JIM			
Green Door			
(US) Dot	6–10–56	1	20
Four Walls			
(US) Dot	9–2–57	20	1
LUKE, ROBIN			
Susie Darlin'			
(US) Dot	15–9–58	5	9
LULU			
Shout (with THE LUVVERS)			
(UK) Decca	*6–6–64*	*7*	*7*
Leave A Little Love			
(UK) Decca	*3–7–65*	*8*	*5*
The Boat That I Row			
(UK) Columbia	*29–4–67*	*6*	*6*

	Date of chart entry	*Highest position reached*	*Number of weeks in charts*
LULU (cont.)			
Let's Pretend			
(UK) Columbia	*29–7–67*	*11*	*4*
To Sir With Love			
(US) Epic	7–10–67	1	11
Me, The Peaceful Heart			
(UK) Columbia	*9–3–68*	*9*	*5*
Boys			
(UK) Columbia	*29–6–68*	*15*	*2*
I'm A Tiger			
(UK) Columbia	*23–11–68*	*11*	*10*
Boom Bang-a-Bang			
(UK) Columbia	*29–3–69*	*4*	*7*
The Man Who Sold The World			
(UK) Polydor	*2–2–74*	*3*	*6*
LUMAN, BOB			
Let's Think About Livin'			
(UK) Warner Brothers	*23–9–60*	*7*	*9*
(US) Warner Brothers	3–10–60	7	7
LUNDBERG, VICTOR			
Open Letter To My Teenage Son			
(US) Liberty	25–11–67	10	3
LYMAN, ARTHUR			
Yellow Bird			
(US) Hi Fi	19–6–61	4	7
LYMON, FRANKIE, AND THE TEENAGERS			
Why Do Fools Fall In Love?			
(US) Gee	3–3–56	7	13
(UK) Columbia	*6–7–56*	*1*	*14*
I Want You To Be My Girl			
(US) Gee	9–6–56	17	1
Baby Baby			
(UK) Columbia	*12–4–57*	*4*	*9*
I'm Not A Juvenile Delinquent			
(UK) Columbia	*12–4–57*	*12*	*4*
LYNCH, KENNY			
Up On The Roof			
(UK) HMV	*6–1–63*	*10*	*6*
You Can Never Stop Me Loving You			
(UK) HMV	*13–7–63*	*10*	*7*
LYNN, BARBARA			
You'll Lose A Good Thing			
(US) Jamie	28–7–62	8	5

	Date of chart entry	*Highest position reached*	*Number of weeks in charts*
LYNN, TAMMI			
I'm Gonna Run Away From You			
(UK) Mojo (re-issue)	*5–6–71*	*4*	*8*
LYNN, VERA			
My Son, My Son			
(UK) Decca	*7–1–55*	*14*	*2*
House With Love In It			
(UK) Decca	*30–11–56*	*17*	*6*
Travellin' Home			
(UK) Decca	*5–7–57*	*20*	*1*
LYNYRD SKYNYRD			
Sweet Home Alabama			
(US) MCA	14–9–74	8	8
LYON, BARBARA			
Stowaway			
(UK) Columbia	*24–6–55*	*12*	*8*
LYTTLETON, HUMPHREY			
Bad Penny Blues			
(UK) Parlophone	*13–7–56*	*19*	*2*
MACK, LONNIE			
Memphis			
(US) Fraternity	29–6–63	5	8
MACKENZIE, GIZELLE			
Hard To Get			
(US) X	25–6–55	5	15
MACKINTOSH, KEN			
Raunchy			
(UK) HMV	*14–2–58*	*19*	*2*
MACRAE, GORDON			
The Secret			
(US) Capitol	20–10–58	18	1
MACRAE, JOSH			
Talkin' Army Blues			
(UK) Rank	*19–6–60*	*12*	*13*
Wild Side Of Life			
(UK) Rank	*20–11–60*	*13*	*6*
Messing About On The River			
(UK) Rank	*22–1–61*	*15*	*3*
MADDOX, JOHNNY			
Crazy Otto Medley			
(US) Dot	12–2–55	2	16

	Date of chart entry	Highest position reached	Number of weeks in charts
MAESTRO, JOHNNY			
Model Girl			
(US) Coed	27–3–61	20	2
[see also BROOKLYN BRIDGE; CRESTS]			
MAIN INGREDIENT			
Everybody Plays The Fool			
(US) RCA	16–9–72	3	8
Just Don't Want To Be Lonely			
(US) RCA	6–4–74	10	7
MAJOR LANCE			
Monkey Time			
(US) Okeh	24–8–63	8	6
Hey Little Girl			
(US) Okeh	16–11–63	13	4
Um Um Um Um Um Um			
(US) Okeh	18–1–64	5	8
Matador			
(US) Okeh	2–5–64	20	2
MAKEBA, MIRIAM			
Pata Pata			
(US) Reprise	18–11–67	12	4
MALO			
Suavecitio			
(US) Warner Brothers	29–4–72	18	2
MALTBY, RICHARD			
Man With The Golden Arm			
(US) Vik	28–4–56	14	3
MAMAS AND PAPAS			
California Dreamin'			
(US) Dunhill	19–2–66	4	10
Monday Monday			
(US) Dunhill	23–4–66	1	8
(UK) RCA	*21–5–66*	*3*	*10*
I Saw Her Again			
(US) Dunhill	9–7–66	5	6
(UK) RCA	*13–8–66*	*11*	*6*
Words Of Love			
(US) Dunhill	31–12–66	5	7
Dedicated To The One I Love			
(US) Dunhill	11–3–67	2	8
(UK) RCA	*22–4–57*	*2*	*10*
Creeque Alley			
(US) Dunhill	20–5–67	5	4
(UK) RCA	*5–8–67*	*9*	*6*

	Date of chart entry	*Highest position reached*	*Number of weeks in charts*
MAMAS AND PAPAS (cont.)			
Twelve Thirty			
(US) Dunhill	16–9–67	20	2
MANCINI, HENRY			
Moon River			
(US) RCA	11–12–61	11	4
How Soon			
(UK) RCA	*17–10–64*	*10*	*4*
Love Theme From 'Romeo And Juliet'			
(US) RCA	24–5–69	1	11
Love Story			
(US) RCA	20–2–71	13	5
MANILOW, BARRY			
Mandy			
(US) Bell	21–12–74	1	8
MANN, BARRY			
Who Put The Bomp In The Bomp Bomp Bomp			
(US) ABC-Paramount	4–9–61	7	5
MANN, JOHNNY, SINGERS			
Up Up And Away			
(UK) Liberty	*29–7–67*	*6*	*7*
MANN, MANFRED			
5-4-3-2-1			
(UK) HMV	*1–2–64*	*5*	*7*
Hubble Bubble Toil And Trouble			
(UK) HMV	*25–4–64*	*11*	*4*
Do Wah Diddy Diddy			
(UK) HMV	*25–7–64*	*1*	*10*
(US) Ascot	19–9–64	1	10
Sha La La			
(UK) HMV	*24–10–64*	*3*	*7*
(US) Ascot	5–12–64	12	7
Come Tomorrow			
(UK) HMV	*23–1–65*	*4*	*7*
Oh No, Not My Baby			
(UK) HMV	*1–5–65*	*11*	*5*
If You Gotta Go, Go Now			
(UK) HMV	*23–9–65*	*2*	*8*
Pretty Flamingo			
(UK) HMV	*30–4–66*	*1*	*7*
Just Like A Woman			
(UK) Fontana	*20–8–66*	*7*	*6*
Semi-detached Suburban Mr. Jones			
(UK) Fontana	*5–11–66*	*2*	*8*

	Date of chart entry	*Highest position reached*	*Number of weeks in charts*
MANN, MANFRED (cont.)			
Ha! Ha! Said The Clown			
(UK) Fontana	*8–4–67*	*4*	*7*
The Mighty Quinn			
(UK) Fontana	*3–2–68*	*1*	*8*
(US) Mercury	23–3–68	10	5
My Name Is Jack			
(UK) Fontana	*29–6–68*	*8*	*5*
Fox On The Run			
(UK) Fontana	*18–1–69*	*5*	*6*
Ragamuffin Man			
(UK) Fontana	*17–5–69*	*8*	*6*
Joybringer			
(UK) Vertigo	*22–8–73*	*9*	*5*
MANTOVANI			
Lonely Ballerina			
(UK) Decca	*11–2–55*	*16*	*4*
Around The World			
(UK) Decca	*7–6–57*	*20*	*1*
Exodus			
(UK) Decca	*26–3–61*	*20*	*1*
MARATHONS			
Peanut Butter			
(US) Arvee	19–6–61	20	1
MARBLES			
Only One Woman			
(UK) Polydor	*19–10–68*	*5*	*8*
MARCELS			
Blue Moon			
(UK) Pye International	*26–3–61*	*1*	*10*
(US) Colpix	27–3–61	1	9
Heartaches			
(US) Colpix	13–11–61	7	4
MARCH, LITTLE PEGGY			
I Will Follow Him			
(US) RCA	13–4–63	1	9
MARDI GRAS			
Too Busy Thinkin' 'Bout My Baby			
(UK) Bell	*16–9–72*	*19*	*1*
MARESCA, ERNIE			
Shout Shout (Knock Yourself Out)			
(US) Seville	5–5–62	6	6

	Date of chart entry	*Highest position reached*	*Number of weeks in charts*
MARINI, MARINO			
Volare			
(UK) Durium	*10–10–58*	*13*	*5*
Come Prima			
(UK) Durium	*10–10–58*	*2*	*17*
MARKETTS			
Out Of Limits			
(US) Warner Brothers	11–1–64	3	7
Batman Theme			
(US) Warner Brothers	5–3–66	17	3
[see also: ROUTERS]			
MAR-KEYS			
Last Night			
(US) Satellite	24–7–61	3	7
MARKHAM, PIGMEAT			
Here Comes The Judge			
(US) Chess	27–7–68	19	1
(UK) Chess	*3–8–68*	*19*	*3*
MARMALADE			
Lovin' Things			
(UK) CBS	*15–6–68*	*6*	*6*
Ob-la-di Ob-la-da			
(UK) CBS	*21–12–68*	*1*	*10*
Baby Make It Soon			
(UK) CBS	*5–7–69*	*9*	*7*
Reflections Of My Life			
(UK) Deram	*10–1–70*	*3*	*7*
(US) London	18–4–70	10	8
Rainbow			
(UK) Decca	*1–8–70*	*3*	*8*
My Little One			
(UK) Decca	*1–5–71*	*15*	*3*
Cousin Norman			
(UK) Decca	*11–9–71*	*6*	*7*
Radancer			
(UK) Decca	*22–4–72*	*6*	*6*
MARTHA AND THE VANDELLAS [*MARTHA REEVES AND THE VANDELLAS]			
Heat Wave			
(US) Gordy	24–8–63	4	9
Quicksand			
(US) Gordy	21–12–63	8	4

	Date of chart entry	*Highest position reached*	*Number of weeks in charts*
MARTHA, etc. (cont.)			
Dancing In The Street			
(US) Gordy	19–9–64	2	8
(UK) Tamla-Motown (re-issue)	*1–2–69*	*4*	*7*
Nowhere To Run			
(US) Gordy	27–3–65	8	5
I'm Ready For Love			
(US) Gordy	26–11–66	9	4
Jimmy Mack			
(US) Gordy	1–4–67	10	7
Honey Chile			
(US) Gordy	16–12–67	11	6
Forget Me Not*			
(UK) Tamla-Motown	*27–2–71*	*11*	*3*
MARTIN, BOBBI			
Don't Forget I Still Love You			
(US) Coral	16–1–65	19	1
For The Love Of Him			
(US) United Artists	25–4–70	13	3
MARTIN, DEAN			
Naughty Lady Of Shady Lane			
(UK) Capitol	*28–1–55*	*5*	*10*
Mambo Italiano			
(UK) Capitol	*4–2–55*	*14*	*2*
Let Me Go Lover			
(UK) Capitol	*25–2–55*	*3*	*9*
Under The Bridges Of Paris			
(UK) Capitol	*4–4–55*	*6*	*8*
Memories Are Made Of This			
(US) Capitol	17–12–55	1	16
(UK) Capitol	*10–2–56*	*1*	*14*
Young And Foolish			
(UK) Capitol	*2–3–56*	*20*	*1*
Return To Me			
(US) Capitol	28–4–58	4	13
(UK) Capitol	*27–6–58*	*2*	*16*
Volare			
(US) Capitol	18–8–58	15	4
(UK) Capitol	*29–8–58*	*2*	*12*
Everybody Loves Somebody			
(US) Reprise	18–7–64	1	11
(UK) Reprise	*18–9–64*	*12*	*7*
The Door Is Still Open To My Heart			
(US) Reprise	24–10–64	6	5
I Will			
(US) Reprise	27–11–65	10	5
Gentle On My Mind			
(UK) Reprise	*1–3–69*	*2*	*12*

	Date of chart entry	Highest position reached	Number of weeks in charts
MARTIN, TONY			
Stranger In Paradise			
(UK) HMV	*22–4–55*	*7*	*13*
Walk Hand In Hand			
(US) RCA	23–6–56	10	2
(UK) HMV	*13–7–56*	*2*	*14*
MARTIN, VINCE, WITH THE TARRIERS			
Cindy Oh Cindy			
(US) Glory	3–11–56	12	10
MARTINDALE, WINK			
Deck Of Cards			
(US) Dot	12–10–59	7	9
(UK) London	*19–12–59*	*19*	*1*
(UK) London (re-issue)	*18–5–63*	*5*	*13*
MARTINO, AL			
Man From Laramie			
(UK) Capitol	*23–9–55*	*19*	*3*
I Love You Because			
(US) Capitol	18–5–63	3	7
Painted, Tainted Rose			
(US) Capitol	7–9–63	15	3
I Love You More Everyday			
(US) Capitol	29–2–64	9	5
Tears And Roses			
(US) Capitol	20–6–64	20	1
Spanish Eyes			
(US) Capitol	8–1–66	15	4
(UK) Capitol (re-issue)	*28–7–73*	*5*	*13*
MARVELLETTES			
Please Mr. Postman			
(US) Tamla	6–11–61	1	11
Playboy			
(US) Tamla	2–6–62	7	7
Beechwood 4-5789			
(US) Tamla	15–9–62	17	3
Don't Mess With Bill			
(US) Tamla	5–2–66	7	6
Hunter Gets Captured By The Game			
(US) Tamla	4–3–67	13	3
When You're Young And In Love			
(UK) Motown	*15–7–67*	*13*	*1*
My Baby Must Be A Magician			
(US) Tamla	10–2–68	17	2

	Date of chart entry	Highest position reached	Number of weeks in charts
MARVIN, HANK. See RICHARD, CLIFF			
MARVIN, LEE			
Wanderin' Star			
(UK) Paramount	*14–2–70*	*1*	*11*
MASAKELA, HUGH			
Grazing In The Grass			
(US) UNI	29–6–68	1	9
MASON, BARBARA			
Yes, I'm Ready			
(US) Arctic	26–6–65	5	7
MATHIS, JOHNNY			
It's Not For Me To Say			
(US) Columbia	10–6–57	5	17
Wonderful Wonderful			
(US) Columbia	22–7–57	17	3
Chances Are			
(US) Columbia	30–9–57	5	17
A Certain Smile			
(US) Columbia	21–7–58	19	1
(UK) Fontana	*3–10–58*	*4*	*14*
Winter Wonderland			
(UK) Fontana	*26–12–58*	*17*	*1*
Someone			
(UK) Fontana	*1–8–59*	*8*	*12*
Small World			
(US) Columbia	10–8–59	20	1
Misty			
(US) Columbia	2–11–59	12	7
(UK) Fontana	*30–1–60*	*13*	*4*
Best Of Everything			
(UK) Fontana	*28–11–59*	*18*	*1*
My Love For You			
(UK) Fontana	*30–9–60*	*14*	*7*
Gina			
(US) Columbia	20–10–62	6	7
What Will Mary Say?			
(US) Columbia	23–2–63	9	7
MATTHEWS SOUTHERN COMFORT			
Woodstock			
(UK) UNI	*17–10–70*	*1*	*8*
MAUGHAN, SUSAN			
Bobby's Girl			
(UK) Philips	*3–11–62*	*3*	*13*

	Date of chart entry	*Highest position reached*	*Number of weeks in charts*
MAURIAT, PAUL			
Love Is Blue			
(US) Philips	27–1–68	1	13
(UK) Philips	*23–3–68*	*12*	*5*
MAXWELL, ROBERT, HIS HARP, HIS ORCHESTRA			
Shangri-La			
(US) Decca	25–4–64	15	4
MAY, BILLY			
Main Title/Man With The Golden Arm			
(UK) Capitol	*4–5–56*	*9*	*6*
MAYFIELD, CURTIS			
Move On Up			
(UK) Buddah	*28–8–71*	*12*	*3*
Freddie's Dead			
(US) Curtom	14–10–72	4	7
Superfly			
(US) Curtom	16–12–72	8	8
[see also: IMPRESSIONS]			
McBETH, DAVID			
Mr. Blue			
(UK) Pye	*31–10–59*	*14*	*2*
McBRIDE, FRANKIE			
Five Little Fingers			
(UK) Emerald	*14–10–67*	*19*	*1*
McCARTNEY, PAUL (*PAUL McCARTNEY'S WINGS; **PAUL McCARTNEY & WINGS)			
Another Day			
(UK) Apple	*6–3–71*	*2*	*9*
(US) Apple (b/w Oh Woman Oh Why)	20–3–71	5	9
Uncle Albert/Admiral Halsey (with LINDA McCARTNEY)			
(US) Apple	28–8–71	1	10
My Love			
(UK) Apple	*21–4–73*	*9*	*6*
(US) Apple	12–5–73	1	10
Live And Let Die			
(UK) Apple	*16–6–73*	*9*	*7*
(US) Apple	4–8–73	2	8

	Date of chart entry	*Highest position reached*	*Number of weeks in charts*
McCARTNEY, PAUL (cont.)			
Helen Wheels			
(UK) Apple	*24–11–73*	*12*	*4*
(US) Apple	22–12–73	10	7
Jet**			
(UK) Apple	*2–3–74*	*7*	*6*
(US) Apple	*2–3–74*	*7*	*7*
Band On The Run**			
(US) Apple	11–5–74	1	10
(UK) Apple	*13–7–74*	*3*	*6*
Junior's Farm**			
(US) Apple (b/w Sally G)	30–11–74	3	9
(UK) Apple	*14–12–74*	*16*	*1*
[see also: BEATLES; WINGS]			
McCOYS			
Hang On Sloopy			
(US) Bang	11–9–65	1	9
(UK) Immediate	*18–9–65*	*5*	*9*
Fever			
(US) Bang	4–12–65	7	7
McCRACKLIN, JIMMY			
The Walk			
(US) Checker	10–3–58	7	5
McCRAE, GEORGE			
Rock Your Baby			
(US) TK	22–6–74	1	7
(UK) Jay Boy	*6–7–74*	*1*	*9*
I Can't Leave You Alone			
(UK) Jay Boy	*19–10–74*	*12*	*6*
McDANIELS, GENE			
One Hundred Pounds Of Clay			
(US) Liberty	10–4–61	3	10
Tower Of Strength			
(US) Liberty	23–10–61	5	8
Chip Chip			
(US) Liberty	17–2–62	10	5
McDEVITT, CHAS (with NANCY WHISKEY)			
Freight Train			
(UK) Oriole	*19–4–57*	*6*	*14*
McGOVERN, MAUREEN			
Morning After			
(US) 20th Century	21–7–73	1	9

	Date of chart entry	Highest position reached	Number of weeks in charts
McGREGOR, BYRON			
Americans			
(US) Janus	19–1–74	4	6
McGRIFF, JIMMY			
I've Gotta Woman			
(US) Sue	24–11–62	20	1
McGUINNESS, FLINT			
When I'm Dead Gone			
(UK) Capitol	*5–12–70*	*2*	*10*
Malt And Barley Blues			
(UK) Capitol	*15–5–71*	*5*	*7*
McGUIRE, BARRY			
Eve Of Destruction			
(US) Dunhill	4–9–65	1	8
(UK) RCA	*18–9–65*	*3*	*10*
McGUIRE SISTERS			
Sincerely			
(US) Coral	15–1–55	1	17
(UK) Vogue-Coral	*15–7–55*	*14*	*4*
No More			
(UK) Vogue-Coral	*4–4–55*	*20*	*1*
Something's Gotta Give			
(US) Coral	11–6–55	6	11
He			
(US) Coral	19–11–55	12	8
Picnic			
(US) Coral	26–5–56	13	8
Sugartime			
(US) Coral	20–1–58	5	15
(UK) Vogue-Coral	*21–2–58*	*14*	*4*
May You Always			
(US) Coral	26–1–59	11	4
Just For Old Times' Sake			
(US) Coral	15–5–61	20	1
McKENZIE, SCOTT			
San Francisco			
(US) Ode	17–6–67	4	8
(UK) CBS	*15–7–67*	*1*	*14*
McLAIN, TOMMY			
Sweet Dreams			
(US) MSL	6–8–66	15	4
McLEAN, DON			
American Pie			
(US) United Artists	18–12–71	1	14
(UK) United Artists	*5–2–72*	*2*	*11*

	Date of chart entry	Highest position reached	Number of weeks in charts
McLEAN, DON (cont.)			
Vincent			
(US) United Artists	15–4–72	12	6
(UK) United Artists	*27–5–72*	*1*	*9*
McNAMARA, ROBIN			
Lay A Little Lovin' On Me			
(US) Steed	1–8–70	11	5
McPHATTER, CLYDE			
A Lover's Question			
(US) Atlantic	10–11–58	6	14
Lover Please			
(US) Mercury	31–3–62	7	8
McTELL, RALPH			
Streets Of London			
(UK) Reprise	*14–12–74*	*2*	*8*
MEAD, SISTER JANET			
Lord's Prayer			
(US) A & M	16–3–74	4	7
MEDICINE HEAD			
One And One Is One			
(UK) Polydor	*19–5–73*	*3*	*7*
Rising Sun			
(UK) Polydor	*18–8–73*	*11*	*5*
MELACHRINO, GEORGE			
Autumn Concerto			
(UK) HMV	*19–10–56*	*19*	*4*
MEL AND TIM			
Backfield In Motion			
(US) Bamboo	8–11–69	10	9
Starting All Over Again			
(US) Stax	28–10–72	19	3
MELANIE			
Lay Down (Candles In The Rain) (with the EDWIN HAWKINS SINGERS)			
(US) Buddah	6–6–70	6	10
Ruby Tuesday			
(UK) Buddah	*24–10–70*	*9*	*7*
Brand New Key			
(US) Neighborhood	4–12–71	1	12
(UK) Buddah	*15–1–72*	*4*	*7*

	Date of chart entry	*Highest position reached*	*Number of weeks in charts*
MELVIN, HAROLD, AND THE BLUE NOTES			
If You Don't Know Me By Now			
(US) Phil. International	11–11–72	3	8
(UK) CBS	*27–1–73*	*9*	*4*
The Love I Lost Pt. 1			
(US) Phil. International	10–11–73	7	9
MENDES, SERGIO, AND BRASIL '66			
Look Of Love			
(US) A & M	8–6–68	4	8
Fool On The Hill			
(US) A & M	31–8–68	6	6
Scarborough Fair			
(US) A & M	14–12–68	16	2
MENZIES, IAN			
Fish Man			
(UK) Pye Nixa	*18–9–60*	*15*	*3*
MERCY			
Love (Can Mek You Happy)			
(US) Sundi	3–5–69	2	9
MERSEYBEATS			
I Think Of You			
(UK) Fontana	*1–2–64*	*5*	*11*
Don't Turn Around			
(UK) Fontana	*2–5–64*	*13*	*5*
Wishin' And Hopin'			
(UK) Fontana	*18–7–64*	*13*	*6*
[see also: MERSEYS]			
MERSEYS			
Sorrow			
(UK) Pye	*18–4–64*	*10*	*6*
MFSB			
TSOP			
(US) Philadelphia International	23–3–74	1	10
MICHAELS, LEE			
Do You Know What I Mean?			
(US) A & M	11–9–71	6	10
MICKEY AND SYLVIA			
Love Is Strange			
(US) Groove	9–2–57	13	8

	Date of chart entry	*Highest position reached*	*Number of weeks in charts*
MIDDLE OF THE ROAD			
Chirpy Chirpy Cheep Cheep *(UK) RCA*	*12–6–71*	*1*	*12*
Tweedle Tweedle Dee *(UK) RCA*	*18–9–71*	*2*	*9*
Soley Soley *(UK) RCA*	*18–12–71*	*5*	*8*
MIDLER, BETTE			
Do You Want To Dance? (US) Atlantic	24–2–73	17	4
Boogie Woogie Bugle Boy (US) Atlantic	30–6–73	8	6
MIGIL FIVE			
Mockingbird Hill *(UK) Pye*	*18–4–64*	*10*	*6*
MIKI AND GRIFF			
Hold Back Tomorrow *(UK) Pye*	*3–10–59*	*20*	*1*
Little Bitty Tear *(UK) Pye*	*24–3–62*	*19*	*1*
MILES, GARY			
Look For A Star (US) Liberty	25–7–60	16	3
MILLER, CHUCK			
House Of Blue Lights (US) Mercury	2–7–55	9	10
MILLER, GARY			
Yellow Rose Of Texas *(UK) Nixa*	*21–10–55*	*13*	*5*
Robin Hood *(UK) Nixa*	*13–1–56*	*10*	*6*
Garden Of Eden *(UK) Pye-Nixa*	*11–1–57*	*14*	*2*
Story Of My Life *(UK) Pye-Nixa*	*17–1–58*	*14*	*5*
MILLER, JODY			
Queen Of The House (US) Capitol	29–5–65	12	3
MILLER, MITCH			
Yellow Rose Of Texas (US) Columbia	6–8–55	1	19
(UK) Philips	*7–10–55*	*2*	*13*

	Date of chart entry	*Highest position reached*	*Number of weeks in charts*
MILLER, MITCH (cont.)			
Song For A Summer Night			
(US) Columbia	25–8–56	10	9
Children's Marching Song			
(US) Columbia	9–2–59	16	5
MILLER, NED			
From A Jack To A King			
(US) Fabor (re-issue)	2–2–63	6	6
(UK) London	*16–3–63*	*2*	*13*
MILLER, ROGER			
Dang Me			
(US) Smash	11–7–64	7	6
Chug-A-Lug			
(US) Smash	17–10–64	9	5
King Of The Road			
(US) Smash	20–2–65	4	9
(UK) Philips	*17–4–65*	*1*	*9*
Engine, Engine No. 9			
(US) Smash	29–5–65	7	4
England Swings			
(US) Smash	4–12–65	8	6
(UK) Philips	*22–1–66*	*13*	*2*
Little Green Apples			
(UK) Mercury	*11–5–68*	*19*	*2*
MILLER, STEVE			
The Joker			
(US) Capitol	8–12–73	1	11
MILLER, SUZI			
Happy Days, Lonely Nights			
(UK) Decca	*21–1–55*	*14*	*2*
MILLICAN AND NESBITT			
Vaya Con Dios			
(UK) Pye	*5–1–74*	*20*	*1*
MILLIE. See SMALL, MILLIE			
MILLS, GARY			
Look For A Star			
(UK) Top Rank	*3–7–60*	*5*	*8*
Top Teen Baby			
(UK) Top Rank	*21–10–60*	*20*	*1*
MILLS, HAYLEY			
Let's Get Together			
(US) Vista	2–10–61	8	7
(UK) Decca	*14–10–61*	*11*	*5*

	Date of chart entry	*Highest position reached*	*Number of weeks in charts*
MIMMS, GARNET, AND THE ENCHANTERS			
Cry Baby			
(US) United Artists	14–9–63	4	8
MINDBENDERS			
A Groovy Kind Of Love			
(UK) Fontana	*29–1–66*	*2*	*10*
(US) Fontana	7–5–66	2	8
Ashes To Ashes			
(UK) Fontana	*17–9–66*	*14*	*3*
[see also: FONTANA, WAYNE, AND THE MINDBENDERS]			
MINEO, SAL			
Start Movin'			
(US) Epic	3–6–57	10	6
(UK) Philips	*26–7–57*	*16*	*6*
MINGRABI, MARCELLO			
Zorba's Dance			
(UK) Durium	*14–8–65*	*6*	*10*
MIRACLES			
Shop Around			
(US) Tamla	9–1–61	2	9
You've Really Got A Hold On Me			
(US) Tamla	26–1–63	8	7
Mickey's Monkey			
(US) Tamla	14–9–63	8	5
Ooo Baby Baby			
(US) Tamla	1–5–65	16	3
Tracks Of My Tears			
(US) Tamla	28–8–65	16	4
(UK) Tamla-Motown (re-issue)	*31–5–69*	*9*	*6*
My Girl Has Gone			
(US) Tamla	20–11–65	14	2
Going To A Go-Go			
(US) Tamla	12–2–66	11	2
(Come Round Here) I'm The One You Need			
(US) Tamla	3–12–66	17	3
(UK) Tamla-Motown (re-issue)	*20–2–71*	*13*	*4*
Do It Baby			
(US) Tamla	5–10–74	13	5
[see also: ROBINSON, SMOKEY, AND THE MIRACLES]			

	Date of chart entry	Highest position reached	Number of weeks in charts
MITCHELL, GUY			
Singing The Blues			
(US) Columbia	3–11–56	1	20
(UK) Philips	*7–12–56*	*1*	*20*
Knee Deep In The Blues			
(US) Columbia	16–2–57	16	3
(UK) Philips	*22–2–57*	*3*	*11*
Rock-a-Billy			
(UK) Philips	*26–4–57*	*1*	*11*
(US) Columbia	27–4–57	13	7
Call Rosie On The Phone			
(UK) Philips	*18–10–57*	*17*	*3*
Heartaches By The Number			
(US) Columbia	2–11–59	1	12
(UK) Philips	*28–11–59*	*5*	*8*
MITCHELL, JONI			
Big Yellow Taxi			
(UK) Reprise	*25–7–70*	*11*	*5*
Help Me			
(US) Asylum	11–5–74	7	6
MIXTURES			
The Pushbike Song			
(UK) Polydor	*23–1–71*	*2*	*13*
MOCEDADES			
Eres Tu (Touch The Wind)			
(US) Tara	2–3–74	9	7
MODUGNO, DOMENICO			
Volare			
(US) Decca	11–8–58	1	13
(UK) Oriole	*5–9–58*	*10*	*8*
MOJOS			
Everything's All Right			
(UK) Decca	*11–4–64*	*9*	*6*
MOMENTS			
Love On A Two Way Street			
(US) Stang	2–5–70	3	10
Sexy Mama			
(US) Stang	23–2–74	17	4
MONKEES			
Last Train To Clarksville			
(US) Colgems	1–10–66	1	10
I'm A Believer			
(US) Colgems	17–12–66	1	12
(UK) RCA	*14–1–57*	*1*	*11*

	Date of chart entry	*Highest position reached*	*Number of weeks in charts*
MONKEES (cont.)			
(I'm Not Your) Steppin' Stone			
(US) Colgems	14–1–67	20	1
A Little Bit Me, A Little Bit You			
(US) Colgems	1–4–67	2	8
(UK) RCA	*8–4–67*	*3*	*8*
Alternate Title			
(UK) RCA	*1–7–67*	*2*	*8*
Pleasant Valley Sunday			
(US) Colgems (b/w*)	5–8–67	3	6
(UK) RCA	*26–8–67*	*11*	*4*
Words*			
(US) Colgems	19–8–67	11	4
Daydream Believer			
(US) Colgems	25–11–67	1	10
(UK) RCA	*2–12–67*	*5*	*12*
Valleri			
(US) Colgems	16–3–68	3	6
(UK) RCA	*6–4–68*	*12*	*5*
D. W. Washburn			
(US) Colgems	6–7–68	19	2
(UK) RCA	*6–7–68*	*17*	*2*
MONOTONES			
Book Of Love			
(US) Argo	14–4–58	5	9
MONRO, MATT			
Portrait Of My Love			
(UK) Parlophone	*18–12–60*	*5*	*8*
My Kind Of Girl			
(UK) Parlophone	*26–2–61*	*5*	*8*
(US) Warwick	31–7–61	18	3
Softly As I Leave You			
(UK) Parlophone	*3–3–62*	*10*	*8*
From Russia With Love			
(UK) Parlophone	*30–11–63*	*20*	*1*
Walk Away			
(UK) Parlophone	*10–10–64*	*5*	*10*
Yesterday			
(UK) Parlophone	*30–10–65*	*8*	*7*
MONROE, GERRY			
Sally			
(UK) Chapter One	*13–6–70*	*4*	*9*
My Prayer			
(UK) Chapter One	*5–12–70*	*9*	*7*
It's A Sin To Tell A Lie			
(UK) Chapter One	*8–5–71*	*13*	*4*

	Date of chart entry	Highest position reached	Number of weeks in charts
MONTE, LOU			
Lazy Mary			
(US) Victor	24–3–58	12	7
Pepino The Italian Mouse			
(US) Reprise	29–12–62	5	5
MONTENEGRO, HUGO			
The Good, The Bad And The Ugly			
(US) RCA	20–4–68	2	10
(UK) RCA	*19–10–68*	*1*	*15*
MONTEZ, CHRIS			
Let's Dance			
(US) Monogram	15–9–62	4	7
(UK) London	*20–10–62*	*2*	*14*
(UK) London (re-issue)	*4–11–72*	*9*	*5*
Some Kinda Fun			
(UK) London	*27–1–63*	*10*	*5*
The More I See You			
(US) A & M	11–6–66	16	3
(UK) Pye	*16–7–66*	*3*	*9*
MOODY BLUES			
Go Now			
(UK) Decca	*2–1–65*	*1*	*9*
(US) London	3–4–65	10	6
Nights In White Satin			
(UK) Deram	*17–2–68*	*19*	*1*
(US) Deram (re-issue)	16–9–72	2	12
(UK) Deram (re-issue)	*16–12–72*	*9*	*6*
Question			
(UK) Threshold	*9–5–70*	*2*	*9*
Isn't Life Strange?			
(UK) Threshold	*27–5–72*	*13*	*4*
I'm Just A Singer (In A Rock And Roll Band)			
(US) Threshold	3–3–73	12	4
MOONEY, ART			
Honey Babe			
(US) MGM	30–4–55	6	16
Nuttin' For Christmas (with BARRY GORDON)			
(US) MGM	24–12–55	7	3
MOORE, BOB			
Mexico			
(US) Monument	25–9–61	7	7

	Date of chart entry	*Highest position reached*	*Number of weeks in charts*
MORGAN, JANE			
Fascination			
(US) Kapp	23–9–57	11	12
The Day The Rains Came Down			
(UK) London	*12–12–58*	*4*	*11*
MORGAN, JAYE P.			
That's All I Want From You			
(US) Victor	1–1–55	5	14
Danger, Heartbreak Ahead			
(US) Victor	9–4–55	18	1
Longest Walk			
(US) Victor	10–9–55	13	7
MORMON TABERNACLE CHOIR			
Battle Hymn Of The Republic			
(US) Columbia	5–10–59	13	5
MORRISON, VAN			
Brown-Eyed Girl			
(US) Bang	9–9–67	10	6
Domino			
(US) Warner Brothers	19–12–70	9	4
[see also: THEM]			
MOTHERLODE			
When I Die			
(US) Buddah	4–10–69	18	2
MOTOWN SPINNERS. See SPINNERS			
MOTT THE HOOPLE			
All The Young Dudes			
(UK) CBS	*19–8–72*	*3*	*6*
Honaloochie Boogie			
(UK) CBS	*7–7–73*	*12*	*3*
All The Way From Memphis			
(UK) CBS	*22–9–73*	*10*	*4*
Roll Away The Stone			
(UK) CBS	*1–12–73*	*8*	*9*
Golden Age Of Rock And Roll			
(UK) CBS	*13–4–74*	*16*	*3*
MOUTH AND MACNEAL			
How Do You Do			
(US) Philips	1–7–72	8	8
I See A Star			
(UK) Decca	*25–5–74*	*8*	*5*

	Date of chart entry	*Highest position reached*	*Number of weeks in charts*
MOVE			
Night Of Fear *(UK) Deram*	*14–1–67*	*2*	*7*
I Can Hear The Grass Grow *(UK) Deram*	*22–4–67*	*5*	*6*
Flowers In The Rain *(UK) Regal Zonophone*	*16–9–67*	*2*	*10*
Fire Brigade *(UK) Regal Zonophone*	*17–2–68*	*3*	*8*
Blackberry Way *(UK) Regal Zonophone*	*18–1–69*	*1*	*8*
Curly *(UK) Regal Zonophone*	*9–8–69*	*12*	*7*
Brontosaurus *(UK) Regal Zonophone*	*9–5–70*	*7*	*6*
Tonight *(UK) Harvest*	*17–7–71*	*11*	*5*
California Man *(UK) Harvest*	*27–5–72*	*7*	*8*
MR. BLOE			
Groovin' With Mr. Bloe *(UK) DJM*	*30–5–70*	*2*	*10*
MUD			
Crazy *(UK) RAK*	*7–4–73*	*12*	*5*
Hypnosis *(UK) RAK*	*4–8–73*	*16*	*2*
Dyna-Mite *(UK) RAK*	*3–11–73*	*4*	*7*
Tiger Feet *(UK) RAK*	*19–1–74*	*1*	*8*
The Cat Crept In *(UK) RAK*	*13–4–74*	*2*	*6*
Rocket *(UK) RAK*	*3–8–74*	*6*	*5*
Lonely This Christmas *(UK) RAK*	*7–12–74*	*1*	*7*
MUDLARKS			
Lollipop *(UK) Columbia*	*2–5–58*	*2*	*9*
Book Of Love *(UK) Columbia*	*13–6–58*	*8*	*7*
MULDAUR, MARIA			
Midnight At The Oasis (US) Reprise	4–5–74	6	8

	Date of chart entry	*Highest position reached*	*Number of weeks in charts*
MUNGO JERRY			
In The Summertime			
(UK) Dawn	*6–6–70*	*1*	*13*
(US) Janus	8–8–70	3	8
Baby Jump			
(UK) Dawn	*20–2–71*	*1*	*8*
Lady Rose			
(UK) Dawn	*5–6–71*	*5*	*7*
You Don't Have To Be In The Army (To Fight In The War)			
(UK) Dawn	*9–10–71*	*13*	*3*
Alright, Alright, Alright			
(UK) Dawn	*21–7–73*	*3*	*6*
Long Legged Woman Dressed In Black			
(UK) Dawn	*27–4–74*	*13*	*5*
MURMAIDS			
Popsicles And Icicles			
(US) Chattahooche	14–12–63	3	9
MURRAY, ANNE			
Snowbird			
(US) Capitol	5–9–70	8	8
Danny's Song			
(US) Capitol	3–3–73	7	9
A Love Song			
(US) Capitol	16–2–74	12	4
You Won't See Me			
(US) Capitol	8–6–74	8	7
MURRAY, RUBY			
Heartbeat			
(UK) Columbia	*7–1–55*	*3*	*11*
Softly Softly			
(UK) Columbia	*28–1–55*	*1*	*23*
Happy Days And Lonely Nights			
(UK) Columbia	*4–2–55*	*6*	*8*
If Anyone Finds This I Love You			
(UK) Columbia	*11–3–55*	*4*	*11*
Let Me Go Lover			
(UK) Columbia	*4–3–55*	*5*	*7*
Evermore			
(UK) Columbia	*1–7–55*	*3*	*17*
I'll Come When You Call			
(UK) Columbia	*14–10–55*	*6*	*7*
You Are My First Love			
(UK) Columbia	*31–8–56*	*16*	*2*
Real Love			
(UK) Columbia	*12–12–58*	*18*	*3*

	Date of chart entry	Highest position reached	Number of weeks in charts
MURRAY, RUBY (cont.)			
Goodbye Jimmy Goodbye			
(UK) Columbia	*20–6–59*	*10*	*7*
MUSIC EXPLOSION			
Little Bit O' Soul			
(US) Laurie	3–6–67	2	11
MUSIC MACHINE			
Talk Talk			
(US) Original Sound	31–12–66	15	4
MYSTICS			
Hushabye			
(US) Laurie	29–6–59	20	1
NAPOLEON XIV			
They're Coming To Take Me Away, Ha Ha			
(US) Warner Brothers	30–7–66	3	4
(UK) Warner Brothers	*20–8–66*	*4*	*6*
NASH, JOHNNY			
Hold Me Tight			
(UK) Regal Zonophone	*24–8–68*	*5*	*10*
(US) JAD	19–10–68	5	9
You Got Soul			
(UK) Major Minor	*25–1–69*	*6*	*6*
Cupid			
(UK) Major Minor	*19–4–69*	*6*	*6*
Stir It Up			
(UK) CBS	*22–4–72*	*13*	*5*
(US) Epic	31–3–73	12	5
I Can See Clearly Now			
(UK) CBS	*8–7–72*	*5*	*9*
(US) Epic	21–10–72	1	10
There Are More Questions Than Answers			
(UK) CBS	*14–10–72*	*9*	*6*
NASHVILLE TEENS			
Tobacco Road			
(UK) Decca	*25–7–64*	*6*	*8*
(US) London	24–10–64	14	4
Google Eyes			
(UK) Decca	*7–11–64*	*10*	*3*
NAZARETH			
Broken Down Angel			
(UK) Mooncrest	*19–5–73*	*9*	*5*
Bad Bad Boy			
(UK) Mooncrest	*28–7–73*	*10*	*5*
This Flight Tonight			
(UK) Mooncrest	*27–10–73*	*11*	*5*

	Date of chart entry	*Highest position reached*	*Number of weeks in charts*
NELSON, RICKY [RICK, after 1961]			
Teenager's Romance			
(US) Verve (b/w*)	27–5–57	8	9
I'm Walkin'*			
(US) Verve	3–6–57	17	3
You're My One And Only Love			
(US) Verve	30–9–57	16	3
Be Bop Baby			
(US) Imperial	21–10–57	5	13
Stood Up			
(US) Imperial (b/w**)	6–1–58	5	8
Waiting In School**			
(US) Imperial	13–1–58	18	3
Believe What You Say			
(US) Imperial (b/w***)	14–4–58	8	3
My Bucket's Got A Hole In It***			
(US) Imperial	14–4–58	18	2
Poor Little Fool			
(US) Imperial	7–7–58	1	12
(UK) London	*22–8–58*	*4*	*13*
Lonesome Town			
(US) Imperial (b/w†)	27–10–58	7	14
I Got A Feeling†			
(US) Imperial	3–11–58	10	8
Someday			
(UK) London	*21–11–58*	*9*	*9*
Never Be Anyone Else But You			
(US) Imperial } (b/w††)	9–3–59	6	9
(UK) London	*18–4–59*	*3*	*18*
It's Late††			
(US) Imperial	23–3–59	9	6
Sweeter Than You			
(US) Imperial } (b/w†††)	20–7–59	9	5
(UK) London	*5–9–59*	*9*	*8*
Just A Little Too Much†††			
(US) Imperial	27–7–59	9	5
I Wanna Be Loved			
(US) Imperial	21–12–59	20	1
Young Emotions			
(US) Imperial	23–5–60	12	6
Travellin' Man			
(US) Imperial } (b/w◇)	8–5–61	1	12
(UK) London	*14–5–61*	*3*	*15*
Hello Mary Lou◇			
(US) Imperial	15–5–61	9	8
A Wonder Like You			
(US) Imperial (b/w◇◇)	6–11–61	11	4
Everlovin'◇◇			
(US) Imperial	13–11–61	16	2
(UK) London	*2–12–61*	*20*	*1*

	Date of chart entry	*Highest position reached*	*Number of weeks in charts*
NELSON, RICK (cont.)			
Young World			
(US) Imperial	24–3–62	5	7
(UK) London	*5–5–62*	*19*	*2*
Teen Age Idol			
(US) Imperial	1–9–62	5	6
It's Up To You			
(US) Imperial	5–1–63	6	6
Fools Rush In			
(US) Decca	19–10–63	12	6
(UK) Brunswick	*2–11–63*	*12*	*5*
For You			
(US) Decca	18–1–64	6	6
(UK) Brunswick	*15–2–64*	*14*	*4*
Garden Party			
(US) Decca	30–9–72	6	8
NELSON, SANDY			
Teen Beat			
(US) Original Sound	21–9–59	4	10
(UK) Top Rank	*31–10–59*	*7*	*11*
Let There Be Drums			
(US) Imperial	4–12–61	7	7
(UK) London	*9–12–61*	*2*	*11*
NEON PHILHARMONIC			
Morning Girl			
(US) Warner Brothers/Seven Arts	7–6–69	17	2
NERVOUS NORVUS			
Transfusion			
(US) Dot	16–6–56	13	5
NEVILLE, AARON			
Tell It Like It Is			
(US) Parlo	24–12–66	2	9
NEWBEATS			
Bread And Butter			
(US) Hickory	29–8–64	2	8
(UK) Hickory	*3–10–64*	*15*	*3*
Everything's All Right			
(US) Hickory	28–11–64	16	3
Run Baby Run			
(US) Hickory	13–11–65	12	5
(UK) London (re-issue)	*13–11–71*	*10*	*6*
NEW CHRISTY MINSTRELS			
Green Green			
(US) Columbia	10–8–63	14	3
Today			
(US) Columbia	6–6–64	17	3

	Date of chart entry	Highest position reached	Number of weeks in charts
NEW COLONY SIX			
Things I'd Like To Say			
(US) Mercury	15–3–69	16	3
NEWLEY, ANTHONY			
Idle On Parade			
(UK) Decca EP	*2–5–59*	*13*	*2*
I've Waited So Long			
(UK) Decca	*2–5–59*	*4*	*13*
Personality			
(UK) Decca	*20–6–59*	*6*	*10*
Why?			
(UK) Decca	*9–1–60*	*1*	*12*
Do You Mind?			
(UK) Decca	*20–3–60*	*2*	*11*
If She Should Come To You			
(UK) Decca	*17–7–60*	*7*	*9*
Strawberry Fair			
(UK) Decca	*20–11–60*	*3*	*6*
And The Heavens Cried			
(UK) Decca	*5–3–61*	*8*	*7*
Pop Goes The Weasel/Bee-Bum			
(UK) Decca	*4–6–61*	*9*	*6*
NEWMAN, THUNDERCLAP			
Something In The Air			
(UK) Track	*21–6–69*	*1*	*8*
NEW SEEKERS			
Look What They've Done To My Song, Ma			
(US) Elektra	10–10–70	14	4
Never-Ending Song Of Love			
(UK) Philips	*24–7–71*	*2*	*12*
I'd Like To Teach The World To Sing			
(UK) Polydor	*25–12–71*	*1*	*14*
(US) Elektra	25–12–71	7	7
Beg, Steal Or Borrow			
(UK) Polydor	*4–3–72*	*2*	*8*
Circles			
(UK) Polydor	*1–7–72*	*4*	*8*
Come Softly To Me			
(UK) Polydor	*20–1–73*	*20*	*1*
Pinball Wizard/See Me Feel Me			
(UK) Polydor	*10–3–73*	*16*	*4*
You Won't Find Another Fool Like Me			
(UK) Polydor	*1–12–73*	*1*	*12*

	Date of chart entry	*Highest position reached*	*Number of weeks in charts*
NEW SEEKERS (cont.)			
I Get A Little Sentimental Over You			
(UK) Polydor	*16–3–74*	*5*	*6*
NEWTON, WAYNE			
Danke Schoen			
(US) Capitol	17–8–63	13	4
Daddy Don't You Walk So Fast			
(US) Chelsea	24–6–72	4	10
NEWTON-JOHN, OLIVIA			
If Not For You			
(UK) Pye International	*3–4–71*	*7*	*6*
Banks Of The Ohio			
(UK) Pye International	*13–11–71*	*5*	*8*
What Is Life?			
(UK) Pye International	*1–4–72*	*16*	*4*
Take Me Home Country Roads			
(UK) Pye International	*10–2–73*	*15*	*4*
Let Me Be There			
(US) MCA	29–12–73	6	10
Long Live Love			
(UK) Pye International	*30–3–74*	*11*	*4*
If You Love Me, Let Me Know			
(US) MCA	1–6–74	5	8
I Honestly Love You			
(US) MCA	7–9–74	1	8
NEW VAUDEVILLE BAND			
Winchester Cathedral			
(UK) Fontana	*24–9–66*	*5*	*9*
(US) Fontana	12–11–66	1	11
Peek A Boo			
(UK) Fontana	*11–2–67*	*7*	*7*
Finchley Central			
(UK) Fontana	*27–5–67*	*11*	*6*
NEW WORLD			
Rose Garden			
(UK) RAK	*13–3–71*	*15*	*5*
Tom Tom Turnaround			
(UK) RAK	*10–7–71*	*6*	*10*
Kara Kara			
(UK) RAK	*8–1–72*	*17*	*1*
Sister Jane			
(UK) RAK	*27–5–72*	*9*	*6*
NEW YORK CITY			
I'm Doing Fine Now			
(US) Chelsea	2–6–73	17	5
(UK) RCA	*25–8–73*	*20*	*2*

	Date of chart entry	*Highest position reached*	*Number of weeks in charts*
NICHOLLS, SUE			
Where Will You Be?			
(UK) Pye	*20–7–68*	*17*	*2*
NILSSON			
Everybody's Talkin'			
(US) RCA	20–9–69	6	6
Without You			
(US) RCA	29–1–72	1	11
(UK) RCA	*19–2–72*	*1*	*13*
Coconut			
(US) RCA	29–7–72	8	6
NINA AND FREDERICK			
Little Donkey			
(UK) Columbia	*20–11–60*	*5*	*6*
Sucu Sucu			
(UK) Columbia	*7–10–61*	*17*	*2*
1910 FRUITGUM COMPANY			
Simon Says			
(US) Buddah	17–2–68	4	9
(UK) Pye International	*6–4–68*	*2*	*12*
1, 2, 3			
(US) Buddah	31–8–68	5	6
Indian Giver			
(US) Buddah	1–3–69	5	7
NITTY GRITTY DIRT BAND			
Mr. Bojangles			
(US) Liberty	30–1–71	9	8
NOBLES, CLIFF AND CO			
The Horse			
(US) Phil L.A. of Soul	15–6–68	2	9
NOONE, PETER AND HERMAN'S HERMITS			
Lady Barbara			
(UK) RAK	*12–12–70*	*13*	*6*
Oh You Pretty Thing			
(UK) RAK	*29–5–71*	*12*	*5*
[see also: HERMAN'S HERMITS]			
NUTTY SQUIRRELS			
Uh! Oh! Pt. 1			
(US) Hanover	7–12–59	14	5
OCEAN			
Put Your Hand In The Hand			
(US) Kama Sutra	10–4–71	2	9

	Date of chart entry	*Highest position reached*	*Number of weeks in charts*
O'CONNOR, DES			
Careless Hands			
(UK) Columbia	*25–11–67*	*6*	*9*
I Pretend			
(UK) Columbia	*15–6–68*	*1*	*15*
1, 2, 3, O'Leary			
(UK) Columbia	*30–11–68*	*4*	*9*
Dick-A-Dum-Dum			
(UK) Columbia	*31–5–69*	*14*	*3*
Loneliness			
(UK) Columbia	*20–12–69*	*18*	*2*
Tips Of My Fingers			
(UK) Columbia	*17–10–70*	*15*	*4*
OFARIM, ESTHER AND ABI			
Cinderella Rockafella			
(UK) Fontana	*24–2–68*	*1*	*9*
One More Dance			
(UK) Philips	*6–7–68*	*13*	*4*
OHIO EXPRESS			
Yummy Yummy Yummy			
(US) Buddah	1–6–68	4	8
(UK) Pye International	*29–9–68*	*5*	*9*
Chewy Chewy			
(US) Buddah	16–11–68	15	7
OHIO PLAYERS			
Funky Worm			
(US) Westbound	12–5–73	15	3
Skin Tight			
(US) Mercury	5–10–74	13	3
O'JAYS			
Backstabbers			
(US) Philadelphia International	26–8–72	3	8
(UK) CBS	*14–10–72*	*14*	*3*
Love Train			
(US) Philadelphia International	17–2–73	1	9
(UK) CBS	*24–3–73*	*9*	*6*
Put Your Hands Together			
(US) Philadelphia International	2–2–74	10	6
For The Love Of Money			
(US) Philadelphia International	18–5–74	9	6
O'KAYSIONS			
Girl Watchers			
(US) ABC	14–9–68	5	9

	Date of chart entry	*Highest position reached*	*Number of weeks in charts*
O'KEEFE, DANNY			
Good Time Charlie's Got The Blues			
(US) Signpost	14–10–72	9	5
OLDFIELD, MIKE			
Tubular Bells (Theme from 'The Exorcist')			
(US) Virgin	13–4–74	7	6
OLIVER			
Good Morning Starshine			
(US) Jubilee	14–6–69	3	9
(UK) CBS	*30–8–69*	*3*	*9*
Jean			
(US) Crewe	13–9–69	2	9
OLYMPICS			
Western Movies			
(US) Demon	18–8–58	8	6
(UK) HMV	*10–10–58*	*12*	*7*
ORBISON, ROY			
Only The Lonely			
(US) Monument	4–7–60	2	10
(UK) London	*14–8–60*	*1*	*16*
Blue Angel			
(UK) London (b/w Today's Teardrops)	*30–10–60*	*13*	*8*
(US) Monument	31–10–60	9	4
Runnin' Scared			
(US) Monument	8–5–61	1	9
(UK) London	*21–5–61*	*9*	*10*
Crying			
(US) Monument	4–9–61	2	8
Dream Baby			
(US) Monument	17–3–62	4	6
(UK) London	*17–3–62*	*2*	*10*
In Dreams			
(US) Monument	2–3–62	7	8
(UK) London	*30–3–63*	*6*	*16*
Falling			
(UK) London	*8–6–63*	*9*	*9*
Blue Bayou			
(UK) London (b/w)*	*28–9–63*	*3*	*12*
Mean Woman Blues*			
(US) Monument	5–10–63	5	8
Pretty Paper			
(US) Monument	28–12–63	15	3
(UK) London	*28–11–64*	*6*	*6*

	Date of chart entry	Highest position reached	Number of weeks in charts
ORBISON, ROY (cont.)			
Borne On The Wind			
(UK) London	*7–3–64*	*15*	*3*
It's Over			
(US) Monument	2–5–64	9	6
(UK) London	*9–5–64*	*1*	*13*
Oh, Pretty Woman			
(US) Monument	12–9–64	1	11
(UK) London	*18–9–64*	*1*	*12*
Goodnight			
(UK) London	*20–2–65*	*14*	*5*
Crawlin' Back			
(UK) London	*4–12–65*	*19*	*1*
Lana			
(UK) London	*2–7–66*	*15*	*5*
Too Soon To Know			
(UK) London	*27–8–66*	*3*	*10*
There Won't Be Many Coming Home			
(UK) London	*17–12–66*	*18*	*2*
ORIGINALS			
Baby, I'm For Real			
(US) Soul	8–11–69	14	6
Bells			
(US) Soul	11–4–70	12	3
ORLANDO, TONY			
Bless You			
(UK) Fontana	*30–9–61*	*7*	*8*
(US) Epic	2–10–61	15	2
Steppin' Out (Gonna Boogie Tonight) (and DAWN)			
(US) Bell	28–9–74	7	6
[see also: DAWN]			
ORLONS			
Wah-Watusi			
(US) Cameo	30–6–62	2	9
Don't Hang Up			
(US) Cameo	10–11–62	4	8
South Street			
(US) Cameo	16–3–63	3	7
Not Me			
(US) Cameo	6–7–63	12	14
Crossfire			
(US) Cameo	2–11–63	19	1
OSMOND, DONNY			
Sweet And Innocent			
(US) MGM	8–5–71	7	9

	Date of chart entry	*Highest position reached*	*Number of weeks in charts*
OSMOND, DONNY (cont.)			
Go Away Little Girl			
(US) MGM	28–8–71	1	11
Hey Girl/I Knew You When			
(US) MGM	11–12–71	9	7
Puppy Love			
(US) MGM	11–3–72	3	8
(UK) MGM	*24–6–72*	*1*	*12*
Too Young			
(US) MGM	1–7–72	13	5
(UK) MGM	*23–9–72*	*5*	*5*
Why			
(US) MGM (b/w Lonely Boy)	7–10–72	13	4
(UK) MGM	*18–11–72*	*3*	*9*
Twelfth Of Never			
(UK) MGM	*10–3–73*	*1*	*9*
(US) MGM	7–4–73	8	6
Young Love			
(UK) MGM	*18–8–73*	*1*	*7*
When I Fall In Love			
(UK) MGM	*17–11–73*	*4*	*8*
(US) MGM (b/w Are You Lonesome Tonight)	5–1–74	14	4
[see also: OSMOND, DONNY AND MARIE]			
OSMOND, DONNY AND MARIE			
I'm Leavin' It Up To You			
(US) MGM	10–8–74	4	7
(UK) MGM	*17–8–74*	*2*	*8*
Morning Side Of The Mountain			
(US) MGM	28–12–74	8	7
OSMOND, LITTLE JIMMY			
Long Haired Lover From Liverpool			
(UK) MGM	*9–12–72*	*1*	*14*
Tweedle Dee			
(UK) MGM	*7–4–73*	*4*	*7*
I'm Gonna Knock On Your Door			
(UK) MGM	*13–4–74*	*11*	*4*
OSMOND, MARIE			
Paper Roses			
(US) MGM	13–10–73	5	9
(UK) MGM	*24–11–73*	*2*	*10*
[see also: OSMOND, DONNY AND MARIE]			
OSMONDS			
One Bad Apple			
(US) MGM	30–1–71	1	10

	Date of chart entry	*Highest position reached*	*Number of weeks in charts*
OSMONDS (cont.)			
Double Lovin'			
(US) MGM	12–6–71	14	4
Yo Yo			
(US) MGM	25–9–71	3	10
Down By The Lazy River			
(US) MGM	5–2–72	4	10
Hold Her Tight			
(US) MGM	22–7–72	14	4
Crazy Horses			
(UK) MGM	*18–11–72*	*2*	*12*
(US) MGM	25–11–72	14	4
Going Home			
(UK) MGM	*21–7–73*	*4*	*6*
Let Me In			
(UK) MGM	*3–11–73*	*2*	*9*
I Can't Stop			
(UK) MCA (re-issue)	*11–5–74*	*12*	*5*
Love Me For A Reason			
(UK) MGM	*24–8–74*	*1*	*7*
(US) MGM	12–10–74	10	3
O'SULLIVAN, GILBERT			
Nothing Rhymed			
(UK) MAM	*12–12–70*	*8*	*7*
We Will			
(UK) MAM	*28–8–71*	*16*	*4*
No Matter How I Try			
(UK) MAM	*4–12–71*	*5*	*9*
Alone Again (Naturally)			
(UK) MAM	*11–3–72*	*3*	*7*
(US) MAM	8–7–72	1	13
Ooh-Wakka-Doo-Wakka-Day			
(UK) MAM	*24–6–72*	*8*	*6*
Clair			
(UK) MAM	*21–10–72*	*1*	*8*
(US) MAM	25–11–72	2	10
Get Down			
(UK) MAM	*24–3–73*	*1*	*8*
(US) MAM	28–7–73	7	8
Out Of The Question			
(US) MAM	5–5–73	17	3
Ooh Baby			
(UK) MAM	*29–9–73*	*18*	*3*
Why Oh Why Oh Why			
(UK) MAM	*17–11–73*	*6*	*10*
Happiness Is You And Me			
(UK) MAM	*2–3–74*	*19*	*3*
Christmas Song			
(UK) MAM	*21–12–74*	*12*	*2*

	Date of chart entry	Highest position reached	Number of weeks in charts
OTIS, JOHNNY SHOW			
Ma (He's Making Eyes At Me) (with MARIE ADAMS AND THE THREE TONS OF JOY)			
(UK) Capitol	*22–11–57*	*2*	*15*
Bye Bye Baby			
(UK) Capitol	*7–2–58*	*20*	*1*
Willie And The Hand Jive			
(US) Capitol	21–7–58	9	8
OUTSIDERS			
Time Won't Let Me			
(US) Capitol	2–4–66	5	7
Respectable			
(US) Capitol	3–9–66	15	2
OVERLANDERS			
Michelle			
(UK) Pye	*22–1–66*	*1*	*7*
OWEN, REG			
Manhattan Spiritual			
(US) Palette	12–1–59	10	7
(UK) Pye International	*7–3–59*	*18*	*3*
PACIFIC GAS AND ELECTRIC			
Are You Ready?			
(US) Columbia	11–7–70	14	5
PAGE, PATTI			
Cross Of Gold			
(US) Mercury	3–12–55	16	3
Go On With The Wedding			
(US) Mercury	4–2–56	11	4
Allegheny Moon			
(US) Mercury	7–7–56	2	17
Mama From The Train			
(US) Mercury	24–11–56	11	8
Old Cape Cod			
(US) Mercury	10–6–57	7	12
Left Right Out Of Your Heart			
(US) Mercury	4–8–58	13	2
Hush Hush Sweet Charlotte			
(US) Columbia	12–6–65	8	5
PAPER DOLLS			
Something Here In My Heart			
(UK) Pye	*20–4–68*	*11*	*5*

	Date of chart entry	Highest position reached	Number of weeks in charts
PAPER LACE			
Billy Don't Be A Hero			
(UK) Bus Stop	*2–3–74*	*1*	*9*
The Night Chicago Died			
(UK) Bus Stop	*11–5–74*	*3*	*6*
(US) Mercury	27–7–74	1	8
Black Eyed Boys			
(UK) Bus Stop	*14–9–74*	*11*	*4*
PARADE			
Sunshine Girl			
(US) A & M	27–5–67	20	1
PARADONS			
Diamonds and Pearls			
(US) Milestone	10–10–60	18	3
PARIS SISTERS			
I Love How You Love Me			
(US) Gregmark	9–10–61	5	8
PARK, SIMON, ORCHESTRA			
Eye Level			
(UK) Columbia	*22–9–73*	*1*	*10*
PARKER, FESS			
Ballad Of Davy Crockett			
(US) Columbia	12–3–55	5	17
PARKER, ROBERT			
Barefootin'			
(US) Nola	28–5–66	7	7
(UK) Island	*3–9–66*	*19*	*1*
PARKINSON, JIMMY			
The Great Pretender			
(UK) Columbia	*2–3–56*	*9*	*10*
Middle Of The House			
(UK) Columbia	*7–12–56*	*20*	*1*
PARKS, MICHAEL			
Long Lonesome Highway			
(US) MGM	18–4–70	20	2
PARLIAMENTS			
(I Wanna) Testify			
(US) Revilot	2–9–67	20	2
PARSONS, BILL			
All American Boy			
(US) Fraternity	19–1–59	2	9

	Date of chart entry	Highest position reached	Number of weeks in charts
PARTRIDGE, DON			
Rosie			
(UK) Columbia	*24–2–68*	*4*	*9*
Blue Eyes			
(UK) Columbia	*8–6–68*	*3*	*8*
PARTRIDGE FAMILY (featuring DAVID CASSIDY)			
I Think I Love You			
(US) Bell	31–10–70	1	14
(UK) Bell	*27–2–71*	*18*	*1*
Doesn't Somebody Want To Be Wanted?			
(US) Bell	27–2–71	6	10
I'll Meet You Halfway			
(US) Bell	29–5–71	9	5
I Woke Up This Morning			
(US) Bell	11–9–71	13	6
It's One Of Those Nights (Yes Love)			
(US) Bell	22–1–72	20	2
(UK) Bell	*18–3–72*	*11*	*4*
Breaking Up Is Hard To Do			
(UK) Bell	*15–5–72*	*3*	*9*
Lookin' Through The Eyes Of Love			
(UK) Bell	*17–2–73*	*9*	*5*
Walking In The Rain			
(UK) Bell	*2–6–73*	*10*	*5*
[see also: DAVID CASSIDY]			
PATIENCE AND PRUDENCE			
Tonight You Belong To Me			
(US) Liberty	1–9–56	6	14
Gonna Get Along Without You Now			
(US) Liberty	15–12–56	12	8
PAUL, BILLY			
Me And Mrs. Jones			
(US) Philadelphia International	2–12–72	1	11
(UK) Epic	*27–1–73*	*12*	*4*
PAUL, LES AND FORD, MARY			
Hummingbird			
(US) Capitol	23–7–55	8	9
PAUL AND PAULA			
Hey Paula			
(US) Philips	19–1–63	1	10
(UK) Philips	*2–3–63*	*8*	*7*

	Date of chart entry	*Highest position reached*	*Number of weeks in charts*
PAUL AND PAULA (cont.)			
Young Lovers			
(US) Philips	6–4–63	6	5
(UK) Philips	*11–5–63*	*9*	*8*
PAYNE, FREDA			
Band Of Gold			
(US) Invictus	20–6–70	3	11
(UK) Invictus	*12–9–70*	*1*	*11*
Bring The Boys Home			
(US) Invictus	17–7–71	12	5
PEACHES AND HERB			
Close Your Eyes			
(US) Date	29–4–67	8	5
For Your Love			
(US) Date	5–8–67	20	1
Love Is Strange			
(US) Date	4–11–67	13	3
PEARLS			
Guilty			
(UK) Bell	*22–6–74*	*10*	*4*
PEARSON, JOHNNY			
Sleepy Shores			
(UK) Penny Farthing	*25–12–71*	*8*	*7*
PEDDLERS			
Birth			
(UK) CBS	*20–9–69*	*17*	*1*
PEERS, DONALD			
Please Don't Go			
(UK) Columbia	*1–2–69*	*4*	*9*
PENGUINS			
Earth Angel			
(US) Dootone	15–1–55	8	11
PEOPLE			
I Love You			
(US) Capitol	15–6–68	14	6
PEPPERS			
Pepper Box			
(UK) Spark	*9–11–74*	*6*	*5*
PERICOLI, EMILIO			
Al Dila			
(US) Warner Brothers	16–6–62	6	7

	Date of chart entry	*Highest position reached*	*Number of weeks in charts*
PERKINS, CARL			
Blue Suede Shoes			
(US) Sun	17–3–56	4	14
(UK) London	*18–5–56*	*10*	*7*
PERSUADERS			
Thin Line Between Love And Hate			
(US) Atco	16–10–71	15	3
PETER AND GORDON			
World Without Love			
(UK) Columbia	*28–3–64*	*1*	*9*
(US) Capitol	23–5–64	1	8
Nobody I Know			
(UK) Columbia	*20–6–64*	*10*	*5*
(US) Capitol	18–7–64	12	4
I Don't Want To See You Again			
(US) Capitol	31–10–64	16	2
I Go To Pieces			
(US) Capitol	6–2–65	9	5
True Love Ways			
(UK) Columbia	*24–4–65*	*2*	*10*
(US) Capitol	22–5–65	14	5
To Know You Is To Love You			
(UK) Columbia	*3–7–65*	*5*	*6*
Baby I'm Yours			
(UK) Columbia	*13–11–65*	*19*	*1*
Woman			
(US) Capitol	19–3–66	14	5
Lady Godiva			
(UK) Columbia	*15–10–66*	*16*	*3*
(US) Capitol	19–11–66	6	6
Knight in Rusty Armour			
(US) Capitol	21–2–67	15	3
PETER, PAUL AND MARY			
If I Had A Hammer			
(US) Warner Brothers	22–9–62	10	5
Puff			
(US) Warner Brothers	30–3–63	2	10
Blowin' In The Wind			
(US) Warner Brothers	20–7–63	2	8
(UK) Warner Brothers	*9–11–63*	*13*	*5*
Don't Think Twice It's All Right			
(US) Warner Brothers	12–10–63	9	4
I Dig Rock And Roll Music			
(US) Warner Brothers	16–9–67	9	5
Leaving On A Jet Plane			
(US) Warner Brothers	22–11–69	1	12
(UK) Warner Brothers	*24–1–70*	*2*	*9*

	Date of chart entry	*Highest position reached*	*Number of weeks in charts*
PETERS AND LEE			
Welcome Home			
(UK) Philips	*9–6–73*	*1*	*15*
Don't Stay Away Too Long			
(UK) Philips	*24–4–74*	*3*	*8*
Rainbow			
(UK) Philips	*7–9–74*	*17*	*2*
PETERSON, PAUL			
She Can't Find Her Keys			
(US) Colpix	28–4–62	19	1
My Dad			
(US) Colpix	29–12–62	6	7
PETERSON, RAY			
Tell Laura I Love Her			
(US) RCA	11–7–60	7	7
Corinna, Corinna			
(US) Dunes	26–12–60	9	7
PHILLIPS, LITTLE ESTHER			
Release Me			
(US) Lenox	24–11–62	8	7
PHILLIPS, PHIL			
Sea Of Love			
(US) Mercury	10–8–59	2	9
PIAF, EDITH			
Milord			
(UK) Columbia	*13–11–60*	*17*	*2*
PICKETT, BOBBY 'BORIS' AND THE CRIPT KICKERS			
Monster Mash			
(US) Garpax	22–9–62	1	9
(US) Parrot (re-issue)	14–7–73	10	7
(UK) London (re-issue)	*22–9–73*	*3*	*6*
PICKETT, WILSON			
In The Midnight Hour			
(UK) Atlantic	*14–10–65*	*12*	*4*
634-5789			
(US) Atlantic	19–3–66	13	4
Land Of A Thousand Dances			
(US) Atlantic	20–8–66	6	5
Funky Broadway			
(US) Atlantic	2–9–67	8	6
She's Lookin' Good			
(US) Atlantic	25–5–68	15	2

	Date of chart entry	*Highest position reached*	*Number of weeks in charts*
PICKETT, WILSON (cont.)			
Hey Jude			
(UK) Atlantic	*15–2–69*	*16*	*1*
Engine Number 9			
(US) Atlantic	14–11–70	14	4
Don't Let The Green Grass Fool You			
(US) Atlantic	27–2–71	17	3
Don't Knock My Love, Pt. 1			
(US) Atlantic	5–6–71	13	5
PICKETTYWITCH			
That Same Old Feeling			
(UK) Pye	*28–2–70*	*5*	*8*
(It's Like A) Sad Old Kinda Movie			
(UK) Pye	*18–7–70*	*16*	*2*
PIGLETS			
Johnny Reggae			
(UK) Bell	*6–11–71*	*3*	*7*
PILOT			
Magic			
(UK) EMI	*16–11–74*	*11*	*5*
PILTDOWN MAN			
McDonald's Cave			
(UK) Capitol	*7–10–60*	*12*	*6*
Piltdown Rides Again			
(UK) Capitol	*1–1–61*	*16*	*2*
Goodnight Mrs. Flintstone			
(UK) Capitol	*5–3–61*	*18*	*3*
PINK FLOYD			
Arnold Layne			
(UK) Columbia	*22–4–67*	*20*	*1*
See Emily Play			
(UK) Columbia	*8–7–67*	*6*	*7*
Money			
(US) Harvest	7–7–73	13	5
PINKERTON'S ASSORTED COLOURS			
Mirror Mirror			
(UK) Decca	*12–2–66*	*9*	*4*
PIONEERS			
Let Your Yeah Be Yeah			
(UK) Trojan	*21–8–71*	*5*	*6*

	Date of chart entry	*Highest position reached*	*Number of weeks in charts*
PIPKINS			
Gimme Dat Ding			
(UK) Columbia	*11–4–70*	*6*	*6*
(US) Capitol	27–6–70	9	5
PIPS			
Every Beat Of My Heart			
(US) Vee Jay	12–6–61	6	7
[see also: KNIGHT, GLADYS AND THE PIPS]			
PITNEY, GENE			
Town Without Pity			
(US) Musicor	20–1–62	13	4
The Man Who Shot Liberty Valance			
(US) Musicor	2–6–62	4	6
Only Love Can Break A Heart			
(US) Musicor	13–10–62	2	8
Half Heaven, Half Heartache			
(US) Musicor	12–1–63	12	6
Mecca			
(US) Musicor	20–4–63	12	5
24 Hours From Tulsa			
(US) Musicor	30–11–63	17	2
(UK) United Artists	*14–12–63*	*5*	*12*
That Girl Belongs To Yesterday			
(UK) United Artists	*14–3–64*	*8*	*7*
It Hurts To Be In Love			
(US) Musicor	19–9–64	7	6
I'm Gonna Be Strong			
(US) Musicor	14–11–64	9	7
(UK) Stateside	*21–11–64*	*2*	*10*
I Must Be Seeing Things			
(UK) Stateside	*27–2–65*	*6*	*6*
Last Chance To Turn Around			
(US) Musicor	12–6–65	13	4
Lookin' Through The Eyes Of Love			
(UK) Stateside	*19–6–65*	*3*	*8*
Princess In Rags			
(UK) Stateside	*20–11–65*	*9*	*8*
Backstage			
(UK) Stateside	*26–2–66*	*4*	*6*
Nobody Needs Your Love			
(UK) Stateside	*18–6–66*	*2*	*9*
Just One Smile			
(UK) Stateside	*26–11–66*	*8*	*6*
Somethin's Gotten Hold Of My Heart			
(UK) Stateside	*25–11–67*	*5*	*9*

	Date of chart entry	Highest position reached	Number of weeks in charts
PITNEY, GENE (cont.)			
Somewhere In The Country			
(UK) Stateside	*4–5–68*	*19*	*2*
She's A Heartbreaker			
(US) Musicor	13–7–68	16	3
PLASTIC ONO BAND.			
See LENNON, JOHN			
PLASTIC PENNY			
Everything I Am			
(UK) Page One	*27–1–68*	*6*	*5*
PLATTERS			
Only You			
(US) Mercury	8–10–55	5	18
(UK) Mercury (b/w)*	*7–9–56*	*5*	*11*
The Great Pretender*			
(US) Mercury	30–12–55	1	17
Magic Touch			
(US) Mercury	7–4–56	4	12
My Prayer			
(US) Mercury	21–7–56	1	16
(UK) Mercury	*2–11–56*	*4*	*10*
You'll Never Know			
(US) Mercury	20–10–56	14	6
I'm Sorry			
(US) Mercury	27–4–57	19	2
(UK) Mercury	*31–5–57*	*18*	*2*
Twilight Time			
(US) Mercury	14–4–58	1	13
(UK) Mercury	*6–6–58*	*3*	*12*
Smoke Gets In Your Eyes			
(US) Mercury	8–12–58	1	13
(UK) Mercury	*17–1–59*	*1*	*19*
Enchanted			
(US) Mercury	20–4–59	12	7
Harbor Lights			
(UK) Mercury	*30–1–60*	*12*	*5*
(US) Mercury	29–2–60	8	8
With This Ring			
(US) Musicor	15–4–67	14	3
PLAYMATES			
Jo Ann			
(US) Roulette	17–2–58	20	1
Beep Beep			
(US) Roulette	10–11–58	4	11
What Is Love			
(US) Roulette	17–8–59	15	4

	Date of chart entry	Highest position reached	Number of weeks in charts
POINTER SISTERS			
Yes We Can			
(US) Blue Thumb	22–9–73	11	7
Fairy Tale			
(US) Blue Thumb	30–11–74	13	3
PONI TAILS			
Born Too Late			
(US) ABC-Paramount	11–8–58	7	9
(UK) HMV	*19–9–58*	*5*	*10*
POOLE, BRIAN, AND THE TREMELOES			
Twist And Shout			
(UK) Decca	*13–7–63*	*4*	*10*
Do You Love Me?			
(UK) Decca	*21–9–63*	*1*	*11*
Candy Man			
(UK) Decca	*15–2–64*	*6*	*7*
Someone, Someone			
(UK) Decca	*30–5–64*	*2*	*10*
Three Bells			
(UK) Decca	*30–1–65*	*17*	*2*
[see also: TREMELOES]			
POPPY FAMILY			
Which Way You Goin', Billy?			
(US) London	16–5–70	2	8
(UK) Decca	*12–9–70*	*7*	*7*
POSEY, SANDY			
Born A Woman			
(US) MGM	27–8–66	12	7
Single Girl			
(US) MGM	24–12–66	12	4
(UK) MGM	*28–1–67*	*15*	*7*
I Take It Back			
(US) MGM	15–7–67	12	5
POURCEL, FRANK			
Only You			
(US) Capitol	11–5–59	9	7
POWELL, COZY			
Dance With The Devil			
(UK) RAK	*22–12–73*	*3*	*10*
Man In Black			
(UK) RAK	*15–6–74*	*18*	*3*
Na Na Na			
(UK) RAK	*24–8–74*	*10*	*6*

	Date of chart entry	Highest position reached	Number of weeks in charts
POWERS, JOEY			
Midnight Mary			
(US) Amy	28–12–63	10	4
PRADO, PERÈZ			
Cherry Pink And Apple Blossom White			
(UK) HMV	*25–3–55*	*1*	*17*
(US) Victor	26–3–55	1	22
Patricia			
(US) Victor	30–6–58	1	15
(UK) RCA	*8–8–58*	*8*	*11*
PREMIERS			
Farmer John			
(US) Warner Brothers	1–8–64	19	1
PRESIDENTS			
5–10–15–20 (25–30 Years of Love)			
(US) Sussex	21–11–70	11	7
PRESLEY, ELVIS			
Heartbreak Hotel			
(US) Victor	24–3–56	1	18
(UK) HMV	*11–5–56*	*2*	*19*
Blue Suede Shoes			
(UK) HMV	*25–5–56*	*9*	*8*
I Want You, I Need You, I Love You			
(US) Victor	9–6–56	3	16
(UK) HMV	*17–8–56*	*14*	*6*
Hound Dog			
(US) Victor } (b/w*)	11–8–56	2	16
(UK) HMV } (b/w*)	*21–9–56*	*2*	*22*
Don't Be Cruel*			
(US) Victor	18–8–56	1	19
Love Me Tender			
(US) Victor	20–10–56	1	17
(UK) HMV	*7–12–56*	*11*	*9*
Blue Moon			
(UK) HMV	*16–11–56*	*9*	*8*
Love Me			
(US) Victor EP	8–12–56	6	12
Too Much			
(US) Victor	2–2–57	2	11
(UK) HMV	*10–5–57*	*6*	*8*
All Shook Up			
(US) Victor	13–4–57	1	17
(UK) HMV	*28–6–57*	*1*	*18*

	Date of chart entry	Highest position reached	Number of weeks in charts
PRESLEY, ELVIS (cont.)			
Teddy Bear			
(US) Victor	1–7–57	1	16
(UK) RCA	*12–7–57*	*3*	*18*
Paralysed			
(UK) HMV	*30–8–57*	*8*	*8*
Let's Have A Party			
*(UK) RCA (b/w**)*	*4–10–57*	*2*	*14*
Jailhouse Rock			
(US) Victor	14–10–57	1	16
(UK) RCA	*24–1–58*	*1*	*13*
Got A Lot Of Living To Do**			
(UK) RCA	*18–10–57*	*17*	*3*
Tryin' To Get To You			
*(UK) HMV (b/w***)*	*1–11–57*	*16*	*3*
Lawdy Miss Clawdy***			
(UK) HMV	*8–11–57*	*15*	*3*
Santa Bring My Baby			
(UK) RCA	*15–11–57*	*7*	*7*
Jailhouse Rock			
(UK) RCA EP	*31–1–58*	*18*	*3*
Don't			
(US) Victor } (b/w†)	3–2–58	1	11
(UK) RCA } (b/w†)	*28–2–58*	*2*	*10*
I Beg Of You†			
(US) Victor	3–2–58	8	3
Wear My Ring Around Your Neck			
(US) Victor	21–4–58	3	10
(UK) RCA	*2–5–58*	*3*	*7*
Hard Headed Woman			
(US) Victor	30–6–58	2	8
(UK) RCA	*25–7–58*	*2*	*8*
King Creole			
(UK) RCA	*3–10–58*	*2*	*10*
I Got Stung			
(US) RCA } (b/w††)	10–11–58	8	10
(UK) RCA } (b/w††)	*24–1–59*	*1*	*12*
One Night††			
(US) RCA	17–11–58	4	11
A Fool Such As I			
(US) RCA } (b/w†††)	6–4–59	2	9
(UK) RCA } (b/w†††)	*25–4–59*	*1*	*14*
I Need Your Love Tonight†††			
(US) RCA	6–4–59	4	8
Big Hunk Of Love			
(US) RCA } (b/w◇)	20–7–59	1	9
(UK) RCA } (b/w◇)	*25–7–59*	*4*	*8*
My Wish Came True ◇			
(US) RCA	3–8–59	12	4

	Date of chart entry	*Highest position reached*	*Number of weeks in charts*
PRESLEY, ELVIS (cont.)			
Stuck On You			
(UK) RCA } (b/w◇◇)	*3-4-60*	*2*	*8*
(US) RCA } (b/w◇◇)	11-4-60	1	11
Fame And Fortune◇◇			
(US) RCA	25-4-60	17	5
The Girl Of My Best Friend/ Mess Of Blues			
(UK) RCA	*24-7-60*	*2*	*15*
It's Now Or Never			
(US) RCA	25-7-60	1	14
(UK) RCA	*30-10-60*	*1*	*13*
Are You Lonesome Tonight?			
(US) RCA } (b/w◇◇◇)	21-22-60	1	12
(UK) RCA } (b/w◇◇◇)	*8-1-61*	*1*	*8*
I Gotta Know◇◇◇			
(US) RCA	12-12-60	20	1
Wooden Heart			
(UK) RCA	*26-2-61*	*1*	*15*
Surrender			
(US) RCA	27-2-61	1	9
(UK) RCA	*14-5-61*	*1*	*11*
Flaming Star			
(US) RCA EP	1-5-61	14	3
I Feel So Bad			
(US) RCA	22-5-61	5	6
(UK) RCA (b/w Wild In The Country)	*2-9-61*	*2*	*8*
Little Sister			
(US) RCA (b/w○)	4-9-61	5	7
(Marie's The Name) His Latest Flame○			
(US) RCA	18-9-61	4	2
(UK) RCA	*28-10-61*	*1*	*8*
Can't Help Falling In Love			
(US) RCA	18-12-61	2	10
(UK) RCA (b/w Rock-A-Hula Baby)	*3-2-62*	*1*	*17*
Good Luck Charm			
(US) RCA	24-3-62	1	10
(UK) RCA	*12-5-62*	*1*	*13*
She's Not You			
(US) RCA	18-8-62	5	7
(UK) RCA	*8-9-62*	*1*	*10*
Return To Sender			
(US) RCA	27-10-62	2	12
(UK) RCA	*8-12-62*	*1*	*10*
One Broken Heart For Sale			
(US) RCA	2-3-63	11	5
(UK) RCA	*16-3-63*	*12*	*4*

	Date of chart entry	Highest position reached	Number of weeks in charts
PRESLEY, ELVIS (cont.)			
(You're The) Devil In Disguise			
(US) RCA	13–7–63	3	8
(UK) RCA	*13–7–63*	*1*	*9*
Bossa Nova Baby			
(UK) RCA	*2–11–63*	*13*	*4*
(US) RCA	9–11–63	8	4
Kiss Me Quick			
(UK) RCA	*28–12–63*	*14*	*6*
Kissin' Cousins			
(US) RCA	14–3–64	12	4
(UK) RCA	*4–7–64*	*10*	*5*
Viva Las Vegas			
(UK) RCA	*28–3–64*	*17*	*4*
Such A Night			
(US) RCA	22–8–64	16	2
(UK) RCA	*29–8–64*	*13*	*5*
Ain't That Loving You, Baby			
(US) RCA (b/w○○)	7–11–64	16	3
(UK) RCA	*7–11–64*	*15*	*3*
Ask Me○○			
(US) RCA	21–11–64	12	4
Do The Clam			
(UK) RCA	*20–3–65*	*19*	*2*
Crying In The Chapel			
(US) RCA	15–5–65	3	10
(UK) RCA	*5–6–65*	*1*	*11*
(Such An) Easy Question			
(US) RCA	10–7–65	11	4
I'm Yours			
(US) RCA	2–10–65	11	4
Tell Me Why			
(UK) RCA	*27–11–65*	*15*	*4*
Puppet On A String			
(US) RCA	18–12–65	14	3
Love Letters			
(UK) RCA	*16–7–66*	*6*	*7*
(US) RCA	23–7–66	19	2
All That I Am			
(UK) RCA	*5–11–66*	*18*	*1*
If Every Day Was Like Christmas			
(UK) RCA	*10–12–66*	*13*	*3*
Guitar Man			
(UK) RCA	*23–3–68*	*19*	*2*
U.S. Male			
(UK) RCA	*25–5–68*	*15*	*3*
If I Can Dream			
(US) RCA	11–1–69	12	6
(UK) RCA	*8–3–69*	*11*	*6*

	Date of chart entry	*Highest position reached*	*Number of weeks in charts*
PRESLEY, ELVIS (cont.)			
In The Ghetto			
(US) RCA	24–5–69	3	9
(UK) RCA	*21–6–69*	*2*	*11*
Suspicious Minds			
(US) RCA	27–9–69	1	11
(UK) RCA	*6–12–69*	*2*	*11*
Don't Cry, Daddy			
(US) RCA (b/w Rubberneckin')	3–1–70	6	7
(UK) RCA	*7–3–70*	*8*	*7*
Kentucky Rain			
(US) RCA	14–3–70	16	3
The Wonder Of You (b/w Mama Liked The Roses)			
(US) RCA	13–6–70	9	7
(UK) RCA	*11–7–70*	*1*	*16*
You Don't Have To Say You Love Me			
(US) RCA (b/w Patch It Up)	21–11–70	11	4
(UK) RCA	*16–1–71*	*9*	*6*
I've Lost You			
(UK) RCA	*28–11–70*	*9*	*8*
There Goes My Everything			
(UK) RCA	*27–3–71*	*6*	*6*
Rags To Riches			
(UK) RCA	*29–5–71*	*9*	*6*
Heartbreak Hotel			
(UK) RCA (re-issue)	*7–8–71*	*10*	*5*
I Just Can't Help Believing			
(UK) RCA	*25–12–71*	*6*	*8*
Until It's Time For You To Go			
(UK) RCA	*15–4–72*	*5*	*5*
American Trilogy			
(UK) RCA	*1–7–72*	*8*	*5*
Burning Love			
(US) RCA	23–9–72	2	9
(UK) RCA	*7–10–72*	*7*	*6*
Always On My Mind			
(UK) RCA	*6–1–73*	*9*	*5*
Separate Ways			
(UK) RCA	*3–2–73*	*20*	*1*
Steamroller Blues			
(US) RCA (b/w○○○)	26–5–73	17	2
Fool○○○			
(UK) RCA	*1–9–73*	*15*	*5*
If You Talk In Your Sleep			
(US) RCA	3–8–74	17	1

	Date of chart entry	Highest position reached	Number of weeks in charts
PRESLEY, ELVIS (cont.)			
Promised Land			
(US) RCA	30–11–74	14	3
My Boy			
(UK) RCA	*30–11–74*	*5*	*8*
PRESTON, BILLY			
That's The Way God Planned It			
(UK) Apple	*12–7–69*	*11*	*6*
Outa-Space			
(US) A & M	3–6–72	2	8
Will It Go Round In Circles			
(US) A & M	2–6–73	1	11
Space Race			
(US) A & M	20–10–73	4	9
Nothing From Nothing			
(US) A & M	24–8–74	1	10
PRESTON, JOHNNY			
Running Bear			
(US) Mercury	28–12–59	1	12
(UK) Mercury	*6–2–60*	*1*	*11*
Cradle Of Love			
(US) Mercury	11–4–60	7	9
(UK) Mercury	*1–5–60*	*2*	*9*
Feel So Fine			
(US) Mercury	1–8–60	14	5
PRESTON, MIKE			
Mr. Blue			
(UK) Decca	*24–10–59*	*9*	*7*
Marry Me			
(UK) Decca	*12–3–61*	*13*	*3*
PRETTY THINGS			
Don't Bring Me Down			
(UK) Fontana	*14–11–64*	*10*	*5*
Honey I Need			
(UK) Fontana	*13–3–65*	*13*	*3*
PRICE, ALAN			
I Put A Spell On You			
(UK) Decca	*16–4–66*	*9*	*5*
Hi-Lili-Hi-Lo			
(UK) Decca	*6–8–66*	*11*	*7*
Simon Smith And His Dancing Bear			
(UK) Decca	*18–3–67*	*4*	*7*

	Date of chart entry	*Highest position reached*	*Number of weeks in charts*
PRICE, ALAN (cont.)			
The House That Jack Built			
(UK) Decca	*12–8–67*	*4*	*7*
Don't Stop The Carnival			
(UK) Decca	*10–2–68*	*13*	*4*
Jarrow Song			
(UK) Warner Brothers	*8–6–74*	*6*	*5*
[see also: ANIMALS; FAME AND PRICE]			
PRICE, LLOYD			
Stagger Lee			
(US) ABC-Paramount	19–1–59	1	12
(UK) HMV	*14–2–59*	*6*	*13*
Where Were You On Our Wedding Day?			
(UK) HMV	*9–5–59*	*15*	*5*
Personality			
(US) ABC-Paramount	25–5–69	2	11
(UK) HMV	*6–6–59*	*9*	*9*
I'm Gonna Get Married			
(US) ABC-Paramount	24–8–59	3	10
(UK) HMV	*19–9–59*	*20*	*2*
Come Into My Heart			
(US) ABC-Paramount	7–12–59	20	1
Lady Luck			
(US) ABC-Paramount	22–2–60	14	7
Question			
(US) ABC-Paramount	8–8–60	19	1
PRICE, RAY			
For The Good Times			
(US) Columbia	19–12–70	11	6
PRIMA, LOUIS			
Wonderland By Night			
(US) Dot	19–12–60	15	6
[see also: SMITH, KEELY]			
PRINCE BUSTER			
Al Capone			
(UK) Blue Beat	*1–4–67*	*18*	*2*
PROBY, P. J.			
Hold Me			
(UK) Decca	*27–6–64*	*3*	*8*
Together			
(UK) Decca	*18–9–64*	*8*	*6*

	Date of chart entry	*Highest position reached*	*Number of weeks in charts*
PROBY, P. J. (cont.)			
Somewhere			
(UK) Liberty	*19–12–64*	*6*	*8*
I Apologise			
(UK) Liberty	*6–3–65*	*11*	*5*
Let The Water Run Down			
(UK) Liberty	*31–7–65*	*19*	*1*
Maria			
(UK) Liberty	*4–12–65*	*8*	*6*
PROCOL HARUM			
A Whiter Shade Of Pale			
(UK) Deram	*3–6–67*	*1*	*11*
(US) Deram	8–7–67	5	9
(UK) Magnify (re-issue)	*27–5–72*	*13*	*4*
Homburg			
(UK) Regal Zonophone	*14–10–67*	*7*	*7*
Conquistador			
(US) A & M	15–7–72	16	4
PROVINE, DOROTHY			
Don't Bring Lulu			
(UK) Warner Brothers	6–1–62	14	2
PUCKETT, GARY, AND THE UNION GAP (* as UNION GAP)			
Woman Woman*			
(US) Columbia	16–12–67	4	11
Young Girl			
(US) Columbia	23–3–68	2	11
(UK) CBS	*4–5–68*	*1*	*12*
(UK) CBS (re-issue)	*6–7–74*	*6*	*6*
Lady Willpower			
(US) Columbia	22–6–68	2	10
(UK) CBS	*7–9–68*	*5*	*10*
Over You			
(US) Columbia	12–10–68	7	7
Don't Give In To Him			
(US) Columbia	12–4–69	15	4
This Girl Is A Woman Now			
(US) Columbia	13–9–69	9	7
PURIFY, JAMES AND BOBBY			
I'm Your Puppet			
(US) Bell	29–10–66	6	7
PURSELL, BILL			
Our Winter Love			
(US) Columbia	9–3–63	9	6
PYRAMIDS			
Penetration			
(US) Best	7–3–64	18	2

	Date of chart entry	*Highest position reached*	*Number of weeks in charts*
PYTHON LEE JACKSON			
In A Broken Dream			
(UK) Young Blood	*7–10–72*	*3*	*6*
QUATRO, SUZIE			
Can The Can			
(UK) RAK	*26–5–73*	*1*	*7*
48 Crash			
(UK) RAK	*4–8–73*	*3*	*5*
Daytona Demon			
(UK) RAK	*17–11–73*	*14*	*4*
Devil Gate Drive			
(UK) RAK	*9–2–74*	*1*	*7*
Too Big			
(UK) (RAK)	*13–7–74*	*14*	*2*
Wild One			
(UK) RAK	*16–11–74*	*7*	*5*
QUEEN			
Seven Seas Of Rye			
(UK) EMI	*23–3–74*	*10*	*6*
Killer Queen			
(UK) EMI	*2–11–74*	*2*	*6*
? AND THE MYSTERIANS			
96 Tears			
(US) Cameo	24–9–66	1	11
QUIN-TONES			
Down The Aisle Of Love			
(US) Hunt	15–9–58	20	1
RADHA KRISHNA TEMPLE			
Hare Krishna Mantra			
(UK) Apple	*20–9–69*	*12*	*5*
RAIDERS. See REVERE, PAUL			
RAINDROPS			
The Kind Of Boy You Can't Forget			
(US) Jubilee	28–9–63	17	1
RAINWATER, MARVIN			
Whole Lotta Woman			
(UK) MGM	*14–3–58*	*1*	*14*
I Dig You Baby			
(UK) MGM	*20–6–58*	*19*	*1*

	Date of chart entry	*Highest position reached*	*Number of weeks in charts*
RAMRODS			
Riders In The Sky			
(UK) London	*5–2–61*	*7*	*9*
RAN-DELLS			
Martian Hop			
(US) Chairman	21–9–63	16	3
RANDY AND THE RAINBOWS			
Denise			
(US) Rust	17–8–63	10	5
RARE EARTH			
Get Ready			
(US) Rare Earth	9–5–70	4	11
(I Know) I'm Losing You			
(US) Rare Earth	12–9–70	7	6
Born To Wander			
(US) Rare Earth	30–1–71	17	2
I Just Want To Celebrate			
(US) Rare Earth	28–8–71	7	6
Hey Big Brother			
(US) Rare Earth	15–1–72	19	2
RASCALS. See YOUNG RASCALS			
RASPBERRIES			
Go All The Way			
(US) Capitol	2–9–72	5	8
I Wanna Be With You			
(US) Capitol	13–1–73	16	3
Overnight Sensation (Hit Record)			
(US) Capitol	2–11–74	18	2
RATTLES			
The Witch			
(UK) Decca	*31–10–70*	*8*	*5*
RAWLS, LOU			
Love Is A Hurtin' Thing			
(US) Capitol	29–10–66	13	5
Your Good Thing (Is About To End)			
(US) Capitol	13–9–69	18	3
Natural Man			
(US) MGM	27–11–71	17	3
RAY, JOHNNIE			
If You Believe			
(UK) Philips	*8–4–55*	*7*	*11*

	Date of chart entry	Highest position reached	Number of weeks in charts
RAY, JOHNNIE (cont.)			
Paths Of Paradise			
(UK) Philips	*20–5–55*	*20*	*1*
Hernando's Hideaway			
(UK) Philips	*7–10–55*	*11*	*5*
Hey There			
(UK) Philips	*14–10–55*	*5*	*9*
Song Of The Dreamer			
(UK) Philips	*28–10–55*	*10*	*5*
Who's Sorry Now?			
(UK) Philips	*17–2–56*	*17*	*2*
Ain't Misbehavin'			
(UK) Philips	*20–4–56*	*17*	*4*
Just Walkin' In The Rain			
(US) Columbia	22–9–56	2	20
(UK) Philips	*12–10–56*	*1*	*18*
You Don't Owe Me A Thing			
(UK) Philips } (b/w*)	*25–1–57*	*12*	*10*
(US) Columbia } (b/w*)	9–2–57	10	6
Look Homeward, Angel*			
(UK) Philips	*22–3–57*	*7*	*10*
Yes Tonight Josephine			
(UK) Philips	*10–5–57*	*1*	*15*
(US) Columbia	27–5–57	18	1
Build Your Love			
(UK) Philips	*13–9–57*	*17*	*3*
RAYBURN, MARGIE			
I'm Available			
(US) Liberty	25–11–57	16	5
RAYS			
Silhouettes			
(US) Cameo	28–10–57	3	15
REBELS			
Wild Weekend			
(US) Swan	16–2–63	8	6
REDBONE			
Witch Queen Of New Orleans			
(UK) Epic	*9–10–71*	*2*	*8*
Come And Get Your Love			
(US) Epic	9–3–74	5	10
REDDING, OTIS			
My Girl			
(UK) Atlantic	*8–1–66*	*11*	*7*
Tramp (with CARLA THOMAS)			
(UK) Stax	*19–8–67*	*18*	*1*

	Date of chart entry	*Highest position reached*	*Number of weeks in charts*
REDDING, OTIS (cont.)			
(Sittin' On The) Dock Of The Bay			
(US) Volt	17–2–68	1	12
(UK) Stax	*9–3–68*	*3*	*8*
Hard To Handle			
(UK) Atlantic	*31–8–68*	*15*	*6*
REDDY, HELEN			
I Don't Know How To Love Him			
(US) Capitol	22–5–71	13	5
I Am Woman			
(US) Capitol	28–10–72	1	11
Peaceful			
(US) Capitol	14–4–73	12	4
Delta Dawn			
(US) Capitol	11–8–73	1	10
Leave Me Alone (Ruby Red)			
(US) Capitol	24–11–73	3	8
Keep On Singing			
(US) Capitol	20–4–74	15	2
You And Me Against The World			
(US) Capitol	17–8–74	9	6
Angie Baby			
(US) Capitol	16–11–74	1	9
REED, JERRY			
Amos Moses			
(US) RCA	20–2–71	8	7
When You're Hot You're Hot			
(US) RCA	12–6–71	9	6
REED, LOU			
Walk On The Wild Side			
(US) RCA	21–4–73	16	4
(UK) RCA	*26–5–73*	*10*	*4*
REESE, DELLA			
Don't You Know			
(US) RCA	19–10–59	2	10
Not One Minute More			
(US) RCA	4–1–60	16	4
REUNION			
Life Is A Rock (But the Radio Rolled Me)			
(US) RCA	26–10–74	8	5
REEVES, JIM			
Four Walls			
(US) Victor	20–5–57	12	7
He'll Have To Go			
(US) RCA	21–1–60	2	16
(UK) RCA	*10–4–60*	*11*	*15*

	Date of chart entry	Highest position reached	Number of weeks in charts
REEVES, JIM (cont.)			
You're The Only Good Thing That's Happened To Me *(UK) RCA*	*2-12-61*	*12*	*1*
Welcome To My World *(UK) RCA*	*29-6-63*	*6*	*10*
I Love You Because *(UK) RCA*	*14-3-64*	*5*	*26*
I Won't Forget You *(UK) RCA*	*4-7-64*	*3*	*19*
There's A Heartache Following Me *(UK) RCA*	*14-11-64*	*6*	*9*
It Hurts So Much *(UK) RCA*	*13-2-65*	*8*	*6*
Not Until The Next Time *(UK) RCA*	*15-5-65*	*13*	*5*
Is It Really Over? *(UK) RCA*	*4-12-65*	*17*	*2*
Distant Drums *(UK) RCA*	*3-9-66*	*1*	*19*
I Won't Come In While He's There *(UK) RCA*	*11-2-67*	*12*	*5*
When Two Worlds Collide *(UK) RCA*	*2-8-69*	*17*	*2*
But You Love Me, Daddy *(UK) RCA*	*27-12-69*	*15*	*6*
REEVES, MARTHA. See MARTHA AND THE VANDELLAS			
REFLECTIONS			
(Just Like) Romeo and Juliet (US) Golden World	16-5-64	6	5
REGAN, JOAN			
Prize Of Gold *(UK) Decca*	*25-3-55*	*6*	*9*
May You Always *(UK) HMV*	*6-6-59*	*12*	*8*
Happy Anniversary *(UK) HMV*	*13-2-60*	*20*	*1*
REGENTS			
Barbara Ann (US) Gee	29-5-61	13	6
REID, NEIL			
Mother Of Mine *(UK) Decca*	*25-12-71*	*2*	*15*

	Date of chart entry	Highest position reached	Number of weeks in charts
RENAY, DIANE			
Navy Blue			
(US) 20th Century Fox	22–2–64	6	6
RENE AND RENE			
The More I Love You			
(US) White Whale	4–1–69	14	3
REPARATA AND THE DELRONS			
Captain Of Your Ship			
(UK) Bell	*6–4–68*	*13*	*5*
REVERE, PAUL, AND THE RAIDERS (featuring MARK LINDSAY)			
Just Like Me			
(US) Columbia	15–1–66	11	5
Kicks			
(US) Columbia	9–4–66	4	9
Hungry			
(US) Columbia	9–7–66	6	6
Great Airplane Strike			
(US) Columbia	29–10–66	20	1
Good Thing			
(US) Columbia	31–12–66	4	7
Him Or Me, What's It Gonna Be?			
(US) Columbia*	20–5–67	5	5
I Had A Dream			
(US) Columbia	16–9–67	17	3
Too Much Talk			
(US) Columbia	9–3–69	19	3
Mr. Sun, Mr. Moon			
(US) Columbia	5–4–69	18	3
Let Me			
(US) Columbia	5–7–69	20	2
Indian Reservations			
(US) Columbia**	12–6–71	1	12
(*no label credit to MARK LINDSAY; **label credit: RAIDERS)			
REYNOLDS, DEBBIE			
Tammy			
(US) Coral	5–8–57	1	18
(UK) Vogue-Coral	*6–9–57*	*2*	*15*
REYNOLDS, JODY			
Endless Sleep			
(US) Demon	16–6–58	5	9

	Date of chart entry	*Highest position reached*	*Number of weeks in charts*
RICH, CHARLIE			
Behind Closed Doors			
(US) Epic	30–6–73	15	4
(UK) Epic (re-issue)	*18–5–74*	*16*	*1*
Most Beautiful Girl			
(US) Epic	17–11–73	1	11
(UK) Epic	*23–2–74*	*2*	*9*
There Won't Be Anymore			
(US) RCA (re-issue)	23–3–74	18	2
A Very Special Love Song			
(US) Epic	30–3–74	11	4
RICHARD, CLIFF (and THE SHADOWS through 1967)			
Move It			
(UK) Columbia	*26–9–58*	*2*	*11*
High Class Baby			
(UK) Columbia	*28–11–58*	*7*	*9*
Never Mind/Mean Streak			
(UK) Columbia	*25–4–59*	*8*	*10*
Livin' Doll			
(UK) Columbia	*11–7–59*	*1*	*18*
Travellin' Light			
(UK) Columbia	*10–10–59*	*1*	*14*
A Voice In The Wilderness			
(UK) Columbia	*16–1–60*	*2*	*10*
Expresso Bongo			
(UK) Columbia EP	*16–1–60*	*8*	*4*
Fall In Love With You/Willie And The Hand Jive			
(UK) Columbia	*20–3–60*	*2*	*11*
Please Don't Tease			
(UK) Columbia	*26–6–60*	*1*	*14*
Nine Times Out Of Ten			
(UK) Columbia	*18–9–60*	*2*	*9*
I Love You			
(UK) Columbia	*27–11–60*	*2*	*11*
Theme For A Dream			
(UK) Columbia	*19–2–61*	*4*	*9*
Gee Whiz, It's You			
(UK) Columbia	*26–3–61*	*8*	*7*
A Girl Like You			
(UK) Columbia	*11–6–61*	*3*	*11*
When The Girl In Your Arms Is The Girl In Your Heart			
(UK) Columbia	*14–10–61*	*2*	*9*
The Young Ones			
(UK) Columbia	*13–1–62*	*1*	*15*

	Date of chart entry	Highest position reached	Number of weeks in charts
RICHARD, CLIFF (cont.)			
Do You Want To Dance?/I'm Looking Out The Window *(UK) Columbia*	*12–5–62*	*2*	*12*
It'll Be Me *(UK) Columbia*	*8–9–62*	*2*	*9*
The Next Time/Bachelor Boy *(UK) Columbia*	*8–12–62*	*1*	*14*
Summer Holiday *(UK) Columbia*	*2–3–63*	*1*	*11*
Lucky Lips *(UK) Columbia*	*18–5–63*	*4*	*8*
It's All In The Game *(UK) Columbia*	*31–8–63*	*2*	*9*
Don't Talk To Him *(UK) Columbia*	*16–11–63*	*2*	*9*
I'm The Lonely One *(UK) Columbia*	*15–2–64*	*8*	*4*
Constantly *(UK) Columbia*	*9–5–64*	*4*	*8*
On The Beach *(UK) Columbia*	*11–7–64*	*7*	*8*
Twelfth Of Never *(UK) Columbia*	*17–10–64*	*8*	*6*
I Could Easily Fall *(UK) Columbia*	*12–12–64*	*6*	*8*
The Minute You're Gone *(UK) Columbia*	*27–3–65*	*1*	*9*
On My Word *(UK) Columbia*	*26–6–65*	*12*	*5*
Wind Me Up *(UK) Columbia*	*20–11–65*	*2*	*12*
Blue Turns To Grey *(UK) Columbia*	*2–4–66*	*15*	*6*
Visions *(UK) Columbia*	*30–7–66*	*7*	*8*
Time Drags By *(UK) Columbia*	*29–10–66*	*10*	*4*
In The Country *(UK) Columbia*	*31–12–66*	*6*	*6*
It's All Over *(UK) Columbia*	*1–4–67*	*9*	*6*
The Day I Met Marie *(UK) Columbia*	*9–9–67*	*10*	*8*
All My Love *(UK) Columbia*	*25–11–67*	*8*	*8*
Congratulations *(UK) Columbia*	*30–3–68*	*1*	*9*
Good Times *(UK) Columbia*	*8–3–69*	*12*	*7*

	Date of chart entry	Highest position reached	Number of weeks in charts
RICHARD, CLIFF (cont.)			
Big Ship			
(UK) Columbia	*14–6–69*	*8*	*5*
Throw Down A Line (with HANK MARVIN)			
(UK) Columbia	*20–9–69*	*7*	*6*
With The Eyes Of A Child			
(UK) Columbia	*20–12–69*	*20*	*2*
Goodbye Sam Hello Samantha			
(UK) Columbia	*13–6–70*	*6*	*10*
Sunny Honey Girl			
(UK) Columbia	*20–2–71*	*19*	*1*
Sing A Song Of Freedom			
(UK) Columbia	*27–11–71*	*13*	*4*
Living In Harmony			
(UK) Columbia	*16–9–72*	*12*	*4*
Power To All Our Friends			
(UK) EMI	*17–3–73*	*4*	*7*
You Keep Me Hangin' On			
(UK) EMI	*1–6–74*	*13*	*3*
RIDDLE, NELSON			
Lisbon Antigua			
(US) Capitol	21–1–56	2	19
RIGHTEOUS BROTHERS			
You've Lost That Lovin' Feelin'			
(US) Philles	2–1–65	1	12
(UK) London	*23–1–65*	*1*	*7*
(UK) London (re-entry)	*1–3–69*	*10*	*7*
Just Once In My Life			
(US) Philles	24–4–65	9	6
Unchained Melody			
(US) Philles	7–8–65	4	8
(UK) London	*11–9–65*	*14*	*3*
Ebb Tide			
(US) Philles	18–12–65	5	6
(You're My) Soul And Inspiration			
(US) Verve	19–3–66	1	10
(UK) Verve	*7–5–66*	*15*	*4*
He			
(US) Verve	2–7–66	18	2
Rock And Roll Heaven			
(US) Haven	29–6–74	3	7
Give It To The People			
(US) Haven	19–10–74	20	2
RILEY, JEANNIE C.			
Harper Valley PTA			
(US) Plantation	31–8–68	1	11
(UK) Polydor	*30–11–68*	*12*	*4*

	Date of chart entry	*Highest position reached*	*Number of weeks in charts*
RIOS, MIGUEL			
Song Of Joy			
(US) A & M	4–7–70	14	5
(UK) A & M	*8–8–70*	*16*	*2*
RIP CHORDS			
Hey Little Cobra			
(US) Columbia	11–1–64	4	8
RITTER, TEX			
Wayward Wind			
(UK) Capitol	*29–6–56*	*8*	*11*
Hillbilly Heaven			
(US) Capitol	28–8–61	20	1
RIVERS, JOHNNY			
Memphis			
(US) Imperial	20–6–64	2	8
Maybellene			
(US) Imperial	5–9–64	12	4
Mountain Of Love			
(US) Imperial	21–11–64	9	6
Midnight Special			
(US) Imperial	13–3–65	20	2
Seventh Son			
(US) Imperial	19–6–65	7	7
Secret Agent Man			
(US) Imperial	2–4–66	3	7
I Washed My Hands In Muddy Water			
(US) Imperial	16–7–66	19	1
Poor Side Of Town			
(US) Imperial	8–10–66	1	10
Baby I Need Your Lovin'			
(US) Imperial	18–2–67	3	8
Tracks Of My Tears			
(US) Imperial	24–6–67	10	4
Summer Rain			
(US) Imperial	16–12–67	14	5
Rockin' Pneumonia And The Boogie Woogie Flu			
(US) United Artists	2–12–72	6	10
RIVIERAS			
California Sun			
(US) Riviera	15–2–64	5	6
ROBBINS, MARTY			
White Sports Coat			
(US) Columbia	29–4–57	3	15

	Date of chart entry	Highest position reached	Number of weeks in charts
ROBBINS, MARTY (cont.)			
El Paso			
(US) Columbia	7-12-59	1	12
(UK) Fontana	*23-1-60*	*17*	*2*
Don't Worry (Like All The Other Times)			
(US) Columbia	20-2-61	3	10
Devil Woman			
(US) Columbia	1-9-62	16	3
(UK) CBS	*27-10-62*	*5*	*11*
Ruby Ann			
(US) Columbia	22-12-62	18	1
ROBERTS, AUSTIN			
Something's Wrong With Me			
(US) Chelsea	25-11-72	12	7
ROBERTS, MALCOLM			
May I Have The Next Dream With You			
(UK) Major Minor	*23-11-68*	*8*	*8*
Love Is All			
(UK) Major Minor	*29-11-69*	*12*	*5*
ROBERTSON, DON			
Happy Whistler			
(US) Capitol	12-5-56	9	11
(UK) Capitol	*18-5-56*	*8*	*7*
ROBIC, IVO			
Morgen			
(US) Laurie	21-9-59	13	6
ROBINSON, FLOYD			
Makin' Love			
(US) RCA	28-9-59	20	1
(UK) RCA	*17-10-59*	*8*	*7*
ROBINSON, SMOKEY AND THE MIRACLES			
The Love I Saw In You was Just A Mirage			
(US) Tamla	8-4-67	20	1
I Second That Emotion			
(US) Tamla	2-12-67	4	10
If You Can Wait			
(US) Tamla	30-3-68	11	6
Don't Cry			
(US) Tamla	15-2-69	8	6

	Date of chart entry	*Highest position reached*	*Number of weeks in charts*
ROBINSON, SMOKEY (cont.)			
Tears Of A Clown			
(UK) Tamla-Motown	*15–8–70*	*1*	*10*
(US) Tamla	7–11–70	1	12
I Don't Blame You At All			
(US) Tamla	15–5–71	18	1
(UK) Tamla-Motown	*26–6–71*	*11*	*5*
[see also: MIRACLES]			
ROCK-A-TEENS			
Woo-Hoo			
(US) Roulette	23–11–59	16	1
ROCKIN' BERRIES			
He's In Town			
(UK) Pye	*31–10–64*	*3*	*7*
Poor Man's Son			
(UK) Piccadilly	*22–5–65*	*5*	*7*
LORD ROCKINGHAM'S XI			
Hoots Mon			
(UK) Decca	*24–10–58*	*1*	*16*
Wee Tom			
(UK) Decca	*7–2–59*	*11*	*3*
ROCKY FELLERS			
Killer Joe			
(US) Scepter	11–5–63	16	3
RODGERS, CLODAGH			
Come Back And Shake Me			
(UK) RCA	*19–4–69*	*3*	*8*
Goodnight Midnight			
(UK) RCA	*26–7–69*	*4*	*8*
Jack In The Box			
(UK) RCA	*27–3–71*	*4*	*6*
RODGERS, JIMMIE			
Honeycomb			
(US) Roulette	2–9–57	1	15
Kisses Sweeter Than Wine			
(US) Roulette	9–12–57	7	10
(UK) Columbia	*20–12–57*	*7*	*10*
Oh Oh I'm Falling In Love Again			
(UK) Columbia	*4–4–58*	*18*	*5*
Secretly			
(US) Roulette	26–5–58	4	10
Are You Really Mine?			
(US) Roulette	25–8–58	10	4
Bimbambay			
(US) Roulette	8–12–58	11	7
English Country Garden			
(UK) Columbia	*30–6–62*	*5*	*9*

	Date of chart entry	Highest position reached	Number of weeks in charts
RODGERS, JULIE			
The Wedding			
(UK) Mercury	*4–9–64*	*3*	*13*
(US) Mercury	19–12–64	10	5
Like A Child			
(UK) Mercury	*2–1–65*	*20*	*1*
ROE, TOMMY			
Sheila			
(US) ABC-Paramount	18–8–62	1	10
(UK) HMV	*22–9–62*	*3*	*10*
The Folk Singer			
(UK) HMV	*30–3–63*	*4*	*9*
Everybody			
(UK) HMV	*12–10–63*	*9*	*5*
(US) ABC-Paramount	9–11–63	3	8
Sweet Pea			
(US) ABC	16–7–66	8	7
Hooray For Hazel			
(US) ABC	15–10–66	6	7
Dizzy			
(US) ABC	1–3–69	1	10
(UK) Stateside	*10–5–69*	*1*	*10*
Jam Up Jelly Tight			
(US) ABC	27–12–69	8	7
ROGERS, EILEEN			
Miracle Of Love			
(US) Columbia	6–10–56	19	2
ROGERS, KENNY, AND THE FIRST EDITION			
Ruby, Don't Take Your Love To Town			
(US) Reprise	19–7–69	6	6
(UK) Reprise	*15–11–69*	*2*	*14*
Something's Burning			
(UK) Reprise	*7–3–70*	*8*	*8*
(US) Reprise	18–4–70	11	5
Tell It All, Brother			
(US) Reprise	15–8–70	17	3
[see also: FIRST EDITION]			
ROLLING STONES			
I Wanna Be Your Man			
(UK) Decca	*7–12–63*	*12*	*9*
Not Fade Away			
(UK) Decca	*7–3–64*	*3*	*9*
It's All Over Now			
(UK) Decca	*11–7–64*	*1*	*11*

	Date of chart entry	Highest position reached	Number of weeks in charts
ROLLING STONES (cont.)			
Time Is On My Side			
(US) London	14–11–64	6	8
Little Red Rooster			
(UK) Decca	*28–11–64*	*1*	*8*
Heart Of Stone			
(US) London	20–1–65	19	1
The Last Time			
(UK) Decca	*13–3–65*	*1*	*9*
(US) London	17–4–65	9	5
(I Can't Get No) Satisfaction			
(US) London	26–6–65	1	10
(UK) Decca	*28–8–65*	*1*	*10*
Get Off Of My Cloud			
(US) London	16–10–65	1	9
(UK) Decca	*30–10–65*	*1*	*8*
As Tears Go By			
(US) London	8–1–66	6	5
19th Nervous Breakdown			
(UK) Decca	*12–2–66*	*2*	*7*
(US) London	5–3–66	2	8
Paint It Black			
(UK) Decca	*21–5–66*	*1*	*7*
(US) London	21–5–66	1	9
Mother's Little Helper			
(US) London	23–7–66	8	6
Have You Seen Your Mother Baby			
(UK) Decca	*1–10–66*	*5*	*6*
(US) London	15–10–66	9	5
Let's Spend The Night Together/ Ruby Tuesday			
(UK) Decca	*28–1–67*	*3*	*7*
(US) London	4–2–67	1	8
Dandelion/We Love You			
(UK) Decca	*26–8–67*	*8*	*6*
(US) London	30–9–67	14	3
Jumping Jack Flash			
(UK) Decca	*1–6–68*	*1*	*9*
(US) London	22–6–68	3	9
Honky Tonk Women			
(UK) Decca	*12–7–69*	*1*	*12*
(US) London	2–8–69	1	12
Brown Sugar			
(UK) Rolling Stones (b/w) Bitch/Let It Rock	*1–5–71*	*2*	*9*
(US) Rolling Stones	8–5–71	1	10
Tumbling Dice			
(UK) Rolling Stones	*29–4–72*	*5*	*6*
(US) Rolling Stones	13–5–72	7	6

	Date of chart entry	*Highest position reached*	*Number of weeks in charts*
ROLLING STONES (cont.)			
Angie			
(UK) Rolling Stones	*8–9–73*	*5*	*5*
(US) Rolling Stones	29–9–73	1	10
It's Only Rock And Roll			
(UK) Rolling Stones	*10–8–74*	*10*	*4*
(US) Rolling Stones	7–9–74	16	3
Doo Doo Doo Doo (Heartbreaker)			
(US) Rolling Stones	9–2–74	15	3
Ain't Too Proud To Beg			
(US) Rolling Stones	14–12–74	17	2
ROMEO, MAX			
Wet Dream			
(UK) Unity	*2–8–69*	*10*	*6*
RONDO, DON			
Two Different Worlds			
(US) Jubilee	17–11–56	19	2
White Silver Sands			
(US) Jubilee	5–7–57	10	8
RONETTES			
Be My Baby			
(US) Philles	14–9–63	2	9
(UK) London	*26–10–63*	*4*	*7*
Baby I Love You			
(UK) London	*1–2–64*	*11*	*7*
RONNIE AND THE HI-LITES			
I Wish That We Were Married			
(US) Joy	12–5–62	16	3
RONNY AND THE DAYTONAS			
G.T.O.			
(US) Mala	29–8–64	4	8
ROOFTOP SINGERS			
Walk Right In			
(US) Vanguard	19–1–63	1	9
(UK) Fontana	*17–2–63*	*10*	*6*
Tom Cat			
(US) Vanguard	4–5–63	20	1
ROSE, DAVID, AND ORCHESTRA			
Stripper			
(US) MGM	2–9–62	1	11
ROSE GARDEN			
Next Plane To London			
(US) Atco	30–12–67	17	1

	Date of chart entry	*Highest position reached*	*Number of weeks in charts*
ROSIE AND THE ORIGINALS			
Angel Baby			
(US) Highland	26–12–60	5	9
ROSS, DIANA			
Reach Out And Touch (Somebody's Hand)			
(US) Motown	6–6–70	20	1
Ain't No Mountain High Enough			
(US) Motown	22–8–70	1	11
(UK) Tamla-Motown	*26–9–70*	*6*	*7*
Remember Me			
(US) Motown	30–1–71	16	3
(UK) Tamla-Motown	*17–4–71*	*7*	*7*
I'm Still Waiting			
(UK) Tamla-Motown	*31–7–71*	*1*	*11*
Surrender			
(UK) Tamla-Motown	*20–11–71*	*10*	*5*
Doobedood'ndoobe			
(UK) Tamla-Motown	*3–6–72*	*12*	*3*
Touch Me In The Morning			
(US) Motown	21–7–73	1	12
(UK) Tamla-Motown	*28–7–73*	*9*	*6*
You're A Special Part Of Me (with MARVIN GAYE)			
(US) Motown	27–10–73	12	4
All Of My Life			
(UK) Tamla-Motown	*19–1–74*	*9*	*6*
Last Time I Saw Him			
(US) Motown	16–2–74	14	3
You Are Everything (with MARVIN GAYE)			
(UK) Tamla-Motown	*30–3–74*	*5*	*7*
My Mistake Was To Love You (with MARVIN GAYE)			
(US) Motown	27–4–74	19	2
[see also: ROSS, DIANA, AND THE SUPREMES; SUPREMES]			
ROSS, DIANA, AND THE SUPREMES			
Reflections			
(US) Motown	19–8–67	2	8
(UK) Tamla-Motown	*16–9–67*	*5*	*8*
In And Out Of Love			
(US) Motown	2–12–67	9	4
(UK) Tamla-Motown	*9–12–67*	*13*	*7*
Love Child			
(US) Motown	26–10–68	1	14
(UK) Tamla-Motown	*7–12–68*	*15*	*9*

	Date of chart entry	*Highest position reached*	*Number of weeks in charts*
ROSS, DIANA, AND THE SUPREMES (cont.)			
I'm Gonna Make You Love Me (with the TEMPTATIONS)			
(US) Motown	14–12–68	2	11
(UK) Tamla-Motown	*8–2–69*	*3*	*7*
I'm Livin' In Shame			
(US) Motown	8–2–69	10	4
(UK) Tamla-Motown	*10–5–69*	*14*	*3*
I Second That Emotion (with the TEMPTATIONS)			
(UK) Tamla-Motown	*4–10–69*	*18*	*2*
Someday We'll Be Together			
(US) Motown	29–11–69	1	12
(UK) Tamla-Motown	*17–1–70*	*13*	*5*
ROSS, JACK			
Cinderella			
(US) Dot	21–4–62	16	2
ROSS, JACKIE			
Selfish One			
(US) Chess	29–8–64	11	5
ROSS, SPENCER			
Tracy's Theme			
(US) Columbia	1–2–60	13	7
ROSSO, NINI			
Il Silenzio			
(UK) Durium	*18–9–65*	*8*	*7*
ROUTERS			
Let's Go			
(US) Warner Brothers	15–12–62	19	2
[see also: MARKETTS]			
ROVER BOYS			
Graduation Days			
(US) ABC-Paramount	23–6–56	20	1
ROWLES, JOHN			
If I Only Had Time			
(UK) MCA	*30–3–68*	*3*	*11*
Not A Word To Mary			
(UK) MCA	*29–6–68*	*12*	*5*
ROXY MUSIC			
Virginia Plain			
(UK) Island	*2–9–72*	*4*	*6*
Pyjamarama			
(UK) Island	*31–3–73*	*10*	*6*

	Date of chart entry	*Highest position reached*	*Number of weeks in charts*
ROXY MUSIC (cont.)			
Street Life			
(UK) Island	*1–12–73*	*9*	*8*
All I Want Is You			
(UK) Island	*19–10–74*	*12*	*6*
ROYAL, BILLY JOE			
Down In The Boondocks			
(US) Columbia	7–8–65	9	6
I Knew You When			
(US) Columbia	30–10–65	14	4
Cherry Hill Park			
(US) Columbia	22–11–69	15	5
ROYAL AIR FORCE BAND			
Dambusters March			
(UK) HMV	*21–10–55*	*18*	*1*
ROYAL GUARDSMEN			
Snoopy vs. The Red Baron			
(US) Laurie	24–12–66	2	9
(UK) Stateside	*4–2–67*	*8*	*8*
Return Of The Red Baron			
(US) Laurie	25–3–67	15	1
ROYAL SCOTS DRAGOON GUARDS BAND			
Amazing Grace			
(UK) RCA	*15–4–72*	*1*	*10*
(US) RCA	10–6–72	11	4
Little Drummer Boy			
(UK) RCA	*16–12–72*	*13*	*4*
ROYAL TEENS			
Short Shorts			
(US) ABC-Paramount	3–2–58	3	8
ROYALTONES			
Poor Boy			
(US) Jubilee	1–12–58	17	1
ROZA, LITA			
Hey There			
(UK) Decca	*7–10–55*	*17*	*2*
Jimmy Unknown			
(UK) Decca	*23–3–56*	*15*	*4*
RUBETTES			
Sugar Baby Love			
(UK) Polydor	*11–5–74*	*1*	*7*

	Date of chart entry	*Highest position reached*	*Number of weeks in charts*
RUBETTES (cont.)			
Tonight			
(UK) Polydor	*27–7–74*	*12*	*5*
Juke Box Jive			
(UK) Polydor	*23–11–74*	*3*	*8*
RUBY AND THE ROMANTICS			
Our Day Will Come			
(US) Kapp	2–3–63	1	8
My Summer Love			
(US) Kapp	29–6–63	16	2
RUFFIN, BRUCE			
Rain			
(UK) Trojan	*22–5–71*	*19*	*2*
Mad About You			
(UK) Rhino	*22–7–72*	*9*	*5*
RUFFIN, DAVID			
My Whole World Ended (The Moment You Left Me)			
(US) Motown	8–3–69	9	5
RUFFIN, JIMMY			
What Becomes Of The Broken Hearted			
(US) Soul	1–10–66	7	9
(UK) Tamla-Motown	*3–12–66*	*8*	*7*
(UK) Tamla-Motown (re-issue)	*10–8–74*	*4*	*8*
I've Passed This Way Before			
(US) Soul	14–1–67	17	3
Farewell Is A Lonely Sound			
(UK) Tamla-Motown	*28–3–70*	*8*	*8*
It's Wonderful To Be Loved By You			
(UK) Tamla-Motown	*31–10–70*	*6*	*9*
I'll Say Forever My Love			
(UK) Tamla-Motown (re-issue)	*18–7–70*	*7*	*8*
RUFUS			
Tell Me Something Good			
(US) ABC	3–8–74	3	7
You Got The Love (featuring CHAKA KAHN)			
(US) ABC	23–11–74	11	6
RUNDGREN, TODD (as RUNT*)			
We Gotta Get You A Woman			
(US) Ampex*	30–1–71	20	3
I Saw The Light			
(US) Bearsville	3–6–72	16	4
Hello It's Me			
(US) Bearsville	24–11–73	5	8

	Date of chart entry	*Highest position reached*	*Number of weeks in charts*
RUSH, MERRILEE			
Angel Of The Morning			
(US) Bell	8–6–68	7	8
RUSSELL, LEON			
Tight Rope			
(US) Shelter	7–10–72	11	5
RYAN, BARRY			
Eloise			
(UK) MGM	*2–11–68*	*2*	*8*
RYAN, MARION			
Love Me Forever			
(UK) Pye Nixa	*24–1–58*	*5*	*10*
It's You That I Love			
(UK) Pye	*18–12–60*	*20*	*1*
RYAN, PAUL AND BARRY			
Don't Bring Me Your Heartaches			
(UK) Decca	*27–11–65*	*13*	*4*
Have Pity On The Boy			
(UK) Decca	*12–2–66*	*18*	*2*
I Love Her			
(UK) Decca	*28–5–66*	*17*	*3*
RYDELL, BOBBY			
Kissin' Time			
(US) Cameo	24–8–59	11	5
We Got Love			
(US) Cameo	16–11–59	6	9
Wild One			
(US) Cameo (b/w*)	22–2–60	2	10
(UK) Columbia	*13–3–60*	*12*	7
Little Bitty Girl*			
(US) Cameo	21–3–60	19	2
Swinging School			
(US) Cameo (b/w**)	23–5–60	5	6
Ding-a-Ling**			
(US) Cameo	30–5–60	18	2
Volare			
(US) Cameo	15–8–60	4	8
Sway			
(US) Cameo	21–11–60	14	6
(UK) Columbia	*1–1–61*	*14*	*2*
Good Time Baby			
(US) Cameo	20–2–61	11	5
I've Got Bonnie			
(US) Cameo	7–4–62	18	1

	Date of chart entry	Highest position reached	Number of weeks in charts
RYDELL, BOBBY (cont.)			
I'll Never Dance Again			
(US) Cameo	30–6–62	14	4
Cha Cha Cha			
(US) Cameo	3–11–62	10	6
Wildwood Days			
(US) Cameo	22–6–63	17	1
Forget Him			
(UK) Cameo Parkway	*15–6–63*	*14*	*7*
(US) Cameo	21–12–63	4	18
RYDER, MITCH, AND THE DETROIT WHEELS			
Jenny Take A Ride			
(US) New Voices	22–1–66	10	4
Little Latin Lupe Lu			
(US) New Voices	9–4–66	17	3
Devil With A Blue Dress On/ Good Golly Miss Molly			
(US) New Voices	5–11–66	4	11
Sock It To Me Baby			
(US) New Voices	25–2–66	6	7
SADLER, BARRY			
Ballad Of The Green Berets			
(US) RCA	19–2–66	1	11
SAFARIS			
Image Of A Girl			
(US) Eldo	11–7–60	6	8
SAILCAT			
Motorcycle Mama			
(US) Elektra	12–8–72	12	5
ST. CECILIA			
Leap Up And Down (Wave Your Knickers In The Air)			
(UK) Polydor	*17–7–71*	*12*	*7*
ST. LOUIS UNION			
Girl			
(UK) Decca	*5–2–66*	*11*	*5*
ST. PETERS, CRISPIAN			
You Were On My Mind			
(UK) Decca	*29–1–66*	*2*	*8*
Pied Piper			
(UK) Decca	*16–4–66*	*5*	*8*
(US) Jamie	16–7–66	4	6

	Date of chart entry	Highest position reached	Number of weeks in charts
SAINTE MARIE, BUFFY			
Soldier Blue			
(UK) RCA	*14–8–71*	*7*	*8*
SAKAMOTO, KYU			
Sukiyaki			
(US) Capitol	25–5–63	1	10
(UK) HMV	*20–7–63*	*6*	*8*
SAKHARIN			
Sugar Sugar			
(UK) RCA	*8–5–71*	*12*	*5*
SAM AND DAVE			
Soul Man			
(US) Stax	7–10–67	2	10
Thank You			
(US) Stax	9–3–68	9	5
Soul Sister, Brown Sugar			
(UK) Stax	*8–2–69*	*15*	*4*
SAM THE SHAM AND THE PHARAOHS			
Wooly Bully			
(US) MGM	8–5–65	2	12
(UK) MGM	*17–7–65*	*11*	*6*
Lil' Red Riding Hood			
(US) MGM	9–7–66	2	9
SAMMES, MICHAEL, SINGERS			
Somewhere My Love			
(UK) HMV	*22–7–67*	*14*	*1*
SANDFORD, CHRIS			
Not Too Little, Not Too Much			
(UK) Decca	*21–12–63*	*17*	*5*
SANDPIPERS			
Guantanamera			
(US) A & M	3–9–66	9	5
(UK) Pye	*1–10–66*	*7*	*9*
Come Saturday Morning			
(US) A & M	30–5–70	17	3
SANDS, JODIE			
With All My Heart			
(US) Chancellor	24–6–57	20	1
Someday			
(UK) HMV	*17–10–58*	*14*	*8*

	Date of chart entry	*Highest position reached*	*Number of weeks in charts*
SANDS, TOMMY			
Teen-Age Crush			
(US) Capitol	2–3–57	3	11
Goin' Steady			
(US) Capitol	24–6–57	19	1
SANTAMARIA, MONGO			
Watermelon Man			
(US) Battle	20–4–63	10	4
SANTANA			
Evil Ways			
(US) Columbia	7–3–70	9	6
Black Magic Woman			
(US) Columbia	5–12–70	4	9
Oye Como Va			
(US) Columbia	27–3–71	13	3
Everybody's Everything			
(US) Columbia	13–11–71	12	4
SANTO AND JOHNNY			
Sleep Walk			
(US) Canadian-American	24–8–59	1	11
(UK) Pye	*10–10–59*	*14*	*2*
SARNE, MIKE			
Come Outside			
(UK) Parlophone	*26–5–62*	*1*	*14*
Will I What?			
(UK) Parlophone	*15–9–62*	*18*	*3*
SARSTEDT, PETER			
Where Do You Go To (My Lovely)?			
(UK) United Artists	*8–2–69*	*1*	*10*
Frozen Orange Juice			
(UK) United Artists	*28–6–69*	*10*	*4*
SAVAGE, EDNA			
Arrivederci Darling			
(UK) Parlophone	*13–1–56*	*19*	*1*
SAXON, AL			
Only Sixteen			
(UK) Fontana	*29–8–59*	*17*	*1*
SAYER, LEO			
The Show Must Go On			
(UK) Chrysalis	*22–12–73*	*2*	*8*
One Man Band			
(UK) Chrysalis	*22–6–74*	*6*	*5*
Long Tall Glasses			
(UK) Chrysalis	*28–9–74*	*4*	*5*

	Date of chart entry	Highest position reached	Number of weeks in charts
SCAFFOLD			
Thank U Very Much			
(UK) Columbia	*9–12–67*	*4*	*8*
Lily The Pink			
(UK) Columbia	*23–11–68*	*1*	*12*
Liverpool Lou			
(UK) Warner Brothers	*15–6–74*	*7*	*4*
SCOTLAND WORLD CUP SQUAD			
Easy Easy			
(UK) Polydor	*29–6–74*	*20*	*1*
SCOTT, BOBBY			
Chain Gang			
(US) Paramount	11–2–56	15	4
SCOTT, FREDDIE			
Hey Girl			
(US) Colpix	24–8–63	10	5
SCOTT, JACK			
My True Love			
(US) Carlton	28–7–58	3	10
(UK) London	*17–10–58*	*9*	*7*
Goodbye Baby			
(US) Carlton	12–1–59	8	7
What In The World's Come Over You			
(US) Top Rank	25–1–60	5	10
(UK) Rank	*27–2–60*	*6*	*8*
Burning Bridges			
(US) Top Rank	16–5–60	3	10
SCOTT, LINDA			
I've Told Every Little Star			
(US) Canadian-American	17–4–61	3	7
(UK) Columbia	*28–5–61*	*9*	*5*
Don't Bet Money Honey			
(US) Canadian-American	14–8–61	9	5
I Don't Know Why			
(US) Canadian-American	11–12–61	12	4
SEALS AND CROFT			
Summer Breeze			
(US) Warner Brothers	11–11–72	6	6
Hummingbird			
(US) Warner Brothers	31–3–73	20	1
Diamond Girl			
(US) Warner Brothers	7–7–73	6	7

	Date of chart entry	*Highest position reached*	*Number of weeks in charts*
SEARCHERS			
Sweets For My Sweet			
(UK) Pye	*13–7–63*	*1*	*11*
Sugar And Spice			
(UK) Pye	*2–11–63*	*2*	*6*
Needles And Pins			
(UK) Pye	*25–1–64*	*1*	*9*
(US) Kapp	28–3–64	13	5
Don't Throw Your Love Away			
(UK) Pye	*18–4–64*	*1*	*8*
(US) Kapp	4–7–64	16	3
Someday We're Gonna Love Again			
(UK) Pye	*25–7–64*	*11*	*5*
When You Walk In The Room			
(UK) Pye	*3–10–64*	*3*	*8*
What Have They Done To The Rain			
(UK) Pye	*19–12–64*	*13*	*6*
Love Potion No. 9			
(US) Kapp	26–12–64	3	8
Goodbye My Love			
(UK) Pye	*13–3–65*	*4*	*5*
He's Got No Love			
(UK) Pye	*24–7–65*	*12*	*5*
Take Me For What I'm Worth			
(UK) Pye	*22–1–66*	*20*	*1*
SECOMBE, HARRY			
On With The Motley			
(UK) Philips	*9–12–55*	*16*	*3*
If I Ruled The World			
(UK) Philips	*21–12–63*	*20*	*1*
This Is My Song			
(UK) Philips	*11–3–67*	*2*	*9*
[see also: GOONS]			
SECRETS			
The Boy Next Door			
(US) Philips	28–12–63	18	2
SEDAKA, NEIL			
Diary			
(US) RCA	26–1–59	14	3
I Go Ape			
(UK) RCA	*2–5–59*	*9*	*10*
Oh, Carol			
(US) RCA	2–11–59	9	8
(UK) RCA	*14–11–59*	*3*	*13*
(UK) RCA (re-issue)	*2–12–72*	*19*	*1*

	Date of chart entry	*Highest position reached*	*Number of weeks in charts*
SEDAKA, NEIL (cont.)			
Stairway To Heaven			
(US) RCA	25–4–60	9	7
(UK) RCA	*8–5–60*	*13*	*6*
You Mean Everything To Me			
(US) RCA	26–9–60	17	3
Calendar Girl			
(US) RCA	16–1–61	4	8
(UK) RCA	*22–1–61*	*10*	*9*
Little Devil			
(UK) RCA	*14–5–61*	*12*	*6*
(US) RCA	22–5–61	11	3
Happy Birthday Sweet 16			
(US) RCA	11–12–61	6	8
(UK) RCA	*16–12–61*	*4*	*12*
Breaking Up Is Hard To Do			
(US) RCA	14–7–62	1	10
(UK) RCA	*11–8–62*	*7*	*10*
Next Door To An Angel			
(US) RCA	27–10–62	5	6
Alice In Wonderland			
(US) RCA	9–3–63	17	3
That's When The Music Takes Me			
(UK) RCA	*24–3–73*	*18*	*1*
Laughter In The Rain			
(UK) Polydor	*20–7–74*	*15*	*3*
(US) Rocket	7–12–74	1	11
SEEKERS			
I'll Never Find Another You			
(UK) Columbia	*30–1–65*	*1*	*11*
(US) Capitol	17–4–65	4	9
World Of Our Own			
(UK) Columbia	*1–5–65*	*3*	*11*
(US) Capitol	10–7–65	19	2
The Carnival Is Over			
(UK) Columbia	*6–11–65*	*1*	*14*
Someday One Day			
(UK) Columbia	*9–4–66*	*11*	*6*
Walk With Me			
(UK) Columbia	*24–9–66*	*10*	*6*
Morningtown Ride			
(UK) Columbia	*3–12–66*	*2*	*10*
Georgy Girl			
(US) Capitol	7–1–67	2	10
(UK) Columbia	*4–3–67*	*3*	*7*
When Will The Good Apple Fall			
(UK) Columbia	*7–10–67*	*11*	*6*

	Date of chart entry	Highest position reached	Number of weeks in charts
SEGER, BOB			
Ramblin' Gamblin' Man			
(US) Capitol	1-2-69	17	5
SELLERS, PETER			
Any Old Iron			
(UK) Parlophone	*20-9-57*	*17*	*2*
Goodness Gracious Me (with Sophia Loren)			
(UK) Parlophone	*13-11-60*	*5*	*9*
Hard Day's Night			
(UK) Parlophone	*8-1-66*	*14*	*4*
[see also: Goons]			
SENATOR BOBBY			
Wild Thing			
(US) Parkway	4-2-67	20	2
SENSATIONS			
Let Me In			
(US) Argo	24-2-62	4	8
SERENDIPITY SINGERS			
Don't Let The Rain Come Down			
(US) Philips	28-3-64	6	9
SEVERINE			
Un Banc, Un Arbre, Une Rue			
(UK) Philips	*15-5-71*	*9*	*4*
SEVILLE, DAVID (*and THE CHIPMUNKS)			
Witch Doctor			
(US) Liberty	21-4-58	1	14
(UK) London	*23-5-58*	*11*	*5*
Chipmunk Song*			
(US) Liberty	15-12-58	1	7
Alvin's Harmonica*			
(US) Liberty	2-3-59	3	7
Ragtime Cowboy Joe*			
(US) Liberty	27-7-59	16	3
(UK) London	*1-8-59*	*11*	*5*
SHADES OF BLUE			
Oh How Happy			
(US) Impact	4-6-66	12	6
SHADOWS			
Apache			
(UK) Columbia	*17-7-60*	*1*	*15*

	Date of chart entry	*Highest position reached*	*Number of weeks in charts*
SHADOWS (cont.)			
Man Of Mystery *(UK) Columbia*	*6–11–60*	*2*	*9*
F.B.I. *(UK) Columbia*	*29–1–61*	*4*	*11*
Frightened City *(UK) Columbia*	*30–4–61*	*3*	*11*
Kon-Tiki *(UK) Columbia*	*2–9–61*	*1*	*9*
The Savage *(UK) Columbia*	*11–11–61*	*9*	*5*
Wonderful Land *(UK) Columbia*	*3–3–62*	*1*	*16*
Guitar Tango *(UK) Columbia*	*11–8–62*	*4*	*9*
Dance On *(UK) Columbia*	*22–12–62*	*1*	*9*
Foottapper *(UK) Columbia*	*16–3–63*	*1*	*10*
Atlantis *(UK) Columbia*	*15–6–63*	*2*	*11*
Shindig *(UK) Columbia*	*28–9–63*	*6*	*7*
Geronimo *(UK) Columbia*	*14–12–63*	*11*	*5*
Theme For Young Lovers *(UK) Columbia*	*21–3–64*	*12*	*6*
Rise And Fall Of Flingel Bunt *(UK) Columbia*	*23–5–64*	*5*	*8*
Genie With The Light Brown Lamp *(UK) Columbia*	*9–1–65*	*17*	*2*
Mary Anne *(UK) Columbia*	*27–2–65*	*17*	*4*
Stingray *(UK) Columbia*	*26–6–65*	*19*	*1*
Don't Make My Baby Blue *(UK) Columbia*	*14–8–65*	*10*	*5*
War Lord *(UK) Columbia*	*25–12–65*	*18*	*2*
[see also: RICHARD, CLIFF]			
SHADOWS OF KNIGHT			
Gloria (US) Dunwich	23–4–66	10	6
SHAG			
Loop Di Love *(UK) UK*	*28–10–72*	*4*	*7*

	Date of chart entry	Highest position reached	Number of weeks in charts
SHAND, JIMMY			
Bluebell Polka			
(UK) Parlophone	*23–12–55*	*18*	*2*
SHANGRI-LAS			
Remember (Walking In The Sand)			
(US) Red Bird	5–9–64	5	8
(UK) Red Bird	*14–11–64*	*14*	*3*
Leader Of The Pack			
(US) Red Bird	24–10–64	1	9
(UK) Red Bird	*30–1–65*	*11*	*4*
(UK) Kama Sutra (re-issue)	*4–11–72*	*3*	*6*
Give Him A Great Big Kiss			
(US) Red Bird	30–1–65	18	2
I Can Never Go Home Any More			
(US) Red Bird	27–11–65	6	6
SHANNON, DEL			
Runaway			
(US) Big Top	3–4–61	1	10
(UK) London	*23–4–61*	*1*	*17*
Hats Off To Larry			
(US) Big Top	26–6–61	5	9
(UK) London	*2–9–61*	*9*	*8*
So Long Baby			
(UK) London	*9–12–61*	*10*	*8*
Hey Little Girl			
(UK) London	*31–3–62*	*2*	*11*
Swiss Maid			
(UK) London	*20–10–62*	*2*	*14*
Little Town Flirt			
(UK) London	*27–1–63*	*4*	*8*
(US) Big Top	16–2–63	12	3
Two Kinds Of Teardrops			
(UK) London	*4–5–63*	*5*	*10*
Keep Searchin'			
(US) Amy	2–1–65	9	7
(UK) Stateside	*23–1–65*	*3*	*8*
SHAPIRO, HELEN			
Don't Treat Me Like A Child			
(UK) Columbia	*14–4–61*	*4*	*8*
You Don't Know			
(UK) Columbia	*2–7–61*	*1*	*14*
Walkin' Back To Happiness			
(UK) Columbia	*23–9–61*	*1*	*16*
Tell Me What He Said			
(UK) Columbia	*24–2–62*	*2*	*12*

	Date of chart entry	*Highest position reached*	*Number of weeks in charts*
SHAPIRO, HELEN (cont.)			
Little Miss Lonely *(UK) Columbia*	*28–7–62*	*8*	*7*
SHARP, DEE DEE			
Mashed Potato Time (US) Cameo	31–3–62	2	12
Gravy (US) Cameo	7–7–62	9	5
Ride (US) Cameo	17–11–62	5	6
Do The Bird (US) Cameo	30–3–63	10	5
SHAW, SANDIE			
(There's) Always Something There To Remind Me *(UK) Pye*	*17–10–64*	*1*	*7*
Girl Don't Come *(UK) Pye*	*19–12–64*	*3*	*9*
I'll Stop At Nothing *(UK) Pye*	*27–2–65*	*4*	*7*
Long Live Love *(UK) Pye*	*22–5–65*	*1*	*9*
Message Understood *(UK) Pye*	*7–10–65*	*6*	*5*
Tomorrow *(UK) Pye*	*12–2–66*	*9*	*5*
Nothing Comes Easy *(UK) Pye*	*4–6–66*	*14*	*4*
Puppet On A String *(UK) Pye*	*25–3–67*	*1*	*13*
You've Not Changed *(UK) Pye*	*21–10–67*	*18*	*4*
Monsieur Dupont *(UK) Pye*	*1–3–69*	*6*	*8*
SHEARING, GEORGE. See NAT 'KING' COLE			
SHEARSTON, GARY			
I Get A Kick Out Of You *(UK) Charisma*	*12–10–74*	*7*	*5*
SHELLEY, PETER			
Gee Baby *(UK) Magnet*	*28–9–74*	*4*	*6*
SHELTON, ANNE			
Arrivederci Darling *(UK) HMV*	*16–12–55*	*17*	*4*

	Date of chart entry	Highest position reached	Number of weeks in charts
SHELTON, ANNE (cont.)			
Seven Days			
(UK) Philips	*20–4–56*	*20*	*2*
Lay Down Your Arms			
(UK) Philips	*31–8–56*	*1*	*13*
Sailor			
(UK) Philips	*15–1–61*	*7*	*5*
SHEP AND THE LIMELITES			
Daddy's Home			
(US) Hull	24–4–61	2	8
SHEPHERD SISTERS			
Alone			
(US) Lance	18–11–57	20	1
(UK) HMV	*22–11–57*	*14*	*3*
SHERMAN, ALLAN			
Hello Muddah, Hello Faddah			
(US) Warner Brothers	10–8–63	2	8
(UK) Warner Brothers	*5–10–63*	*14*	*5*
SHERMAN, BOBBY			
Little Woman			
(US) Metromedia	13–9–69	3	9
La La La (If I Had You)			
(US) Metromedia	20–12–69	9	6
Easy Come Easy Go			
(US) Metromedia	14–3–70	9	8
Julie, Do Ya Love Me			
(US) Metromedia	29–8–70	5	9
Cried Like A Baby			
(US) Metromedia	13–3–71	16	3
SHIELDS			
You Cheated			
(US) Dot	6–10–58	15	4
SHIRELLES			
Will You Love Me Tomorrow			
(US) Scepter	26–12–60	1	12
(UK) Top Rank	*29–1–61*	*3*	*11*
Dedicated To The One I Love			
(US) Scepter	13–2–61	3	11
Mama Said			
(US) Scepter	1–5–61	4	7
Baby, It's You			
(US) Scepter	13–1–62	8	9
Soldier Boy			
(US) Scepter	14–4–62	1	10

	Date of chart entry	*Highest position reached*	*Number of weeks in charts*
SHIRELLES (cont.)			
Everybody Loves A Lover (US) Scepter	19–1–63	19	2
Foolish Little Girl (US) Scepter	27–4–63	4	7
SHOWADDYWADDY			
Hey Rock And Roll *(UK) Bell*	*1–6–74*	*2*	*8*
Rock And Roll Lady *(UK) Bell*	*31–8–74*	*15*	*4*
SHOCKING BLUE			
Venus (US) Colossus	27–12–69	1	11
(UK) Penny Farthing	*14–2–70*	*8*	*5*
SHONDELL, TROY			
This Time (US) Liberty	2–10–61	6	10
(UK) London	*25–11–61*	*14*	*1*
SHOWSTOPPERS			
Ain't Nothing But A Houseparty *(UK) Beacon*	*30–3–68*	*11*	*9*
SIFFRE, LABI			
It Must Be Love *(UK) Pye International*	*11–12–71*	*14*	*6*
Crying, Laughing, Loving, Lying *(UK) Pye International*	*15–4–72*	*11*	*4*
SILHOUETTES			
Get A Job (US) Ember	27–1–58	1	9
SILKIE			
You've Got To Hide Your Love Away (US) Fontana	13–11–65	10	4
SIMEONE, HARRY, CHORALE			
Little Drummer Boy (US) 20th Century Fox	5–1–59	13	2
(US) 20th Century Fox (re-entry)	28–12–59	15	1
SIMMONS, GENE			
Haunted House (US) Hi	5–9–64	11	6

	Date of chart entry	*Highest position reached*	*Number of weeks in charts*
SIMON, CARLY			
That's The Way I've Always Heard It Should Be			
(US) Elektra	26–6–71	10	6
Anticipation			
(US) Elektra	22–1–72	13	6
You're So Vain			
(US) Elektra	23–12–72	1	12
(UK) Elektra	*2–1–73*	*3*	*8*
The Right Thing To Do			
(UK) Elektra	*12–5–73*	*17*	*1*
(US) Elektra	19–5–73	17	2
Mockingbird (with JAMES TAYLOR)			
(US) Elektra	2–3–74	5	8
Haven't Got Time For The Pain			
(US) Elektra	15–6–74	14	2
SIMON, JOE			
Chokin' Kind			
(US) SS7	26–4–69	13	5
Drowning In The Sea Of Love			
(US) Spring	1–1–72	11	7
Power Of Love			
(US) Spring	9–9–72	11	4
Step By Step			
(UK) Mojo	*14–7–73*	*14*	*3*
Theme From 'Cleopatra Jones'			
(US) Spring	22–8–73	18	3
SIMON, PAUL			
Mother And Child Reunion			
(UK) CBS	*26–2–72*	*5*	*7*
(US) Columbia	4–3–72	4	8
Me And Julio Down By The Schoolyard			
(UK) CBS	*27–5–72*	*15*	*3*
Kodachrome			
(US) Columbia	9–6–73	2	18
Take Me To The Mardi Gras			
(UK) CBS	*30–6–73*	*7*	*5*
Loves Me Like A Rock			
(US) Columbia	25–8–73	2	10
[see also: SIMON AND GARFUNKEL]			
SIMON AND GARFUNKEL			
Sounds Of Silence			
(US) Columbia	18–12–65	1	8
Homeward Bound			
(US) Columbia	5–3–66	5	7
(UK) CBS	*16–4–66*	*9*	*7*

	Date of chart entry	Highest position reached	Number of weeks in charts
I Am A Rock			
(US) Columbia	21–5–66	3	8
(UK) CBS	*2–7–66*	*17*	*2*
Hazy Shade Of Winter			
(US) Columbia	26–11–66	13	4
At The Zoo			
(US) Columbia	15–4–67	16	3
Scarborough Fair			
(US) Columbia	23–3–68	11	5
Mrs. Robinson			
(US) Columbia	11–5–68	1	10
(UK) CBS	*20–7–68*	*4*	*7*
Mrs. Robinson			
(UK) CBS EP	*8–2–69*	*9*	*1*
The Boxer			
(US) Columbia	19–4–69	7	8
(UK) CBS	*10–5–69*	*6*	*7*
Bridge Over Troubled Water			
(US) Columbia	14–2–70	1	12
(UK) CBS	*28–2–70*	*1*	*13*
Cecilia			
(US) Columbia	2–5–70	4	9
El Condor Pasa			
(US) Columbia	24–10–70	18	3
SIMONE, NINA			
I Loves You Porgy			
(US) Bethlehem	5–10–59	18	2
Ain't Got No – I Got Life			
(UK) RCA	*16–11–68*	*2*	*12*
To Love Somebody			
(UK) RCA	*1–2–69*	*5*	*5*
SINATRA, FRANK			
Learnin' The Blues			
(US) Capitol	28–5–55	2	18
(UK) Capitol	*5–8–55*	*2*	*15*
You My Love			
(UK) Capitol	*10–6–55*	*13*	*6*
Not As A Stranger			
(UK) Capitol	*2–9–55*	*18*	*1*
Love And Marriage			
(US) Capitol	12–11–55	5	14
(UK) Capitol	*13–1–56*	*3*	*8*
Love Is The Tender Trap			
(UK) Capitol	*20–1–56*	*2*	*9*
Songs For Swingin' Lovers			
(UK) Capitol LP	*22–6–56*	*12*	*5*
Hey Jealous Lover			
(US) Capitol	3–11–56	6	14

	Date of chart entry	*Highest position reached*	*Number of weeks in charts*
SINATRA, FRANK (cont.)			
Can I Steal A Little Love			
(US) Capitol	2–3–57	20	1
All The Way			
(US) Capitol	2–12–57	15	7
(UK) Capitol	*13–12–57*	*3*	*16*
Witchcraft			
(UK) Capitol	*14–2–58*	*12*	*6*
(US) Capitol	24–2–58	20	1
High Hopes			
(UK) Capitol	*19–9–59*	*9*	*10*
River, Stay 'Way From My Door			
(UK) Capitol	*12–6–60*	*16*	*2*
Nice 'n' Easy			
(UK) Capitol	*11–9–60*	*20*	*1*
Ole McDonald			
(UK) Capitol	*20–11–60*	*14*	*4*
Granada			
(UK) Reprise	*23–9–61*	*13*	*3*
Strangers In The Night			
(UK) Reprise	*21–5–66*	*1*	*13*
(US) Reprise	4–6–66	1	8
That's Life			
(US) Reprise	3–12–66	4	8
My Way			
(UK) Reprise	*10–5–69*	*5*	*9*
Love's Been Good To Me			
(UK) Reprise	*25–10–69*	*8*	*7*
Somethin' Stupid (with NANCY SINATRA)			
(US) Reprise	1–4–67	1	10
(UK) Reprise	*1–4–67*	*1*	*11*
My Way			
(UK) Reprise (re-entry)	*2–1–71*	*18*	*1*
I Will Drink The Wine			
(UK) Reprise	*20–3–71*	*16*	*2*
SINATRA, NANCY			
These Boots Are Made For Walkin'			
(UK) Reprise	*5–2–66*	*1*	*10*
(US) Reprise	12–2–66	1	10
How Does That Grab You Darlin'			
(US) Reprise	7–5–66	7	4
(UK) Reprise	*14–5–66*	*19*	*1*
Sugar Town			
(US) Reprise	10–12–66	5	8
(UK) Reprise	*4–2–67*	*8*	*5*

	Date of chart entry	Highest position reached	Number of weeks in charts
SINATRA. NANCY (cont.)			
Love Eyes			
(US) Reprise	22–4–67	15	2
You Only Live Twice			
(UK) Reprise	*15–7–67*	*11*	*4*
Jackson (with LEE HAZLEWOOD)			
(US) Reprise	22–7–67	14	4
Lady Bird (with LEE HAZLEWOOD)			
(US) Reprise	18–11–67	20	1
Did You Ever? (with LEE HAZLEWOOD)			
(UK) Reprise	*4–9–71*	*2*	*9*
[see also: SINATRA, FRANK]			
SINGING DOGS			
Oh Susanna			
(UK) Nixa EP	*25–11–55*	*13*	*4*
SINGING NUN			
Dominique			
(US) Philips	16–11–63	1	11
(UK) Philips	*14–12–63*	*7*	*7*
SIR DOUGLAS QUINTET			
She's About A Mover			
(US) Tribe	22–5–65	13	4
(UK) London	*10–7–65*	*15*	*3*
SKELLERN, PETER			
You're A Lady			
(UK) Decca	*30–9–72*	*3*	*7*
SKIP AND FLIP			
It Was I			
(US) Brent	10–8–59	11	6
Cherry Pie			
(US) Brent	2–5–60	11	6
SKYLARK			
Wildflower			
(US) Capitol	21–4–73	9	9
SKYLINERS			
Since I Don't Have You			
(US) Calico	30–3–59	12	6
SLADE			
Get Down And Get With It			
(UK) Polydor	*7–8–71*	*16*	*4*
Coz I Luv You			
(UK) Polydor	*6–11–71*	*1*	*9*
Look Wot You Dun			
(UK) Polydor	*12–2–72*	*4*	*8*

	Date of chart entry	*Highest position reached*	*Number of weeks in charts*
SLADE (cont.)			
Take Me Bak 'Ome			
(UK) Polydor	*10–6–72*	*1*	*9*
Mama Weer All Crazee Now			
(UK) Polydor	*2–9–72*	*1*	*7*
Gudbuy T'Jane			
(UK) Polydor	*25–11–73*	*2*	*9*
Cum On Feel The Noize			
(UK) Polydor	*3–3–73*	*1*	*8*
Skweeze Me Pleeze Me			
(UK) Polydor	*30–6–73*	*1*	*6*
My Friend Stan			
(UK) Polydor	*6–10–73*	*2*	*6*
Merry Christmas Everybody			
(UK) Polydor	*8–12–73*	*1*	*6*
Everyday			
(UK) Polydor	*6–4–74*	*3*	*5*
Bangin' Man			
(UK) Polydor	*6–7–74*	*3*	*5*
Far Far Away			
(UK) Polydor	*19–10–74*	*2*	*5*
SLEDGE, PERCY			
When A Man Loves A Woman			
(US) Atlantic	7–5–66	1	8
(UK) Atlantic	*28–5–66*	*4*	*9*
Warm And Tender Love			
(US) Atlantic	27–8–66	17	2
It Tears Me Up			
(US) Atlantic	17–12–66	20	1
Take Time To Know Her			
(US) Atlantic	27–4–68	11	5
SLIM HARPO			
Baby Scratch My Back			
(US) Excello	19–3–66	16	3
SLY AND THE FAMILY STONE			
Dance To The Music			
(US) Epic	9–3–68	8	9
(UK) CBS	*3–8–68*	*7*	*7*
Everyday People			
(US) Epic	18–1–69	1	11
Hot Fun In The Summertime			
(US) Epic	27–9–69	2	8
Thank You (Falettin Me Be Mice Elf Agin)/Everybody Is A Star			
(US) Epic	24–1–70	1	8

	Date of chart entry	Highest position reached	Number of weeks in charts
SLY AND THE FAMILY STONE (cont.)			
Family Affair			
(US) Epic	20–11–71	1	11
(UK) Epic	*5–2–72*	*15*	*3*
Runnin' Away			
(UK) Epic	*6–5–72*	*17*	*2*
If You Want Me To Stay			
(US) Epic	4–8–73	12	8
SMALL, MILLIE			
My Boy Lollipop			
(UK) Fontana	*11–4–64*	*2*	*10*
(US) Smash	13–6–64	2	7
SMALL FACES			
Whatcha Gonna Do About It			
(UK) Decca	*30–9–65*	*14*	*5*
Sha La La La Lee			
(UK) Decca	*19–2–66*	*3*	*8*
Hey Girl			
(UK) Decca	*21–5–66*	*10*	*5*
All Or Nothing			
(UK) Decca	*20–8–66*	*1*	*8*
My Mind's Eye			
(UK) Decca	*26–11–66*	*4*	*8*
Here Comes The Nice			
(UK) Immediate	*24–6–67*	*12*	*6*
Itchycoo Park			
(UK) Immediate	*19–8–67*	*3*	*11*
(US) Immediate	27–1–68	16	3
Tin Soldier			
(UK) Immediate	*23–12–67*	*9*	*8*
Lazy Sunday			
(UK) Immediate	*27–4–68*	*2*	*7*
Universal			
(UK) Immediate	*27–7–68*	*16*	*5*
[see also: FACES; HUMBLE PIE]			
SMITH			
Baby It's You			
(US) Dunhill	11–10–69	5	9
SMITH, HUEY, AND THE CLOWNS			
Don't You Just Know It			
(US) Ace	7–4–58	9	7
SMITH, HURRICANE			
Don't Let It Die			
(UK) Columbia	*19–6–71*	*2*	*8*

	Date of chart entry	Highest position reached	Number of weeks in charts
SMITH, HURRICANE (cont.)			
Oh Babe, What Would You Say			
(UK) Columbia	*13–5–72*	*4*	*8*
(US) Capitol	13–1–73	3	8
SMITH, KEELEY			
That Old Black Magic (with LOUIS PRIMA)			
(US) Capitol	15–12–58	18	1
You're Breaking My Heart			
(UK) Reprise	*3–4–65*	*14*	*5*
SMITH, O.C.			
Son Of Hickory Holler's Tramp			
(UK) CBS	*15 6 68*	*2*	*9*
Little Green Apples			
(US) Columbia	28–9–68	2	10
SMITH, SAMMI			
Help Me Make It Through The Night			
(US) Mega	13–2–71	8	7
SMITH, SOMETHIN', AND THE REDHEADS			
It's A Sin To Tell A Lie			
(US) Epic	14–5–55	7	16
SMITH, WHISTLING JACK			
I Was Kaiser Bill's Batman			
(UK) Deram	*18–3–67*	*5*	*7*
(US) Deram	3–6–67	20	1
SMITH BROTHERS			
I'm In Favour of Friendship			
(UK) Decca	*22–7–55*	*20*	*1*
SOMMERS, JOANIE			
Johnny Get Angry			
(US) Warner Brothers	30–6–62	7	7
SONNY			
Laugh At Me			
(UK) Atlantic	*4–9–65*	*9*	*6*
(US) Atco	11–9–65	10	5
[see also: SONNY AND CHER]			
SONNY AND CHER			
I Got You Babe			
(US) Atco	7–8–65	1	8
(UK) Atlantic	*21–8–65*	*1*	*10*

	Date of chart entry	*Highest position reached*	*Number of weeks in charts*
SONNY AND CHER (cont.)			
Baby Don't Go			
(US) Reprise	25–9–65	8	5
(UK) Reprise	*30–9–65*	*11*	*5*
Just You			
(US) Atco	9–10–65	20	1
But You're Mine			
(US) Atco	30–10–65	15	4
(UK) Atlantic	*6–11–65*	*17*	*2*
What Now My Love			
(US) Atco	19–2–66	14	3
(UK) Atlantic	*12–3–66*	*13*	*5*
Little Man			
(UK) Atlantic	*17–9–66*	*4*	*6*
The Beat Goes On			
(US) Atco	4–2–67	6	6
All I Ever Need Is You			
(US) Kapp	27–11–71	7	7
(UK) MCA	*29–1–72*	*8*	*7*
A Cowboy's Work Is Never Done			
(US) Kapp	25–3–72	8	8
SOUL. JIMMY			
If You Wanna Be Happy			
(US) S.P.Q.R.	27–4–63	1	9
SOUL SURVIVORS			
Expressway To Your Heart			
(US) Crimson	7–10–67	4	9
SOUNDS NICE			
Love At First Sight			
(UK) Parlophone	*4–10–69*	*18*	*3*
SOUNDS ORCHESTRAL			
Cast Your Fate To The Wind			
(UK) Piccadilly	*2–1–65*	*5*	*10*
(US) Parkway	24–4–65	10	6
SOUTH, JOE			
Games People Play			
(US) Capitol	15–2–69	12	6
(UK) Capitol	*15–3–69*	*6*	*8*
Walk A Mile In My Shoes			
(US) Capitol	31–1–70	12	6
SOUTHLANDERS			
Alone			
(UK) Decca	*29–11–57*	*17*	*6*

	Date of chart entry	*Highest position reached*	*Number of weeks in charts*
SPANKY AND OUR GANG			
Sunday Will Never Be The Same			
(US) Mercury	10–6–67	9	5
Lazy Day			
(US) Mercury	18–11–67	14	5
Like To Get To Know You			
(US) Mercury	18–5–68	17	4
SPARKS			
This Town Ain't Big Enough For The Both Of Us			
(UK) Island	*18–5–74*	*2*	*6*
Amateur Hour			
(UK) Island	*27–7–74*	*7*	*5*
Never Turn Your Back on Mother Earth			
(UK) Island	*2–11–74*	*13*	*4*
SPENCE, JOHNNY			
Theme from 'Dr. Kildare'			
(UK) Parlophone	*31–3–62*	*15*	*6*
SPINNERS (*MOTOWN SPINNERS; †DETROIT SPINNERS)			
It's A Shame			
(US) V.I.P.	3–10–70	14	3
*(UK) Tamla-Motown**	*19–12–70*	*20*	*2*
I'll Be Around/How Could I Let You Get Away			
(US) Atlantic	28–10–72	3	7
Could It Be I'm Falling In Love			
(US) Atlantic	3–2–73	4	8
(UK) Atlantic†	*12–5–73*	*11*	*5*
One Of A Kind (Love Affair)			
(US) Atlantic	9–6–73	11	5
Ghetto Child			
(UK) Atlantic†	*13–10–73*	*7*	*6*
Mighty Love			
(US) Atlantic	23–3–74	20	1
I'm Coming Home			
(US) Atlantic	22–6–74	18	2
Love Don't Love Nobody			
(US) Atlantic	9–11–74	15	2
[see also: WARWICKE, DIONNE AND THE SPINNERS]			
SPIRAL STAIRCASE			
More Today Than Yesterday			
(US) Columbia	31–5–69	12	4

	Date of chart entry	Highest position reached	Number of weeks in charts
SPLINTER			
Costafine Town			
(UK) Dark Horse	*30–11–74*	*17*	*3*
SPOTNIKS			
Hava Nagila			
(UK) Oriole	*17–2–63*	*13*	*4*
SPRINGFIELD, DUSTY			
I Only Want To Be With You			
(UK) Philips	*7–12–63*	*4*	*12*
(US) Philips	22–2–64	12	4
Stay Awhile			
(UK) Philips	*29–2–64*	*13*	*6*
I Just Don't Know What To Do With Myself			
(UK) Philips	*21–7–64*	*3*	*9*
Wishin' And Hopin'			
(US) Philips	18–7–64	6	7
Losing You			
(UK) Philips	*21–11–64*	*9*	*5*
In The Middle Of Nowhere			
(UK) Philips	*10–7–65*	*8*	*6*
Some Of Your Lovin'			
(UK) Philips	*7–10–65*	*8*	*6*
Little By Little			
(UK) Philips	*19–2–66*	*17*	*3*
You Don't Have To Say You Love Me			
(UK) Philips	*9–4–66*	*1*	*10*
(US) Philips	11–6–66	4	8
Goin' Back			
(UK) Philips	*16–7–66*	*10*	*7*
All I See Is You			
(UK) Philips	*24–9–66*	*9*	*7*
(US) Philips	22–10–66	20	1
I'll Try Anything			
(UK) Philips	*14–3–67*	*13*	*4*
Give Me Time			
(UK) Philips	*8–7–67*	*19*	*1*
I Close My Eyes			
(UK) Philips	*27–7–68*	*4*	*6*
Son Of A Preacher Man			
(UK) Philips	*21–12–68*	*9*	*6*
(US) Atlantic	4–1–69	10	6
[see also: SPRINGFIELDS]			
SPRINGFIELD, RICK			
Speak To The Sky			
(US) Capitol	23–9–72	14	5

	Date of chart entry	Highest position reached	Number of weeks in charts
SPRINGFIELDS			
Bambino			
(UK) Philips	*6–1–62*	*15*	*1*
Silver Threads And Golden Needles			
(US) Philips	22–9–62	20	2
Island Of Dreams			
(UK) Philips	*20–1–63*	*5*	*15*
SPRINGWATER			
I Will Return			
(UK) Polydor	*6–11–71*	*5*	*6*
STAFFORD, JIM			
Spiders And Snakes			
(US) MGM	19–1–74	3	9
(UK) MGM	*11–5–74*	*14*	*4*
My Girl Bill			
(US) MGM	25–5–74	12	4
(UK) MGM	*27–7–74*	*20*	*2*
Wildwood Weed			
(US) MGM	27–7–74	7	7
STAFFORD, JO			
Suddenly There's A Valley			
(US) Columbia	12–11–55	16	3
(UK) Philips	*9–12–55*	*12*	*6*
It's Almost Tomorrow			
(US) Columbia	21–1–56	19	2
STAFFORD, TERRY			
Suspicion			
(US) Crusader	21–3–64	3	9
STAMPEDERS			
Sweet City Woman			
(US) Bell	25–9–71	8	7
STANDELLS			
Dirty Water			
(US) Tower	2–7–66	11	4
STANG, ARNOLD			
Ivy Will Cling			
(UK) Fontana	*5–12–59*	*18*	*1*
STAPLE SINGERS			
Respect Yourself			
(US) Stax	27–11–71	12	6

	Date of chart entry	Highest position reached	Number of weeks in charts
STAPLE SINGERS (cont.)			
I'll Take You There			
(US) Stax	29–4–72	1	10
If You're Ready, Go With Me			
(US) Stax	24–11–73	9	6
STAPLETON, CYRIL			
Elephant Tango			
(UK) Decca	*27–5–55*	*19*	*4*
Blue Star			
(UK) Decca	*23–9–55*	*2*	*12*
The Italian Theme			
(UK) Decca	*6–4–56*	*18*	*1*
Children's Marching Song			
(US) London	2–2–59	13	4
STARDUST, ALVIN			
My Coo Coo Ca Choo			
(UK) Magnet	*24–11–73*	*2*	*11*
Jealous Mind			
(UK) Magnet	*23–2–74*	*1*	*6*
Red Dress			
(UK) Magnet	*11–5–74*	*7*	*5*
You You You			
(UK) Magnet	*7–9–74*	*6*	*6*
Tell Me Why			
(UK) Magnet	*14–12–74*	*16*	*3*
STARGAZERS			
Somebody			
(UK) Decca	*11–3–55*	*20*	*1*
Crazy Otto Rag			
(UK) Decca	*3–6–55*	*18*	*3*
Close The Door			
(UK) Decca	*9–9–55*	*6*	*9*
Twenty Tiny Fingers			
(UK) Decca	*11–11–55*	*4*	*11*
STARR, EDWIN			
SOS/Headline News			
(UK) Polydor (re-issue)	*18–1–69*	*11*	*5*
25 Miles			
(US) Gordy	29–3–69	6	6
War			
(US) Gordy	1–8–70	1	11
(UK) Tamla-Motown	*24–10–70*	*3*	*8*
STARR, FREDDIE			
It's You			
(UK) Tiffany	*2–3–74*	*9*	*6*

	Date of chart entry	Highest position reached	Number of weeks in charts
STARR, KAY			
Rock And Roll Waltz			
(US) Victor	7–1–56	1	18
(UK) HMV	*17–2–56*	*1*	*18*
STARR, RINGO			
It Don't Come Easy			
(UK) Apple	*24–4–71*	*4*	*8*
(US) Apple	15–5–71	4	9
Back Off Boogaloo			
(UK) Apple	*8–4–72*	*2*	*7*
(US) Apple	22–4–72	9	5
Photograph			
(US) Apple	27–10–73	1	9
(UK) Apple	*10–11–73*	*8*	*5*
You're Sixteen			
(US) Apple	5–1–74	1	10
(UK) Apple	*23–2–74*	*4*	*7*
Oh My My			
(US) Apple	30–3–74	5	7
Only You			
(US) Apple	14–12–74	6	6
STATLER BROTHERS			
Flowers On The Wall			
(US) Columbia	25–12–65	4	5
STATUS QUO			
Pictures Of Matchstick Men			
(UK) Pye International	*10–2–68*	*7*	*7*
(US) Cadet Concept	27–7–68	12	4
Ice In The Sun			
(UK) Pye International	*21–9–68*	*8*	*6*
Down The Dustpipe			
(UK) Pye	*20–6–70*	*12*	*6*
Paper Plane			
(UK) Vertigo	*27–1–73*	*8*	*5*
Mean Girl			
(UK) Pye	*26–5–73*	*20*	*1*
Caroline			
(UK) Vertigo	*29–9–73*	*5*	*8*
Break The Rules			
(UK) Vertigo	*18–5–74*	*8*	*4*
Down Down			
(UK) Vertigo	*14–12–74*	*1*	*7*
STEALERS WHEEL			
Stuck In The Middle With You			
(US) A & M	14–4–73	6	9
(UK) A & M	*2–6–73*	*8*	*6*

	Date of chart entry	*Highest position reached*	*Number of weeks in charts*
STEAM			
Na Na Hey Hey Kiss Him Goodbye			
(US) Fontana	15–11–69	1	11
(UK) Fontana	*7–3–70*	*9*	*5*
STEELE, TOMMY			
Rock With The Cave Man			
(UK) Decca	*2–11–56*	*13*	*3*
Singing The Blues			
(UK) Decca	*21–12–56*	*1*	*10*
Knee Deep In The Blues			
(UK) Decca	*22–2–57*	*15*	*4*
Butterfingers			
(UK) Decca	*17–5–57*	*8*	*15*
Shiralee			
(UK) Decca	*23–8–57*	*11*	*3*
Water Water/Handful Of Songs			
(UK) Decca	*30–8–57*	*5*	*13*
Nairobi			
(UK) Decca	*7–3–58*	*3*	*10*
Happy Guitar			
(UK) Decca	*25–4–58*	*20*	*1*
Only Man On The Island			
(UK) Decca	*18–7–58*	*16*	*3*
Come On, Let's Go			
(UK) Decca	*21–11–58*	*9*	*11*
Give Give Give/Tallahassie Lassie			
(UK) Decca	*15–8–59*	*17*	*3*
Little White Bull			
(UK) Decca	*28–11–59*	*6*	*10*
What A Mouth			
(UK) Decca	*26–6–60*	*5*	*7*
The Writing On The Wall			
(UK) Decca	*12–8–61*	*18*	*1*
STEELEYE SPAN			
Gaudete			
(UK) Chrysalis	*22–12–73*	*14*	*3*
STEELY DAN			
Do It Again			
(US) ABC	20–1–73	6	7
Reeling In The Years			
(US) ABC	28–4–73	11	6
Rikki Don't Lose That Number			
(US) ABC	29–6–74	4	7

	Date of chart entry	*Highest position reached*	*Number of weeks in charts*
STEPPENWOLF			
Born To Be Wild			
(US) Dunhill	3–8–68	2	9
Magic Carpet Ride			
(US) Dunhill	2–11–68	3	9
Rock Me			
(US) Dunhill	22–3–69	10	6
STEVENS, CAT			
Matthew And Son			
(UK) Deram	*14–1–67*	*2*	*7*
I'm Gonna Get Me A Gun			
(UK) Deram	*22–4–67*	*6*	*5*
A Bad Night			
(UK) Deram	*26–8–67*	*20*	*1*
Lady D'Arbanville			
(UK) Island	*11–7–70*	*8*	*8*
Wild World			
(US) A & M	27–3–71	11	5
Peace Train			
(US) A & M	16–10–71	7	8
Morning Has Broken			
(UK) Island	*15–1–72*	*9*	*4*
(US) A & M	6–5–72	6	8
Sitting			
(US) A & M	30–12–72	16	3
Can't Keep It In			
(UK) Island	*20–1–73*	*13*	*4*
Oh Very Young			
(US) A & M	11–5–74	10	6
Another Saturday Night			
(US) A & M	14–9–74	6	5
(UK) Island	*28–9–74*	*19*	*1*
STEVENS, CONNIE			
Sixteen Reasons			
(US) Warner Brothers	4–4–60	3	11
(UK) Warner Brothers	*15–5–60*	*12*	*4*
[see also: BYRNES, ED]			
STEVENS, DODIE			
Pink Shoelaces			
(US) Crystalette	16–3–59	3	12
STEVENS, RAY			
Ahab The Arab			
(US) Mercury	14–7–62	5	8
Harry The Hairy Ape			
(US) Mercury	13–7–63	17	3
Gitarzan			
(US) Monument	3–5–69	8	8

	Date of chart entry	*Highest position reached*	*Number of weeks in charts*
STEVENS, RAY (cont.)			
Everything Is Beautiful			
(US) Barnaby	2–5–70	1	9
(UK) CBS	*23–5–70*	*6*	*8*
Bridget The Midget			
(UK) CBS	*20–3–71*	*2*	*9*
The Streak			
(US) Barnaby	27–4–74	1	11
(UK) Janus	*1–6–74*	*1*	*7*
STEVENSON, B. W.			
My Maria			
(US) RCA	8–9–73	9	7
STEWART, BILLY			
Summertime			
(US) Chess	20–8–66	10	4
STEWART, ROD			
Maggie May/Reason To Believe			
(US) Mercury	4–9–71	1	13
(UK) Mercury	*19–8–72*	*1*	*7*
You Wear It Well			
(UK) Mercury	*19–8–72*	*1*	*7*
(US) Mercury	7–10–72	13	3
Angel/What Made Milwaukee Famous			
(UK) Mercury	*25–11–72*	*4*	*5*
Oh No, Not My Baby			
(UK) Mercury	*15–9–73*	*6*	*5*
Farewell/Bring It On Home To Me – You Send Me			
(UK) Mercury	*12–10–74*	*7*	*4*
[see also: Faces, Python Lee Jackson]			
STEWART, SANDY			
My Coloring Book			
(US) Colpix	2 2–63	20	1
STILLS, STEPHEN			
Love The One You're With			
(US) Atlantic	16–1–71	14	4
[see also: Buffalo Springfield; Crosby, Stills and Nash, CSN&Y]			
STOLLER, RHET			
Chariot			
(UK) Decca	*8–1–61*	*19*	*1*

	Date of chart entry	Highest position reached	Number of weeks in charts
STOLOFF, MORRIS			
Moonglow And Theme From 'Picnic'			
(US) Decca	5–5–56	2	17
(UK) Brunswick	*1–6–56*	*7*	*8*
STONE PONEYS			
Different Drum			
(US) Capitol	30–12–67	13	6
STORIES			
Brother Louie			
(US) Kama Sutra	28–7–73	1	11
STORM, GALE			
I Hear You Knocking			
(US) Dot	29–10–55	2	17
Teen-Age Prayer			
(US) Dot (b/w*)	31–12–55	9	11
Memories Are Made Of This*			
(US) Dot	7–1–56	16	2
Why Do Fools Fall In Love			
(US) Dot	10–3–56	15	9
Ivory Tower			
(US) Dot	12–5–56	10	11
Dark Moon			
(US) Dot	13–5–57	5	14
STRANGELOVES			
I Want Candy			
(US) Bang	24–7–65	11	4
STRAWBERRY ALARM CLOCK			
Incense And Peppermint			
(US) UNI	21–10–67	1	12
STRAWBS			
Lay Down			
(UK) A & M	*25–11–72*	*12*	*3*
Part Of The Union			
(UK) A & M	*27–1–73*	*2*	*9*
STREISAND, BARBRA			
People			
(US) Columbia	30–5–64	5	9
Second Hand Rose			
(UK) CBS	*19–2–66*	*14*	*2*
Stoney End			
(US) Columbia	26–12–70	6	8
The Way We Were			
(US) Columbia	5–1–74	1	12

	Date of chart entry	*Highest position reached*	*Number of weeks in charts*
STRING-A-LONGS			
Wheels			
(UK) London	*12–2–61*	*12*	*5*
(US) Warwick	13–2–61	3	8
STRUNK, JED			
Daisy A Day			
(US) MGM	5–5–73	14	4
STYLISTICS			
You Are Everything			
(US) Avco	11–12–71	9	10
Betcha By Golly Wow			
(US) Avco	25–3–72	3	10
(UK) Avco	*22–7–72*	*13*	*4*
I'm Stone In Love With You			
(UK) Avco	*11–11–72*	*9*	*5*
(US) Avco	18–11–72	10	6
Break Up To Make Up			
(US) Avco	10–3–73	5	7
Rockin' Roll Baby			
(US) Avco	8–12–73	14	4
(UK) Avco	*26–1–74*	*6*	*6*
You Make Me Feel Brand New			
(US) Avco	4–5–74	2	11
(UK) Avco	*27–7–74*	*2*	*9*
Let's Put It All Together			
(US) Avco	14–9–74	18	2
(UK) Avco	*2–11–74*	*9*	*5*
SUGARLOAF			
Green-Eyed Lady			
(US) Liberty	26–9–70	3	10
SUNNY AND THE SUNGLOWS			
Talk To Me			
(US) Tear Drop	19–10–63	11	5
SUNNY SIDERS			
Hey Mr. Banjo			
(US) Kapp	4–6–55	20	4
SUNNY			
Doctor's Orders			
(UK) CBS	*13–4–74*	*7*	*5*
SUPREMES			
Where Did Our Love Go?			
(US) Motown	25–7–64	1	11
(UK) Stateside	*11–9–64*	*3*	*10*

	Date of chart entry	Highest position reached	Number of weeks in charts
SUPREMES (cont.)			
Baby Love			
(US) Motown	17–10–64	1	10
(UK) Stateside	*31–10–64*	*1*	*10*
(UK) Tamla-Motown (re-issue)	*14–9–74*	*12*	*3*
Come See About Me			
(US) Motown	28–11–64	1	11
Stop! In The Name Of Love			
(US) Motown	6–3–65	1	9
(UK) Tamla-Motown	*10–4–65*	*6*	*6*
Back In My Arms Again			
(US) Motown	15–5–65	1	8
Nothing But Heartaches			
(US) Motown	21–8–65	11	4
I Hear A Symphony			
(US) Motown	6–11–65	1	8
My World Is Empty Without You			
(US) Motown	5–2–66	5	6
Love Is Like An Itching In My Heart			
(US) Motown	14–5–66	9	5
You Can't Hurry Love			
(US) Motown	27–8–66	1	9
(UK) Tamla-Motown	*17–9–66*	*3*	*8*
You Keep Me Hangin' On			
(US) Motown	12–11–66	1	8
(UK) Tamla-Motown	*10–12–66*	*8*	*7*
Love Is Here And Now You're Gone			
(US) Motown	11–2–67	1	8
(UK) Tamla-Motown	*25–3–67*	*17*	*3*
The Happening			
(US) Motown	15–4–67	1	8
(UK) Tamla-Motown	*27–5–67*	*6*	*8*
Up The Ladder To The Roof			
(US) Motown	4–4–70	10	6
(UK) Tamla-Motown	*30–5–70*	*6*	*6*
Stoned Love			
(US) Motown	5–12–70	7	8
(UK) Tamla-Motown	*30–1–71*	*3*	*9*
River Deep Mountain High (with the FOUR TOPS)			
(US) Motown	26–12–70	14	5
(UK) Tamla-Motown	*10–7–71*	*11*	*6*
Nathan Jones			
(US) Motown	12–6–71	16	4
(UK) Tamla-Motown	*4–9–71*	*5*	*7*

	Date of chart entry	*Highest position reached*	*Number of weeks in charts*
SUPREMES (cont.)			
Floy Joy			
(US) Motown	26–2–72	16	3
(UK) Tamla-Motown	*18–3–72*	*9*	*6*
Automatically Sunshine			
(UK) Tamla-Motown	*29–7–72*	*10*	*4*
[see also: ROSS, DIANA AND THE SUPREMES]			
SURFARIS			
Wipe Out			
(US) Dot	6–7–63	2	9
(UK) London	*3–8–63*	*5*	*9*
(US) Dot (re-issue)	17–9–66	16	4
SWAN, BILLY			
I Can Help			
(US) Monument	9–11–74	1	7
(UK) Monument	*21–12–74*	*6*	*6*
SWEET			
Funny Funny			
(UK) RCA	*10–4–71*	*13*	*6*
Co-Co			
(UK) RCA	*19–6–71*	*2*	*10*
Poppa Joe			
(UK) RCA	*26–2–72*	*11*	*5*
Little Willy			
(UK) RCA	*24–6–72*	*4*	*8*
(US) Bell (re-issue)	7–4–73	3	9
Wig Wam Bam			
(UK) RCA	*23–9–72*	*4*	*7*
Blockbuster			
(UK) RCA	*13–1–73*	*1*	*10*
Hell Raiser			
(UK) RCA	*5–5–73*	*2*	*6*
Ballroom Blitz			
(UK) RCA	*22–9–73*	*2*	*6*
Teenage Rampage			
(UK) RCA	*19–1–74*	*2*	*6*
Six Teens			
(UK) RCA	*20–7–74*	*9*	*4*
SWEET DREAMS			
Honey Honey			
(UK) Bradleys	*17–8–74*	*10*	*6*
SWEET INSPIRATIONS			
Sweet Inspiration			
(US) Atlantic	27–4–68	18	3

	Date of chart entry	*Highest position reached*	*Number of weeks in charts*
SWEET SENSATION			
Sad Sweet Dreamer			
(UK) Pye	*28–9–74*	*1*	*7*
SWINGING BLUE JEANS			
Hippy Hippy Shake			
(UK) HMV	*4–1–64*	*2*	*9*
Good Golly Miss Molly			
(UK) HMV	*4–4–64*	*11*	*5*
You're No Good			
(UK) HMV	*20–6–64*	*3*	*7*
SWINGING MEDALLIONS			
Double Shot (Of My Baby's Love)			
(US) Smash	18–6–66	17	3
SYLVIA			
Pillow Talk			
(US) Vibration	5–5–73	3	11
(UK) London	*21–7–73*	*14*	*4*
SYLVIA			
Y Viva España			
(UK) Sonet	*24–8–74*	*4*	*8*
SYNDICATE OF SOUND			
Little Girl			
(US) Bell	2–7–66	8	4
TAMS			
What Kind Of Fool (Do You Think I Am)			
(US) ABC-Paramount	1–2–64	9	5
Hey Girl Don't Bother Me			
(UK) Probe (re-issue)	*21–8–71*	*1*	*11*
TARRIERS			
Banana Boat Song			
(US) Glory	29–12–56	6	20
(UK) Philips	*8–3–57*	*8*	*6*
[see also: MARTIN, VINCE]			
TAYLOR, FELICE			
I Feel Love Coming On			
(UK) President	*18–11–67*	*11*	*6*
TAYLOR, JAMES			
Fire And Rain			
(US) Warner Brothers	10–10–70	3	10

	Date of chart entry	Highest position reached	Number of weeks in charts
TAYLOR, JAMES (cont.)			
You've Got A Friend			
(US) Warner Brothers	26–6–71	1	10
(UK) Warner Brothers	*11–9–71*	*4*	*9*
Don't Let Me Be Lonely Tonight			
(US) Warner Brothers	6–1–73	14	4
[see also: SIMON, CARLY]			
TAYLOR, JOHNNIE			
Who's Making Love			
(US) Stax	16–11–68	5	9
Take Care Of Your Homework			
(US) Stax	22–2–69	20	1
I Believe In You (You Believe In Me)			
(US) Stax	28–7–73	11	8
Cheaper To Keep Her			
(US) Stax	10–11–73	15	4
TAYLOR, LITTLE JOHNNY			
Part Time Love			
(US) Galaxy	5–10–63	19	2
TAYLOR, R. DEAN			
Gotta See Jane			
(UK) Tamla Motown	*20–7–68*	*17*	*3*
Indiana Wants Me			
(US) Rare Earth	17–10–70	5	8
(UK) Tamla Motown	*1–5–71*	*2*	*9*
There's A Ghost In My House			
(UK) Tamla Motown (re-issue)	*25–5–74*	*3*	*7*
TAYLOR, VINCE			
I'll Be Your Hero/Jet Black Machine			
(UK) Palette	*18–9–60*	*16*	*4*
T-BONES			
No Matter What Shape (Your Stomach's In)			
(US) Liberty	8–1–66	3	8
TEDDY BEARS			
To Know Him Is To Love Him			
(US) Dore	20–10–58	1	15
(UK) London	*10–1–59*	*2*	*10*
TEE SET			
Ma Belle Amie			
(US) Colossus	14–2–70	5	8

	Date of chart entry	*Highest position reached*	*Number of weeks in charts*
TEMPERANCE SEVEN			
You're Driving Me Crazy			
(UK) Parlophone	*26–3–61*	*1*	*10*
Pasadena			
(UK) Parlophone	*4–6–61*	*4*	*12*
Hardhearted Hannah			
(UK) Parlophone	*30–9–61*	*19*	*2*
The Charleston			
(UK) Parlophone	*2–12–61*	*14*	*2*
TEMPO, NINO AND STEVENS, APRIL			
Deep Purple			
(US) Atco	12–10–63	1	9
(UK) London	*7–12–63*	*17*	*2*
Whispering			
(US) Atco	4–1–64	11	6
(UK) London	*8–2–64*	*20*	*1*
TEMPTATIONS			
The Way You Do The Things You Do			
(US) Gordy	28–3–64	11	6
My Girl			
(US) Gordy	30–1–65	1	10
It's Growing			
(US) Gordy	1–5–65	18	3
Since I Lost My Baby			
(US) Gordy	28–8–65	17	2
My Baby			
(US) Gordy	20–11–65	13	2
Ain't Too Proud To Beg			
(US) Gordy	25–6–66	13	5
Beauty Is Only Skin Deep			
(US) Gordy	10–9–66	3	6
(UK) Tamla Motown	*12–11–66*	*18*	*1*
(I Know) I'm Losing You			
(US) Gordy	10–12–66	8	6
(UK) Tamla Motown	*14–1–67*	*19*	*2*
All I Need Is You			
(US) Gordy	27–5–67	8	5
You're My Everything			
(US) Gordy	26–8–67	6	6
(Loneliness Made Me Realize) It's You That I Need			
(US) Gordy	28–10–67	14	5
I Wish It Would Rain			
(US) Gordy	27–1–68	4	5
I Could Never Love Another			
(US) Gordy	1–6–68	13	5

	Date of chart entry	Highest position reached	Number of weeks in charts
TEMPTATIONS (cont.)			
Cloud Nine			
(US) Gordy	7–12–68	6	8
(UK) Tamla Motown	*13–9–69*	*15*	*3*
Runaway Child, Running Wild			
(US) Gordy	8–3–69	6	8
Get Ready			
(UK) Tamla Motown (re-sisue)	*22–3–69*	*10*	*5*
Don't Let The Joneses Get You Down			
(US) Gordy	28–6–69	20	1
I Can't Get Next To You			
(US) Gordy	6–9–69	1	13
(UK) Tamla Motown	*31–1–70*	*13*	*5*
Psychedelic Shack			
(US) Gordy	7–2–70	7	7
Ball Of Confusion			
(US) Gordy	13–6–70	3	11
(UK) Tamla Motown	*10–10–70*	*7*	*7*
Just My Imagination			
(US) Gordy	27–2–71	1	11
(UK) Tamla Motown	*19–6–71*	*8*	*8*
Superstar (Remember How You Got Where You Are)			
(US) Gordy	18–12–71	18	2
Take A Look Around			
(UK) Tamla Motown	*6–5–72*	*13*	*5*
Papa Was A Rolling Stone			
(US) Gordy	4–11–72	1	9
(UK) Tamla Motown	*20–1–73*	*14*	*4*
Masterpiece			
(US) Gordy	31–3–73	7	6
[see also: SUPREMES]			
10cc			
Donna			
(UK) UK	*7–10–72*	*2*	*9*
Rubber Bullets			
(UK) UK	*2–6–73*	*1*	*9*
The Dean And I			
(UK) UK	*8–9–73*	*10*	*4*
Wall Street Shuffle			
(UK) UK	*29–6–74*	*10*	*5*
TEN YEARS AFTER			
Love Like A Man			
(UK) Deram	*18–7–70*	*10*	*6*
TERRELL, TAMMI. See GAYE, MARVIN			

	Date of chart entry	*Highest position reached*	*Number of weeks in charts*
TERRY DACTYL AND THE DINOSAURS			
Seaside Shuffle			
(UK) UK (re-issue)	*22–7–72*	*2*	*8*
TEX, JOE			
Hold What You've Got			
(US) Dial	16–1–65	5	6
Skinny Legs And All			
(US) Dial	9–12–67	10	7
I Gotcha			
(US) Dial	11–3–72	2	13
THEM			
Baby Please Don't Go			
(UK) Decca	*16–1–65*	*10*	*6*
Here Comes The Night			
(UK) Decca	*3–4–65*	*2*	*8*
THIN LIZZY			
Whisky In The Jar			
(UK) Decca	*10–2–76*	*6*	*6*
THOMAS, B. J.			
I'm So Lonesome I Could Cry (with the TRIUMPHS)			
(US) Scepter	19–3–66	8	8
Hooked On A Feeling			
(US) Scepter	28–12–68	5	7
Raindrops Keep Falling On My Head			
(US) Scepter	6–12–69	1	15
I Just Can't Help Believing			
(US) Scepter	25–7–70	9	7
No Love At All			
(US) Scepter	10–4–71	16	2
Rock And Roll Lullaby			
(US) Scepter	18–3–72	15	4
THOMAS, CARLA			
Gee Whiz			
(US) Atlantic	13–3–61	10	5
B-A-B-Y			
(US) Stax	15–10–66	14	4
[see also: REDDING, OTIS]			
THOMAS, IRMA			
Wish Some One Would Care			
(US) Imperial	9–5–64	17	3

	Date of chart entry	*Highest position reached*	*Number of weeks in charts*
THOMAS, NICKY			
Love Of The Common People			
(UK) Trojan	*4–7–70*	*9*	*7*
THOMAS, RUFUS			
Walking The Dog			
(US) Stax	16–11–63	10	6
Do The Funky Chicken			
(UK) Stax	*23–5–70*	*18*	*2*
THOMAS, TIMMY			
Why Can't We Live Together			
(US) Glades	6–1–73	3	8
(UK) Mojo	*24–3–73*	*12*	*4*
THOMPSON, SUE			
Sad Movies (Make Me Cry)			
(US) Hickory	9–10–61	5	7
Norman			
(US) Hickory	13–1–62	3	9
James (Hold The Ladder Steady)			
(US) Hickory	3–11–62	17	3
THORNE, KEN			
Theme From 'Legion's Last Patrol'			
(UK) HMV	*3–8–63*	*4*	*9*
THREE DEGREES			
Year Of Decision			
(UK) Philadelphia	*4–5–74*	*13*	*4*
International	4–5–74	13	4
When Will I See You Again?			
(UK) Philadelphia International	*20–7–74*	*1*	*10*
(US) Philadelphia International	9–11–74	2	9
THREE DOG NIGHT			
One			
(US) Dunhill	7–6–69	5	10
Easy To Be Hard			
(US) Dunhill	23–8–69	4	10
Eli's Coming			
(US) Dunhill	15–11–69	10	10
Celebrate			
(US) Dunhill	14–3–70	15	5
Mama Told Me Not To Come			
(US) Dunhill	13–6–70	1	11
(UK) Stateside	*22–8–70*	*3*	*8*

	Date of chart entry	Highest position reached	Number of weeks in charts
THREE DOG NIGHT (cont.)			
Out In The Country			
(US) Dunhill	10–10–70	15	3
One Man Band			
(US) Dunhill	2–1–71	19	2
Joy To The World			
(US) Dunhill	3–4–71	1	13
Liar			
(US) Dunhill	7–8–71	7	7
Old Fashioned Love Song			
(US) Dunhill	27–11–71	4	8
Never Been To Spain			
(US) Dunhill	15–1–72	5	8
Family Of Man			
(US) Dunhill	15–4–72	12	5
Black And White			
(US) Dunhill	2–9–72	1	6
Pieces Of April			
(US) Dunhill	13–1–73	19	1
Shambala			
(US) Dunhill	9–6–73	3	11
Let Me Serenade You			
(US) Dunhill	1–12–73	17	2
The Show Must Go On			
(US) Dunhill	20–4–74	4	9
Sure As I'm Sitting Here			
(US) Dunhill	10–8–74	16	2
THREE KAYES			
Ivory Tower			
(UK) HMV	*8–6–56*	*20*	*1*
[see also: KAYE SISTERS]			
TILLOTSON, JOHNNY			
Poetry In Motion			
(US) Cadence	31–10–60	2	9
(UK) London	*20–11–60*	*1*	*12*
Without You			
(US) Cadence	4–9–61	7	6
It Keeps Right On A-Hurtin'			
(US) Cadence	26–5–62	3	9
Send Me The Pillow You Dream On			
(US) Cadence	15–9–62	17	2
You Can Never Stop Me Loving You			
(US) Cadence	7–9–63	18	3
Talk Back Trembling Lips			
(US) MGM	14–12–63	7	6

	Date of chart entry	Highest position reached	Number of weeks in charts
TIN TIN			
Toast And Marmalade For Tea			
(US) Atco	29–5–71	20	1
TINY TIM			
Tip-Toe Through The Tulips			
(US) Reprise	29–6–68	17	1
TITANIC			
Sultana			
(UK) CBS	*9–10–71*	*5*	*7*
TODD, ART AND DOTTY			
Chanson d'Amour			
(US) Era	5–5–58	13	8
TOKENS			
Tonight I Fell In Love			
(US) Warwick	1–5–61	15	4
The Lion Sleeps Tonight			
(US) RCA	4–12–61	1	11
(UK) London	*13–1–62*	*16*	*4*
TOPOL			
If I Were A Rich Man			
(UK) CBS	*17–6–67*	*9*	*3*
TORME, MEL			
Mountain Greenery			
(UK) Vogue Coral	*18–5–56*	*4*	*17*
Comin' Home Baby			
(UK) London	*20–1–63*	*13*	*3*
TORNADOES			
Telstar			
(UK) Decca	*15–9–62*	*1*	*20*
(US) London	24–11 62	1	11
Globotrotter			
(UK) Decca	*20–1–63*	*5*	*7*
Robot			
(UK) Decca	*13–4–63*	*17*	*2*
Ice Cream Man			
(UK) Decca	*29–6–63*	*18*	*2*
TOROK, MITCHELL			
When Mexico Gave Up The Rhumba			
(UK) Brunswick	*5–10–56*	*6*	*15*

	Date of chart entry	Highest position reached	Number of weeks in charts
TOWER OF POWER			
So Very Hard To Go			
(US) Warner Brothers	14–7–73	17	3
TOWNSEND, ED			
For Your Love			
(US) Capitol	12–5–58	15	6
TOYS			
A Lover's Concerto			
(US) DynoVoice	9–10–65	2	8
(UK) Stateside	*20–11–65*	*5*	*9*
Attack			
(US) DynoVoice	22–1–66	18	2
TRAFFIC			
Paper Sun			
(UK) Island	*17–6–67*	*5*	*5*
Hole In My Shoe			
(UK) Island	*23–9–67*	*2*	*10*
Here We Go Round The Mulberry Bush			
(UK) Island	*9–12–67*	*8*	*7*
TRASHMEN			
Surfin' Bird			
(US) Garrett	4–1–64	4	7
TRAVIS AND BOB			
Tell Him No			
(US) Sandy	13–4–59	8	6
TREMELOES			
Here Comes My Baby			
(UK) CBS	*18–2–67*	*4*	*6*
(US) Epic	13–5–67	13	5
Silence Is Golden			
(UK) CBS	*6–5–67*	*1*	*10*
(US) Epic	29–7–67	11	5
Even The Good Times Are Bad			
(UK) CBS	*12–8–67*	*5*	*9*
Suddenly You Love Me			
(UK) CBS	*27–1–68*	*6*	*8*
Helule Helule			
(UK) CBS	*25–5–68*	*14*	*5*
My Little Lady			
(UK) CBS	*5–10–68*	*6*	*7*
Hello World			
(UK) CBS	*19–4–69*	*14*	*2*

	Date of chart entry	*Highest position reached*	*Number of weeks in charts*
TREMELOES (cont.)			
(Call Me) Number One			
(UK) CBS	*1–11–69*	*2*	*11*
Me And My Life			
(UK) CBS	*26–9–70*	*4*	*9*
TRENT, JACKIE			
Where Are You Now My Love			
(UK) Pye	*8–5–65*	*1*	*7*
T. REX			
Ride A White Swan			
(UK) Fly	*21–11–70*	*2*	*14*
Hot Love			
(UK) Fly	*6–3–71*	*1*	*12*
Bang A Gong (Get It On)			
(UK) Fly	*17–7–71*	*1*	*9*
(US) Reprise	19–2–72	10	6
Jeepster			
(UK) Fly	*20–11–71*	*2*	*10*
Telegram Sam			
(UK) T. Rex	*29–1–72*	*1*	*7*
Debora/One Inch Rock (re-issue)			
(UK) MagniFly	*15–4–72*	*7*	*6*
Metal Guru			
(UK) T. Rex	*13–5–72*	*1*	*8*
Children Of The Revolution			
(UK) T. Rex	*16–9–72*	*2*	*7*
Solid Gold Easy Action			
(UK) EMI-MARC	*9–12–72*	*2*	*8*
20th Century Boy			
(UK) EMI-MARC	*10–3–73*	*3*	*6*
Groover			
(UK) EMI-MARC	*16–6–73*	*4*	*5*
Truck On (Tyke)			
(UK) EMI-MARC	*1–12–73*	*12*	*6*
TROGGS			
Wild Thing			
(UK) Fontana	*14–5–66*	*2*	*7*
(US) Atco & Fontana	9–7–66	1	8
With A Girl Like You			
(UK) Fontana	*23–7–66*	*1*	*8*
I Can't Control Myself			
(UK) Page One	*8–10–66*	*2*	*9*
Anyway That You Want Me			
(UK) Page One	*31–12–66*	*8*	*6*
Give It To Me			
(UK) Page One	*11–3–67*	*12*	*4*
Night Of The Long Grass			
(UK) Page One	*17–6–67*	*17*	*2*

	Date of chart entry	Highest position reached	Number of weeks in charts
TROGGS (cont.)			
Love Is All Around			
(UK) Page One	*4–11–67*	*5*	*7*
(US) Fontana	4–5–68	7	5
TROY, DORIS			
Just One Look			
(US) Atlantic	13–7–63	10	6
TUCKER, TOMMY			
Hi-Heel Sneakers			
(US) Checker	14–3–64	11	4
TUNE WEAVERS			
Happy Happy Birthday Baby			
(US) Checker	30–9–57	5	9
TURNER, IKE AND TINA			
It's Gonna Work Out Fine			
(US) Sue	18–9–61	14	2
River Deep Mountain High			
(UK) London	*18–6–66*	*3*	*9*
A Love Like Yours			
(UK) London	*26–11–66*	*16*	*3*
Proud Mary			
(US) Liberty	6–3–71	4	7
Nutbush City Limits			
(UK) United Artists	*22–9–73*	*4*	*7*
TURNER, JESSIE LEE			
Little Space Girl			
(US) Carlton	9–2–59	20	1
TURNER, SAMMY			
Lavender Blue			
(US) Big Top	27–7–59	3	8
Always			
(UK) London	*14–11–59*	*20*	*1*
(US) Big Top	30–11–59	19	1
TURNER, SPYDER			
Stand By Me			
(US) MGM	28–1–67	12	5
TURTLES			
It Ain't Me Babe			
(US) White Whale	4–9–65	8	5
You Baby			
(US) White Whale	26–3–66	20	1
Happy Together			
(US) White Whale	11–3–67	1	10
(UK) London	*15–4–67*	*12*	*6*

	Date of chart entry	Highest position reached	Number of weeks in charts
TURTLES (cont.)			
She'd Rather Be With Me			
(US) White Whale	3–6–67	3	6
(UK) London	*24–6–67*	*4*	*10*
You Know What I Mean			
(US) White Whale	9–9–67	12	4
She's My Girl			
(US) White Whale	16–12–67	14	3
Eleanore			
(US) White Whale	19–10–68	6	7
(UK) London	*16–11–68*	*7*	*5*
You Showed Me			
(US) White Whale	1–2–69	6	7
TWINKLE			
Terry			
(UK) Decca	*19–12–64*	*4*	*9*
TWITTY, CONWAY			
It's Only Make Believe			
(US) MGM	6–10–58	1	14
(UK) MGM	*14–11–58*	*1*	*14*
Hey Little Lucy			
(UK) MGM	*16–5–69*	*20*	*1*
Mona Lisa			
(UK) MGM	*15–8–59*	*6*	*13*
Danny Boy			
(US) MGM	2–11–59	10	7
Lonely Blue Boy			
(US) MGM	1–2–60	6	6
TYMES			
So Much In Love			
(US) Parkway	29–6–63	1	9
Wonderful Wonderful			
(US) Parkway	14–9–63	7	5
Somewhere			
(US) Parkway	1–2–64	19	1
People			
(UK) Direction	*8–2–69*	*16*	*2*
You Little Trustmaker			
(US) RCA	28–9–74	12	4
(UK) RCA	*19–10–74*	*18*	*3*
UNDISPUTED TRUTH			
Smiling Faces Sometimes			
(US) Gordy	21–8–71	3	9
UNIT 4+2			
Concrete And Clay			
(UK) Decca	*20–3–65*	*3*	*9*
(You've) Never Been In Love Like This Before			
(UK) Decca	*5–6–65*	*14*	*4*

	Date of chart entry	*Highest position reached*	*Number of weeks in charts*
UPSETTERS			
Return Of Django			
(UK) Upsetter	*18–10–69*	*5*	*8*
VALANCE, RICKY			
Tell Laura I Love Her			
(UK) Columbia	*21–8–60*	*1*	*11*
VALE, JERRY			
You Don't Know Me			
(US) Columbia	18–8–56	14	10
VALENS, RICHIE			
Donna			
(US) Del-Fi	29–12–58	2	14
(UK) London	*28–3–59*	*20*	*2*
VALENTE, CATERINA			
The Breeze And I			
(US) Decca	16–4–55	3	11
(UK) Polydor	*19–8–55*	*5*	*14*
VALENTINE, DICKIE			
Finger Of Suspicion			
(UK) Decca	*7–1–55*	*1*	*12*
Mr. Sandman			
(UK) Decca	*7–1–55*	*5*	*9*
A Blossom Fell			
(UK) Decca	*18–2–55*	*9*	*10*
I Wonder			
(UK) Decca	*3–6–55*	*4*	*15*
Christmas Alphabet			
(UK) Decca	*25–11–55*	*1*	*7*
Old Pianna Rag			
(UK) Decca	*16–12–55*	*20*	*3*
Christmas Island			
(UK) Decca	*14–12–56*	*8*	*3*
One More Sunrise			
(UK) Pye	*24–10–59*	*14*	*4*
VALINO, JOE			
Garden Of Eden			
(US) Vik	24–11–56	12	9
VALLI, FRANKIE			
Can't Take My Eyes Off You			
(US) Philips	10–6–67	2	11
I Make A Fool Of Myself			
(US) Philips	30–9–67	18	2
You're Ready Now			
(UK) Philips (re-issue)	*16–1–71*	*11*	*6*

[see also: FOUR SEASONS]

	Date of chart entry	*Highest position reached*	*Number of weeks in charts*
VAN DYKE, LEROY			
Walk On By			
(US) Mercury	27–11–61	5	10
(UK) Mercury	*13–1–62*	*5*	*12*
VANILLA FUDGE			
(You Keep Me) Hangin' On			
(UK) Atlantic	*16–9–67*	*18*	*2*
(US) Atco	3–8–68	6	7
VANITY FARE			
I Live For The Sun			
(UK) Page One	*28–9–68*	*20*	*1*
Early In The Morning			
(UK) Page One	*9–8–69*	*10*	*6*
(US) Page One	3–1–70	12	6
Hitchin' A Ride			
(UK) Page One	*7–2–70*	*16*	*3*
(US) Page One	13–6–70	5	9
VAUGHAN, FRANKIE			
Happy Days And Lonely Nights			
(UK) HMV	*28–1–55*	*12*	*3*
Tweedle Dee			
(UK) Philips	*22–4–55*	*17*	*1*
Seventeen			
(UK) Philips	*2–12–55*	*18*	*3*
My Boy Flat Top			
(UK) Philips	*3–2–56*	*20*	*2*
Green Door			
(UK) Philips	*9–11–56*	*2*	*15*
Garden Of Eden			
(UK) Philips	*11–1–57*	*1*	*12*
Man On Fire/Wanderin' Eyes			
(UK) Philips	*4–10–57*	*6*	*11*
Gotta Have Somethin' In The Bank, Frank (with the KAYE SISTERS)			
(UK) Philips	*1–11–57*	*8*	*8*
Kisses Sweeter Than Wine			
(UK) Philips	*27–12–57*	*8*	*8*
Can't Get Along Without You/ We Are Not Alone			
(UK) Philips	*7–3–58*	*11*	*3*
Kewpie Doll			
(UK) Philips	*16–5–58*	*10*	*9*
Come Softly To Me			
(UK) Philips	*25–4–59*	*9*	*8*
Heart Of A Man			
(UK) Philips	*25–7–59*	*6*	*12*

	Date of chart entry	Highest position reached	Number of weeks in charts
VAUGHAN, FRANKIE (cont.)			
Tower Of Strength			
(UK) Philips	*11–11–61*	*1*	*12*
Don't Stop–Twist			
(UK) Philips	*10–2–62*	*14*	*5*
Loop De Loop			
(UK) Philips	*10–2–63*	*5*	*7*
Hello Dolly			
(UK) Philips	*27–6–64*	*18*	*3*
There Must Be A Way			
(UK) Philips	*16–9–67*	*7*	*14*
VAUGHAN, MALCOLM			
Every Day Of My Life			
(UK) HMV	*1–7–55*	*5*	*16*
With Your Love			
(UK) HMV	*27–1–56*	*18*	*3*
St. Theresa Of The Roses			
(UK) HMV	*16–11–56*	*3*	*18*
Chapel Of The Roses			
(UK) HMV	*10–5–57*	*13*	*7*
My Special Angel			
(UK) HMV	*29–11–57*	*3*	*14*
To Be Loved			
(UK) HMV	*4–4–58*	*14*	*8*
More Than Ever			
(UK) HMV	*17–10–58*	*5*	*13*
Wait For Me			
(UK) HMV	*28–2–59*	*15*	*6*
VAUGHAN, SARAH			
Make Yourself Comfortable			
(US) Mercury	1–1–55	8	9
How Important Can It Be			
(US) Mercury	5–3–55	18	1
Whatever Lola Wants			
(US) Mercury	23–4–55	12	11
Broken-Hearted Melody			
(US) Mercury	31–8–59	7	8
(UK) Mercury	*26–9–59*	*9*	*10*
Passing Strangers (with BILLY ECKSTINE)			
(UK) Mercury	*26–4–69*	*17*	*3*
VAUGHN, BILLY			
Melody Of Love			
(US) Dot	1–1–55	2	21
Shifting Whispering Sands			
(US) Dot	24–9–55	5	14
(UK) London	*27–1–56*	*20*	*1*

	Date of chart entry	*Highest position reached*	*Number of weeks in charts*
Theme From 'The Threepenny Opera'			
(UK) London	*23–3–56*	*12*	*5*
Sail Along, Silv'ry Moon			
(US) Dot	27–1–58	5	13
Look For A Star			
(US) Dot	1–8–60	19	1
Swingin' Star			
(US) Dot	1–9–62	13	2
VEE, BOBBY			
Devil Or Angel			
(US) Liberty	19–9–60	6	9
Rubber Ball			
(US) Liberty	19–12–60	6	9
(UK) London	*8–1–61*	*3*	*7*
More Than I Care To Say			
(UK) London	*23–4–61*	*3*	*9*
How Many Tears			
(UK) London	*12–8–61*	*13*	*5*
Take Good Care Of My Baby			
(US) Liberty	4–9–61	1	8
(UK) London	*28–10–61*	*1*	*11*
Run To Him			
(US) Liberty	27–11–61	2	11
(UK) London	*6–1–62*	*10*	*9*
Please Don't Ask About Barbara			
(US) Liberty	31–3–62	15	2
Sharing You			
(US) Liberty	16–6–62	15	4
(UK) Liberty	*16–6–62*	*10*	*8*
Punish Me			
(US) Liberty	13–10–62	20	1
Forever Kind Of Love			
(UK) Liberty	*15–12–62*	*13*	*5*
The Night Has A Thousand Eyes			
(US) Liberty	5–1–63	3	8
(UK) Liberty	*17–2–63*	*3*	*8*
Charms			
(US) Liberty	27–4–63	13	4
Come Back When You Grow Up (with the STRANGERS)			
(US) Liberty	26–8–67	3	9
VENTURES			
Walk, Don't Run			
(US) Dolton	1–8–60	2	12
(UK) London	*11–9–60*	*8*	*7*

	Date of chart entry	*Highest position reached*	*Number of weeks in charts*
VENTURES (cont.)			
Perfidia			
(US) Dolton	28–11–60	15	6
(UK) London	*4–12–60*	*5*	*7*
Walk, Don't Run '64			
(US) Dolton	8–8–64	8	5
Hawaii Five-O			
(US) Liberty	19–4–69	4	7
VERNE, LARRY			
Mr. Custer			
(US) Era	5–9–60	1	8
VERNON GIRLS			
Lover Please			
(UK) Decca	*16–6–62*	*16*	*2*
VIENNA PHILHARMONIC ORCHESTRA			
Theme From 'Onedin Line'			
(UK) Decca	*15–1–72*	*15*	*2*
VILLAGE STOMPERS			
Washington Square			
(US) Epic	19–10–63	2	9
VINCENT, GENE			
Be-Bop-a-Lula			
(US) Capitol	14–7–56	9	10
(UK) Capitol	*24–8–56*	*16*	*2*
Blue Jean Bop			
(UK) Capitol	*9–11–56*	*16*	*1*
Lotta Lovin'			
(US) Capitol	7–10–57	14	7
Pistol Packing Mama			
(UK) Capitol	*12–6–60*	*11*	*4*
VINTON, BOBBY			
Roses Are Red			
(US) Epic	23–6–62	1	12
(UK) Columbia	*18–8–62*	*15*	*2*
Rain Rain Go Away			
(US) Epic	22–9–62	12	4
Blue On Blue			
(US) Epic	8–6–63	3	8
Blue Velvet			
(US) Epic	31–8–63	1	10
There! I've Said It Again			
(US) Epic	14–12–63	1	10
My Heart Belongs To Only You			
(US) Epic	21–3–64	9	4

	Date of chart entry	*Highest position reached*	*Number of weeks in charts*
VINTON, BOBBY (cont.)			
Tell Me Why			
(US) Epic	6–6–64	13	4
Clinging Vine			
(US) Epic	5–9–64	17	3
Mr. Lonely			
(US) Epic	21–11–64	1	11
Long Lonely Nights			
(US) Epic	3–4–65	17	2
Coming Home Soldier			
(US) Epic	24–12–66	11	6
Please Love Me Forever			
(US) Epic	21–10–67	6	9
I Love How You Love Me			
(US) Epic	23–11–68	9	10
Sealed With A Kiss			
(US) Epic	19–8–72	19	2
VIPERS			
Don't You Rock Me Daddy-O			
(UK) Parlophone	*1–2–57*	*10*	*6*
Cumberland Gap			
(UK) Parlophone	*29–3–57*	*10*	*4*
VIRTUES			
Guitar Boogie Shuffle			
(US) Hunt	30–3–59	5	9
(UK) HMV	*16–5–59*	*19*	*3*
VISCOUNTS			
Shortnin' Bread			
(UK) Pye	*14–10–60*	*13*	*4*
Who Put The Bomp			
(UK) Nixa	*7–10–61*	*15*	*1*
VOGUES			
You're The One			
(US) Co and Co	16–10–65	4	6
Five O'Clock			
(US) Co and Co	25–12–65	4	9
Turn Around, Look At Me			
(US) Reprise	20–7–68	7	8
My Special Angel			
(US) Reprise	21–9–68	7	7
WADE, ADAM			
Take Good Care Of Her			
(US) Coed	3–4–61	7	8
Writing On The Wall			
(US) Coed	5–6–61	5	7
As If I Didn't Know			
(US) Coed	21–8–61	10	4

	Date of chart entry	*Highest position reached*	*Number of weeks in charts*
WADSWORTH MANSION			
Sweet Mary			
(US) Sussex	13–2–71	7	5
WAINWRIGHT III, LOUDON			
Dead Skunk			
(US) Columbia	17–3–73	16	4
WALKER, JUNIOR, AND THE ALL STARS			
Shotgun			
(US) Soul	13–3–65	4	8
(I'm A) Road Runner			
(US) Soul	11–6–66	20	2
(UK) Tamla Motown	*26–4–69*	*12*	*6*
How Sweet It Is			
(US) Soul	24–9–66	18	1
What Does It Take To Win Your Love			
(US) Soul	28–6–69	4	9
(UK) Tamla Motown	*5–11–69*	*13*	*5*
These Eyes			
(US) Soul	13–12–69	16	3
Walk In The Night			
(UK) Tamla Motown	*23–9–72*	*16*	*4*
Take Me Girl, I'm Ready			
(UK) Tamla Motown	*17–2–73*	*16*	*2*
WALKER, SCOTT			
Jackie			
(UK) Philips	*6–1–68*	*20*	*1*
Joanna			
(UK) Philips	*18–5–68*	*7*	*7*
Lights of Cincinatti			
(UK) Philips	*28–6–69*	*13*	*5*
[see also: WALKER BROTHERS]			
WALKER BROTHERS			
Love Her			
(UK) Philips	*19–6–65*	*20*	*1*
Make It Easy On Yourself			
(UK) Philips	*28–8–65*	*1*	*10*
(US) Smash	4–12–65	16	1
My Ship Is Coming In			
(UK) Philips	*11–12–65*	*3*	*10*
The Sun Ain't Gonna Shine Anymore			
(UK) Philips	*12–3–66*	*1*	*8*
(US) Smash	14–5–66	13	4

	Date of chart entry	Highest position reached	Number of weeks in charts
WALKER BROTHERS (cont.)			
(Baby) You Don't Have To Tell Me			
(UK) Philips	*30–7–66*	*13*	*2*
Another Tear Falls			
(UK) Philips	*8–10–66*	*12*	*3*
WALLACE, JERRY			
How Time Flies			
(US) Challenge	22–9–58	11	4
Primrose Lane			
(US) Challenge	21–9–59	8	11
In The Misty Moonlight			
(US) Challenge	12–9–64	19	2
WAR			
Slippin' Into Darkness			
(US) United Artists	6–5–72	16	4
World Is A Ghetto			
(US) United Artists	20–1–73	7	6
Cisco Kid			
(US) United Artists	7–4–73	2	7
Gypsy Man			
(US) United Artists	18–8–73	8	6
Me and Baby Brother			
(US) United Artists	5–1–74	15	5
WARD, BILLY			
Stardust			
(US) Liberty	29–7–57	13	11
(UK) Brunswick	*13–9–57*	*13*	*6*
WARD, CLIFFORD T.			
Gaye			
(UK) Charisma	*21–7–73*	*8*	*5*
WARD, MICHAEL			
Let There Be Peace On Earth			
(UK) Philips	*27–10–73*	*15*	*3*
WARD, ROBIN			
Wonderful Summer			
(US) Dot	23–11–63	14	5
WARWICK, DIONNE			
Anyone Who Had A Heart			
(US) Scepter	18–1–64	8	6
Walk On By			
(UK) Pye International	*2–5–64*	*9*	*9*
(US) Scepter	23–5–64	6	8
You'll Never Get To Heaven			
(UK) Pye International	*15–8–64*	*20*	*1*

	Date of chart entry	*Highest position reached*	*Number of weeks in charts*
WARWICK, DIONNE (cont.)			
Reach Out For Me			
(US) Scepter	28–11–64	20	1
Message To Michael			
(US) Scepter	30–4–66	8	6
Alfie			
(US) Scepter	24–6–67	15	4
I Say A Little Prayer			
(US) Scepter	18–11–67	4	8
Valley Of The Dolls			
(US) Scepter	10–2–68	2	9
Do You Know The Way to San José?			
(US) Scepter	11–5–68	10	4
(UK) Pye International	*25–5–68*	*8*	*8*
Promises Promises			
(US) Scepter	30–11–68	19	2
This Girl's In Love With You			
(US) Scepter	1–3–69	7	7
You've Lost That Lovin' Feeling			
(US) Scepter	25–10–69	16	3
I'll Never Fall In Love Again			
(US) Scepter	17–1–70	6	7
Then Came You (and THE SPINNERS)			
(US) Atlantic	24–8–74	1	11
WASHINGTON, DINAH			
What A Difference A Day Makes			
(US) Mercury	27–7–59	8	8
Unforgettable			
(US) Mercury	9–11–59	17	3
September In The Rain			
(UK) Mercury	*25–11–61*	*16*	*2*
[see also: BENTON, BROOK]			
WATTS 103rd STREET RHYTHM BAND (*featuring CHARLES WRIGHT)			
Do Your Thing			
(US) Warner Brothers	19–4–69	11	4
Love Land			
(US) Warner Brothers*	4–7–70	16	3
Express Yourself			
(US) Warner Brothers*	3–10–70	12	5
WAYNE, THOMAS			
Tragedy			
(US) Fernwood	9–3–59	5	8

	Date of chart entry	Highest position reached	Number of weeks in charts
WEATHERLY, JIM			
The Need To Be			
(US) Buddah	2–11–74	11	4
WEATHERMEN			
It's The Same Old Song			
(UK) B & C	*13–2–71*	*19*	*2*
WEBER, JOAN			
Let Me Go, Lover			
(US) Columbia	1–1–55	1	10
(UK) Philips	*18–2–55*	*16*	*1*
WEEDON, BERT			
Guitar Boogie Shuffle			
(UK) Top Rank	*9–5–59*	*6*	*8*
Sorry Robbie			
(UK) Rank	*13–11–60*	*18*	*1*
WE FIVE			
You Were On My Mind			
(US) A & M	21–8–65	3	9
WEIR, FRANK			
Caribbean Holiday			
(UK) Oriole	*28–8–60*	*18*	*4*
WEISSBERG, ERIC, AND DELIVERANCE			
Duelling Banjos			
(US) Warner Brothers	3–2–73	2	10
(UK) Warner Brothers	*21–4–73*	*17*	*2*
WELCH, LENNY			
Since I Fell For You			
(US) Cadence	23–11–63	4	10
WELK, LAWRENCE			
Calcutta			
(US) Dot	9–1–61	1	11
(UK) RCA	*5–2–61*	*19*	*1*
WELLS, MARY			
The One Who Really Loves You			
(US) Motown	12–5–62	8	7
You Beat Me To The Punch			
(US) Motown	15–9–62	9	5
Two Lovers			
(US) Motown	29–12–62	7	7

	Date of chart entry	Highest position reached	Number of weeks in charts
WELLS, MARY (cont.)			
Laughing Boy			
(US) Motown	30–3–63	15	2
My Guy			
(US) Motown	18–4–64	1	11
(UK) Stateside	*6–6–64*	*5*	*8*
(UK) Tamla Motown (re-issue)	*29–7–72*	*14*	*3*
[see also: GAYE, MARVIN]			
WEST, KEITH			
Excerpt From A Teenage Opera			
(UK) Parlophone	*26–8–66*	*2*	*11*
WESTON, KIM. See GAYE, MARVIN			
WET WILLIE			
Keep On Smilin'			
(US) Capricorn	27–7–74	10	5
WHITCOMB, IAN			
You Turn Me On			
(US) Tower	26–6–65	8	6
WHITE, BARRY			
I'm Gonna Love You Just A Little Bit More, Baby			
(US) 20th Century	19–5–73	3	9
Never Never Gonna Give Ya Up			
(US) 20th Century	1–12–73	7	11
(UK) Pye International	*23–2–74*	*14*	*4*
Can't Get Enough Of Your Love			
(US) 20th Century	24–8–74	1	6
(UK) Pye International	*7–9–74*	*8*	*6*
You Are My First My Last My Everything			
(UK) 20th Century	*9–11–74*	*1*	*8*
(US) 20th Century	30–11–74	2	9
WHITE, TONY JOE			
Polk Salad Annie			
(US) Monument (re-issue)	2–8–69	8	6
WHITE PLAINS			
My Baby Loves Lovin'			
(UK) Deram	*21–2–70*	*9*	*6*
(US) Deram	13–6–70	13	6

	Date of chart entry	Highest position reached	Number of weeks in charts
WHITE PLAINS (cont.)			
I've Got You On My Mind			
(UK) Deram	*16–5–70*	*17*	*4*
Julie Do Ya Love Me?			
(UK) Deram	*14–11–70*	*8*	*9*
When You Are A King			
(UK) Deram	*3–7–71*	*13*	*5*
WHITFIELD, DAVID			
Santo Natale			
(UK) Decca	*7–1–55*	*5*	*2*
Beyond The Stars			
(UK) Decca	*11–2–55*	*8*	*9*
Mama			
(UK) Decca	*27–5–55*	*12*	*11*
Everywhere			
(UK) Decca	*8–7–55*	*3*	*20*
When You Lose The One You Love			
(UK) Decca	*25–11–55*	*7*	*11*
My September Love			
(UK) Decca	*2–3–56*	*5*	*21*
Adoration Waltz			
(UK) Decca	*25–1–57*	*9*	*8*
On The Street Where You Live			
(UK) Decca	*20–6–58*	*16*	*8*
WHITMAN, SLIM			
Rosemarie			
(UK) London	*15–7–55*	*1*	*19*
Indian Love Call			
(UK) London	*29–7–55*	*8*	*12*
China Doll			
(UK) London	*23–9–55*	*15*	*2*
Tumbling Tumbleweeds			
(UK) London	*9–3–56*	*19*	*2*
I'm A Fool			
(UK) London	*13–4–56*	*16*	*3*
Serenade			
(UK) London	*3–8–56*	*8*	*8*
I'll Take You Home Again, Kathleen			
(UK) London	*19–4–57*	*5*	*11*
Happy Anniversary			
(UK) United Artists	*26–10–74*	*14*	*2*
WHITTAKER, ROGER			
Leavin' (Durham Town)			
(UK) Columbia	*6–12–69*	*12*	*9*
I Don't Believe In If Any More			
(UK) Columbia (re-issue)	*9–5–70*	*8*	*8*

	Date of chart entry	*Highest position reached*	*Number of weeks in charts*
WHO			
I Can't Explain			
(UK) Brunswick	*27–3–65*	*8*	*6*
Anyway, Anyhow, Anywhere			
(UK) Brunswick	*19–6–65*	*10*	*6*
My Generation			
(UK) Brunswick	*13–11–65*	*2*	*10*
Substitute			
(UK) Reaction	*19–3–66*	*5*	*9*
I'm A Boy			
(UK) Reaction	*10–9–66*	*2*	*10*
Happy Jack			
(UK) Reaction	*24–12–66*	*3*	*7*
Pictures Of Lily			
(UK) Track	*6–5–67*	*4*	*6*
I Can See For Miles			
(UK) Track	*11–11–67*	*10*	*4*
(US) Decca	11–11–67	9	5
Pinball Wizard			
(UK) Track	*5–4–69*	*4*	*8*
(US) Decca	17–5–69	19	3
The Seeker			
(UK) Track	*16–5–70*	*19*	*1*
See Me, Feel Me			
(US) Decca	28–11–70	12	2
Won't Get Fooled Again			
(UK) Track	*31–7–71*	*9*	*5*
(US) Decca	4–9–71	15	4
Let's See Action			
(UK) Track	*27–11–71*	*16*	*3*
Join Together			
(UK) Track	*8–7–72*	*9*	*7*
(US) Decca	2–9–72	17	2
5.15			
(UK) Track	*20–10–73*	*20*	*1*
WILDE, MARTY			
Endless Sleep			
(UK) Philips	*18–7–58*	*4*	*12*
Donna			
(UK) Philips	*21–3–59*	*4*	*13*
Teenager In Love			
(UK) Philips	*6–6–59*	*2*	*13*
Sea Of Love			
(UK) Philips	*26–9–59*	*4*	*12*
Bad Boy			
(UK) Philips	*5–12–59*	*6*	*8*
Little Girl			
(UK) Philips	*25–12–60*	*17*	*4*

	Date of chart entry	Highest position reached	Number of weeks in charts
WILDE, MARTY (cont.)			
Rubber Ball			
(UK) Philips	*15–1–61*	*10*	*4*
Jezebel			
(UK) Philips	*16–6–62*	*19*	*2*
WILLIAMS, ANDY			
Canadian Sunset			
(US) Cadence	1–9–56	8	12
Butterfly			
(US) Cadence	2–3–57	1	13
(UK) London	*26–4–57*	*1*	*12*
I Like Your Kind Of Love			
(US) Cadence	17–6–57	9	7
(UK) London	*12–7–57*	*16*	*2*
Are You Sincere?			
(US) Cadence	3–3–58	10	6
Promise Me Love			
(US) Cadence	6–10–58	17	2
Hawaiian Wedding Song			
(US) Cadence	2–2–59	11	10
Lonely Street			
(US) Cadence	28–9–59	5	10
Village Of St. Bernadette			
(US) Cadence	4–1–60	7	7
Can't Get Used To Losing You			
(US) Columbia	30–3–63	2	9
(UK) CBS	*20–4–63*	*2*	*11*
Hopeless			
(US) Columbia	20–7–63	13	4
A Fool Never Learns			
(US) Columbia	8–2–64	13	5
Almost There			
(UK) CBS	*23–9–65*	*2*	*10*
Can't Keep My Eyes Off You			
(UK) CBS	*6–4–68*	*5*	*9*
Happy Heart			
(UK) CBS	*28–6–69*	*19*	*1*
Can't Help Falling In Love			
(UK) CBS	*14–3–70*	*3*	*11*
It's So Easy			
(UK) CBS	*5–9–70*	*13*	*4*
Home Lovin' Man			
(UK) CBS	*28–11–70*	*7*	*9*
Love Story (Where Do I Begin?)			
(US) Columbia	20–3–71	9	6
(UK) CBS	*3–4–71*	*4*	*8*
Solitaire			
(UK) CBS	*19–1–74*	*4*	*8*

	Date of chart entry	*Highest position reached*	*Number of weeks in charts*
WILLIAMS, BILLY			
I'm Gonna Sit Right Down And Write Myself A Letter			
(US) Coral	8–7–57	6	12
WILLIAMS, DANNY			
Moon River			
(UK) HMV	*4–11–61*	*2*	*14*
Jeannie			
(UK) HMV	*10–2–62*	*14*	*4*
Wonderful World Of The Young			
(UK) HMV	*28–4–62*	*8*	*7*
White On White			
(US) United Artists	25–4–64	9	5
WILLIAMS, LARRY			
Short Fat Fanny			
(US) Specialty	15–7–57	6	12
Bony Moronie			
(US) Specialty	30–12–57	18	4
(UK) London	*24–1–58*	*11*	*7*
WILLIAMS, MASON			
Classical Gas			
(US) Warner Brothers	20–7–68	2	8
(UK) Warner Brothers	*21–9–68*	*9*	*8*
WILLIAMS, MAURICE AND THE ZODIACS			
Stay			
(US) Herald	31–10–60	1	8
(UK) Top Rank	*25–12–60*	*11*	*5*
WILLIAMS, OTIS, AND THE CHARMS			
Ivory Tower			
(US) Deluxe	28–4–56	12	8
[see also: CHARMS]			
WILLIAMS, ROGER			
Autumn Leaves			
(US) Kapp	27–8–55	1	24
Near You			
(US) Kapp	22–9–58	10	9
Born Free			
(US) Kapp	5–11–66	7	9
WILLIS, CHUCK			
C C Rider			
(US) Atlantic	1–7–57	12	6
What Am I Living For			
(US) Atlantic	7–4–58	15	2

	Date of chart entry	*Highest position reached*	*Number of weeks in charts*
WILSON, AL			
Show And Tell			
(US) Rocky Road	15–12–73	1	11
WILSON, JACKIE			
Reet Petite			
(UK) Coral	*29–11–57*	*6*	*11*
Lonely Teardrops			
(US) Brunswick	26–12–58	7	12
That's Why			
(US) Brunswick	27–4–59	13	4
I'll Be Satisfied			
(US) Brunswick	3–8–59	20	1
Night			
(US) Brunswick (b/w*)	18–4–60	4	10
Doggin' Around*			
(US) Brunswick	9–5–60	15	1
(You Were Made) For All My Love			
(US) Brunswick (b/w**)	15–8–60	12	4
A Woman, A Lover, A Friend**			
(US) Brunswick	15–8–60	15	2
My Empty Arms			
(US) Brunswick	23–1–61	9	4
Please Tell Me Why			
(US) Brunswick	17–4–61	20	1
I'm Comin' On Back To You			
(US) Brunswick	10–7–61	19	1
Baby Work Out			
(US) Brunswick	30–3–63	5	7
Whispers			
(US) Brunswick	5–11–66	11	6
(Your Love Keeps Lifting Me) Higher And Higher			
(US) Brunswick	9–9–67	6	7
(UK) MCA (re-issue)	*31–5–69*	*11*	*6*
I Get The Sweetest Feeling			
(UK) MCA (re-issue)	*26–8–72*	*9*	*6*
WILSON, J. FRANK			
Last Kiss			
(US) Josie	3–10–64	2	10
WILSON, NANCY			
(You Don't Know) How Glad I Am			
(US) Capitol	1–8–64	11	4
WINDING, KAI			
More			
(US) Verve	3–8–63	8	6

	Date of chart entry	*Highest position reached*	*Number of weeks in charts*
WINGS			
Give Ireland Back To The Irish			
(UK) Apple	*11–3–72*	*16*	*3*
Mary Had A Little Lamb			
(UK) Apple	*3–6–72*	*9*	*7*
Hi Hi Hi			
(UK) Apple (b/w C Moon)	*6–1–73*	*5*	*6*
(US) Apple	13–1–73	10	5
[see also: PAUL MCCARTNEY'S WINGS]			
WINSTONS			
Color Him Father			
(US) Metromedia	28–6–69	7	7
WINTER, EDGAR, GROUP			
Frankenstein			
(US) Epic	28–4–73	1	10
(UK) Epic	*23–6–73*	*18*	*1*
Free Ride			
(US) Epic	29–9–73	14	4
WISDOM, NORMAN			
Wisdom Of A Fool			
(UK) Columbia	*15–3–57*	*13*	*4*
WITHERS, BILL			
Ain't No Sunshine			
(US) Sussex	28–8–71	3	9
Lean On Me			
(US) Sussex	10–6–72	1	10
(UK) A & M	*9–9–72*	*18*	*2*
Use Me			
(US) Sussex	23–9–72	2	7
WIZZARD			
Ball Park Incident			
(UK) Harvest	*6–1–73*	*6*	*6*
See My Baby Jive			
(UK) Harvest	*28–4–73*	*1*	*10*
Angel Fingers			
(UK) Harvest	*1–9–73*	*1*	*8*
I Wish It Could Be Christmas Everyday			
(UK) Harvest	*8–12–73*	*4*	*6*
Rock And Roll Winter			
(UK) Warner Brothers	*4–5–74*	*6*	*4*
WOMACK, BOBBY			
Looking For A Love			
(US) United Artists	30–3–74	10	6

	Date of chart entry	Highest position reached	Number of weeks in charts
WOMBLES			
Wombling Song			
(UK) CBS	*9–2–74*	*4*	*7*
Remember You're A Womble			
(UK) CBS	*13–4–74*	*3*	*9*
Banana Rock			
(UK) CBS	*6–7–74*	*9*	*5*
Minuetto Allegretto			
(UK) CBS	*2–11–74*	*16*	*3*
Wombling Merry Christmas			
(UK) CBS	*21–12–74*	*6*	*3*
WONDER, STEVIE (*LITTLE)			
Fingertips Pt. 2			
(US) Tamla*	6–7–63	1	10
Uptight (Everything's Alright)			
(US) Tamla	5–2–66	3	6
(UK) Motown	*26–2–66*	*14*	*3*
Nothing's Too Good For My Baby			
(US) Tamla	14–5–66	20	1
Blowin' In The Wind			
(US) Tamla	13–8–66	9	5
A Place In The Sun			
(US) Tamla	10–12–66	9	5
(UK) Motown	*21–1–67*	*20*	*1*
I Was Made To Love Her			
(US) Tamla	8–7–67	2	9
(UK) Motown	*5–8–67*	*5*	*9*
I'm Wondering			
(US) Tamla	28–10–67	12	3
Shoo-Be-Doo-Be-Doo-Da-Day			
(US) Tamla	4–5–68	9	6
For Once In My Life			
(US) Tamla	16–11–68	2	11
(UK) Motown	*4–1–69*	*3*	*11*
I Don't Know Why**			
(UK) Motown	*19–4–69*	*14*	*4*
My Cherie Amour			
(US) Tamla (b/w**)	5–7–69	4	8
(UK) Motown	*2–8–69*	*4*	*9*
Yester-Me, Yester-You, Yesterday			
(US) Tamla	22–11–69	7	6
(UK) Motown	*22–11–69*	*2*	*9*
Never Had A Dream Come True			
(UK) Tamla Motown	*11–4–70*	*6*	*7*

	Date of chart entry	Highest position reached	Number of weeks in charts
WONDER, STEVIE (cont.)			
Signed Sealed Delivered (I'm Yours)			
(US) Tamla	18–7–70	3	10
(UK) Tamla Motown	*1–8–70*	*15*	*5*
Heaven Help Us All			
(US) Tamla	14–11–70	9	6
We Can Work It Out			
(US) Tamla	24–4–71	13	3
If You Really Love Me			
(US) Tamla	18–9–71	8	8
(UK) Tamla Motown	*19–2–72*	*20*	*2*
Superstition			
(US) Tamla	23–12–72	1	10
(UK) Tamla Motown	*10–2–73*	*11*	*5*
You Are The Sunshine Of My Life			
(US) Tamla	14–4–73	1	10
(UK) Tamla Motown	*26–5–73*	*7*	*5*
Higher Ground			
(US) Tamla	8–9–73	4	9
Living In The City			
(US) Tamla	15–12–73	8	9
(UK) Tamla Motown	*2–2–74*	*15*	*4*
He's Misstra Know It All			
(UK) Tamla Motown	*27–4–74*	*10*	*5*
Don't You Worry 'Bout A Thing			
(US) Tamla	18–5–74	16	3
You Haven't Done Nothin'			
(US) Tamla	31–8–74	1	11
Boogie On Reggae Woman			
(US) Tamla	21–12–74	3	9
WONDER WHO			
Don't Think Twice			
(US) Philips	11–12–65	12	4
WOOD, BRENTON			
Gimme Little Sign			
(US) Double Shot	23–9–67	9	7
(UK) Liberty	*3–2–68*	*8*	*7*
WOOD, ROY			
Dear Elaine			
(UK) Harvest	*8–9–73*	*18*	*1*
Forever			
(UK) Harvest	*22–12–73*	*8*	*8*
Going Down The Road			
(UK) Harvest	*29–6–74*	*13*	*3*

[see also: ELECTRIC LIGHT ORCHESTRA; MOVE; WIZZARD]

	Date of chart entry	Highest position reached	Number of weeks in charts
WOOLEY, SHEB			
Purple People Eater			
(US) MGM	2–6–58	1	9
(UK) MGM	*26–6–58*	*12*	*6*
WRAY, LINK			
Rumble			
(US) Cadence	19–5–58	16	5
WRIGHT, BETTY			
Clean Up Woman			
(US) Alston	1–1–72	6	8
WRIGHT, CHARLES. See WATTS 103rd STREET RHYTHM BAND			
WRIGHT, PERCY			
Man In The Raincoat			
(US) Unique	9–7–55	18	4
WRIGHT, RUBY			
Three Stars			
(UK) Parlophone	*23–5–59*	*8*	*6*
WYNETTE, TAMMY			
Stand By Your Man			
(US) Epic	1–2–69	19	1
WYNTER, MARK			
Image Of A Girl			
(UK) Decca	*21–8–60*	*11*	*7*
Kicking Up The Leaves			
(UK) Decca	*27–11–60*	*19*	*1*
Dream Girl			
(UK) Decca	*19–2–61*	*18*	*2*
Venus In Blue Jeans			
(UK) Pye	*20–10–62*	*4*	*9*
Go Away Little Girl			
(UK) Pye	*6–1–63*	*6*	*6*
It's Almost Tomorrow			
(UK) Pye	*30–11–63*	*4*	*12*
YARBROUGH, GLENN			
Baby The Rain Must Fall			
(US) RCA	8–5–65	12	5
YARDBIRDS			
For Your Love			
(UK) Columbia	*27–3–65*	*2*	*7*
(US) Epic	12–6–65	6	7

	Date of chart entry	*Highest position reached*	*Number of weeks in charts*
YARDBIRDS (cont.)			
Heart Full Of Soul			
(UK) Columbia	*26–6–65*	*2*	*9*
(US) Epic	4–9–65	9	5
Evil Hearted You/Still I'm Sad			
(UK) Columbia	*21–10–65*	*3*	*6*
I'm A Man			
(US) Epic	11–12–65	17	1
Shapes Of Things			
(UK) Columbia	*12–3–66*	*3*	*7*
(US) Epic	23–4–66	11	4
Over Under Sideways Down			
(UK) Columbia	*11–6–66*	*10*	*5*
(US) Epic	30–7–66	13	4
YES			
Roundabout			
(US) Atlantic	25–3–72	13	5
YOUNG, BARRY			
One Has My Name			
(US) Dot	18–12–65	13	3
YOUNG, FARON			
Hello Walls			
(US) Capitol	22–5–61	12	5
Four In The Morning			
(UK) Mercury	*12–8–72*	*3*	*10*
YOUNG, JIMMY			
Unchained Melody			
(UK) Decca	*6–5–55*	*1*	*18*
Man From Laramie			
(UK) Decca	*16–9–55*	*1*	*12*
Someone On Your Mind			
(UK) Decca	*23–12–55*	*13*	*5*
Chain Gang			
(UK) Decca	*16–3–56*	*9*	*5*
More			
(UK) Decca	*12–10–56*	*4*	*14*
Miss You			
(UK) Columbia	*2–11–63*	*15*	*4*
YOUNG, KAREN			
Nobody's Child			
(UK) Major Minor	*27–9–69*	*6*	*13*
YOUNG, KATHY AND THE INNOCENTS			
A Thousand Stars			
(US) Indigo	14–11–60	3	12

	Date of chart entry	Highest position reached	Number of weeks in charts
YOUNG, NEIL			
Heart Of Gold			
(US) Reprise	26–2–72	1	10
(UK) Reprise	*1–4–72*	*10*	*5*
[See also: BUFFALO SPRINGFIELD; CROSBY STILLS NASH & YOUNG]			
YOUNGBLOODS			
Get Together			
(US) RCA (re-issue)	16–8–69	5	9
YOUNG-HOLT LIMITED			
Soulful Street			
(US) Brunswick	21–12–68	3	9
YOUNG IDEA			
With A Little Help From My Friends			
(UK) Columbia	*15–7–61*	*10*	*1*
YOUNG RASCALS (*RASCALS)			
Good Lovin'			
(US) Atlantic	9–4–66	1	9
You Better Run			
(US) Atlantic	16–7–66	20	2
I've Been Lonely Too Long			
(US) Atlantic	18–3–67	16	3
Groovin'			
(US) Atlantic	6–5–67	1	10
(UK) Atlantic	*17–6–67*	*8*	*9*
Girl Like You			
(US) Atlantic	29–7–67	10	6
How Can I Be Sure			
(US) Atlantic	30–9–67	4	7
It's Wonderful			
(US) Atlantic	13–1–68	20	1
Beautiful Morning			
(US) Atlantic*	27–4–68	3	9
People Got To Be Free			
(US) Atlantic*	3–8–68	1	11
YURO, TIMI			
Hurt			
(US) Liberty	7–8–61	4	7
What's A Matter Baby			
(US) Liberty	25–8–62	12	3
ZACHARIAS, HELMUT			
When The White Lilacs Bloom Again			
(US) Decca	22–9–56	16	4
Tokyo Melody			
(UK) Polydor	*14–11–64*	*9*	*5*

	Date of chart entry	*Highest position reached*	*Number of weeks in charts*
ZACHARLE, JOHN			
Dinner With Drac			
(US) Cameo	24–3–58	6	3
ZAGER AND EVANS			
In The Year 2525			
(US) RCA	5–7–69	1	10
(UK) RCA	*16–8–69*	*1*	*9*
ZAVARONI, LENA			
Ma, He's Makin' Eyes At Me			
(UK) Phillips	*11–2–74*	*10*	*6*
ZOMBIES			
She's Not There			
(UK) Decca	*4–9–64*	*12*	*6*
(US) Parrot	14–11–64	2	9
Tell Her No			
(US) Parrot	6–2–65	6	6
Time Of The Season			
(US) Date	8–3–69	3	8

AMERICAN CHART-TOPPERS, 1955–74

				Weeks at No. 1
1955				
Jan 1	Chordettes	Mr. Sandman	Cadence	3
Jan 22	Joan Weber	Let Me Go, Lover	Columbia	2
Feb 5	Fontane Sisters	Hearts Of Stone	Dot	1
Feb 12	McGuire Sisters	Sincerely	Coral	6
Mar 26	Bill Hayes	Ballad Of Davy Crockett	Cadence	5
May 30	Perèz Prado	Cherry Pink And Apple Blossom White	Victor	10
July 9	Bill Haley and His Comets	Rock Around The Clock	Decca	8
Sept 3	Mitch Miller	Yellow Rose Of Texas	Columbia	5
Oct 8	Four Aces	Love Is A Many Splendored Thing	Decca	1
Oct 15	Mitch Miller	Yellow Rose Of Texas	Columbia	1
Oct 22	Four Aces	Love Is A Many Splendored Thing	Decca	1
Oct 29	Roger Williams	Autumn Leaves	Kapp	2
Nov 12	Four Aces	Love Is A Many Splendored Thing	Decca	3
Dec 3	Tennessee Ernie Ford	16 Tons	Capitol	6
1956				
Jan 14	Dean Martin	Memories Are Made Of This	Capitol	5
Feb 18	Platters	Great Pretender	Mercury	2
Mar 3	Kay Starr	Rock And Roll Waltz	Victor	3
Mar 24	Les Baxter	Poor People Of Paris	Capitol	6
May 3	Elvis Presley	Heartbreak Hotel	Victor	7
June 16	Gogi Grant	Wayward Wind	Era	7
Aug 4	Pat Boone	I Almost Lost My Mind	Dot	2
Aug 18	Platters	My Prayer	Mercury	5
Sept 15	Elvis Presley	Don't Be Cruel	Victor	7
Nov 3	Jim Lowe	Green Door	Dot	3
Nov 17	Elvis Presley	Love Me Tender	Victor	3
Dec 8	Guy Mitchell	Singing The Blues	Columbia	2
Dec 22	Elvis Presley	Love Me Tender	Victor	1
Dec 29	Guy Mitchell	Singing the Blues	Columbia	7
1957				
Feb 9	Pat Boone	Don't Forbid Me	Dot	1
Feb 16	Tab Hunter	Young Love	Dot	6
Mar 30	Andy Williams	Butterfly	Cadence	3

				Weeks at No. 1
1957—(cont.)				
Apr 20	Elvis Presley	All Shook Up	Victor	8
June 10	Pat Boone	Love Letters In The Sand	Dot	5
July 15	Elvis Presley	Teddy Bear	Victor	7
Sept 2	Debbie Reynolds	Tammy	Coral	5
Oct 7	Jimmie Rodgers	Honeycomb	Roulette	2
Oct 21	Everly Brothers	Wake Up Little Susie	Cadence	2
Nov 4	Elvis Presley	Jailhouse Rock	Victor	6
Dec 9	Sam Cooke	You Send Me	Keen	3
Dec 30	Pat Boone	April Love	Dot	1
1958				
Jan 6	Danny and the Juniors	At The Hop	ABC-Paramount	7
Feb 24	Silhouettes	Get A Job	Ember	2
Mar 10	Elvis Presley	Don't	Victor	1
Mar 17	Champs	Tequila	Challenge	5
Apr 21	Platters	Twilight Time	Mercury	1
Apr 28	David Seville	Witch Doctor	Liberty	3
May 19	Everly Brothers	All I Have To Do Is Dream	Cadence	3
June 9	Sheb Wooley	Purple People Eater	MGM	6
July 21	Coasters	Yakety Yak	Atco	1
July 28	Perèz Prado	Patricia	Victor	1
Aug 4	Ricky Nelson	Poor Little Fool	Imperial	2
Aug 18	Domenico Modugno	Volare	Decca	1
Aug 25	Elegants	Little Star	Apt	1
Sept 1	Domenico Modugno	Volare	Decca	4
Sept 29	Tommy Edwards	It's All In The Game	MGM	6
Nov 10	Conway Twitty	It's Only Make Believe	MGM	1
Nov 17	Kingston Trio	Tom Dooley	Capitol	1
Nov 24	Conway Twitty	It's Only Make Believe	MGM	1
Dec 1	Teddy Bears	To Know Him Is To Love Him	Dore	3
Dec 22	David Seville and the Chipmunks	Chipmunk Song	Liberty	4
1959				
Jan 19	Platters	Smoke Gets In Your Eyes	Mercury	3
Feb 9	Lloyd Price	Stagger Lee	ABC-Paramount	4
Mar 9	Frankie Avalon	Venus	Chancellor	5

				Weeks at No. 1
Apr 13	Fleetwoods	Come Softly To Me	Dolphin	4
May 11	Dave (Baby) Cortez	Happy Organ	Clock	1
May 18	Wilbert Harrison	Kansas City	Fury	2
June 1	Johnny Horton	Battle Of New Orleans	Columbia	6
July 13	Paul Anka	Lonely Boy	ABC-Paramount	4
Aug 10	Elvis Presley	Big Hunk O'Love	RCA	2
Aug 24	Browns	Three Bells	RCA	4
Sept 21	Santo and Johnny	Sleep Walk	Canadian-American	2
Oct 5	Bobby Darin	Mack The Knife	Atco	6
Nov 16	Fleetwoods	Mr. Blue	Dolton	1
Nov 23	Bobby Darin	Mack The Knife	Atco	3
Dec 14	Guy Mitchell	Heartaches By The Number	Columbia	2
Dec 28	Frankie Avalon	Why	Chancellor	1
1960				
Jan 4	Marty Robbins	El Paso	Columbia	2
Jan 18	Johnny Preston	Running Bear	Mercury	3
Feb 8	Mark Dinning	Teen Angel	MGM	2
Feb 22	Percy Faith	Theme From 'Summer Place'	Columbia	9
Apr 25	Elvis Presley	Stuck On You	RCA	4
May 23	Everly Brothers	Cathy's Clown	Warner Brothers	5
June 27	Connie Francis	Everybody's Somebody's Fool	MGM	2
July 11	Hollywood Argyles	Alley-Oop	Lute	1
July 18	Brenda Lee	I'm Sorry	Decca	3
Aug 8	Brian Hyland	Itsy Bitsy Teenie Weenie Yellow Polka Dot Bikini	Leader	1
Aug 15	Elvis Presley	It's Now Or Never	RCA	5
Sept 19	Chubby Checker	The Twist	Parkway	1
Sept 26	Connie Francis	My Heart Has A Mind Of Its Own	MGM	2
Oct 10	Larry Verne	Mr. Custer	Era	1
Oct 17	Drifters	Save The Last Dance For Me	Atlantic	1
Oct 24	Brenda Lee	I Want To Be Wanted	Decca	1
Oct 31	Drifters	Save The Last Dance For Me	Atlantic	2
Nov 14	Ray Charles	Georgia On My Mind	ABC-Paramount	1

				Weeks at No. 1
1960—(cont.)				
Nov 21	Maurice Williams and the Zodiacs	Stay	Herald	1
Nov 28	Elvis Presley	Are You Lonesome Tonight?	RCA	6
1961				
Jan 9	Bert Kaempfert	Wonderland By Night	Decca	3
Jan 30	Shirelles	Will You Love Me Tomorrow?	Scepter	2
Feb 13	Lawrence Welk	Calcutta	Dot	2
Feb 27	Chubby Checker	Pony Time	Parkway	3
Mar 20	Elvis Presley	Surrender	RCA	2
Apr 3	Marcels	Blue Moon	Colpix	3
Apr 24	Del Shannon	Runaway	Big Top	4
May 22	Ernie K. Doe	Mother-in-Law	Minit	1
May 29	Ricky Nelson	Travellin' Man	Imperial	1
June 5	Roy Orbison	Runnin' Scared	Monument	1
June 12	Ricky Nelson	Travellin' Man	Imperial	1
June 19	Pat Boone	Moody River	Dot	1
June 26	Gary 'U.S.' Bonds	Quarter To Three	Le Grand	2
July 10	Bobby Lewis	Tossin' And Turnin'	Belone	7
Aug 28	Joe Dowell	Wooden Heart	Smash	1
Sept 4	Highwaymen	Michael	United Artists	2
Sept 18	Bobby Vee	Take Good Care Of My Baby	Liberty	3
Oct 9	Ray Charles	Hit The Road, Jack	ABC-Paramount	2
Oct 23	Dion	Runaround Sue	Laurie	2
Nov 6	Jimmy Dean	Big Bad John	Columbia	5
Dec 11	Marvelettes	Please Mr Postman	Tamla	1
Dec 18	Tokens	The Lion Sleeps Tonight	RCA	3
1962				
Jan 13	Chubby Checker	The Twist	Parkway	2
Jan 27	Joey Dee and the Starliters	Peppermint Twist	Roulette	3
Feb 17	Gene Chandler	Duke Of Earl	Vee Jay	3
Mar 10	Bruce Channel	Hey! Baby	Smash	3
Mar 31	Connie Francis	Don't Break The Heart That Loves You	MGM	1
Apr 7	Shelley Fabares	Johnny Angel	Colpix	2
Apr 21	Elvis Presley	Good Luck Charm	RCA	2

			Weeks at No. 1
1962—(cont.)			
May 5 Shirelles	Soldier Boy	Scepter	3
May 26 Acker Bilk	Stranger On The Shore	Atco	1
June 2 Ray Charles	I Can't Stop Loving You	ABC-Paramount	5
July 7 David Rose and Orchestra	The Stripper	MGM	1
July 14 Bobby Vinton	Roses Are Red	Epic	4
Aug 11 Neil Sedaka	Breaking Up Is Hard To Do	RCA	2
Aug 25 Little Eva	The Locomotion	Dimension	1
Sept 1 Tommy Roe	Sheila	ABC-Paramount	2
Sept 15 Four Seasons	Sherry	Vee Jay	5
Oct 20 Bobby 'Boris' Pickett and the Crypt Kickers	The Monster Mash	Garpax	2
Nov 3 Crystals	He's A Rebel	Philles	2
Nov 17 Four Seasons	Big Girls Don't Cry	Vee Jay	5
Dec 22 Tornadoes	Telstar	London	3
1963			
Jan 12 Steve Lawrence	Go Away Little Girl	Columbia	2
Jan 26 Rooftop Singers	Walk Right In	Vanguard	2
Feb 9 Paul and Paula	Hey Paula	Philips	3
Mar 2 4 Seasons	Walk Like A Man	Vee Jay	3
Mar 23 Ruby and the Romantics	Our Day Will Come	Kapp	1
Mar 30 Chiffons	He's So Fine	Laurie	4
Apr 27 Little Peggy March	I Will Follow Him	RCA	3
May 18 Jimmy Soul	If You Wanna Be Happy	S.P.Q.R.	2
June 1 Lesley Gore	It's My Party	Mercury	2
June 15 Kyu Sakamoto	Sukiyaki	Capitol	3
July 6 David Essex	Easier Said Than Done	Roulette	2
July 20 Jan and Dean	Surf City	Liberty	2
Aug 3 Tymes	So Much In Love	Parkway	1
Aug 10 Stevie Wonder	Fingertips, Pt. 2	Tamla	3
Aug 31 Angels	My Boyfriend's Back	Smash	3
Sept 21 Bobby Vinton	Blue Velvet	Epic	3
Oct 12 Jimmy Gilmer and the Fireballs	Sugar Shack	Dot	5
Nov 16 Nino Tempo and April Stevens	Deep Purple	Atco	1

Date	Artist	Title	Label	*Weeks at No. 1*
1963—(cont.)				
Nov 23	Dale and Gracie	I'm Leavin' It Up To You	Montel-Michele	2
Dec 7	Singing Nun	Dominique	Philips	4
1964				
Jan 4	Bobby Vinton	There I've Said It Again	Epic	4
Feb 1	Beatles	I Want To Hold Your Hand	Capitol	7
Mar 21	Beatles	She Loves You	Swan	2
Apr 4	Beatles	Can't Buy Me Love	Capitol	5
May 9	Louis Armstrong	Hello Dolly	Kapp	1
May 16	Mary Wells	My Guy	Motown	2
May 30	Beatles	Love Me Do	Tollie	1
June 6	Dixie Cups	Chapel Of Love	Red Bird	3
June 27	Peter and Gordon	World Without Love	Capitol	1
July 4	Beach Boys	I Get Around	Capitol	2
July 18	Four Seasons	Rag Doll	Philips	2
Aug 1	Beatles	Hard Day's Night	Capitol	2
Aug 15	Dean Martin	Everybody Loves Somebody	Reprise	1
Aug 22	Supremes	Where Did Our Love Go?	Motown	2
Sept 5	Animals	House Of The Rising Sun	MGM	3
Sept 26	Roy Orbison	Oh Pretty Woman	Monument	3
Oct 17	Manfred Mann	Do Wah Diddy Diddy	Ascot	2
Oct 31	Supremes	Baby Love	Motown	4
Nov 28	Shangri-Las	Leader Of The Pack	Red Bird	1
Dec 5	Lorne Greene	Ringo	RCA	1
Dec 12	Bobby Vinton	Mr. Lonely	Epic	1
Dec 19	Supremes	Come See About Me	Motown	1
Dec 26	Beatles	I Feel Fine	Capitol	3
1965				
Jan 16	Supremes	Come See About Me	Motown	1
Jan 23	Petula Clark	Downtown	Warner Brothers	2
Feb 6	Righteous Brothers	You've Lost That Lovin' Feeling	Philles	2
Feb 20	Gary Lewis and the Playboys	This Diamond Ting	Liberty	2
Mar 6	Temptations	My Girl	Gordy	1
Mar 13	Beatles	8 Days A Week	Capitol	2

				Weeks at No. 1
1965—(cont.)				
Mar 27	Supremes	Stop! In The Name Of Love	Motown	2
Apr 10	Freddie and the Dreamers	I'm Telling You Now	Tower	2
Apr 24	Wayne Fontana and the Mindbenders	Game Of Love	Fontana	1
May 1	Herman's Hermits	Mrs. Brown You've Got A Lovely Daughter	MGM	3
May 22	Beatles	Ticket To Ride	Capitol	1
May 29	Beach Boys	Help Me Rhonda	Capitol	2
June 12	Supremes	Back In My Arms Again	Motown	1
June 19	Four Tops	I Can't Help Myself	Motown	1
June 26	Byrds	Mr. Tambourine Man	Columbia	1
July 3	Four Tops	I Can't Help Myself	Motown	1
July 10	Rolling Stones	Satisfaction	London	4
Aug 7	Herman's Hermits	I'm Henry VIII I Am	MGM	1
Aug 14	Sonny and Cher	I Got You Babe	Atco	3
Sept 4	Beatles	Help	Capitol	3
Sept 25	Barry McGuire	Eve Of Destruction	Dunhill	1
Oct 2	McCoys	Hang On Sloopy	Bang	1
Oct 9	Beatles	Yesterday	Capitol	4
Nov 6	Rolling Stones	Get Off Of My Cloud	London	2
Nov 20	Supremes	I Hear A Symphony	Motown	2
Dec 4	Byrds	Turn Turn Turn	Columbia	3
Dec 25	Dave Clark Five	Over And Over	Epic	1
1966				
Jan 1	Simon and Garfunkel	Sounds Of Silence	Columbia	1
Jan 8	Beatles	We Can Work It Out	Capitol	2
Jan 22	Simon and Garfunkel	Sounds Of Silence	Columbia	1
Jan 29	Beatles	We Can Work It Out	Capitol	1
Feb 5	Petula Clark	My Love	Warner Brothers	2
Feb 19	Lou Christie	Lightning Strikes	MGM	1
Feb 26	Nancy Sinatra	These Boots Are Made For Walking	Reprise	1

			Weeks at No. 1
1966—(cont.)			
Mar 5 Barry Sadler	Ballad Of The Green Berets	RCA	5
Apr 9 Righteous Brothers	You're My Soul And Inspiration	Verve	3
Apr 30 Young Rascals	Good Lovin'	Atlantic	1
May 7 Mamas and Papas	Monday Monday	Dunhill	3
May 28 Percy Sledge	When A Man Loves A Woman	Atlantic	2
June 11 Rolling Stones	Paint It Black	London	2
June 25 Beatles	Paperback Writer	Capitol	1
July 2 Frank Sinatra	Strangers In The Night	Reprise	1
July 9 Beatles	Paperback Writer	Capitol	1
July 16 Tommy James and the Shondells	Hanky Panky	Roulette	2
July 30 Troggs	Wild Thing	Atco & Fontana	2
Aug 13 Lovin' Spoonful	Summer In The City	Kama Sutra	3
Sept 3 Donovan	Sunshine Superman	Epic	1
Sept 10 Supremes	You Can't Hurry Love	Motown	2
Sept 24 Association	Cherish	Valiant	3
Oct 15 Four Tops	Reach Out I'll Be There	Motown	2
Oct 29 ? and the Mysterians	96 Tears	Cameo	1
Nov 5 Monkees	Last Train To Clarksville	Colgems	1
Nov 12 Johnny Rivers	Poor Side Of Town	Imperial	1
Nov 19 Supremes	You Keep Me Hanging On	Motown	2
Dec 3 New Vaudeville Band	Winchester Cathedral	Fontana	1
Dec 10 Beach Boys	Good Vibrations	Capitol	1
Dec 17 New Vaudeville Band	Winchester Cathedral	Fontana	2
Dec 31 Monkees	I'm A Believer	Colgems	7
1967			
Feb 18 Buckinghams	Kind Of A Drag	USA	2
Mar 4 Rolling Stones	Ruby Tuesday	London	1
Mar 11 Supremes	Love Is Here And Now You're Gone	Motown	1
Mar 18 Beatles	Penny Lane	Capitol	1

			Weeks at No. 1
1967—(cont.)			
Mar 25 Turtles	Happy Together	White Whale	3
Apr 15 Frank and Nancy Sinatra	Somethin' Stupid	Reprise	4
May 13 Supremes	The Happening	Motown	1
May 20 Young Rascals	Groovin'	Atlantic	2
June 3 Aretha Franklin	Respect	Atlantic	2
June 17 Young Rascals	Groovin'	Atlantic	2
July 1 Association	Windy	Warner Brothers	4
July 29 Doors	Light My Fire	Elektra	3
Aug 19 Beatles	All You Need Is Love	Capitol	1
Aug 26 Bobbie Gentry	Ode To Billie Joe	Capitol	4
Sept 23 Box Tops	The Letter	Mala	4
Oct 21 Lulu	To Sir, With Love	Epic	5
Nov 25 Strawberry Alarm Clock	Incense And Peppermint	UNI	1
Dec 2 Monkees	Daydream Believer	Colgems	4
Dec 30 Beatles	Hello Goodbye	Capitol	3
1968			
Jan 20 John Fred and his Playboy Band	Judy In Disguise	Paula	2
Feb 3 Lemon Pipers	Green Tambourine	Buddah	1
Feb 10 Paul Mauriat	Love Is Blue	Philips	5
Mar 16 Otis Redding	Dock Of The Bay	Volt	4
Apr 13 Bobby Goldsboro	Honey	United Artists	5
May 18 Archie Bell and the Drells	Tighten Up	Atlantic	2
June 1 Simon and Garfunkel	Mrs. Robinson	Columbia	3
June 22 Herb Alpert and the Tijuana Brass	This Guy's In Love With You	A & M	4
July 20 Hugh Masekela	Grazing In The Grass	UNI	2
Aug 3 Doors	Hello I Love You	Elektra	2
Aug 17 Rascals	People Got To Be Free	Atlantic	5
Sept 21 Jeannie C. Riley	Harper Valley PTA	Plantation	1
Sept 28 Beatles	Hey Jude	Apple	9
Nov 30 Diana Ross and the Supremes	Love Child	Motown	2
Dec 14 Marvin Gaye	I Heard It Through The Grapevine	Tamla	7

				Weeks at No. 1
1969				
Feb 1	Tommy James and the Shondells	Crimson And Clover	Roulette	2
Feb 15	Sly and the Family Stone	Everyday People	Epic	4
Mar 15	Tommy Roe	Dizzy	ABC	4
Apr 12	5th Dimension	Aquarius/Let The Sun Shine In	Soul City	6
May 24	Beatles	Get Back	Apple	5
June 28	Henry Mancini	Love Theme From 'Romeo And Juliet'	RCA	2
July 12	Zager and Evans	In The Year 2525	RCA	6
Aug 23	Rolling Stones	Honky Tonk Woman	London	4
Sept 20	Archies	Sugar Sugar	Calendar	4
Oct 18	Temptations	I Can't Get Next To You	Gordy	2
Nov 1	Elvis Presley	Suspicious Minds	RCA	1
Nov 8	5th Dimension	Wedding Bell Blues	Soul City	3
Nov 29	Beatles	Come Together/ Something	Apple	1
Dec 6	Steam	Na Na Hey Hey Kiss Him Goodbye	Fontana	2
Dec 20	Peter, Paul and Mary	Leaving On A Jet Plane	Warner Brothers	1
Dec 27	Diana Ross and the Supremes	Someday We'll Be Together	Motown	1
1970				
Jan 3	B. J. Thomas	Raindrops Keep Falling On My Head	Scepter	4
Jan 31	Jackson 5	I Want You Back	Motown	1
Feb 7	Shocking Blue	Venus	Colossus	1
Feb 14	Sly and the Family Stone	Thank You Falettin Me Be Mice Elf Agin	Epic	2
Feb 28	Simon and Garfunkel	Bridge Over Troubled Water	Columbia	6
Apr 11	Beatles	Let It Be	Apple	2
Apr 25	Jackson 5	ABC	Motown	2
May 9	Guess Who	American Woman/ No Sugar Tonight	RCA	3
May 30	Ray Stevens	Everything Is Beautiful	Barnaby	2

				Weeks at No. 1
1970—(cont.)				
June 13	Beatles	Long And Winding Road/ For You Blue	Apple	2
June 27	Jackson 5	The Love You Save/I Found That Girl	Motown	2
July 11	Three Dog Night	Mama Told Me Not To Come	Dunhill	2
July 25	Carpenters	Close To You	A & M	4
Aug 22	Bread	Make It With You	Elektra	1
Aug 29	Edwin Starr	War	Gordy	3
Sept 19	Diana Ross	Ain't No Mountain High Enough	Motown	3
Oct 10	Neil Diamond	Cracklin' Rosie	UNI	1
Oct 17	Jackson 5	I'll Be There	Motown	5
Nov 21	Partridge Family	I Think I Love You	Bell	3
Dec 12	Smokey Robinson and the Miracles	Tears Of A Clown	Tamla	2
Dec 26	George Harrison	My Sweet Lord/ Isn't It A Pity	Apple	4
1971				
Jan 23	Dawn	Knock Three Times	Bell	3
Feb 13	Osmonds	One Bad Apple	MGM	5
Mar 20	Janis Joplin	Me And Bobby McGee	Columbia	2
Apr 3	Temptations	Just My Imagination	Gordy	2
Apr 17	Three Dog Night	Joy To The World	Dunhill	6
May 29	Rolling Stones	Brown Sugar	Rolling Stones	2
June 12	Honey Cone	Want Ads	Hot Wax	1
June 19	Carole King	It's Too Late/I Feel The Earth Move	Ode	5
July 24	Raiders	Indian Reservation	Columbia	1
July 31	James Taylor	You've Got A Friend	Warner Brothers	1
Aug 7	Bee Gees	How Can You Mend A Broken Heart	Atco	4
Sept 4	Paul McCartney	Uncle Albert/ Admiral Halsey	Apple	1

				Weeks at No. 1
1971—(cont.)				
Sept 11	Donny Osmond	Go Away Little Girl	MGM	3
Oct 2	Rod Stewart	Maggie May/ Reason To Believe	Mercury	5
Nov 6	Cher	Gypsies, Tramps And Thieves	Kapp	2
Nov 20	Isaac Hayes	Shaft	Enterprise/ MGM	2
Dec 4	Sly and the Family Stone	Family Affair	Epic	3
Dec 25	Melanie	Brand New Me	Neighbor-hood	3
1972				
Jan 15	Don McLean	American Pie	United Artists	4
Feb 12	Al Green	Let's Stay Together	Hi	1
Feb 19	Nilsson	Without You	RCA	4
Mar 18	Neil Young	Heart Of Gold	Reprise	1
Mar 25	America	Horse With No Name	Warner Brothers	3
Apr 15	Roberta Flack	First Time Ever I Saw Your Face	Atlantic	6
May 27	Chi-Lites	Oh Girl	Brunswick	1
June 3	Staple Singers	I'll Take You There	Stax	1
June 10	Sammy Davis Jr.	Candy Man	MGM	3
July 1	Neil Diamond	Song Sung Blue	UNI	1
July 8	Bill Withers	Lean On Me	Sussex	3
July 29	Gilbert O'Sullivan	Alone Again (Naturally)	MAM	4
Aug 26	Looking Glass	Brandy (You're A Fine Girl)	Epic	1
Sept 2	Gilbert O'Sullivan	Alone Again (Naturally)	MAM	2
Sept 16	Three Dog Night	Black And White	Dunhill	1
Sept 23	Mac Davis	Baby Don't Get Hooked On Me	Columbia	3
Oct 14	Michael Jackson	Ben	Motown	1
Oct 21	Chuck Berry	My Ding-A-Ling	Chess	2
Nov 4	Johnny Nash	I Can See Clearly Now	Epic	4
Dec 2	Temptations	Papa Was A Rolling Stone	Gordy	1
Dec 9	Helen Reddy	I Am Woman	Capitol	1
Dec 16	Billy Paul	Me And Mrs. Jones	Philadelphia Intern'l	3

				Weeks at No. 1
1973				
Jan 6	Carly Simon	You're So Vain	Elektra	3
Jan 27	Stevie Wonder	Superstition	Tamla	1
Feb 3	Elton John	Crocodile Rock	MCA	3
Feb 24	Roberta Flack	Killing Me Softly	Atlantic	4
Mar 24	O'Jay's	Love Train	Philadelphia Intern'l	1
Mar 31	Roberta Flack	Killing Me Softly	Atlantic	1
Apr 7	Vicki Lawrence	The Night The Lights Went Out In Georgia	Bell	2
Apr 21	Dawn	Tie A Yellow Ribbon Round The Old Oak Tree	Bell	4
May 19	Stevie Wonder	You Are The Sunshine Of My Life	Tamla	1
May 26	Edgar Winter Group	Frankenstein	Epic	1
June 2	Paul McCartney and Wings	My Love	Apple	4
June 30	George Harrison	Give Me Love	Apple	1
July 7	Billy Preston	Will It Go Round In Circles	A & M	2
July 21	Jim Croce	Bad, Bad Leroy Brown	ABC	2
Aug 4	Maureen McGovern	Morning After	20th Century	2
Aug 18	Diana Ross	Touch Me In The Morning	Motown	1
Aug 25	Stories	Brother Louie	Kama Sutra	2
Sept 8	Marvin Gaye	Let's Get It On	Motown	1
Sept 15	Helen Reddy	Delta Dawn	Capitol	1
Sept 22	Marvin Gaye	Let's Get It On	Motown	1
Sept 29	Grand Funk Railroad	We're An American Band	Capitol	1
Oct 6	Cher	Half-Breed	MCA	2
Oct 20	Rolling Stones	Angie	Rolling Stones	1
Oct 27	Gladys Knight and the Pips	Midnight Train To Georgia	Buddah	2
Nov 10	Eddie Kendricks	Keep On Truckin'	Tamla	2
Nov 24	Ringo Starr	Photograph	Apple	1
Dec 1	Carpenters	Top Of The World	A & M	2

			Weeks at No. 1
1973—(cont.)			
Dec 15 Charlie Rich	Most Beautiful Girl In The World	Epic	2
Dec 29 Jim Croce	Time In A Bottle	ABC	2
1974			
Jan 12 Steve Miller	The Joker	Capitol	1
Jan 19 Al Wilson	Show And Tell	Rocky Road	1
Jan 26 Ringo Starr	You're Sixteen	Apple	1
Feb 2 Barbra Streisand	The Way We Were	Columbia	1
Feb 9 Love Unlimited Orchestra	Love's Theme	20th Century	1
Feb 16 Barbra Streisand	The Way We Were	Columbia	2
Mar 2 Terry Jacks	Seasons In The Sun	Bell	3
Mar 23 Cher	Dark Lady	MCA	1
Mar 30 John Denver	Sunshine On My Shoulder	RCA	1
Apr 6 Blue Swede	Hooked On A Feeling	EMI	1
Apr 13 Elton John	Bennie And The Jets	MCA	1
Apr 20 MFSB	TSOP	Philadelphia Intern'l	2
May 4 Grand Funk	The Locomotion	Capitol	2
May 18 Ray Stevens	The Streak	Barnaby	3
June 8 Paul McCartney and Wings	Band On The Run	Apple	1
June 15 Bo Donaldson and the Heywoods	Billy Don't Be A Hero	ABC	2
June 29 Gordon Lightfoot	Sundown	Reprise	1
July 6 Hues Corporation	Rock The Boat	RCA	1
July 13 George McCrae	Rock Your Baby	TK	2
July 27 John Denver	Annie's Song	RCA	2
Aug 10 Roberta Flack	Feel Like Makin' Love	Atlantic	1
Aug 17 Paper Lace	The Night Chicago Died	Mercury	1
Aug 24 Paul Anka (with Odia Coates)	(You're) Having My Baby	United Artists	3
Sept 14 Eric Clapton	I Shot The Sheriff	RSO	1
Sept 21 Barry White	Can't Get Enough Of Your Love Baby	20th Century	1
Sept 28 Andy Kim	Rock Me Gently	Capitol	1

				Weeks at No. 1
Oct 5	Olivia Newton-John	I Honestly Love You	MCA	2
Oct 19	Billy Preston	Nothing From Nothing	A & M	1
Oct 26	Dionne Warwicke and the Spinners	Then Came You	Atlantic	1
Nov 2	Stevie Wonder	You Haven't Done Nothin'	Tamla	1
Nov 9	Bachman Turner Overdrive	You Ain't Seen Nothing Yet	Mercury	1
Nov 16	John Lennon	Whatever Gets You Through The Night	Apple	1
Nov 23	Billy Swan	I Can Help	Monument	2
Dec 7	Carl Douglas	Kung Fu Fighting	20th Century	2
Dec 21	Harry Chapin	Cat's In The Cradle	Elektra	1
Dec 28	Helen Reddy	Angie Baby	Capitol	1

BRITISH CHART-TOPPERS, 1955–74

				Weeks at No. 1
1955				
Jan 7	Dickie Valentine	Finger Of Suspicion	Decca	1
Jan 14	Rosemary Clooney	Mambo Italiano	Philips	3
Feb 4	Eddie Fisher	I Need You Now	HMV	2
Feb 18	Ruby Murray	Softly Softly	Columbia	3
Mar 11	Tennessee Ernie Ford	Give Me Your Word	Capitol	7
Apr 29	Perèz Prado	Cherry Pink And Apple Blossom White	HMV	2
May 13	Tony Bennett	Stranger In Paradise	Philips	2
May 27	Eddie Calvert	Cherry Pink And Apple Blossom White	Columbia	4
June 24	Jimmy Young	Unchained Melody	Decca	3
July 15	Alma Cogan	Dreamboat	HMV	2
July 29	Slim Whitman	Rosemarie	London	11
Oct 14	Jimmy Young	Man From Laramie	Decca	4
Nov 11	Johnston Brothers	Hernandos Hideaway	Decca	2
Nov 25	Bill Haley and the Comets	Rock Around The Clock	Brunswick	3
Dec 16	Dickie Valentine	Christmas Alphabet	Decca	3
1956				
Jan 6	Bill Haley and the Comets	Rock Around The Clock	Brunswick	2
Jan 20	Tennessee Ernie Ford	Sixteen Tons	Capitol	4
Feb 17	Dean Martin	Memories Are Made Of This	Capitol	4
Mar 16	Dream Weavers	It's Almost Tomorrow	Brunswick	2
Mar 30	Kay Starr	Rock And Roll Waltz	HMV	1
Apr 6	Dream Weavers	It's Almost Tomorrow	Brunswick	1
Apr 13	Winifred Attwell	Poor People Of Paris	Decca	3
May 4	Ronnie Hilton	No Other Love	HMV	6
June 15	Pat Boone	I'll Be Home	London	5
July 20	Frankie Lymon and the Teenagers	Why Do Fools Fall In Love	Columbia	3

				Weeks at No. 1
1956—(cont.)				
Aug 10	Doris Day	Whatever Will Be Will Be	Philips	6
Sept 21	Anne Shelton	Lay Down Your Arms	Philips	4
Oct 19	Frankie Laine	Woman In Love	Philips	4
Nov 16	Johnnie Ray	Just Walkin' In The Rain	Philips	7
1957				
Jan 4	Guy Mitchell	Singing The Blues	Philips	1
Jan 11	Tommy Steele	Singing The Blues	Decca	1
Jan 18	Guy Mitchell	Singing The Blues	Philips	1
Jan 25	Frankie Vaughan	Garden Of Eden	Philips	4
Feb 22	Tab Hunter	Young Love	London	7
Apr 12	Lonnie Donegan	Cumberland Gap	Pye Nixa	5
May 17	Guy Mitchell	Rock-a-Billy	Philips	1
May 24	Andy Williams	Butterfly	London	2
June 7	Johnnie Ray	Yes Tonight Josephine	Philips	3
June 28	Lonnie Donegan	Gamblin' Man/ Putting On The Style	Nixa	2
July 12	Elvis Presley	All Shook Up	HMV	7
Aug 30	Paul Anka	Diana	Columbia	9
Nov 1	Crickets	That'll Be The Day	Vogue-Coral	3
Nov 22	Harry Belafonte	Mary's Boy Child	RCA	7
1958				
Jan 10	Jerry Lee Lewis	Great Balls Of Fire	London	2
Jan 24	Elvis Presley	Jailhouse Rock	RCA	3
Feb 14	Michael Holliday	The Story Of My Life	Columbia	2
Feb 28	Perry Como	Magic Moments	RCA	8
Apr 25	Marvin Rainwater	Whole Lotta Woman	MGM	3
May 16	Connie Francis	Who's Sorry Now?	MGM	6
June 27	Vic Damone	On The Street Where You Live	Philips	2
July 4	Everly Brothers	All I Have To Do Is Dream/ Claudette	London	7
Aug 22	Kalin Twins	When	Brunswick	5
Sept 26	Connie Francis	Carolina Moon/ Stupid Cupid	MGM	6
Nov 7	Tommy Edwards	It's All In The Game	MGM	3
Nov 28	Lord Rockingham's XI	Hoots Mon	Decca	3

			Weeks at No. 1
1958—(cont.)			
Dec 19 Conway Twitty	It's Only Make Believe	MGM	5
1959			
Jan 24 Elvis Presley	I Got Stung/One Night	RCA	5
Feb 22 Platters	Smoke Gets In Your Eyes	Mercury	5
Apr 4 Russ Conway	Side Saddle	Columbia	2
Apr 18 Buddy Holly	It Doesn't Matter Anymore	Coral	2
May 2 Elvis Presley	A Fool Such As I	RCA	7
June 20 Russ Conway	Roulette	Columbia	1
June 27 Bobby Darin	Dream Lover	London	5
Aug 1 Cliff Richard	Livin' Doll	Columbia	4
Aug 29 Craig Douglas	Only Sixteen	Rank	7
Oct 17 Cliff Richard	Travellin' Light	Columbia	7
Dec 5 Adam Faith	What Do You Want	Parlophone	6
1960			
Jan 9 Emile Ford	What Do You Want To Make Those Eyes At Me For?	Pye	1
Jan 16 Anthony Newley	Why	Decca	6
Feb 27 Adam Faith	Poor Me	Parlophone	1
Mar 6 Johnny Preston	Running Bear	Mercury	2
Mar 20 Lonnie Donegan	My Old Man's A Dustman	Pye	5
Apr 24 Everly Brothers	Cathy's Clown	Warner	9
June 26 Jimmy Jones	Good Timin'	MGM	4
July 24 Cliff Richard	Please Don't Tease	Columbia	3
Aug 14 Shadows	Apache	Columbia	6
Sept 23 Ricky Valance	Tell Laura I Love Her	Columbia	2
Oct 7 Roy Orbison	Only The Lonely	London	3
Oct 30 Elvis Presley	It's Now Or Never	RCA	8
Dec 25 Johnny Tillotson	Poetry In Motion	London	3
1961			
Jan 15 Elvis Presley	Are You Lonesome Tonight?	RCA	4
Feb 12 Everly Brothers	Walk Right Back	Warner	4
Mar 12 Elvis Presley	Wooden Heart	RCA	4
Apr 2 Allisons	Are You Sure?	Fontana	2
Apr 16 Temperance Seven	You're Driving Me Crazy	Parlophone	2
Apr 30 Marcels	Blue Moon	Pye Int.	2

			Weeks at No. 1
1961—(cont.)			
May 14 Del Shannon	Runaway	London	1
May 14 Elvis Presley	Surrender	RCA	5
June 18 Del Shannon	Runaway	London	1
June 25 Everly Brothers	Temptation	Warner	4
July 29 Eden Kane	Well I Ask You	Decca	1
Aug 5 Helen Shapiro	You Don't Know	Columbia	2
Aug 19 John Leyton	Johnny Remember Me	Top Rank	5
Sept 23 Shadows	Kon-Tiki	Columbia	1
Sept 30 Highwaymen	Michael Row The Boat	HMV	1
Oct 7 Helen Shapiro	Walkin' Back To Happiness	Columbia	4
Nov 4 Elvis Presley	His Latest Flame	RCA	3
Nov 25 Bobby Vee	Take Good Care Of My Baby	London	1
Dec 2 Frankie Vaughan	Tower Of Strength	Philips	2
Dec 23 Acker Bilk	Stranger On The Shore	Columbia	4
1962			
Jan 20 Cliff Richard	The Young Ones	Columbia	5
Feb 24 Elvis Presley	Rock A Hula Baby/Can't Help Falling In Love With You	RCA	4
Mar 24 Shadows	Wonderful Land	Columbia	8
May 19 B. Bumble and the Stingers	Nut Rocker	Top Rank	1
May 26 Elvis Presley	Good Luck Charm	RCA	5
June 30 Mike Sarne	Come Outside	Parlophone	2
July 14 Ray Charles	I Can't Stop Loving You	HMV	2
July 28 Frank Ifield	I Remember You	Columbia	7
Sept 15 Elvis Presley	She's Not You	RCA	3
Oct 6 Tornadoes	Telstar	Decca	5
Nov 10 Frank Ifield	Lovesick Blues	Columbia	5
Dec 15 Elvis Presley	Return To Sender	RCA	3
1963			
Jan 6 Cliff Richard	The Next Time/ Bachelor Boy	Columbia	3
Jan 27 Shadows	Dance On	Columbia	1
Feb 3 Jet Harris/Tony Meehan	Diamonds	Decca	3
Feb 24 Frank Ifield	Wayward Wind	Columbia	3
Mar 16 Cliff Richard	Summer Holiday	Columbia	2
Mar 30 Shadows	Foottapper	Columbia	1
Apr 6 Gerry and the Pacemakers	How Do You Do It?	Columbia	4

				Weeks at No. 1
1963—(cont.)				
May 4	Beatles	From Me To You	Parlophone	7
June 22	Gerry and the Pacemakers	I Like It	Columbia	4
July 20	Frank Ifield	Confessin'	Columbia	2
Aug 3	Elvis Presley	Devil In Disguise	RCA	1
Aug 10	Searchers	Sweets For My Sweet	Pye	2
Aug 24	Billy J. Kramer and the Dakotas	Bad To Me	Parlophone	3
Sept 14	Beatles	She Loves You	Parlophone	4
Oct 12	Brian Poole and the Tremeloes	Do You Love Me?	Decca	3
Nov 2	Gerry and the Pacemakers	You'll Never Walk Alone	Columbia	4
Nov 30	Beatles	She Loves You	Parlophone	2
Dec 14	Beatles	I Want To Hold Your Hand	Parlophone	5
1964				
Jan 18	Dave Clark Five	Glad All Over	Columbia	2
Feb 1	Searchers	Needles And Pins	Pye	3
Feb 22	Bachelors	Diane	Decca	1
Feb 29	Cilla Black	Anyone Who Had A Heart	Parlophone	3
Mar 21	Billy J. Kramer and the Dakotas	Little Children	Parlophone	2
Apr 4	Beatles	Can't Buy Me Love	Parlophone	3
Apr 25	Peter and Gordon	World Without Love	Columbia	2
May 9	Searchers	Don't Throw Your Love Away	Pye	2
May 23	Four Pennies	Juliet	Philips	1
May 30	Cilla Black	You're My World	Parlophone	4
June 27	Roy Orbison	It's Over	London	2
July 11	Animals	The House Of The Rising Sun	Columbia	1
July 18	Rolling Stones	It's All Over Now	Decca	1
July 25	Beatles	Hard Day's Night	Parlophone	3
Aug 15	Manfred Mann	Doo Wah Diddy Diddy	HMV	2
Aug 29	Honeycombs	Have I The Right?	Pye	2
Sept 11	Kinks	You Really Got Me	Pye	2
Sept 26	Herman's Hermits	I'm Into Something Good	Columbia	2
Oct 10	Roy Orbison	Oh, Pretty Woman	London	2
Oct 24	Sandie Shaw	(There's) Always Something There To Remind Me	Pye	3

Date	Artist	Title	Label	Weeks at No. 1
1964—(cont.)				
Nov 14	Roy Orbison	Oh, Pretty Woman	London	1
Nov 21	Supremes	Baby Love	Stateside	2
Dec 5	Rolling Stones	Little Red Rooster	Decca	1
Dec 12	Beatles	I Feel Fine	Parlophone	5
1965				
Jan 16	Georgie Fame	Yeh Yeh	Columbia	2
Jan 30	Moody Blues	Go Now	Decca	1
Feb 6	Righteous Brothers	You've Lost That Lovin' Feeling	London	2
Feb 20	Kinks	Tired Of Waiting For You	Pye	1
Feb 27	Seekers	I'll Never Find Another You	Columbia	2
Mar 13	Tom Jones	It's Not Unusual	Decca	1
Mar 20	Rolling Stones	The Last Time	Decca	3
Apr 10	Unit 4+2	Concrete And Clay	Decca	1
Apr 17	Cliff Richard	The Minute You're Gone	Columbia	1
Apr 24	Beatles	Ticket To Ride	Parlophone	3
May 15	Roger Miller	King Of The Road	Philips	1
May 22	Jackie Trent	Where Are You Now My Love	Pye	1
May 29	Sandie Shaw	Long Live Love	Pye	3
June 19	Elvis Presley	Crying In The Chapel	RCA	2
June 26	Hollies	I'm Alive	Parlophone	3
July 24	Byrds	Mr. Tambourine Man	CBS	2
Aug 7	Beatles	Help	Parlophone	3
Aug 28	Sonny and Cher	I Got You Babe	Atlantic	2
Sept 11	Rolling Stones	Satisfaction	Decca	2
Sept 23	Walker Brothers	Make It Easy On Yourself	Philips	1
Sept 30	Ken Dodd	Tears	Columbia	5
Nov 6	Rolling Stones	Get Off Of My Cloud	Decca	3
Nov 27	Seekers	The Carnival Is Over	Columbia	3
Dec 18	Beatles	Day Tripper/We Can Work It Out	Parlophone	5
1966				
Jan 22	Spencer Davis Group	Keep On Runnin'	Fontana	1
Jan 29	Overlanders	Michelle	Pye	3
Feb 19	Nancy Sinatra	These Boots Are Made For Walking	Reprise	4
Mar 3	Walker Brothers	Sun Ain't Gonna Shine Anymore	Philips	4

				Weeks at No. 1
1966—(cont.)				
Apr 16	Spencer Davis Group	Somebody Help Me	Fontana	2
Apr 30	Dusty Springfield	You Don't Have To Say You Love Me	Philips	1
May 7	Manfred Mann	Pretty Flamingo	HMV	3
May 28	Rolling Stones	Paint It Black	Decca	1
June 4	Frank Sinatra	Strangers In The Night	Reprise	3
June 25	Beatles	Paperback Writer	Parlophone	2
July 9	Kinks	Sunday Afternoon	Pye	2
July 23	Georgie Fame	Get Away	Columbia	1
July 30	Chris Farlowe	Out Of Time	Immediate	1
Aug 6	Troggs	With A Girl Like You	Fontana	2
Aug 20	Beatles	Eleanor Rigby/ Yellow Submarine	Parlophone	4
Sept 17	Small Faces	All Or Nothing	Decca	1
Sept 24	Jim Reeves	Distant Drums	RCA	5
Oct 29	Four Tops	Reach Out I'll Be There	Motown	3
Nov 19	Beach Boys	Good Vibrations	Capitol	2
Dec 3	Tom Jones	Green Green Grass Of Home	Decca	6
1967				
Jan 14	Monkees	I'm A Believer	RCA	4
Feb 18	Pet Clark	This Is My Song	Pye	2
Mar 4	Engelbert Humperdinck	Release Me	Decca	6
Apr 15	Frank and Nancy Sinatra	Somethin' Stupid	Reprise	2
Apr 29	Sandie Shaw	Puppet On A String	Pye	3
May 20	Tremeloes	Silence Is Golden	CBS	3
June 10	Procol Harum	A Whiter Shade Of Pale	Deram	6
July 22	Beatles	All You Need Is Love	Parlophone	3
Aug 12	Scott MacKenzie	San Francisco	CBS	4
Sept 9	Engelbert Humperdinck	The Last Waltz	Decca	5
Oct 14	Bee Gees	Massachussetts	Polydor	4
Nov 11	Foundations	Baby Now That I've Found You	Pye	2
Nov 25	Long John Baldry	Let The Heartaches Begin	Pye	2
Dec 9	Beatles	Hello Goodbye	Parlophone	7

				Weeks at No. 1
1968				
Jan 27	Georgie Fame	The Ballad Of Bonnie And Clyde	CBS	1
Feb 3	Love Affair	Everlasting Love	CBS	2
Feb 17	Manfred Mann	The Mighty Quinn	Fontana	2
Mar 2	Esther and Abi Ofarim	Cinderella Rockafella	Fontana	3
Mar 23	Dave Dee & Co.	Legend Of Xanadu	Fontana	1
Mar 30	Beatles	Lady Madonna	Parlophone	2
Apr 13	Cliff Richard	Congratulations	Columbia	2
Apr 27	Louis Armstrong	Wonderful World	Stateside	4
May 25	Union Gap	Young Girl	CBS	4
June 22	Rolling Stones	Jumping Jack Flash	Decca	2
July 6	Equals	Baby Come Back	President	3
July 27	Des O'Connor	I Pretend	Columbia	1
Aug 3	Tommy James and the Shondells	Mony Mony	Roulette	2
Aug 17	The Crazy World of Arthur Brown	Fire	Track	1
Aug 24	Tommy James and the Shondells	Mony Mony	Roulette	1
Aug 31	Beach Boys	Do It Again	Capitol	1
Sept 7	Bee Gees	I Gotta Get A Message To You	Polydor	1
Sept 14	Beatles	Hey Jude	Apple	2
Sept 28	Mary Hopkins	Those Were The Days	Apple	6
Nov 9	Joe Cocker	With A Little Help From My Friends	Regal Zonophone	1
Nov 16	Hugo Montenegro	The Good, The Bad And The Ugly	RCA	4
Dec 14	Scaffold	Lily The Pink	Columbia	3
1969				
Jan 4	Marmalade	Ob-La-Di-Ob-La-Da	CBS	1
Jan 11	Scaffold	Lily The Pink	Columbia	1
Jan 18	Marmalade	Ob-La-Di-Ob-La-Da	CBS	2
Feb 1	Fleetwood Mac	Albatross	Blue Horizon	1
Feb 8	Move	Blackberry Way	Regal Zonophone	1
Feb 15	Amen Corner	Half As Nice	Immediate	2
Mar 1	Peter Sarstedt	Where Do You Go To My Lovely	United Artists	4
Mar 29	Marvin Gaye	I Heard It Thru' The Grapevine	Tamla Motown	3
Apr 19	Desmond Dekker and the Aces	The Israelites	Pyramid	1

			Weeks at No. 1
1969—(cont.)			
Apr 26 Beatles	Get Back	Apple	6
June 7 Tommy Roe	Dizzy	Stateside	1
June 14 Beatles	Ballad Of John And Yoko	Apple	3
July 5 Thunderclap Newman	Something In The Air	Track	3
July 26 Rolling Stones	Honky Tonk Woman	Decca	5
Aug 30 Zager and Evans	In The Year 2525	RCA	3
Sept 20 Creedence Clearwater Revival	Bad Moon Rising	Liberty	3
Oct 11 Jane Birkin and Serge Gainsbourg	Je T'Aime Moi Non Plus	Major Minor	1
Oct 18 Bobbie Gentry	I'll Never Fall In Love Again	Capitol	1
Oct 25 Archies	Sugar Sugar	RCA	8
Dec 20 Rolf Harris	Two Little Boys	Columbia	6
1970			
Jan 31 Edison Lighthouse	Love Grows	Bell	5
Mar 7 Lee Marvin	Wanderin' Star	Paramount	4
Apr 4 Simon and Garfunkel	Bridge Over Troubled Water	CBS	2
Apr 18 Dana	All Kinds Of Everything	Rex	2
May 2 Norman Greenbaum	Spirit In The Sky	Reprise	2
May 16 England World Cup Squad	Back Home	Pye	3
June 6 Christie	Yellow River	CBS	1
June 13 Mungo Jerry	In The Summertime	Dawn	8
Aug 1 Elvis Presley	The Wonder Of You	RCA	6
Sept 12 Smokey Robinson and the Miracles	The Tears Of A Clown	Motown	1
Sept 19 Freda Payne	Band Of Gold	Invictus	6
Oct 31 Matthews Southern Comfort	Woodstock	UNI	3
Nov 21 Jimi Hendrix	Voodoo Chile	Track	1
Nov 28 Dave Edmunds	I Hear You Knocking	MAM	7
1971			
Jan 9 Clive Dunn	Grandad	Columbia	3
Jan 31 George Harrison	My Sweet Lord	Apple	5
Mar 6 Mungo Jerry	Baby Jump	Dawn	2

				Weeks at No. 1
1971—(cont.)				
Mar 20	T Rex	Hot Love	Fly	6
May 1	Dave and Ansell Collins	Double Barrel	Technique	2
May 15	Dawn	Knock Three Times	Bell	5
June 19	Middle of the Road	Chirpy Chirpy Cheep Cheep	RCA	5
July 24	T Rex	Get It On	Fly	4
Aug 21	Diana Ross	I'm Still Waiting	Motown	3
Sept 18	Tams	Hey Girl Don't Bother Me	Probe	3
Oct 9	Rod Stewart	Maggie May	Mercury	5
Nov 13	Slade	Cos I Luv You	Polydor	4
Dec 11	Benny Hill	Ernie	Columbia	4
1972				
Jan 8	New Seekers	I'd Like To Teach The World To Sing	Polydor	4
Feb 5	T Rex	Telegram Sam	T Rex	2
Feb 19	Chicory Tip	Son Of My Father	CBS	4
Mar 18	Nilsson	Without You	RCA	4
Apr 15	Royal Scots Dragoon Guards Band	Amazing Grace	RCA	5
May 20	T Rex	Metal Guru	T Rex	4
June 10	Don McLean	Vincent	UA	2
July 1	Slade	Take Me Back 'Ome	Polydor	1
July 8	Donny Osmond	Puppy Love	MGM	5
Aug 12	Alice Cooper	School's Out	Warner	3
Sept 2	Rod Stewart	You Wear It Well	Mercury	1
Sept 9	Slade	Mama Weer All Crazee Now	Polydor	3
Sept 30	David Cassidy	How Can I Be Sure	Bell	2
Oct 14	Lieutenant Pigeon	Mouldy Old Dough	Decca	4
Nov 11	Gilbert O'Sullivan	Clair	MAM	2
Nov 25	Chuck Berry	My Ding-A-Ling	Chess	4
Dec 23	Little Jimmy Osmond	Long Haired Lover From Liverpool	MGM	5
1973				
Jan 27	Sweet	Blockbuster	RCA	5
Mar 3	Slade	Cum On Feel The Noize	Polydor	4
Mar 31	Donny Osmond	Twelfth Of Never	MGM	1
Apr 7	Gilbert O'Sullivan	Get Down	MAM	2

			Weeks at No. 1
1973—(cont.)			
Apr 21 Dawn	Tie A Yellow Ribbon Round The Old Oak Tree	Bell	4
May 19 Wizzard	See My Baby Jive	Harvest	4
June 16 Suzie Quatro	Can The Can	RAK	1
June 23 10cc	Rubber Bullets	UK	1
June 30 Slade	Skweeze Me, Pleeze Me	Polydor	3
July 21 Peters and Lee	Welcome Home	Philips	1
July 28 Garry Glitter	I'm The Leader Of The Gang	Bell	4
Aug 25 Donny Osmond	Young Love	MGM	4
Sept 22 Wizzard	Angel Fingers	Harvest	1
Sept 29 Simon Park Orchestra	Eye Level	Columbia	4
Oct 27 David Cassidy	Daydreamer	Bell	3
Nov 17 Gary Glitter	I Love You Love Me Love	Bell	4
Dec 15 Slade	Merry Christmas Everybody	Polydor	5
1974			
Jan 19 New Seekers	You Won't Find Another Fool Like Me	Polydor	1
Jan 26 Mud	Tiger Feet	RAK	4
Feb 23 Suzi Quatro	Devil Gate Drive	RAK	2
Mar 9 Alvin Stardust	Jealous Mind	Magnet	1
Mar 16 Paper Lace	Billy Don't Be A Hero	Bus Stop	3
Apr 6 Terry Jacks	Seasons In The Sun	Bell	4
May 4 Abba	Waterloo	Epic	2
May 18 Rubettes	Sugar Baby Love	Polydor	4
June 15 Ray Stevens	The Streak	Janus	1
June 22 Gary Glitter	Always Yours	Bell	1
June 29 Charles Azvanour	She	Barclay	4
July 27 George McCrae	Rock Your Baby	Jay Boy	3
Aug 17 Three Degrees	When Will I See You Again	Philadelphia Intern'l	2
Aug 31 Osmonds	Love Me For A Reason	MGM	3
Sept 21 Carl Douglas	Kung Fu Fighting	Pye	3
Oct 12 John Denver	Annie's Song	RCA	1
Oct 19 Sweet Sensation	Sad Sweet Dreamer	Pye	1
Oct 26 Ken Boothe	Everything I Own	Trojan	3
Nov 16 David Essex	I'm Gonna Make You A Star	CBS	3

1974—(cont.)			Weeks at No. 1
Dec 7 Barry White	You're My First, My Last, My Everything	20th Century	2
Dec 14 Mud	Lonely This Christmas	RAK	3

ROLL CALL OF HIT MAKERS IN AMERICA AND BRITAIN, 1955–74

Number of hits altogether	*Artist*	*Number of hits in US*	*Number of hits in UK*
88	Elvis Presley	58	70
49	Cliff Richard	—	49
39	Beatles	37	23
32	Diana Ross/and Supremes[1]	26	22
28	Pat Boone	23	22
	Connie Francis	22	19
	Ricky Nelson	27	9
27	Marvin Gaye	24	7
	Temptations	24	9
26	Lonnie Donegan	2	26
25	Beach Boys	20	12
	Perry Como	14	17
	Herman's Hermits/Peter Noone	14	18
	Stevie Wonder	22	14
24	Everly Brothers	17	19
	Aretha Franklin	24	4
	Brenda Lee	19	13
	Rolling Stones	20	18
23	Hollies	7	22
22	Four Seasons/Frankie Valli	21	8
	Four Tops	17	15
	Frank Sinatra	9	19
19	Paul Anka	18	8
	Nat 'King' Cole	11	10
	Billy Fury	—	19
	Tom Jones	10	19
	Gene Pitney	10	11
	Supremes[1]	18	13
	Andy Williams	12	11
18	Fats Domino	15	8
	Roy Orbison	10	16
	Three Dog Night	18	1
	Frankie Vaughan	—	18
	Roy Wood/Move/Wizzard	—	18

Number of hits altogether	*Artist*	*Number of hits in US*	*in UK*
17	Ray Charles	16	5
	Dave Clark Five	14	9
	Duane Eddy	6	17
16	Kinks	6	16
	Brook Benton	16	—
	Eric Burdon/and Animals/and War	11	11
	David Cassidy/Partridge Family	6	12
	Sam Cooke	15	4
	Bobby Darin	14	10
	Adam Faith	—	16
	Gladys Knight/and Pips	14	2
	Manfred Mann	3	16
15	James Brown	15	1
	Neil Diamond	15	4
	Drifters	11	7
	Buddy Holly/Crickets	15	1
	Dusty Springfield	5	14
	Who	5	14
	Jackie Wilson	13	3
14	Bee Gees	11	9
	Cilla Black	—	14
	Carpenters	13	6
	Chubby Checker	14	4
	Jackson Five	11	7
	Jim Reeves	2	13
	Smokey Robinson/and Miracles	14	4
	Bobby Rydell	14	2
	Tommy Steele	—	14
	Bobby Vinton	14	1
	Dionne Warwicke	13	3
13	Marc Bolan/and T. Rex	1	13
	Bill Haley and His Comets	7	11
	Curtis Mayfield/Impressions[2]	12	1
	Neil Sedaka	11	10
	Slade	—	13
	Bobby Vee	10	8
12	Chicago	11	2
	Russ Conway	—	12
	Dion/and Belmonts/Di Mucci	12	2
	Fifth Dimension	12	2
	Elton John	11	10
	Dean Martin	6	10
	Johnny Mathis	8	6
	Gilbert O'Sullivan	4	11
	Johnnie Ray	3	12
	Johnny Rivers	12	—

Number of hits altogether	*Artist*	*Number of hits in US*	*in UK*
	Simon and Garfunkel	11	6
11	Chuck Berry	9	5
	Englebert Humperdinck	5	11
	Frankie Laine	1	11
	Paul McCartney/and Wings	9	10
	Donny Osmond	10	7
	Platters	11	6
	Paul Revere/and Raiders	11	—
	Searchers	3	10
	Cat Stevens	6	7
10	Bachelors	2	10
	David Bowie	1	10
	Max Bygraves	—	10
	Alma Cogan	—	10
	Creedence Clearwater Revival	10	6
	Dave Dee, Dozy, Beaky, Mick and Tich	—	10
	Ronnie Hilton	—	10
	Impressions[2]	10	—
	Tommy James/and Shondells	10	1
	Gary Lewis and The Playboys	10	—
	Little Richard	4	9
	Lulu	1	9
	Monkees	9	7
	Ruby Murray	—	10
	Osmonds	7	5
	Peter and Gordon	8	6
	Small Faces	1	10
	Rod Stewart/Faces	3	10
	Sweet	1	10

NOTES:

1. 13 titles by the Supremes are listed both under the group and under Diana Ross, whose voice was featured but not credited on the label.
2. 9 titles by the Impressions are listed both under the group and under Curtis Mayfield, whose voice was featured but not credited on the label.